Spanish

in PLAIN ENGLISH

Raymond W. Lowry

New York   Chicago   San Francisco   Lisbon   London   Madrid   Mexico City
Milan   New Delhi   San Juan   Seoul   Singapore   Sydney   Toronto

1 2 3 4 5 6 7 8 9 10 11 12 13 14 15 16 17 18 19 20 21   DOC/DOC   0 9

ISBN 978-0-07-146488-8
MHID   0-07-146488-3

McGraw-Hill books are available at special quantity discounts to use as premiums and sales promotions or for use in corporate training programs. To contact a representative, please visit the Contact Us pages at www.mhprofessional.com.

This book is printed on acid-free paper.

CONTENTS

THIS BOOK'S PURPOSE AND PROMISE
An Important Note to Self-Directed Learners

It's unquestionably true: unless you've spent your life staring into a corner, building sand castles, or otherwise not paying much attention to the world around you, you *already*—perhaps without being conscious of the fact—possess an essential familiarity with the Spanish language. Indeed, you already employ a significant number of Spanish terms in your everyday speech and understand many more! For in fact, modern English is heavily and increasingly interlaced with Spanish terminology: words that are often incorrectly assumed to be English, while in fact they've been Spanish—or originally Latin or Italian—from the start, drawn into our polyglot tongue by centuries of cultural interchange. If you doubt that assertion, it will be demonstrated momentarily.

The purpose of this book is to assist you in readily adding to that preexisting base of acquaintance. To help you, in short, *learn more* Spanish, *faster and more thoroughly and confidently*, than you have believed possible. And give you a basic working knowledge of the structure and syntax of the language as well.

Your desire to better comprehend and speak Spanish may arise from any of numerous sources: perhaps you have friends of Latin extraction, Spanish-speaking neighbors, coworkers, or employees with whom you want to improve your communicability. Perhaps you're fascinated by the history, culture, literature, art, music, dance, or the unique cuisine of one or more Spanish-rooted cultures. Maybe you have an urge to travel to Spain, Mexico, Central or South America, or the Philippines—or perhaps you have already been to one or more of those destinations, and long to return with the capability of more easily and effectively conversing with their natives in their own fiery, staccato tongues.

Whatever the impetus, the fact that you *are* motivated, and thus especially alert and attentive to Spanish, assures that this book's principal thesis is almost certainly true: you *do* already own a larger Spanish vocabulary than you've imagined, and are well positioned to advance more quickly and easily toward a growing mastery of *la lengua española* than you've supposed, via the unique means offered within this volume. Here's the promised demonstration: you *do* recognize and understand at least a majority of the following words, don't you?—*amigo, amor, bandido, bueno, carne, casa, diablo, feliz, gato, huevo, hombre, leche, madre, mañana, número, olé, oro, padre, pollo, salsa, sí, sol, tía, usted, vista, verde.* If your answer is in the affirmative, then you're almost certainly well acquainted with a large fraction of the 200-plus words contained in this book's initial compendium, **LISTA DE TÉRMINOS Y FRASES FAMILIARES (List of Familiar Terms and Phrases)**, and truly possess a meaningful head start in the relatively painless task of building an even more comprehensive Spanish vocabulary.

"Relatively painless?" Well, yes! For this book's unique feature is its primary focus on *cognate* English-Spanish terminology. That is, words that are either spelled and / or pronounced identically, almost identically, or with a high degree of similarity in both languages. An English ambulance, for example, is a Spanish **ambulancia**; the English term *abbreviation* equates to *abreviatura* in Spanish; and an accident in Milwaukee, Miami, or Missoula is no more or less likely to be serious as an **accidente** in Madrid, Mexico City, or Montevideo. In short, cognates are far easier to master than same-meaning words that bear little or no resemblance to one another—and there are literally *thousands* of English / Spanish cognates that can be readily incorporated into your basic Spanish vocabulary! A substantial number of important terms contain no similarity at all across the linguistic divide, of course, and eventually many of them will be important for you to learn as well. But they will be far more easily and eagerly mastered once you've got a few hundred—or a thousand or more!—cognates securely stowed away in your mental bilingual lexicon.

In short, this book's approach is to work from easy to not so easy, rather than the other way around. Here, we want to start you off *fast*, and let your already possessed and easily broadened vocabulary serve as a base for the more difficult words and grammatical structures that, in time, will round out your learning. If that sounds like a fair and attractive proposition, fellow learner . . . well, read on! And welcome to the world of easiest-to-master conversational Spanish!

HOW TO USE THIS BOOK
TO BEST ADVANTAGE

Except for the few who are blessed with inborn linguistic superskill, for most of us *no* foreign language is truly easy to learn: all are as complex—and often as inconsistent—as we humans who invented them. Relatively speaking, however, Spanish is one of the easiest of all nonnative languages for an English speaker to master. Not only does it have a structural logic less replete with exceptions and self-contradictions than many, but *it's full to overflowing with cognates*: words that are identical or highly similar across the linguistic divide. The cognate factor constitutes the greatest advantage that any learner of Spanish possesses: he or she can amass a relatively vast vocabulary—the essential foundation of language acquisition—with less arduous effort than is required for almost any other tongue! Indeed, most English speakers already know between scores and hundreds of Spanish words, often without their conscious awareness.

This book, uniquely, is an instructional tool that focuses upon that "easier-ness" of Spanish vocabulary acquisition. Like any tool, of course, it can either be utilized skillfully, to the learner's greatest advantage, or mis-used and / or underutilized, to his or her loss. The suggestions that follow, then, constitute an "Owner's Manual" on the best possible usage of this potentially powerful tool.

1. The single greatest assistance the learner can give him- / herself is to get the essentials of *pronunciation* in mind and mouth *first*. Before *all* else: before the easiness of cognate-rich vocabulary, even, and certainly before becoming enmeshed in the complexities of grammatical formality and syntactical structure. *First*, learn how the language "sounds and says"; *first*, train the ears and mind and mouth!

In the case of Spanish, this is a somewhat more challenging task than for the other Romance languages. Because of its widespread diffusion—westward from Madrid into the Caribbean, all of Mexico and Central

America, most of South America, and onward to Manila (and now, increasingly, the United States)—*español* has developed numerous local flavors, just like English. The essential vocabulary remains the same from one Spanish-speaking culture or subculture to the next, but pronunciational regionalism has infused the basic tongue with variants. Still, a *basic* sound, cadence, and stress pattern underlie, and in the end supersede, the panoply of local pronunciational distinctions. It is vitally important for the learner to master these fundamentals from the outset as the basis of his or her progress toward real bilingual competence.

It would be impossible to overstress the importance of this: go *first* to this book's pronunciation chapter, and carefully read and heed both its suggestions and detailed descriptions. Only then, *after* absorbing an essential familiarity with the basic vocal / aural character of the Spanish tongue, can you effectively progress toward the absorption of the vocabulary itself. In most cases, a mere two or three hours of listening, learning, and vocal practice, as specified in the pronunciation guide, will suffice to give you a sense of pronunciational confidence. Failure to develop an acute ear and adept tongue from the outset would be a continual obstacle to your progress; and eventually, it would become a handicap in need of difficult unlearning and correction.

2. Then, with the matter of "sound" confidently in ear, you'll be ready to begin absorbing the cognate-rich Spanish vocabulary. Not all of the several thousand cognates at the heart of this book will be of need or of interest to you, of course. So, especially as you begin to build vocabulary, *be selective*! After you're sure of all the terms in the book's initial list, **LISTA DE TÉRMINOS Y FRASES FAMILIARES (List of Familiar Terms and Phrases)**—none of which are repeated elsewhere in this volume—turn with highlighter in hand to the main list, **LISTA DE TÉRMINOS IDÉNTICOS Y SIMILARES (List of Identical and Similar Terms)**, which constitutes this book's core. Select a dozen or two everyday nouns and adjectives from across its alphabetic spectrum. For example, from *abundance* (abundancia) and *accusation* (acusación), through *curious* (curioso), *decent* (decente), *generous* (generoso), *necessity* (necesidad), *radiant* (radiante), and *student* (estudiante), on to *zebra* (cebra), *zone* (zona), and so forth. Then choose another dozen. Then another. Then yet another, adding a few everyday verbs into the mix as you go along.

While you can afford to ignore the masculine / feminine coding at first, at some point during your buildup of nouns and adjectives you'll need to turn to the chapter on grammar and become comfortable with the wildly irrational issue of gender. You'll have no choice in that: it must be done. But *don't* immerse yourself in the issue of verb conjugations yet! That comes last, when you've amassed a substantial lexicon of nouns, adjectives, and infinitives; and you're *eager* to begin learning how to make the "action" words assume real, grammatically correct vivacity.

Yes, verbs come last. Because they must be conjugated for most effective conversational use, and because conjugation is every language's most complex morass, verbs are by far the toughest to master. In infinitive form, as presented herein (as in all language-reference books), they're a snap; but in conjugated form—well, that's a considerably knottier problem. But when you're ready—after, say, you've got two or three hundred easy nouns and adjectives in hand, your effort toward verb mastery will seem a worthy price to pay.

3. Finally, as you begin to build and augment your core Spanish vocabulary, do not forget the time-tested / experience-proven value of a "flash" system of memory-embedding, review, and self-testing! If you're computer adept, you can create such a tool within your PC with either a database, spreadsheet, or word-processing program; or by using one of the many notebook-type applications widely available. (At least one, in all likelihood, is embedded within your computer's operating system itself.) Alternatively—and portably!—hand-lettered 2″ x 4″ cards (English on one side, Spanish with pronunciation key, gender code, and perhaps even pluralization on the other) never lose their effectiveness. In either case, the very act of transposing words into such a system is, in and of itself, a valuable aid to learning and retention. And of course, the value of a ready-review tool cannot be overstated.

FORMAT & SYMBOLOGY

All entries in this book follow the same pattern: an extra space separates the English from the Spanish or the Spanish from the English portions of each word set; the English or Spanish call word—depending on which word list you're consulting—is always shown in boldface text and its English or Spanish counterpart, in regular text. A phonetic representation of the Spanish term's pronunciation is appended to each entry, within parentheses and in italics.

Masculine and feminine nouns are signified throughout by an "*m.*" or an " *f.*"—unless they are plural, in which case they are signified by an "*m. pl.*" or an "*f. pl.*"—and bigender terms by "*m. & f.*" Occasionally, you may find an *n.* (for *noun*) to distinguish the noun meaning of the word from that of a different part of speech. Adjectives (always shown in the masculine form!) are denoted by (adj.), usually positioned after the adjective itself; and verbs (always shown in the infinitive form) by "to." Adverbs, conjunctions, pronouns, prepositions, and colloquial expressions are assumed to be self-identifying and / or unimportant to be so distinguished in the present context, and thus bear no such denotations.

In instances where noncognate English terms *also directly translate* to the Spanish word, they will conjoin the cognate in immediate succession, separated by slashes. Thus, the entry

abandon / forsake / give up / renounce (to) abandonar (ah-<u>b</u>ahn-doh-NAHR)

indicates that in addition to the closely cognate term at the far left, the annexed terms *are also directly translatable* by the Spanish word. In more instances than not, a string of English words separated by slashes will be closely related and synonymous within itself—*but not always!* For example, the following entries

front / forehead (!) *f.* frente (FREHN-teh)

phrase / sentence *f.* frase (FRAH-seh)

(railway) station / season (*of the year*) (!)
f. estación (ehs-tah-SYOHN)

illustrate that English terms with considerably different meanings can own the same translation into Spanish. Terms with notably nonsynonymous additional meanings are flagged with a parenthesized explanation point, as noted in two of the entries immediately above. *The learner must be particularly alert to these word strings,* and must remember to make a separate "flash" device entry for each elemental pair.

Similarly, where more than a single Spanish word is a direct translation of the English term(s) at the left, a slash separates them. Again, the diligent student will provide him- / herself with a "flash" device for *every* word-pairing listed!

Symbolic markings in this book are as follows:

- Where a "bomb" (💣) symbol is appended to an entry, it refers to a subtle spelling differentiation between the English and Spanish terms that might be overlooked without the symbol.

- Where space permits, arrows embracing a ↺word or fragment↻ indicate an important similarity (including location of the stressed syllable) between related Spanish word forms. Where minor spelling differences are noted, the part of the word that is missing from the hyphenated *-fragment* is drawn from the original, and subsequent characters indicate the alteration. Thus the line

> **friend**   *m.* amigo (ah-MEE-goh) ↺*f.* -ga↻

indicates that the noun exists in both genders and that the spelling of the feminine form is ***amiga***. Similarly, the entry

> **negative (*reply or value*)**   *f.* negativa
> (neh-gah-TEE-<u>b</u>ah) ↺(adj.) -vo↻

indicates that the English noun-related adjective *negative* is spelled ***negativo*** in Spanish. And entries

> **diligence**   *f.* diligencia (dee-lee-HEHN-syah)
> ↺(adj.) **diligent** -nte↻

> **physics (*science of*)**   *f.* física (FEE-see-kah)
> ↺(adj.) **physical** -co↻

demonstrate that differing forms need not be identical, but rather only closely related to warrant the memory-convenience of single-line placement.

- Arrows embracing a ☐ check symbol specify that a related word form is *identical* to the listed term, even if the English correspondent differs. Thus, the entries

> **human**   *m.* humano (oo-MAH-noh) ↺(adj.) ☐↻

> **contrary**   *m.* contrario (kohn-TRAH-ryoh) ↺(adj.) ☐↻

> **parallel**   *m.* paralelo (pah-rah-LEH-loh) ↺(adj.) ☐↻

carnivore   *m.* carnívoro (kahr-NEE-<u>b</u>oh-roh)
 ↺(adj.) **carnivorou**s ☐↺

coward   *m. & f.* cobarde (koh-BAHR-<u>d</u>eh)
 ↺(adj.) **cowardly / craven** ☐↺ ♠※

indicate that the Spanish adjectives meaning *human, contrary, parallel, carnivorous,* and *cowardly / craven* are spelled and pronounced in exactly the same way as their Spanish corresponding nouns.

- In instances where it's possible to offer significant additional intelligence or clarification about a given word or closely related (but not necessarily cognate) term, it will be provided directly below the entry, flagged by the international "Information" symbol, ①. Because these notes contain an important wealth of additional vocabulary, data, and understanding, the learner is urged to pay careful attention to their content. Again, much of this information is worthy of being added to the user's collection of "flash" devices.

- Finally, a boxed double-headed arrow symbol ⬄ is appended to words that are pronounced differently in "classic" Castilian and Latin American Spanish. More information in this regard is provided in the following chapter on pronunciation.

SPANISH PRONUNCIATION

The Spanish language is more widely dispersed than any other tongue save English; and in the half millennium of its diffusion, it has lost much of its original uniformity in pronunciation. Today *español* is a language that owns a significant variety of regional norms. Thus, a **gentleman**—caballero (kah-<u>b</u>ah-YEH-roh) in one Spanish-speaking community becomes a (kah-bah-LYEH-roh) in another Spanish-speaking community, and something else still in yet another. One of them will be just as **feliz** (feh-LEES), or happy, as the other is (feh-LEETH). And so on. Linguistic diffusion, in short, has been a mighty wrecker of Spanish pronunciational purity, and an ongoing impetus toward local change and diversity. Like English, Spanish has become a very variously spoken tongue indeed!

Despite vocal differentiation, tens of thousands of *gringos* very effectively learn Spanish every year. Despite the various pronunciations they may have been taught by instructors (or textbook authors!) arising from different local traditions, they are able to communicate with each other with unmistakable clarity. Just as a highborn Londoner, a Cockney laborer, a Scottish bagpiper, a Canadian banker, a Boston attorney, a house painter from Biloxi, a wheat farmer from Kansas, a young New Delhi computer technician, a sheep broker from Christchurch, and a surfer from Melbourne can readily understand one another's English despite their wildly variant intonations, so also can Spaniards, Mexicans, Venezuelans, Puerto Ricans, Argentineans, Colombians, Cubans, Chileans, and older Filipinos—and everyone else in the Spanish-speaking world—comprehend each other without missing a beat. They simply think of each other's variant pronunciations as somewhat odd and "charming."

In this volume, rigid scholastic "historic correctness" in this regard (usually outdated at best) is disregarded in favor of on-the-ground reality, and no one pronunciational regionalism preferred over another. Neither will any variant be blithely ignored (a standard classroom and textbook practice) as though it didn't exist. Rather, the primary differentiations will be carefully delineated; and the one that predominates—that is, *the one that is most widely used* in everyday social intercourse across the broad spectrum of Spanish culture—will then be recommended in each case, and thenceforth used in phonetic description. Thus, the learner will be alerted to the pronunciational differences that he or she may encounter from place to place, while gaining a firm grasp on those that are most likely to be correct in the broadest range of circumstances and locales.

ONE CRUCIAL DIFFERENCE

As far as pronunciation goes, this volume is primarily concerned with Latin American *español*, the Spanish that developed in the New World and is spoken in Central and South America and in the Caribbean, rather than Castilian Spanish—the original mother tongue, widely known as *castellano*, rooted in the heart of Spain. However, because some users may wish to learn *castellano* as well as Latin American Spanish—or perhaps need the former to the exclusion of the latter—*both* pronunciations will be detailed in the course of our letter-by-letter review, below. While space-limitation precludes the inclusion of alternative pronunciations for every affected word in this book's various compendia, at least a symbolic reminder—a double-ended arrow ⬌ pointing eastward toward Spain and westward toward the Americas—will be appended to each such term, alerting readers to words that they may wish to annotate to reflect proper *castellano* pronunciation. Those learners not interested in Castilian Spanish might be well advised to avoid potential confusion by ignoring these symbols and differences altogether!

TRAINING YOUR EAR

Even though the distinctions noted above are unavoidably evident in the language-recording industry (some readers bring a classic Castilian enunciation to the microphone, for example, while others express one of their native Latin American intonations—such as Cuban, Puerto Rican, or Peruvian), the learner will nonetheless gain greatly from an introductory immersion into the general sound of contemporary *español*. While the pronunciation of some characters will almost inevitably differ from the one that is offered herein, the fundamental pace, cadence, and stress of the language are virtually identical—as is the pronunciation of *most* alphabet sounds—across all regional divides. One needs to become familiar with them at an early point for confident progress to be assured. Therefore, as one of this book's users, you are *urged in the strongest possible terms* to follow the prescription outlined below before undertaking attainment of Spanish vocabulary and understanding of the language's underlying grammatical structure. Do *not* begin amassing words until you've learned how they actually sound and "say" in general.

From your own audio collection, or from a friend's, or from your local library, or from the bookstore where you purchased this book, obtain a tape or CD that contains spoken Spanish and *listen* to it. That's all you have to do for the time being: just listen. Do not at this point try to learn words or phrases or "understand" anything at all. *Just listen!* Unhook the phone, dim the lights, close your eyes, lean your head back, and simply let the speaker's voice wash over and imbue you for thirty minutes at least. Or, better yet, a full hour. Just *hearing.*

The ideal recording for this ear-training exercise would be one that contains no English at all—the recounting of a story, a news report, a conversational interchange, or the reading of a book in Spanish. However, it may be difficult to find such all-Spanish recordings in any but the largest metropolitan centers (or on the Internet, of course). So you'll very possibly end up with an instructional audio in which English words and phrases are presented first, followed by their Spanish equivalents, spoken somewhat more slowly than normal. No great matter: you're not now concerned with meaning at all, but rather simply with *sound.* Your sole objective is to become initially familiar with the general "shape," intonation, stress, and rise-and-fall cadence of Spanish vocalization. Nothing else.

At the conclusion of your listening session, take an hour's or a day's break, and then return to the recording and listen again. Then again. And, if possible, yet again, until you've experienced a total of two to four hours of "immersion" listening. *Every minute you invest in such listening will pay itself back* in time saved from future uncertainty, confusion, and misunderstanding.

Count yourself done when the general sound of Spanish has begun to become so familiar and well imbedded in your mind that its few "weird" vocalizations cease to seem odd at all, and you can begin to confidently anticipate both the sound, pace, and feel of the language as it unfolds from word to word. You're beginning to get bored? Good! You're progressing: it's becoming "old hat"!

And with that—*at least four* listening sessions of a half hour to one hour each well embedded in your ear—you're done with initial "ear training," and ready to begin "seeing and saying" Spanish.

If you have access to a PBS channel that regularly airs a Spanish instructional series (usually late at night and / or during weekend hours) or to a cable system that offers extensive Spanish news and / or programming, videotape and watch / listen to several such programs for several half-hour sessions at least. If you continue to do so, or repeatedly listen to your tapes / CDs during your vocabulary-building period, your understanding, competence, and skill will all be steadily strengthened, and your progress accelerated and solidified.

TRAINING YOUR EYES AND MOUTH

Now, with listening done, turn to the two sections in this chapter that immediately follow, "The Matter of Stress" and "'Saying' the Spanish Alphabet," and carefully study the pronunciation overviews offered there. You'll find that the issue of which syllable to stress is very simple indeed. The majority of alphabetic characters, too, present little challenge. They pronounce either identically or almost identically to their English counterparts, and they can be dispensed with in a matter of minutes. Mastering the "tricky" letters and diphthongs is a bit more of a chore, however, and will require your concentrated—and probably repeated—attention. When you reach the "difficult" letters . . . well, that's where the real work begins.

Upon completion of your initial review of those matters, return HERE for suggestions regarding practice and implementation of your mounting knowledge. From that point forward, you will probably want to alternate back-and-forth between specific-letter re-review and practice.

Having completed your first alphabetic letter-by-letter pronunciation review, now open the book toward the middle to any two-page spread. There, working at an unhurried pace *and pointedly ignoring* both the leftmost *boldface English word* on each line and *the light-face Spanish word* that follows, move slowly from entry to entry, *focusing solely on each term's phonetic representation*—that is, the parenthesized syllable-by-syllable rendition of each line's Spanish word. Your objective is to attempt to vocalize (say aloud!) that representation in mimicry of the type and quality of sound you've recently heard issue from your loudspeakers or headphones, and in accordance with the specific pronunciation guidance offered in the detailed review.

For now, pay no attention whatsoever to words, their actual spellings or meanings. Your sole concern should be with *sound*— that is, with an attempt to match your mouth to the phonetic representation given for each entry, pointedly including the ALL-CAPS accentuated syllable. It is likely that in some instances, particularly in your first few minutes of trying, your mouth will resist some of the constructions found; but press on. Millions of people don't find these sounds arduous at all, and many thousands more successfully learn how to form them every year. There's nothing even vaguely "impossible" here; just some seeming strangeness and modest difficulty at the start. It will soon abate!

Remaining unhurried—and unconcerned, for the moment, whether you're getting it precisely right (you're almost certainly *not,* at least some of the time)—continue your out-loud pronunciational effort from top to bottom of at least two full pages, and preferably three or four. Then call it quits for a while. Total investment thus far: between thirty and forty-five minutes. You may not realize it yet, but you've just made a huge step *into Spanish*!

As soon as practicable, return to a spread of pages within this book's **LISTA DE TÉRMINOS IDÉNTICOS Y SIMILARES (List of Identical and Similar Terms)**. For variety's sake, pick a different alphabetical section this time; and repeat your out-loud enunciation of the phonetics found there. This time, however, you are going to look carefully at the *Spanish word* on each line before vocalizing its phonic representation. You still don't care about the word's *meaning* (although in many instances, now, that will be self-evident), but you do want to start to make a firm connection between the word's actual spelling and its phoneticized representation. Between spelling and sound, in short.

Continue your reading-and-pronouncing effort for, again, two full pages at least, and preferably several more. By now, you should be beginning to master the production of some of the more difficult sounds specified by the phonetic code. When you're satisfied with your progress (again, a half-hour minimum is advised), take another break before returning to . . .

Give yourself an initial *acceleration test*. Again selecting a random beginning point and again completely ignoring both the spelling and the meaning of the term, pick a two- or three-syllable word as your starting point, and rather than merely attempting to pronounce it as the phonetic guide suggests, practice doing so at a faster and faster rate, until it's emerging from your mouth as a unified whole rather than a jerky syllable-by-syllable construction. This may seem particularly difficult at first, especially in the case of terms that contain distinctly "un-English" pronunciations. But keep at it, and slowly, surely, you *will* begin to become not only the master of virtually any construction that falls beneath your eye, but moreover a *rapid-*master, capable of expressing whole words rather than slowly enunciated syllable-by-syllable constructs.

Stay with your one chosen word until a dozen or more increasingly rapid repetitions have forced your mouth into the required shapes and movements to get it spoken with quick confidence. Then move on to another word, and another and another, repeating in each case the same progress from slow / careful pronunciation to confident rapid-fire *expression* of the whole-unit term—that is, with a smoothly ever-diminishing space between syllables. Just as your out-loud reading of the words of *this* English paragraph would be, through years of familiarity and everyday practice, essentially without lengthy intraword breaks, so also do you want to attain the point where your expression of Spanish terms will be similarly unified and unpaused except between the whole words themselves.

You're undoubtedly some distance from that level of expertise still—but you *are* headed in that direction! One word at a time. Over and over. And soon, you'll find that each new word—even those difficult five- and six-syllable monsters—becomes all the easier to attain and really, deeply master. Hard? Not really. All it takes, like any other skill, is *practice* . . . *practice* . . . *practice*! For thirty minutes . . . an hour . . . maybe two.

And by that point you really *will* be becoming comfortable and expert—not only beginning to hear Spanish words as they're spoken in everyday conversation, but moreover noticing that these pleasing sounds are issuing from *your* mouth and understanding! It's an important point to have achieved!

In sum, in less than a half-dozen hours you've not only *absorbed* a new sound structure, but you've also begun to be comfortable with its use—and you're almost ready, now, to begin building your cognate-based Spanish vocabulary with accuracy and confidence. This chapter's concluding sections will finalize and solidify your understanding of the basics of Spanish pronunciation, and leave you fully ready to begin absorbing *language*.

THE MATTER OF STRESS

Spanish words, like those of every language, contain variable syllable-to-syllable accentuation, or stress. Thankfully, in all variant iterations of *español* (including *castellano*), the structural rules regarding stress are identical and far simpler than they are for many tongues; indeed, they are so simple that they can be learned in seconds.

- If a word concludes with a VOWEL, an *N*, or an *S*, it is to be stressed on its penultimate (next-to-last) syllable. Period! Thus: **letter**—letra (LEH-trah); **word**—palabra (pah-LAH-brah); **phrase / sentence**—frase (FRAH-seh); **verb**—verbo (BEHR-boh); and **consonants**—consonantes (kohn-soh-NAHN-tehs).

- All other Spanish words, unless accent-marked otherwise (see below), *are* stressed on their final syllable. Period! Thus: **to speak**—hablar (ah-BLAHR); **to converse**—conversar (kohn-behr-SAHR); and **vocal**—vocal (boh-KAHL).

- If for any reason a word's proper stress falls elsewhere than as described above, an acute accent mark ['] will appear above the vowel in its properly stressed syllable. Thus: **expression**—expresión (ehs-preh-SYOHN); **syllable**—sílaba (SEE-lah-bah); and **term / word**—término (TEHR-mee-noh).

An acute accent occasionally serves a secondary purpose; that is, it does not invariably relate solely to a word's proper stress point. Sometimes it's also used to distinguish between words that are identical in spelling, but own different meanings. The best example of this is the distinction between the words *el* and *él*. The first of these is the very common masculine singular definite article, *the*; the second, accented version specifies *he*. In all such instances, the two words pronounce identically: the "distinguishing" (rather than "stress-indicating") accent mark sets the two meanings of the same word apart in the written form of the language, something that the context takes care of in speech.

"SAYING" THE SPANISH ALPHABET

Spanish possesses all the letters contained in the English alphabet plus two, three, or four more: all linguistic authorities agree that by tradition and / or logical requirement, **LL (YEH)** and **Ñ (EH-nyeh)** need to be classified as individual letters; some also argue in favor of the same designation for the two-unit characters **CH (CHEH)** and **RR (EH-rreh)**— an argument honored here by their separate listings. Thirty in all! Lest the learner be discouraged by this superabundance, however, note that all four of the "extra" letters are easy to pronounce and that two others of the thirty—**K** and **W** (both imports to Spanish from other tongues)—are used so little as to be virtually invisible, practically speaking.

Of the remainder, many are easy to master, as their pronunciation is either identical with or very close to the English norm. That is good, because the others are "tricky" at best, or . . . well, very problematic and variant indeed!

Ready, then? The full Spanish alphabet, together with each letter's phonetic name-pronunciation and representative contextual pronunciation(s), is listed below. The listing sequence is from easiest-to-absorb by an English speaker, through somewhat more challenging—often because of the complexity of diphthong treatment—to really problematical, potentially confusing, variously pronounced, and most-difficult-to-master. *To help confirm and solidify your absorption of the sounds produced by the letters of the Spanish alphabet, you are urged to generate a self-testing "flash" device for each one!*

The "Easy" Letter Sounds

CH (CHEH)   A two-character "letter"? Yes! In case you slipped past the discussion several paragraphs above, many Spanish linguists and dictionaries consider the **CH** combination to be a distinct member of the alphabetic system. Quite apart from the history and rationale of this distinction, it's an easy "letter" to learn: it always and unvaryingly pronounces exactly as does an English *CH* combination—as in *change, check, child, choke,* or *chunk.*

F (EH-feh)   Easy again. The Spanish **F** is always identical in value to its English counterpart.

K (KAH)   This letter is a rarely seen import to the Spanish alphabet. In all cases it pronounces exactly as does the English *K.*

L (EH-leh)   Widely used in Spanish, the stand-alone **L** is pronounced exactly as in English.

M (EH-meh)   As in English. Always. No exceptions.

N (EH-neh)   The Spanish "naked" **N** (i.e., without an overtopping tilde) is pronounced exactly as in English.

Ñ (EH-nyeh)   Even though the *tilde-N* is a character unknown to English, its pronunciation is so straightforward and unvarying that its mastery proves to be very easy indeed. Simply put, the Spanish **Ñ** always pronounces as an English *N* + *Y*-sound combined with the vowel that immediately follows. The complete sound will be: *ña* (NYAH), *ñe* (NYEH), *ñi* (NYEEH), *ño* (NYOH), or *ñu* (NYOO). Easy! "Spanish **Ñ** as in *canyon* or *onion.*"

P (PEH)   Easy again! The Spanish **P** is always and invariably pronounced exactly as in the English words *pass, pea, pink, plow, pod, prom,* or *punch.*

R (EH-reh) and **RR (EH-rreh)**   The Spanish **R** is essentially identical to its English counterpart, with the notable distinction of sometimes being "rolled," or "trilled." The rolled **R** is universal among speakers of both Latin American Spanish and *castellano.* The **R**-roll is pronounced when the **R** occurs at the beginning of a word, and in the case of the double **RR**, of course. (In this volume, as a visual reminder that the **RR** inevitably receives a doubly emphatic trill, it is represented, phonetically, as **RR**.

For many students, accustomed since infancy to the flat *R* of English speech, learning to relax and flutter the front of the tongue so as to produce an **R**-roll initially proves to be difficult. With a few minutes of persistent practice, however, the skill can be achieved. Once gained, the Spanish **RR** becomes very straightforward, natural, and easy, indeed. Summary: rrrrroll your Spanish **RR**s!

T (TEH)   Again, exactly as in English.

W (DOH-bleh-beh)   This rarely seen imported-to-Spanish character meets many different pronunciational fates in the mouths of its occasional users. If you stick to the standard English pronunciation, you'll be judged correct far more often than not (it is, after all, *your* letter, not theirs!), and you will always be understood. "Spanish *W* as in English *whiskey*, *wine*, and *why*."

The "Tricky" Letter Sounds

The letters in this subsection include the Spanish vowels (*vocales*), which are *A, E, I, O,* and *U.* Each of these owns an essentially easy pronunciation, unless it occurs in a diphthong or is followed by a *Y.* In most of these latter cases the "easy" pronunciational standard changes considerably, as the two characters essentially combine to form a unified, altered sound.

In English, any combination of vowels is considered a diphthong. In Spanish, only the combination of a strong (*fuerte*) vowel (*A*, *E*, or *O*) with a weak (*débil*) one (*I* or *U*) yields a *diptongo.* Thus the combination of an *A* and an *E*, for example, is not a Spanish diphthong, but rather an instance in which each vowel retains its individual pronunciational value, and the space between them constitutes a distinct syllable break. (True diphthongs always unify within a single syllable.) Also not a diphthong is one in which an accent mark appears over the weak vowel; in such instances, the accent nullifies "diphthong status," and the two vowels segregate into separate syllables and revert to their singular pronunciations.

Because diphthongs are, in effect, separate and uniquely pronounced characters within the Spanish pronunciational alphabet, the learner is strongly urged to create a ready-review "flash" device for each one, as

well as for stand-alone letters. A flasher for each of the nondiphthongs—
e.g., "AE—NOT A DIPHTHONG!"—is also a good idea, as it's vital
that eye recognition and mental understanding of the effect of all vowel
combinations become automatic and instantaneous.

A (AH) At root, the Spanish alphabet's initial letter yields a very easy
pronunciation indeed. Simply put, when not conjoined with another
vowel into diphthong form, it invariably pronounces like an English soft
a, as in *mamma* or *papa*. So fix this one easily and firmly in mind: "Spanish
A as in *aah! bah!* and *father*," except in . . .

The *A*-diphthongs. The three vowel linkages in which Spanish *A*
plays an initial-letter role are as follows:

- **AI**, which pronounces with an English long-*i* sound—a quick, tightly
  compressed conjoining of the *AH* and *EE* intonations, represented
  phonetically as *EYE*. Thus: **air**—aire (EYE-reh) and **to isolate**—aislar
  (eyez-LAHR).

- **AU**, which pronounces like an English *AOW* sound, again melding
  the sounds ordinarily made by the two vowels. Thus: **to howl /
  wail**—aullar (aow-YAHR) and **absent**—ausente (aow-SEHN-teh).

- **AY**, when *Y* functions as a vowel, pronounces identically with the *AI*
  pairing, intoning with an English long-*i* sound. Thus: **there are**—hay
  (*EYE*).

C (SEH) Pronunciation of the Spanish *C* is context-dependent. It
pronounces with different intonations in combination with different
partner-letters.

- When followed by an *A*, *O*, *U*, or any *CONSONANT* except *H*, a
  Spanish *C* sounds exactly like the familiar English hard *c*, as in *case*,
  cover, or *cuddle*. This sound is represented phonetically as *K*. Thus:
  to accompany—acompañar (ah-kohm-pah-NYAHR), **clarinet**—
  clarinete (klah-ree-NEH-teh), **crocodile**—cocodrilo (koh-koh-
  DREE-loh), **to cure**—curar (koo-RAHR), and **house**—casa
  (KAH-sah).

- **CE** and **CI** combinations pronounce like an English soft *c*, as in English *century* and *cinch*; this is phonetically rendered as *S*. Thus: **celestial**—celestial (seh-lehs-TYAHL); **central**—central (sehn-TRAHL);

cigar—cigarro (see-GAH-rroh); **international**—internacional (een-tehr-nah-syoh-NAHL); and employing both pronunciations, **lesson**—lección (lehk-SYOHN).

⇔ In *castellano*, **CE** and **CI** are pronounced with a wildly anti-intuitive *TH* sound! Thus, instead of the first two intonations noted immediately above: (theh-lehs-TYAHL) and (thehn-TRAHL).

E (EH) Like the other Spanish vowels, the pronunciation of a Spanish *E* is in most locales essentially simple: apart from its diphthong forms, it pronounces like an English short *e*. It yields an aspirated *EH* sound, as in the English words *bet, debt, men,* or *petty*. Thus: **coffee pot**—cafetera (kah-feh-TEH-rah), **echo**—eco (EH-koh), **minor**—menor (meh-NOHR), and **sincere**—sincero (seen-SEH-roh). But then come the "dips" . . .

The *E*-diphthongs. The two-vowel unions in which Spanish *E* plays an initial-letter role are as follows:

- **EI**, which pronounces with an English long-*a* intonation: a tight, fast consolidation of the *EH* and *EE* sounds produced by the partners in nonintegrated contexts. This sound is phonetically represented as *AY*. Representative examples are **baseball**—béisbol (BAYS-<u>b</u>ohl), **six**—seis (SAYS), and **thirty**—treinta (TRAYN-tah).

- **EU**, which is pronounced as "EHW." For example, **Europe**—Europa (ehw-ROH-pah).

- **EY**, a letter combination that pronounces like the **EI** diphthong, with a long-*a* (AY) intonation. Thus: **law**—ley (LAY) and **king**—rey (RAY).

G (HEH) Like *C*, the Spanish *G* is a context-dependent two-voiced character. In most instances, *G* sounds exactly like an English hard *g*. Thus: **gallop**—galope (gah-LOH-peh); **global**—global (gloh-<u>B</u>AHL); **gum**—goma (GOH-mah*)*; **miracle**—milagro (mee-LAH-groh); **organ**—órgano (OHR-gah-noh); and **program**—programa (proh-GRAH-mah).

- In dramatic contrast, when Spanish *G* is immediately followed by an *E* or an *I*, its intonation becomes identical with that of a Spanish *J,* which in turn is a somewhat harsh and guttural version of the English *h,* as detailed below at letter *J.* Thus: **gem**—gema (HEH-mah), **general**—general (heh-neh-RAHL), **agent**—agente (ah-HEHN-teh), and **to mourn**—afligirse (ah-flee-HEER-seh). The adjective **gigantic**—gigante (hee-GAHN-teh) exemplifies both of these very distinct pronunciations within the same term.

H (AH-cheh) Pronunciation of the Spanish *H* is "tricky" because it's often hard for new learners to remember that it doesn't pronounce at all! Never! It is always silent. Except in combination with a *C,* it is absolutely mute. Unvoiced. Essentially nonexistent; not even vocally *hinted* at! No exceptions!

Given the hundreds of Spanish words that begin with this character, the hundreds more that include it within their bodies without a conjoining *C,* and the many, many words that contain an English almost-*h* sound as part and parcel of their makeup (produced by letters other than *H*), this may seem an anomaly of inscrutable depth. So be it. That's the way it *is*: One doesn't hear the letter *H*; one doesn't say it. One must only remember to ignore it!

I (EE) On its own, the Spanish *I* pronounces like an English long *e,* as in *lien* or *machine.* Always! Thus: **agriculture**—agricultura (ah-gree-kool-TOO-rah), **fatigue**—fatiga (fah-TEE-gah), **lantern**—linterna (leen-TEHR-nah), **princess**—princesa (preen-SEH-sah), and **tyrant**—tirano (tee-RAH-noh).

In combination with other vowels, the Spanish *I* loses all trace of its "long-*e*-ness," but because it is a *débil* (weak) vowel at the mercy of its superiors, it assumes a new uniformity.

The *I*-diphthongs. The four vowel linkings in which Spanish *I* plays an initial-letter role are as follows:

- **IA**, in which the two letters condense their individual pronunciations (*EE* and *AH*), yielding an English *y* + *ah*-sound. Thus: **diabetic**—diabético (dyah-BEH-tee-koh) and **fiasco / failure**—fiasco (FYAHS-koh).

- **IE** follows the same pattern, yielding *YEH*. Thus **piece**—pieza (PYEH-sah) and **grandson**—nieto (NYEH-toh).

- **IO**, similarly, pronounces **YOH**. As in **near-sighted** / **myopic**—miope (MYOH-peh) and **biography**—biografía (byoh-grah-FEE-ah). Note that in the latter word, the concluding -*ÍA* combination is not a dipthong, owing to the presence of the accent mark on the weak vowel, *I*.

- **IU,** completing the established pattern, pronounces **YOO.** Thus: **diurnal** / **daytime**—diurno (DYOOR-noh) and **widow**—viuda (BYOO-<u>d</u>ah).

J (HO-tah)   In essence, the Spanish **J** is fairly simple: it never issues with what an English speaker knows as a *j*-sound, but rather sounds almost like an English *h*. (Think of a baseball player named Jesús (heh-SOOS).) Indeed, it's so close to an *h*-sound that the learner is perfectly safe in accepting that as a general substitution, and being done with the issue. Thus, "Spanish *J* as in English *hat, heat, hit, hot,* or *hut*."

If you wish to speak with fully authentic pronunciation, however, there's a bit more work to be done. The "almost-*h*" intonation of a Spanish *J* is distinctly harsher and more guttural than the gentle, breathy openness of a purely English *h*. An English speaker projects the beginning of that sound from his voice box to the front of his mouth over a tongue that remains absolutely inactive until called upon to produce the remainder of the sound. The initiation of the Spanish *J* = *H*-sound, in contrast, is forced over an active tongue, its back slightly fluttering against the posterior hard palate. The resulting sound—almost a forceful, quasi-Germanic semigargle, or the beginning of a thick "spitting" sound—is utterly unknown to English, and frankly sounds. . . well, almost coarse, to ears accustomed to the softer American and British intonation.

With minimal practice, a fully correct Spanish *J* becomes easy; and it will earn widespread admiration from Spanish-speakers unaccustomed to hearing a foreigner "get it right." Otherwise, one can simply be satisfied with a plain-vanilla *h*-sound, and move on to more pressing matters.

LL (YEH)   Again, a two-letter combination officially deemed to be a separate alphabetic character. In this case, there is no English *ll*-like sound at all in general Latin American pronunciation, but rather the issuance of an English *y*-sound combined with the vowel that invariably follows. None of these are even modestly difficult to form in the English-accustomed mouth. Thus: **butter**—mantequilla (mahn-teh-KEE-yah); **hen**—gallina (gah-YEE-nah), and **passageway**—pasillo (pah-SEE-yoh). An example of the differing pronunciation of the **L** and **LL** characters within the same word: **moth**—polilla (poh-LEE-yah).

⇔ In *castellano*, an **LL** is called an *lyeh*, and is pronounced with an intrinsic **L**-sound, closely bound to an English *y* intonation combined with the following vowel. Simply put, it is identical to the Latin American pronunciation save for the leading **L** intonation. The best English-equivalent example is the *lli* combination in the English word *million*. In *castellano*, the examples in the paragraph above would pronounce (mahn-teh-KEE-lyah), (gah-LYEE-nah), (pah-SEE-lyoh), and (poh-LEE-lyah). And of course, the term *castellano* itself would be (kahs-tee-LYAH-noh).

!!! REGIONALISM! Although not one of the "big bad three" of pronunciational anomalies, it is worth noting that in the southern-most South American nations (Argentina, Paraguay, and Uruguay), the **LL** is often—but not without exceptions—pronounced like an English *J*.

O (OH)   Except in diphthongs, the Spanish **O** is invariably pronounced like an English long *o*, as in *boat, comb, hope, mole*, or *toad*. It never makes an **AH**-sound as found in such English terms as *bottle,* or an **OO**-sound as in English *move,* or an **UH**-sound as in *cover* or *shove*. It's simply, always, equivalent to a round, free-flowing *o*. Thus: **deep**—hondo (OHN-doh); **graph**—gráfica (GRAH-fee-kah); **north**—norte (NOHR-teh); and **oasis**—oasis (oh-AH-sees). Almost as easy to master are . . .

The O-diphthongs. The two vowel pairings in which Spanish **O** plays an initial-letter role are as follows:

- **OI**, which pronounces like an English *oy,* as in *boy* or *toy.* Thus: **boycot**—boicot (boy-KOHT) and **bribe**—coima (KOY-mah).

- **OU** is an uncommon diphthong that can best be described as almost retaining the sound of its separate constituents, albeit in condensed form. Thus: **seiner**—bou (BOW).

- **OY**, a letter combination that pronounces exactly as it sounds in English. Thus: **today**—hoy (OY).

Q (KOO)   The Spanish **Q** is highly similar to its English counterpart, with one important distinction. The difference lies in its ending. In English, we always pair the Q with a *U,* and give the combination an essential *KW*-sound, as in *quart, queen, quiet, quote.* The Spanish **Q** is also invariably paired with a **U**, and just as invariably initiates with an English *K* intonation. But it ends there. Literally! It does not trail a **W**-sound behind it, or impart any sound value to the trailing **U**, but rather jumps from the initial **K** intonation to the sound of the letter following the **U.** Thus **cheese**—queso (KEH-soh) and **keel**—quilla (KEE-yah). In sum: Spanish **Q** like plain-and-simple English *K.*

S (EH-seh)   The Spanish **S** usually pronounces exactly as it does in English, with a sibilant *s*-sound, as in *sassy.* Thus: **before**—antes (AHN-tehs), **scale**—escala (ehs-KAH-lah), and **until**—hasta (AHS-tah). However,

- When followed by letters **B**, **D**, **G**, **L**, **M**, **N**, or **V**, or usually, when embraced by *VOWELS ON EITHER SIDE*, the **S** takes on an English *z* intonation, as found in the English terms *design* and *mechanism.* Thus: **baptism**—bautismo (baow-TEEZ-moh), **disadvantageous**— desventajoso   (dehz-<u>b</u>ehn-tah-HOH-soh),   and   **measure / appraisal**—tasa (TAH-zah). Note that when the latter of a pair of embracing vowels is an **O** that ends the word, an emphatic **S**-sound, rather than **Z**, is usually preferred. Thus **kiss**—beso (*BEH-soh*).

!!! **REGIONALISM!** When preceding a consonant, or at the end of a word, many Spanish speakers enunciate a single **S** with a drawn-out "hissy" intonation that is almost equivalent to the strength of a rolled **R**, e.g. **oasis**—oasis (oh-AH-seess). Although that practice is not followed here, the learner will never be "wrong" if he / she finds it preferable to be especially emphatic with his / her pronunciation of **S.**

U (OO)   The Spanish **U** is "tricky" only because of the complexity of two of its diphthong variants. On its own, embraced by consonants, it produces a consistent English double-*o* sound, as it does in such English words as *cuckoo, dune, judicial, lure,* and *tune.* Thus: **cockroach**—cucaracha (koo-kah-RAH-cha); **furtive**—furtivo (foor-TEE-<u>b</u>oh), **moon**—luna

(LOO-nah), and **pulmonary**—pulmonar (pool-moh-NAHR). But then come . . .

The U-diphthongs. The four diphthongs in which Spanish **U** plays an initial-letter role all share the same characteristic . . . with exceptions. Namely, in each case the **U** loses all trace of its "oo-ness," adopts an English *w* intonation, and combines the latter with the partner vowel's essential sound. Thus:

- **UA** pronounces as an English **WAH**. Thus: **annual**—anual (ah-NWAHL), **tongue**—lengua (LEHN-gwah), and **water**—agua (AH-gwah).

- **UE** pronounces **WEH**. Thus: **new**—nuevo (NWEH-boh), **port**—puerto (PWEHR-toh), and **town**—pueblo (PWEH-bloh).

!!! **EXCEPTIONS!** When a **UE** or a **UI** is preceded by either a **G** or a **Q**, the **U** falls silent and pronunciation jumps directly from the preceding letter to the following **E**. Thus: **banker**—banquero (bahn-KEH-roh), **cheese**—queso (KEH-soh), **war**—guerra (GEH-rrah), **architect**—arquitecto (ahr-kee-TEHK-toh), **butter**—mantequilla (mahn-teh-KEE-yah), and **machine**—máquina (MAH-kee-nah). Note that in these cases, the same effect is produced by the standards outlined for the letters **G** and **Q**, above.

!!! **EXCEPTIONS EXCEPTION!** The exceptions noted above do not apply when an otherwise-silenced **U** is topped by a *diaeresis*—that is, a two-dot mark—and the **U** is replaced by a **Ü**. In these cases the exceptions are nullified, and the **UE** and **UI** revert to standard pronunciations. Thus: **blond / fair**—güero (GWEH-roh), and **penguin**—pingüino (peen-GWEE-noh).

- **UO** pronounces **WOH**. Thus: **ancient**—antiguo (ahn-TEE-gwoh), **continual / continuous**—continuo (kohn-TEE-nwoh), and **quota**—cuota (KWOH-tah).

- **UY** at end of word pronounces **WEE**. Thus: **very**—muy (MWEE).

Of course, returning to our initial review of diphthongs in general, if and when an otherwise-diphthonged **U** is topped by an acute accent mark **(Ú)**, its diphthong status is broken, and both the **U** and its conjoining vowel segregate into separate syllables and pronounce as stand-alones. Thus: **trunk / chest**—baúl (bah-OOL).

X (EH-kees) Because the Spanish **X** owns four (!) distinct pronunciations, it might at first glance appear to be a very troublesome letter indeed. A fairly simple set of rules defines which preference prevails in any given circumstance, however; and because over ninety-five percent of all such terms are covered by the first two of those standards, the letter is merely "tricky" rather than truly difficult to master. Specifically,

- In words beginning with an ***EX*** + *VOWEL* combination, the combination intones with an ***EHGS***-sound. Thus: **exact**—exacto (ehg-SAHK-toh); **exempt**—exento (ehg-SEHN-toh); **existence**—existencia (ehg-sees-TEHN-syah). REMEMBER that because a Spanish *H* is always silent, this rule also embraces terms that initiate with an *EX* + *H* + *VOWEL* linkage. Thus, **exhibition**—exhibición (ehg-see-bee-SYOHN).

- In words beginning with an ***EX*** + *CONSONANT* (except ***H***) combination, the **X** is pronounced with an emphatic ***ESS***-intonation. Thus: **excellent**—excelente (ehs-seh-LEHN-teh), **exclusive**—exclusivo (ehs-skloo-SEE-boh), **to excuse**—excusar (ehs-skoo-SAHR), **expectation**—expectación (ehs-spehk-tah-SYOHN), **explosive**—explosivo (ehs-sploh-SEE-boh), **extension**—extensión (ehs-stehn-SYOHN), and **exterior**—exterior (ehs-steh-RYOHR).

- In those few cases where the **X** occurs other than as described above, the familiar English-like **eks** pronunciation usually and most widely prevails. Thus: **annex**—anexo (ah-NEK-soh), **boxer**—*boxeador* (bohk-seh-ah-**DOHR**), **oxygen**—oxígeno (ohk-SEE-heh-noh), **reflection**—reflexión (reh-flek-SYOHN), and **sex**—sexo (SEHK-soh).

- In a small number of words imported into Spanish from indigenous native populations—almost invariably the names of regions, towns, or native deities—an **X** pronounces with an ***SH***-sound. Thus: **Ixtapa**—Ixtapa (eesh-TAH-pah).

!!! **REGIONALISM!** In several locales, the first three of the foregoing formulas are only loosely and inconsistently held to. The ubiquitous term *taxi,* for example, can vary in sound from (TAHG-see) to (TAHS-see) to (TAHK-see), not only from region to region, but almost from block to block! This occasional variability should not deter the learner from preferring and maintaining the above prescriptions as the basis of his or her own pronunciation.

Y (ee-GRYEH-gah)   The slightly variable pronunciation of the Spanish **Y** when preceded by a vowel has been covered in the diphthongs subsection under each vowel's entry. When followed by a vowel, the **Y** invariably owns an English soft *y* sound combined with the intonation of its subsequent companion. Thus: **beach**—playa (PLAH-yah), **jewel**—joya (HOH-yah), **legend**—leyenda (leh-YEHN-dah), **majority**—mayoría (mah-yoh-REE-ah),   **ray / beam**—rayo   (RAH-yoh),   and   **aid / asstance**—ayuda (ah-YOO-dah).

• When standing alone in the one-letter conjunction **and**—y (EE), the Spanish **Y** sounds like an English long *e.*

Z (SEH-tah)   Simply put, a Spanish **Z** never pronounces like its English counterpart. *Castellano* does not employ the "buzzed-*z*" pronunciation familiar to English and nor does Latin American Spanish. In Latin American Spanish the **Z** invariably sounds like an English *s,* as in *save, sense,* and *soft.* Thus: **alliance**—alianza (ah-LYAHN-sah), **light**—luz (loos), **plaza**—plaza (PLAH-sah), and **zone**—zona (SOH-nah). As for the folks in Spain, on the other hand . . .

⇔ *Castellano* treats letter **Z** as yet another opportunity to employ the **TH**-sound. Thus the words cited immediately above pronounce (ah-LYAHN-thah), (LOOTH), (PLAH-thah), and (THO-nah).

The "Difficult" Letter Sounds

The three remaining Spanish characters have been sending linguistic scholars, teachers, textbook authors, and language-learners alike into hair-pulling agonies for years.

Historically, in most regional traditions, each of these letters owns a "dual personality," being pronounced in some intraword positions with one enunciation, and in other positions with a different and distinctly un-

English sound. The difficulty of producing that secondary sound has led to the adoption by many teachers of a compromise that is close to the sound produced in Spanish, but by no means fully accurate.

None of the aforementioned traditions is absolutely consistent throughout the Spanish-speaking world: some communities hold to one letter's most widespread pair of pronunciations, while others modify or ignore them. Still other regions choose to deviate from the norm regarding a different character's enunciations. In short, consistency is utterly absent, and it would take a box full of different colored markers to even half-accurately depict this uneven preference dispersion on a map.

The foregoing patterns are today in accelerating evolutionary flux, under the prevalent influence of English media, population shift, and increasing intercultural exchange and accommodation.

A learner preferring to avoid this entire morass has an easy "out." To wit, he or she can simply choose to pronounce each of these letters in all positions and circumstances *as he / she would normally do in English!* This common practice will assure at least slight incorrectness in more cases than not, but in no instance at the risk of being misunderstood. All other alternatives assure being more correct in a broader variety of locales much more of the time.

B (BEH)   A Spanish **B** always sounds like an English **B** at the beginning of any word, or when preceded by an **M** or an **N**. Thus **balcony**— balcón (bahl-KOHN), **to combine**—combinar (kohm-<u>b</u>ee-NAHR), and **embassy**—embajada (ehm-<u>b</u>ah-HAH-<u>d</u>ah).

- With few exceptions, in all other positions and combinations, in more Spanish-speaking cultures than not, a very real pronunciational distinction does exist. *In this book, phonetic representation of these instances is indicated by an underscored* **B** (**<u>b</u>**). Thus **globe**—globo (GLOH-<u>b</u>oh) and **habit**—hábito (AH-<u>b</u>ee-toh).

- What is the "correct" secondary pronunciation? None actually exists! More specifically, in some regions an English-like **V**-sound prevails, while in others (a majority) a difficult-to-reproduce **B / V**-enunciation is the norm.

The learner who wishes to be "most correct, most of the time" will take the trouble to learn how to create a unified **B / V**-sound: a delicate lips-almost-closed-then-opened action to produce a subtle *BUH* intonation instantaneously combined with a *VUH* exhalation coming from behind lower-lip / upper-teeth contact. This is not an easy sound for the English-accustomed mouth to produce! Several score attempts, however, several days in succession, will lead to its mastery. Or, finally, most simply— and most commonly incorrect—an English-like *B* pronunciation can be utilized in all cases. No native Spanish speaker would be surprised by that choice!

D (DEH) Almost everything noted about the Spanish *B*, above, can be said about the *D* as well. It traditionally and still-generally owns two context-dependent pronunciations, one of which is identical to its English counterpart, and the other at considerable variance therefrom. That variance is inconsistently noted across the broad spectrum of Spanish society.

Herein, again, are the following conclusions and suggestions.

- A Spanish *D* always sounds like an English *D* at the beginning of any word or when preceded by an *L*, *M*, or *N*. Thus: **lady**—dama (DAH-mah), **day**—día (DEE-ah), **kettle**—caldera (kahl-<u>D</u>EH-rah), and **big**—grande (GRAHN-deh).

- Admitting a few idiosyncratic exceptions, in most other positions and combinations, in more regions than not, a real pronunciational distinction does exist between the enunciation above and the "second" intonation. *In this book, phonetic representation of these instances is indicated by an underscored D (<u>d</u>).* Thus: **you**—usted (oos-TEH<u>D</u>), **abdomen**—abdomen (ah<u>b</u>-<u>D</u>HOH-mehn), **city**—ciudad (syoo-<u>D</u>AH<u>D</u>), and **cellar / grocery store**—bodega (boh-<u>D</u>EH-gah).

What is the "correct" secondary pronunciation? A clear majority of authorities assert that the second *D* is equivalent to an English *TH*-sound, while an opposing group of scholars insist that the second *D* is one "with teeth," as described below.

Herein, we strongly side with the second school, and suggest that, again, the learner who wishes to be "most correct, most of the time" will take the effort to master the alternative described immediately above: the dental *D*, or "*D* with teeth." This is a pronunciation that is absolutely resistant to unambiguous phonetic depiction (in this volume, it's represented with an underscored *D*), but in fact is fairly easy to master. Specifically, it's a **D**-sound produced in a very un-English manner: a **D** intonation formed behind and then expelled from a tongue-between-teeth position. This being one of the two closely related ways we English speakers normally produce our *TH*-sound, the longstanding confusion is easily understood: the only difference is the nature of the tone being released by the withdrawing tongue. The Spanish **D**-with-teeth is a subtle admixture combination of those two sounds, albeit with clearly more *D* than *TH* intonation. Although it initially seems impossible to produce, a mere several dozen attempts and repetitions will bring gratifying mastery!

Students wishing an easier approach will opt for the *TH* alternative wherever they encounter an underscored **D**, while those willing to be less often correct will simply employ an English-like **D**-sound across the board. Again, no native Spanish speaker will be taken aback by that!

V (BEH *or* **OO-<u>b</u>eh)**   Spanish *V* always sounds like an English *B* at the beginning of a word or when preceded by an **M** or an **N**. Elsewhere the **B / V** combination discussed with regard to the letter **B**-sound above is the norm.

THE BASICS OF
SPANISH GRAMMAR

Simplicity, of course, cannot be expected within any tongue's grammatical makeup, pointedly including that of Spanish. Between the
nonintuitive assignment of noun genders, the need to make articles
and adjectives match the gender of the nouns they modify, the various
forms of adverbs, the deeply complex and often irregular verb conjugations—and yes, from time to time a flagrant inconsistency and / or self-
contradiction—the intricacies of Spanish grammar can be very taxing
indeed.

Owing to such complexities, it cannot be within the scope of this
book—which is, at root, an easy vocabulary builder rather than a comprehensive instructional text—to offer an all-inclusive, highly detailed analysis of the structure and rules of Spanish grammar. Practical comprehension
of the whole of *any* language's convoluted and often inconsistent architecture can only be gained through intensive study with knowledgeable
teachers and / or scholarly texts addressing and illustrating that issue alone;
and of course, through practice, practice, practice—culminating in extend-
ed conversational experience, preferably "on the ground," within that
tongue's home milieu.

As a guide to understanding the basic grammatical underpinnings of
Spanish, however, a general overview of its formal structure is offered on
the following pages. Enough, surely, to enable the attentive learner, utiliz-
ing the substantial cognate vocabulary he or she will have amassed from
within these pages, to become a competent, *effective* communicator, if not
an invariably and fluently "correct" one yet. Attainment of the latter status
must depend upon the ambitious learner's attention to more comprehensive direction than can be afforded here.

NOUNS
Gender

Spanish nouns—words that identify persons, places, and things—are unlike English nouns in that they are mysteriously assigned a gender. They are identified as either masculine or feminine or both, as in a very small number of cases, with far-reaching implications regarding their proper use and that of associated articles and modifiers. The student who fails to learn a noun's gender along with its spelling and pronunciation will severely hinder his or her advancement toward correct understanding and use of the Spanish language!

GENDER UNDERSTANDING #1. With only a few obvious exceptions (see *Gender Understanding #2*), linguistic gender bears no relationship whatsoever to sexual gender. In the overwhelming majority of cases, a Spanish noun's gender assignment does not arise from any intrinsically male or female quality owned or implied by the animate or inanimate entity the word designates; but rather, it is rooted in an abstract and often seemingly illogical standard lost in the mists of bygone time. Gender, in sum, is an arbitrary convention that the learner must accept and master on a word-by-word basis, sans any attempt to make sense of it at all.

GENDER UNDERSTANDING #2. Nouns referring to unmistakably male or female persons or animals are reliably gender-linked; this is often referred to as "natural" gender. Thus, the Spanish words for *boy, man, brother, husband, father, son, grandson, nephew, uncle, actor, colonel, general, monk, waiter,* and *lion* are all masculine; while those for *girl, woman, sister, wife, mother, daughter, granddaughter, niece, aunt, actress, nun, waitress,* and *lioness* are all feminine. This is the only class of nouns where such self-evident gender linkage occurs. Many of these terms differ from their opposite-sex counterparts only in their single-letter ending; thus, **boy**—muchacho and **girl**—muchacha; **son**—hijo and **daughter**—hija; **brother**—hermano and **sister**—hermana; **uncle**—tío and **aunt**—tía; **monk**—monje and **nun**—monja. Of course, there's an exception: **father**—padre and **mother**—madre are first-letter changers!

The relatively few nouns that own dual-gender assignment include such obvious either / or terms as **patient**—paciente; **student**—estudiante; and **rival**—rival.

GENDER UNDERSTANDING #3. The great preponderance of nouns relating to time are masculine. Thus, the Spanish terms for *time, clock, moment, second, minute, calendar, day, month, year, century,* and *millennium* are all masculine, as are names of days, months, and seasons except for the word *spring*. The other five exceptions to this general rule are the words for *hour, morning, night, midnight,* and *week*.

GENDER UNDERSTANDING #4. A word's spelling often indicates its gender.

- With very few exceptions, nouns ending in **-O** or **-OR** are masculine. Thus: **book**—libro; **census**—censo; **effect**—efecto; **garlic**—ajo; **actor**—actor; **depositor**—depositador; and **farmer**—agricultor are all masculine. An exception to the **-O** = masculine rule is the word **hand**—mano. Feminine noun **labor**—labor is one of the few that violate the **-OR** = masculine rule.

- With very few exceptions, nouns ending in **-A** or **-IÓN** are feminine. Thus: **jar**—jarra; **kettle**—caldera; **malice**—malicia; **idea**—noción; and **legislation**—legislación are all feminine. Among the small number of exceptions to the **-A** = feminine rule are the words **priest**—cura; **day**—día; and **map**—mapa, all of which are masculine despite their **-A** endings.

- With no exceptions, nouns ending in **-DAD**, **-ED**, **-IE**, or **-UMBRE** are feminine. Thus: **necessity**—necesidad; **penalty**—penalidad; **reality**—realidad; **truth**—verdad; **university**—universidad; **mercy**—merced; **wall**—pared; **series**—serie; **surface**—superficie; and **regret**—pesadumbre are all feminine.

Pluralization

Pluralizing Spanish nouns is relatively simple and straightforward. With very few exceptions, one simply adds an **-S** or an **-ES**, almost exactly as in English, as follows:

- Virtually all Spanish nouns that terminate in an unstressed vowel or an accented **É**, form their plural by adding an **-S**. Thus: **(one) friend**—amigo / **(two or more) friends**—amigos; **(one) house**—casa / **(two or more) houses**—casas; **(one) street**—calle / **(two or more) streets**—calles; **(one) café**—café / **(two or more) cafés**—cafés; and **(one) committee**—comité / **(two or more) committees**—comités.

- Most other nouns—that is, those ending in a stressed vowel except **É** or those ending in any consonant except **S** or **Z**—form their plural by adding **-ES**. Thus: **(one) menu**—menú / **(two or more) menus**—menúes; **(one) city**—ciudad / **(two or more) cities** ciudades; **(one) kindness**—favor / **(two or more) kindnesses**—favores; **(one) thief**—ladrón / **(two or more) thieves**—ladrones; **(one) ox**—buey / **(two or more) oxen**—bueyes. Of the very few nouns that deviate from the this rule of stressed terminal vowel, only **dad**—papá and **mom**— mamá are worthy of mention: both violate the scheme and form their plural simply by adding an **-S**.

- Singular nouns ending in **-S** (rare) form their plural according to where the stress falls in the word. If the stress falls *ahead* of the final syllable (that is, the one containing the terminal **-S**), the existing **-S** ending remains unchanged. The spelling remains identical in both singular and plural forms. If the terminating **-S** is part of the stressed syllable, however, then the plural is formed by adding an **-ES**. Thus: **(one) Thursday**—jueves is identical to **(two or more) Thursdays**—jueves, whereas **(one) month**—mes becomes **(two or more) months**—meses.

- Nouns ending in **-Z** (rare) form their plural by changing **Z** to **C** and adding **-ES**. Thus: **(one) actress**—actriz becomes **(two or more) actresses**—actrices, and **(one) disguise**—disfraz becomes **(two or more) disguises**—disfraces.

ARTICLES
Definite Articles

In English, we simply use *THE* to indicate a specific person or persons, place or places, thing or things. End of story: a single all-purpose designator does the job. Like the other Romance languages, however, Spanish is a bit more complicated in this regard, requiring no fewer than four terms to fulfill the same function. Which is to be used in any given context depends upon both the gender and singular / plural status of the noun to which it refers.

- *THE* before masculine singular nouns is **EL.** Thus, **the bull**—
  el toro

- *THE* before masculine plural nouns is **LOS.** Thus, **the men**—
  los hombres.

- *THE* before most feminine singular nouns is **LA.** Thus, **the nurse**—
  la enfermera.

- *THE* before feminine plural nouns is **LAS.** Thus, **the women**—
  las mujeres.

Definite articles are used with much greater frequency in Spanish than in English. Whereas we would ordinarily say "She went downtown," "He has had dinner," "His leg is injured," and "I'm looking forward to spring," a Spanish speaker would normally include an article before the noun in each one of those expressions (*the* downtown, *the* dinner, *the* leg, *the* spring). While there are some syntactical constructions that allow for their omission, the beginning learner will never be seriously wrong to include them in all cases, and learn the subtlety of their occasional omission as he or she progresses toward fluency.

Definite Quasi Articles

Technically speaking, the terms *THAT* and *THOSE* are adjectives rather than articles when used as specific identifiers. However, their usage is so closely akin to the "pointing" function of *THE* and so distinct from the usual adjectival employment (where the Spanish adjective generally follows its associated noun)—besides being very simple to comprehend and master—that they are included here as a matter of convenience.

- *THAT* before masculine singular nouns is *ESE*. Thus, **that cat**— ese gato.

- *THAT* before feminine singular nouns is *ESA*. Thus, **that family**— esa familia.

- *THOSE* before masculine plural nouns is *ESOS*. Thus, **those habits**—esos hábitos.

- *THOSE* before feminine plural is *ESAS*. Thus, **those limes**— esas limas.

There are two additional adjectives related to *ESE*: *ESTE* (*ESTA*, *ESTOS*, *ESTAS*), meaning *this*; and *AQUEL* (*AQUELLA*, *AQUEL-LOS*, *AQUELLAS*), meaning *that over there*. These are used in the same way as *ESE*, but are not used in this text.

Indefinite Articles

English uses indefinite article *A* and *AN* when referring to a person, place, or thing. It uses *A* when the noun that follows starts with a consonant (a lake, a table, a chair, a policeman), and it uses *AN* when the noun that follows starts with a vowel (an apple, an elephant, an oyster, an ant, an almond). The indefinite article in Spanish, too, has two forms: *UN* and *UNA*. Whereas English uses one form or the other depending on whether the noun that follows starts with a consonant or a vowel, Spanish uses one form or the other depending on whether the noun that follows is masculine or feminine.

- *A / AN* = *UN* before masculine nouns. Thus, **a market**— un mercado.

- *A / AN* = *UNA* before feminine nouns. Thus, **a necessity**— una necesidad.

Partitive Articles

Very simple, too, are the Spanish equivalents of the English partitive (indefinite, plural) articles *SOME* and *SEVERAL*. Again, a single term in two gender-specific forms is used in Spanish.

- *SOME / SEVERAL* before masculine nouns: **UNOS**. Thus, **some / several refugees**—unos refugiados.

- *SOME / SEVERAL* before feminine nouns: **UNAS**. Thus, **some / several tombs**—unas tumbas.

ADJECTIVES

The use of Spanish adjectives—words that generally describe, define, or limit associated nouns—differs in several essential respects from the use of English adjectives. Most importantly, a Spanish adjective must match, or must be made to match, the noun it modifies in both gender and number. Furthermore, it must be positioned in such a way in relationship to the noun it modifies as to indicate a general qualification of that noun or a specific one.

GENDER MATCHING. A small number of Spanish adjectives are considered "neutral," or "neuter." So they can be used with either masculine or feminine nouns without consideration of the noun's gender. The vast majority of adjectives, however, occur in both masculine (generally ending in **-O**) and feminine (generally ending in **-A**) versions. In this volume, adjectives are invariably shown in the masculine form, appropriate for use "as-is" to modify masculine singular nouns. The adjective **fat**—gordo, for example, can be applied without modification to any appropriate masculine noun, as in **a fat man**—un hombre gordo, or **a fat dog**—un perro gordo.

The feminine form of any masculine adjective ending in **-O** is identical to its masculine form except that it ends in **-A** rather than **-O**. Thus: **a fat woman**—una mujer gorda; **a fat cow**—una vaca gorda.

While the **-O / -A** distinction covers almost the whole of the adjectival gender-matching issue, there are several minor exceptions.

- Adjectives that end in **-ÁN**, **-ÓN**, or **-OR** in the masculine are the same in the feminine except that they drop the accent if they have one and add an **-A** at the end. Thus: **a talkative man**—un hombre hablador / **a talkative woman**—una mujer habladora; **an easygoing professor** (*male*)—un professor bonachón / **an easygoing professor** (*female*)—una profesora bonachona; **a lazy young man**—un joven haragán / **a lazy young woman**—una joven hiragana.

- Adjectives of nationality that end in an *ACCENTED VOWEL + CONSONANT* in the masculine drop the accent and add an **-A** to the consonant in the feminine. Thus: **the English bishop**—el obispo inglés arrived with **an English nun**—una monja inglesa; and **the Danish restaurant**—el restaurante danés served **Danish beer**—cerveza danesa.

- The relatively few other types of adjectives that are not being treated here—most notably, those that end in **-E**—are neutral and have the same form both in the masculine and in the feminine. Thus **a sad man**—un hombre triste is the same as **a sad woman**—una mujer triste and **an easy walk**—un paseo fácil is identical to **an easy task**—una tarea fácil.

NUMBER MATCHING. Like gender, an adjective's status as singular or plural must also be made to match that of the noun it modifies. Adjectives pluralize exactly as nouns do, usually by adding an **-S** or **-ES** (see NOUNS / Pluralization, above). Thus: **the thin man**—el hombre delgado becomes **the thin men**—los hombres delgados; **the kind girl**—la muchacha amable becomes **the kind girls**—las muchachas amables; **the ugly car**—el automóvil feo becomes **the ugly cars**—los automóviles feos; and **the happy nurse**—la enfermera feliz becomes **the happy nurses**—las enfermeras felices.

ADJECTIVAL POSITION. The examples above have illustrated a marked difference between the positioning of adjectives in English versus the positioning of adjectives in Spanish. While in English an adjective almost always precedes the noun it modifies, in Spanish the reverse is true:

in all but a handful of exceptions, the adjective follows the noun it refers to. Thus, an English pompous politician would be a Spanish **político pomposo**. The exceptions follow:

- If the adjective is specific to a named person or thing, it will generally precede the object of its qualification. Thus: **the beautiful actress Greta Garbo**—la hermosa actriz Greta Garbo; **the beautiful Cadillac at the corner**—el bello Cadillac en la esquina.

- If the adjective identifies a quality obviously inherent to the affected noun (the height of a specific man, the whiteness of snow, the blackness of coal), as opposed to a quality assumed or adopted by the noun (the thinness or obesity of a man, the dirtiness of "old" snow, the size of a lump of coal), it will generally precede the noun. Thus: **the hard pavement**—el duro pavimento; **the white snow**—la blanca nieve.

- If the adjective is one of limitation more than description, it precedes the noun. Thus: **the two songs**—las dos canciones; **the last train of the night**—el último tren de la noche.

- If the adjective is one of a small class of "position-definition shifters," it will precede or follow its affected noun depending upon its intended meaning. The most significant members of this class are *grande*, *pobre*, and *único*.

- *GRANDE*—or *GRAN* before a singular noun—means *great* (when used) before a noun; (when used) after a noun it means *big / large*. Thus: **a great (wonderful) wife**—una gran esposa; **the big river**—el río grande.

- *POBRE* means *unfortunate* before a noun; after a noun it means *poor* (in wealth). Thus: **the unfortunate orphan girl**—la pobre huérfana; **the poor farmer**—el agricultor pobre.

- *ÚNICO* means *only* before a noun; after a noun it means *unique*. Thus: **the only bus**—el único autobús; **a unique performance**—una ejecución única.

ADJECTIVAL ABBREVIATIONS #1. A small number of Spanish adjectives assume abbreviated forms by dropping their concluding **-O** when they are positioned before masculine singular nouns (only!), as per the standards noted above. These are: **anyone / someone**—alguno, which shortens to *algún* (with accent added); **bad / evil**—malo, which shortens to *mal*; **fine / good**—bueno, which shortens to *buen*; **no / none**—ninguno, which shortens to *ningún* (accent added); **prime / first**—primero, which shortens to *primer*; and finally, **third**—tercero, which abbreviates to *tercer*. Again for emphasis, these abbreviated forms are appropriate only when they precede a masculine singular noun.

ADJECTIVAL ABBREVIATIONS #2: Two anomalies are *grande*, which shortens to *gran* when positioned before any (masculine or feminine) singular noun, as shown above; and *ciento*, which abbreviates to *cien* before any masculine or feminine noun.

ADVERBS

In English, a majority of adverbs—words that modify verbs, adjectives, or other adverbs in terms of time, place, manner, degree, intensity, or cause—are formed by adding the suffix *-LY* to an adjective. Thus adjective *abundant* becomes adverb *abundantly*. In Spanish, an even larger majority of adverbs are formed almost as easily: by adding the suffix *-MENTE* to an adjectival form. Thus adjective *abundante* becomes adverb *abundantemente*.

There are exceptions in both languages, of course; and when a Spanish adverb deviates from the norm, it is listed herein. In all other cases, cognate adverbs are not included in this book in the belief that the learner will quickly understand how to form them from adjectives via the addition of the *-MENTE* ending.

One small but significant "wrinkle" pertains to the foregoing: in all instances and contexts, Spanish uses the feminine form of an adjective as the basis of constructing an adverb. Thus the masculine form of the adjective **adverse**—adverso must be changed to its feminine counterpart (*adversa*) before being transformed into **adversely**—adversamente. Similarly, **aggressive**—agresivo is altered to *agresiva* before becoming **aggressively**—agresivamente; and **approximate**—aproximado must become *aproximada* prior to further mutation into **approximately**—aproximadamente. In most instances this is merely the changing of an *O* to an *A*;

adjectives that in the masculine do not terminate in an **-O**, require no alteration prior to the addition of the **-MENTE** suffix.

PRONOUNS

One cannot, of course, speak useful Spanish (or any other language!) without the constant use of pronouns. After all, we communicate much more about ourselves and others than about things.

Spanish pronouns—embracing such varieties as personal, prepositional, possessive, relative, reflexive, interrogative, demonstrative, and indefinite—constitute one of the language's most complex grammatical subsystems. So much so that with its scores of contextual variants, any attempt to offer more than the narrowest summary overview is considerably beyond this book's purpose and available space. Thus, save for the very abbreviated review and listing below, the learner must, when ready, direct his or her attention to an instructive text that treats this vitally important class of words comprehensively.

SUBJECT-OF-VERB PRONOUNS. Distinct subject–verb segregation—as exemplified by such English constructions as *I am; you are; he cooked; she determined; we will fly; they will argue*—is rarely employed in Spanish (or any other Romance language), inasmuch as a verb's conjugation unambiguously identifies its subject in most instances. Only when emphatic clarity, dramatic emphasis, or vivid contrast is needed are subject-of-verb pronouns brought into conversational play. In those instances, the singular and plural terms are as follows.

I—yo (yoh)

you *(familiar / intimate)*—tú (too)

you *(usual / formal)*—usted (oos-TEH<u>D</u>)

he—él (ehl)

she—ella (EH-yah)

it—él (ehl) or ella (EH-yah)

we—nosotros (noh-SOH-trohs)

you *(familiar / intimate)*—vosotros★ (<u>b</u>oh-SOH-trohs)

you *(usual / formal)*—ustedes★ (oos-TEH-<u>d</u>ehs)

they *(all masculine or masculine and feminine mixed)*—ellos (EH-yohs)

they *(all feminine)*—ellas (EH-yahs)

★*Vosotros* is used in Spain; *ustedes* is used in Latin America.

The learner is again cautioned that the above listing is but a fractional representation of the Spanish pronoun universe and that it is distinctly limited in terms of correct use. As soon as sufficient basic vocabulary has been attained to yield a growing sense of strength and confidence, he or she is urged to seek further intelligence elsewhere regarding this vital category of the Spanish tongue.

VERBS

Lastly, we come very briefly to the complicated matter of verbs. In Spanish, as in many languages, the complexity of verbs is considerable. They not only specify an action; but by one or another conjugated form and / or modifier, they also indicate the past, present, variously conditional, ongoing or future context of that action; its indicative, subjunctive, or imperative mood; the singularity or plurality of the actor(s) or acted-upon(s); and his / her / their / its sex or inanimate gender. All in a one- or two-word construct, which can assume any one of an astronomical number of forms!

While it is clearly beyond the scope of the present volume to decipher and teach this complicated tangle of variants, the following basics are offered to give the learner an introductory practical understanding of Spanish verb structure and use.

- In Spanish, as in all languages, the fundamental form of every verb is its *infinitive*—that is, the form that specifies only the verb's essential action (to abstain, to eat, to make, to speak), without indication of who or what is executing the action or being acted upon, or the action's "mood," or time frame. As is common practice in dictionaries and other language compendia, all verbs in this book's lists are shown in this infinitive form. The student who learns the more frequently used of these infinitives will at the very least be able to effectively communicate his or her essential needs—if not with the smooth, polished, and grammatically correct fluency of one who has truly mastered the language.

- In their infinitive form Spanish verbs terminate in an *-AR*, *-ER*, or *-IR* construct; immediately preceding that two-letter ending is the verb's "root." It is by a verb's terminating doublet that the basic form of its conjugation is determined, and upon its root that the conjugation is structured. Regular (as opposed to irregular) Spanish *-AR* verbs, for example, typically form the first person present indicative by adding an **-O** to the verb's root. Thus, **to accept**—aceptar becomes **I accept**—acepto; **to want**—desear becomes **I want**—deseo; and **to speak**—hablar becomes **I speak**—hablo.

Were all Spanish verbs as regular as are most that end in **-AR**, and were there only a handful of contextual variables rather than the fourteen (!) that the Romance languages employ (each with six subvariables!), there would be room in this volume to cover this critical element of Spanish grammar with comprehensive thoroughness. Alas, the topic is not so simple, as attested to by the many textbooks that focus on nothing but verbs. Two that this author has used and can heartily recommend are ***Spanish Verb Drills***, by Vivienne Bey; and ***The Big Red Book of Spanish Verbs***, by Ronni L. Gordon and David L. Sillman. The former is an easier, more basic treatment, ideal for novices, while the latter is a highly detailed and richly comprehensive technical overview of over five hundred verbs in their multitude of conjugations, variants, and irregularities. The learner is encouraged to rely upon such sources for enlightenment regarding, and mastery of, this complex yet fundamental and vitally important part of the Spanish grammatical structure.

LISTA DE TÉRMINOS
Y FRASES FAMILIARES
List of Familiar Terms and Phrases

This word list is composed of words that have been adopted into English directly from Spanish—*adobe, mesa, río, siesta*—or of terms such as *barrio, conquistador, luna, noche,* and *toro* that have become generally familiar throughout the English-speaking world via various cultural media. Thus, despite the relatively few cognates within this group, for most learners it will be the easier of the book's two compendia: a helpful reminder / refresher regarding a Spanish minivocabulary that, at least subconsciously, is already well known.

In many instances, familiarity with these words is much greater than awareness of their Spanish origin. Ask the average American, Canadian, or Briton where the term *chocolate* comes from, for example, and you'll likely be met with a blank stare, suggesting that he or she is wholly unaware of the fact that it is a direct adoption from the·Spanish lexicon, and thus every bit as useable in Seville or Santo Domingo as in St. Louis or Stratford-upon-Avon. Very likely you, too, will find many wholly familiar words here whose Spanish source will seem surprising; and will thereby instantly broaden your reading and conversational strength (and confidence!) in the language of El Cid, Cervantes, and Juan Q. Público.

As some of these terms are importantly fundamental on an everyday basis—e.g., *man, woman, to speak,* and so forth—and none will be duplicated elsewhere in this volume, it is important that any unknown words herein be incorporated into the learner's basic vocabulary before moving on.

adiós *m.* (ah-DYOHS)   farewell / leave-taking / good-bye

adobe *m.* (ah-DOH-beh)   sun-dried brick

agua *f.* (AH-gwah)   water

Americano *m.* (ah-meh-ree-KAH-noh)   American ⟲*f.* -na⟲

amigo *m.* (ah-MEE-goh)   friend / chum / pal ⟲*f.* -ga⟲

amor *m.* (ah-MOHR)   love / loved one / beloved

año *m.* (AH-nyoh)   year (*in general*) / grade (*in school*)

armada *f.* (ahr-MAH-dah)   navy / fleet

arriba (ah-RREE-bah)   above / up / upstairs / upward!

arroyo *m.* (ah-RROH-yoh)   brook / creek / stream / rivulet / gutter (!)

arroz *m.* (ah-RROHS)   rice

asado (adj.) (ah-SAH-doh)   roasted

avenida *f.* (ah-beh-NEE-dah)   avenue

bandera *f.* (bahn-DEH-rah)   flag

bandido *m.* (bahn-DEE-doh)   bandit / outlaw

baño *m.* (BAH-nyoh)   bath / bathroom

barrio *m.* (BAH-rryoh)   neighborhood / district / quarter

bebida *f.* (beh-BEE-dah)   drink / beverage

béisbol *m.* (BAYS-bohl)   baseball

bello (adj.) (BEH-yoh)   beautiful / pleasing to the eye

beso *m.* (BEH-soh)   kiss

biblioteca *f.* (bee-blyoh-TEH-kah)   library

bien (BYEHN)   well / properly / correctly / right / good / quite / very

¡Bienvenido! (byehn-beh-NEE-doh)   welcome!

blanco (adj.) (BLAHN-koh)   white / blank

boca *f.* (BOH-kah)   mouth

bodega *f.* (boh-DEH-gah)   grocery store / storeroom / wine cellar

borracho (adj.) (boh-RRAH-choh)   drunk / intoxicated

brea *f.* (BREH-ah)   pitch / tar

bueno (adj.) (BWEH-noh)   good / fine / well

¡Buenos días! (BWEH-nohs DEE-ahs)   Good morning! / Good day!

¡Buenas noches! (BWEH-nahs NOH-chehs)   Good evening! / Good night!

¡Buenas tardes! (BWEH-nahs TAHR-dehs)   Good afternoon!

¡Buena suerte! (BWEH-nah SWEHR-teh)   Good luck!

burro *m.* (BOO-rroh)   burro / donkey / ass

caballero *m.* (kah-bah-YEH-roh)   gentleman / horseman / knight

cabaña *f.* (kah-BAH-nyah)   cabin / cottage / hut / (small) beach house

café *m.* (kah-FEH)   coffee / café / small restaurant

caldera *f.* (kahl-DEH-rah)   kettle / boiler

calle *f.* (KAH-yeh)   street / road

camarero *m.* (kah-mah-REH-roh)   waiter ◑*f.* **waitress** -ra◑

camino *m.* (kah-MEE-noh)   road / lane / path / pathway / way

campesino *m.* (kahm-peh-SEE-noh)   peasant / farmworker

campo *m.* (KAHM-poh)   countryside / rural region / field / realm / sphere of action (!)

canon *m.* (kah-NYOHN)   canyon / gorge / cannon (!)

cantina *f.* (kahn-TEE-nah)   tavern / bar / barroom / canteen / mess hall

carne *f.* (KAHR-neh)   meat / flesh

casa *f.* (KAH-sah)   house / household / home / business enterprise (!)

cerveza *f.* (sehr-BEH-sah)   beer

chocolate *m.* (choh-koh-LAH-teh)   chocolate / hot chocolate

cigarro *m.* (see-GAH-rroh)   cigar

cigarillo *m.* (see-gah-RREE-yoh)   cigarette

cine *m.* (SEE-neh)   cinema / movies / movie house / film industry

ciudad *f.* (syoo-DAD)   city / large town

comida *f.* (koh-MEE-dah)   food / meal / dinner

compañero *m.* (kohm-pah-NYEH-roh)   companion / classmate / pal / partner / playmate / teammate

conquistador *m.* (kohn-kees-tah-DOHR)   conqueror

corona *f.* (koh-ROH-nah)   crown / wreath

corral *m.* (koh-RRAHL)   pen / farmyard / stockyard / playpen (!)

correo *m.* (koh-RREH-oh)   mail / post office / postal system

coyote *m.* (koh-YOH-teh)   coyote

crucifijo *m.* (kroo-see-FEE-hoh)   crucifix

cruz *f.* (KROOS)   cross

cucaracha *f.* (koo-kah-RAH-cha)   cockroach / roach

cueva *f.* (KWEH-<u>b</u>ah)   cave / cavern

dama *f.* (DAH-mah)   lady

de (DEH)   of / from

de nada (deh NAH-<u>d</u>ah)   you're welcome [LITERALLY: "of nothing"]

día *m.* (DEE-ah)   day (*daytime or 24-hour period*)

diablo *m.* (DYAH-<u>b</u>loh)   devil

dinero *m.* (dee-NEH-roh)   money

Dios *m.* (DYOHS)   God

dorado (adj.) (doh-RAH-<u>d</u>oh)   golden

dulce (adj.) (DOOL-seh)   sweet / mild / gentle / mellow ◌*m.* candy ▯◌

España *f.* (ehs-PAH-nyah)   Spain

español *m.* (ehs-pah-NYOHL)   Spanish (*language*) / Spaniard (*male*)
    ◌**Spaniard (*female*)** española (ehs-pah-NYOH-lah) ▯◌
    ◌(adj.) **Spanish** ▯◌

estado *m.* (ehs-TAH-<u>d</u>oh)   nation / state / condition / state (*of health, mind, etc.*)

Estados Unidos *m.* (ehs-TAH-<u>d</u>ohs oo-NEE-<u>d</u>ohs)   United States (of America)

favor *m.* (fah-<u>B</u>OHR)   favor / kindness
    ① To say "please": **por favor** (pohr fah-<u>B</u>OHR)

felicidad *f.* (feh-lee-see-<u>D</u>AH<u>D</u>)   happiness / bliss

feliz (adj.) (feh-LEES)   happy / glad / merry

¡Feliz Año Nuevo! (feh-LEES AH-nyoh NWEH-<u>b</u>oh)   Happy New Year!

¡Feliz Navidad! (feh-LEES nah-<u>b</u>ee-<u>D</u>AH<u>D</u>)   Merry Christmas!

fiesta *f.* (FYEHS-tah)   party / fête / festival

flor *f.* (FLOHR)   flower / bloom / blossom

fresco (adj.) (FREHS-koh)   fresh (*not stale*) / cool / chilled / chilly

frío *m.* (FREE-oh)   cold / chill ↻(adj.) **cold / chilly / frigid** ▢↻

frito (adj.) (FREE-toh)   fried

fuego *m.* (FWEH-goh)   fire

fuente *f.* (FWEHN-teh)   fountain / spring (*of water*) / fount / source

fuerte (adj.) (FWEHR-teh)   forceful / powerful / strong / tough / intense / loud

fútbol *m.* (FOOT-bohl)   soccer

galería *f.* (gah-leh-REE-ah)   gallery / balcony / (broad) porch / (wide) corridor

gato *m.* (GAH-toh)   cat / automobile jack (!)

gordo (adj.) (GOHR-doh)   fat / obese

¡Gracias! (GRAH-syahs)   Thank you! / Thanks!

grande (adj.) (GRAHN-deh)   big / great / large / grand

gringo *m.* (GREEN-goh)   foreigner / American / Yankee ↻*f.* -ga↻

guacamole *m.* (gwah-kah-MOH-leh)   avocado paste

guerra *f.* (GEH-rrah)   war

habla *f.* (AH-blah)   speech (*oral expression, not formal oration*)

hacienda *f.* (ah-SYEHN-dah)   farm / ranch / estate

harina *f.* (ah-REE-nah)   flour

hasta (AHS-tah)   until

¡Hasta la vista! (AHS-tah lah BEES-tah)   See you again!

¡Hasta luego! (AHS-tah LWEH-goh)   So long! / See you later!

¡Hola! (oh-LAH)   Hello! / Hi! / Greetings!

hombre *m.* (OHM-breh)   man

huevo *m.* (WHEH-boh)   egg

infante *m.* (een-FAHN-teh) infant ↻*f.* -ta↻

infierno *m.* (een-FYEHR-noh)   hell / inferno

inglés (adj.) (een-GLEHS)   English

isla *f.* (EES-lah)   island

jamón *m.* (hah-MOHN)   ham

jefe *m.* (HEH-feh)   boss / chief / leader / head man

Jesús (heh-SOOS)   Jesus (*sometimes used as a given name for a male*)

lago *m.* (LAH-goh)   lake

lápiz *m.* (LAH-pees)   pencil / crayon

lava *f.* (LAH-<u>b</u>ah)   lava

latino (adj.) (lah-TEE-noh)   Latino / Latin / Latin American

leche *m.* (LEH-cheh)   milk

libertad *f.* (lee-<u>b</u>ehr-TAH<u>D</u>)   liberty / freedom

libro *m.* (LEE-<u>b</u>roh)   book

lobo *m.* (LOH-<u>b</u>oh)   wolf

loco (adj.) (LOH-koh)   crazy / insane / looney / (mentally, emotionally) mad

lo siento (loh SYEHN-toh)   I'm sorry

luna *f.* (LOO-nah)   moon

luego (LWEH-goh)   then (*subsequently*)

luz *f.* (LOOS)   light / illumination

machete *m.* (mah-CHEH-teh)   machete / field knife / cane knife

macho *m.* (MAH-choh)   male ♺(adj.) **male / manly / virile / tough** ☐♺

madre *f.* (MAH-<u>d</u>reh)   mother

maestro *m.* (mah-EHS-troh)   teacher / master artist or artisan

maíz *m.* (mah-EES)   maize / corn

mal *m.* (MAHL)   evil / wrong ♺(adj.) **bad** malo (MAH-loh) ☐♺

mañana (mah-NYAH-nah)   tomorrow ♺*f.* **morning** ☐♺

mano *f.* (MAH-noh)   hand

mantequilla *f.* (mahn-teh-KEE-yah)   butter

mar *m. & f.* (MAHR)   sea

marijuana *f.* (mah-ree-HWAH-nah)   marijuana

mariposa *f.* (mah-ree-POH-sah)   butterfly

más (MAHS)   more / further (*to greater extent*) / plus

matador *m.* (mah-tah-<u>D</u>OHR)   bullfighter

mayor (adj.) (mah-YOHR)   larger / senior / elder / older / major

medio *m.* (MEH-<u>d</u>yoh)   half / middle / center / medium (*referring to communication*) (!)

mercado *m.* (mehr-KAH-<u>d</u>oh)   market

mesa *f.* (MEH-sah)   table / plateau / tableland

milagro *m.* (mee-LAH-groh)   miracle

momento *m.* (moh-MEHN-toh)   moment

montaña *f.* (mohn-TAH-nyah)   mountain

muchacho *m.* (moo-CHAH-choh)   boy ↻*f.* **girl** -cha↻

mucho (adj.) (MOO-choh)   much

muerte *f.* (MWEHR-teh)   death ↻(adj.) **dead** -rto↻

mujer *f.* (moo-HEHR)   woman

mundo *m.* (MOON-doh)   world

muy (MWEE)   very

nada *f.* (NAH-<u>d</u>ah)   nothing / nothingness / nil

Navidad *f.* (nah-<u>b</u>ee-<u>D</u>AH<u>D</u>)   Christmas

negro (adj.) (NEH-groh)   black

niño *m.* (NEE-nyoh)   boy child ↻*f.* **girl child** -ña↻

ninguno / ningún (adj.) (neen-GOO-noh / neen-GOON)   none / not any

noche *f.* (NOH-cheh)   night / nighttime

nombre *m.* (NOHM-breh)   name / noun (!)

norte *m.* (NOHR-teh)   north

nuevo (adj.) (NWEH-<u>b</u>oh)   new

número *m.* (NOO-meh-roh)   number (*numeral or quantity*)

nunca (NOON-kah)   never

océano *m.* (oh-SEH-ah-noh)   ocean

ocupado (adj.) (oh-koo-PAH-<u>d</u>oh)   occupied / busy / engaged / taken / in use

¡Ole! (oh-LEH [*The E is held until it almost becomes a diphthong, "-AY"!*])   Great! / Superb! / Keep it up!

oro *m.* (OH-roh)   gold

otro (OH-troh)   other / another

pacífico (adj.) (pah-SEE-fee-koh)   peaceful / peaceable

padre *m.* (PAH-<u>d</u>reh)   father / sire / priest (!)

palabra *f.* (pah-LAH-<u>b</u>rah)   word

paloma *f.* (pah-LOH-mah)   pigeon / dove

pan *m.* (PAHN)   bread

pantalones *m.* (pahn-tah-LOH-nehs)   pants / trousers

papa *m.* (PAH-pah)   pope / (white) potato (!)

papá *m.* (pah-PAH)   father / poppa / pop / dad

papi *m.* (PAH-pee)   daddy

paseo *m.* (pah-SEH-oh)   stroll / pleasure walk

patio *m.* (PAH-tyoh)   patio / courtyard

paz *f.* (PAHS)   peace

pequeño (adj.) (peh-KEH-nyoh)   little / small / slight

pensión *f.* (pehn-SYOHN)   pension / retirement income / boarding house

peón *m.* (peh-OHN)   laborer / farm worker / pawn (*chess*)

¡Perdón! (pehr-<u>D</u>OHN)   Pardon me! / Excuse me! / I'm sorry!

persona *f.* (pehr-SOH-nah)   person

pescado *m.* (pehs-KAH-<u>d</u>oh)   fish (*as food*)

picante (adj.) (pee-KAHN-teh)   piquant / peppery / highly seasoned / spicy

pistola *f.* (pees-TOH-lah)   pistol / handgun / spray gun (!)

pistolero *m.* (pees-toh-LEH-roh)   gunman

playa *f.* (PLAH-yah)   beach

plaza *f.* (PLAH-sah)   plaza / public square

pluma *f.* (PLOO-mah)   feather / quill / pen

poco *m.* (POH-koh)   small amount ○(adj.) **not much** □○

pollo *m.* (POH-yoh)   chicken

¿por qué? (pohr KEH)   why?

porque (POHR-keh)   because / in order that

pórtico *m.* (POHR-tee-koh)   porch / covered porch

posada *f.* (poh-SAH-<u>d</u>ah)   inn / (small) hotel / lodging

primero / primer (adj.) (pree-MEH-roh / pree-MEHR) first / prime / leading

pronto (adj.) (PROHN-toh) prompt / quick / rapid / speedy / ready

pueblo *m.* (PWEH-<u>b</u>loh) small town / village / populace (!) / (the) people (!)

puerto *m.* (PWEHR-toh) port / harbor

queso *m.* (KEH-soh) cheese

rancho *m.* (RAHN-choh) ranch / farm / hut (!) / settlement (!) / camp (!)

relleno *m.* (reh-YEH-noh) stuffing ↻(adj.) **stuffed** ☐↻

real (adj.) (reh-AHL) regal / royal / real / true

rey *m.* (RAY) king

rico (adj.) (REE-koh) rich / wealthy

río *m.* (REE-oh) river

rodeo *m.* (roh-<u>D</u>EH-oh) rodeo / roundup / roping contest

rojo (adj.) (ROH-hoh) red

ropa *f.* (ROH-pah) clothing

sal *f.* (SAHL) salt / wit (!)

salsa *f.* (SAHL-sah) salsa / sauce / gravy

salvador *m.* (sahl-<u>b</u>ah-<u>D</u>OHR) savior / rescuer

santo *m.* (SAHN-toh) saint ↻(adj.) **holy / saintly** ☐↻

seco (adj.) (SEH-koh) dry / dried

secoya *f.* (seh-KOH-yah) sequoia / redwood

señor *m.* (seh-NYOHR) gentleman / mister / sir / lord / master

señora *f.* (seh-NYOH-rah) lady / mistress / madam / (married) woman / missus (*dialect*)

señorita *f.* (seh-nyoh-REE-tah) young lady / Miss / (unmarried) young woman

sí (SEE) yes

siempre (SYEHM-preh) always / ever / at all times

sierra *f.* (SYEH-rrah) mountain range / mountain chain / saw (!)

siesta *f.* (SYEHS-tah) nap

sol *m.* (SOHL) sun / sunlight / sunshine

soledad *f.* (soh-leh-DAHD)   solitude / loneliness

sombrero *m.* (sohm-BREH-roh)   hat

taco *m.* (TAH-koh)   taco

también (tahm-BYEHN)   also / as well / likewise / too

tarántula *f.* (tah-RAHN-too-lah)   tarantula

tequila *f.* (teh-KEE-lah)   (particular Mexican) liquor

tío *m.* (TEE-oh)   uncle ↺ *f.* **tía** (TEE-ah) aunt↺

tierra *f.* (TYEH-rrah)   dirt / earth / ground / land / soil / (planet) earth

tienda *f.* (TYEHN-dah)   shop / store / tent (!)

toro *m.* (TOH-roh)   bull

torta *f.* (TOHR-tah)   cake

tortilla *f.* (tohr-TEE-yah)   tortilla / omelet (!)

trabajo *m.* (trah-BAH-hoh)   work / labor / task

triste (adj.) (TREES-teh)   sad / sorrowful / moody / blue / dismal / mournful

vaquero *m.* (bah-KEH-roh)   cowboy / herdsman

veranda *f.* (beh-RAHN-dah)   porch

verdad *f.* (behr-DAHD)   truth / veracity

verde (adj.) (BEHR-deh)   green / unripe / inexperienced

vía *f.* (BEE-ah)   road / route / way
  ① As a preposition *vía* means *via, by means of, by way of*

vida *f.* (BEE-dah) life

viejo (adj.) (BYEH-hoh)   old

vino *m.* (BEE-noh)   wine

vista *f.* (BEES-tah)   view / (range of) view / scene / eyesight / (sense of) vision

yanqui *m. & f.* (YAHN-kee)   Yankee / American

yo (YOH)   I (*me, myself*) / ego

LISTA DE TÉRMINOS IDÉNTICOS Y SIMILARES
List of Identical and Similar Terms

Now we come to the big one—*la lista grande e importante*: the register of five thousand-plus words that because of their high degree of similarity across the lingual divide, can most readily be absorbed by English-speaking students of contemporary Spanish. Even a casual reader's perusal of this immense collection would provide both a substantial increase in his or her Spanish vocabulary and a greatly improved familiarity with Spanish pronunciation. The serious learner who utilizes it as the basis of an ongoing and systematic language-acquisition program will find it both invaluable and continually encouraging. So, let's get to it!

—A—

abandon / forsake / give up / renounce (!) (to)   abandonar (ah-<u>b</u>ahn-doh-NAHR)

abandoned / forlorn (adj.)   abandonado (ah-<u>b</u>ahn-doh-NAH-<u>d</u>oh)

abandonment   *m.* abandono (ah-<u>b</u>ahn-DOH-noh)

abbreviate / abridge / shorten (to)   abreviar (ah-<u>b</u>reh-<u>B</u>YAHR)

abbreviation   *f.* abreviación (ah-<u>b</u>reh-<u>b</u>yah-SYOHN)

aberration   *f.* aberración (ah-<u>b</u>eh-rrah-SYOHN)

abhor (to)   aborrecer (ah-<u>b</u>oh-rreh-SEHR)

abhorrence   *m.* aborrecimiento (ah-<u>b</u>oh-rreh-see-MYEHN-toh)

abhorrent (adj.)   aborrecible (ah-<u>b</u>oh-rreh-SEE-<u>b</u>leh)

ability / dexterity / skill   *f.* habilidad (ah-<u>b</u>ee-lee-<u>D</u>AH<u>D</u>) 💣

able / skilled / skillful (adj.)   hábil (AH-<u>b</u>eel) 💣

abnegation / self-denial *f.* abnegación (ah<u>b</u>-neh-gah-SYOHN)

abnormal (adj.) anormal (ah-nohr-MAHL)

abnormality *f.* anormalidad (ah-nohr-mah-lee-<u>D</u>AH<u>D</u>)

abolish (to) abolir (ah-<u>b</u>oh-LEER)

abominate / loathe (to) abominar (ah-<u>b</u>oh-mee-NAHR)

abomination *f.* abominación (ah-<u>b</u>oh-mee-nah-SYOHN)

abort / miscarry (!) (to) abortar (ah-<u>b</u>ohr-TAHR)

abound (to) abundar (ah-<u>b</u>oon-DAHR)

abrasive (adj.) abrasivo (ah-<u>b</u>rah-SEE-<u>b</u>oh)

abscess *m.* absceso (ah<u>b</u>s-SEH-soh)

absence *f.* ausencia (aow-SEHN-syah) ↻(adj.) **absent / away** -nte↻

absolute / out-and-out / utter (adj.) absoluto (ah<u>b</u>-soh-LOO-toh)

absorbed / engrossed / rapt (adj.) absorto (ah<u>b</u>-SOHR-toh)

absorbency *f.* absorbencia (ah<u>b</u>-sohr-<u>B</u>EHN-syah)

abstain / refrain from (to) abstenerse (ah<u>b</u>s-teh-NEHR-seh)

abstinence *f.* abstinencia (ah<u>b</u>s-tee-NEHN-syah)

abstract (adj.) abstracto (ah<u>b</u>s-TRAHK-toh)

abstraction *f.* abstracción (ah<u>b</u>s-trahk-SYOHN)

absurd / ridiculous (adj.) absurdo (ah<u>b</u>-SOOR-<u>d</u>oh)

absurdity *m.* absurdo (ah<u>b</u>-SOOR-<u>d</u>oh)

abundance / plenty *f.* abundancia (ah-<u>b</u>oon-DAHN-syah)

abundant / plentiful (adj.) abundante (ah-<u>b</u>oon-DAHN-teh)

abuse *m.* abuso (ah-<u>B</u>OO-soh)

abuse / misuse (to) abusar (ah-<u>b</u>oo-SAHR)

abuser *m.* abusador (ah-<u>b</u>oo-sah-<u>D</u>OHR) ↻*f.* –ra ↻

abusive (adj.) abusivo (ah-<u>b</u>oo-SEE-<u>b</u>oh)

academic *m.* académico (ah-kah-<u>D</u>EH-mee-koh) ↻*f.* –ca↻

academic / scholastic (adj.) académico (ah-kah-<u>D</u>EH-mee-koh)

academy *f.* academia (ah-kah-<u>D</u>EH-myah)

accede / agree to (to) acceder (ahk-seh-<u>D</u>EHR)

accelerate / hasten / quicken (to)   acelerar (ah-seh-leh-RAHR) 💣

acceleration / speedup   *f.* aceleración (ah-seh-leh-rah-SYOHN) 💣

accent (*mark*)   *m.* acento (ah-SEHN-toh) 💣

accent / accentuate / stress (to)   acentuar (ah-sehn-TWAHR) 💣

accept / approve (to)   aceptar (ah-sehp-TAHR) 💣

acceptable (adj.)   aceptable (ah-sehp-TAH-<u>b</u>leh) 💣

acceptance (*receipt of*)   *f.* aceptación (ah-sehp-tah-SYOHN) 💣

access   *m.* acceso (ahk-SEH-soh)

accessible (adj.)   accesible (ahk-seh-SEE-<u>b</u>leh)

accessories / furnishings   *m.* accesorios (ahk-seh-SOH-ryohs)

accident / mishap   *m.* accidente (ahk-see-<u>D</u>EHN-teh)

accidental / unintentional / coincidental (adj.)   accidental (ahk-see-<u>D</u>EHN-tahl)

acclamation / acclaim   *f.* aclamación (ah-klah-mah-SYOHN) 💣

accompany / escort / attach to (to)   acompañar (ah-kohm-pah-NYAHR) 💣

accomplice   *m. & f.* cómplice (KOHM-plee-seh) 💣

accord / agreement   *m.* acuerdo (ah-KWEHR-<u>d</u>oh)

accordion   *m.* acordeón (ah-kohr-<u>d</u>eh-OHN) 💣

account (*financial*) / bill   *f.* cuenta (KWEHN-tah) 💣
   ① **"The check, please."** "La cuenta, por favor."

account / story / tale   *m.* cuento (KWEHN-toh) 💣

accountant   *m.* contador (kohn-tah-<u>D</u>OHR) 💣

accounting   *f.* contabilidad (kohn-tah-<u>b</u>ee-lee-<u>D</u>AH<u>D</u>) 💣

accredit (to)   acreditar (ah-kreh-<u>d</u>ee-TAHR)

accumulate / store / amass / hoard (to)   acumular (ah-koo-moo-LAHR)

accumulation   *f.* acumulación (ah-koo-moo-lah-SYOHN)

accusation / charge / indictment   *f.* acusación (ah-koo-sah-SYOHN)

accuse / charge / indict (to)   acusar (ah-koo-SAHR)

accused / defendant   *m.* acusado (ah-koo-SAH-<u>d</u>oh) ↻*f.* -da↻

accuser / prosecutor *m.* acusador (ah-koo-sah-DOHR) ◑*f.* -ra◒

accustom (*oneself to*) (to) acostumbrarse (ah-kohs-toom-BRAHR-seh)

acidic / sour (adj.) ácido (AH-see-doh)

acquire (to) adquirir (ahd-kee-REER) ●⁜

acquisition *f.* adquisición (ahd-kee-see-SYOHN) ●⁜

acrobat *m. & f.* acróbata (ah-KROH-bah-tah)

acrobatic (adj.) acrobático (ah-kroh-BAH-tee-koh)

act (*personal action*) / deed *m.* acto (AHK-toh)

action (*deed*) *f.* acción (ahk-SYOHN)

active (adj.) activo (ahk-TEE-boh)

activity *f.* actividad (ahk-tee-bee-DAHD)

actor *m.* actor (ahk-TOHR) ◑*f.* -triz◒

acupuncture *f.* acupuntura (ah-koo-poon-TOO-rah)

adapt (to) adaptar (ah-dahp-TAHR)

adaptability / resiliance *f.* adaptabilidad (ah-dahp-tah-bee-lee-DAHD)

adaptable (adj.) adaptable (ah-dahp-TAH-bleh)

adapter (*device*) *m.* adaptador (ah-dahp-tah-DOHR)

addict *m.* adicto (ah-DEEK-toh) ◑*f.* -ta◒ ●⁜

addiction *f.* adicción (ah-deek-SYOHN) ●⁜

addition (*supplement*) *f.* adición (ah-dee-SYOHN) ●⁜
  ① The math process: **addition**—*f.* suma (SOO-mah)

additional / further (adj.) adicional (ah-dee-syoh-NAHL) ●⁜

adequate / appropriate / suitable (adj.) adecuado (ah-deh-KWAH-doh)

adhere / cohere / stick to (to) adherirse (ahd-eh-REER-seh)

adherence *f.* adherencia (ahd-eh-REHN-syah)

adhesive *m.* adhesivo (ahd-eh-SEE-boh) ◒(adj.) **adhesive / sticky** ☐◒

adjacent (adj.) adyacente (ahd-yah-SEHN-teh)

adjust (to) ajustar (ah-hoos-TAHR)

adjustable (adj.) ajustable (ah-hoos-TAH-bleh)

administer / manage (to) administrar (ahd-mee-nees-TRAHR)

administration / management   *f.* administración (ah<u>d</u>-mee-nees-trah-SYOHN)

administrator / manager   *m.* administrador (ah<u>d</u>-mee-nees-trah-<u>D</u>OHR) ○*f.* -ra○

admiration   *f.* admiración (ah<u>d</u>-mee-rah-SYOHN)

admirable (adj.)   admirable (ah<u>d</u>-mee-RAH-<u>b</u>leh)

admire (to)   admirar (ah<u>d</u>-mee-RAHR)

admirer   *m.* admirador (ah<u>d</u>-mee-rah-<u>D</u>OHR) ○*f.* -ra○

admissible (adj.)   admisible (ah<u>d</u>-mee-SEE-<u>b</u>leh)

admission of / admittance to (*place or event*)   *f.* admisión (ah<u>d</u>-mee-SYOHN)

admit to (*place, event, or fact*) (to)   admitir (ah<u>d</u>-mee-TEER)

adolescence   *f.* adolescencia (ah-<u>d</u>oh-lehs-SEHN-syah)

adolescent / teenager   *m. & f.* adolescente (ah-<u>d</u>oh-lehs-SEHN-teh) ○(adj.) []○

adopt (to)   adoptar (ah-<u>d</u>ohp-TAHR)

adoption   *f.* adopción (ah-<u>d</u>ohp-SYOHN)

adorable / lovable (adj.)   adorable (ah-<u>d</u>oh-RAH-<u>b</u>leh)

adoration / worship   *f.* adoración (ah-<u>d</u>oh-rah-SYOHN)

adore / worship   (to) adorar (ah-<u>d</u>oh-RAHR)

adorn / beautify / bedeck / decorate / trim (to)   adornar (ah-<u>d</u>ohr-NAHR)

adornment   *m.* adorno (ah-<u>D</u>OHR-noh)

adrenaline   *f.* adrenalina (ah-<u>d</u>reh-nah-LEE-nah)

adulation / flattery   *f.* adulación (ah-<u>d</u>oo-lah-SYOHN)

adulator / flatterer / toady   *m.* adulador (ah-<u>d</u>oo-lah-<u>D</u>OHR) ○*f.* -ra○

adult   *m. & f.* adulto (ah-<u>D</u>OOL-toh) ○*f.* -ta○ ○(adj.) []○

adulterer   *m.* adúltero (ah-<u>D</u>OOL-teh-roh) ○*f.* -ra○

adultery   *m.* adulterio (ah-<u>d</u>ool-TEH-ryoh)

advance / progression   *m.* avance (ah-<u>B</u>AHN-seh) ○

advance (to) avanzar   *m.* (ah-<u>b</u>ahn-SAHR) ○

advanced / developed (adj.)   avanzado (ah-<u>b</u>ahn-SAH-<u>d</u>oh) ○

advantage / benefit / head start   *f.* ventaja (behn-TAH-hah) ○

advantageous (adj.)   ventajoso (behn-tah-HOH-soh) 💣

adventure / (amorous) affair / escapade   *f.* aventura (ah-<u>b</u>ehn-TOO-rah)

adventurous (adj.)   aventurero (ah-<u>b</u>ehn-too-REH-roh)

adversary / opponent   *m.* adversario (ah<u>d</u>-<u>b</u>ehr-SAH-ryoh) ◑*f.* -ia◐

adverse (adj.)   adverso (ah<u>d</u>-<u>B</u>EHR-soh)

adversity / hardship   *f.* adversidad (ah<u>d</u>-<u>b</u>ehr-see-<u>D</u>AH<u>D</u>)

advocate / attorney / lawyer   *m.* abogado (ah-<u>b</u>oh-GAH-<u>d</u>oh) ◑*f.* -da◐

advocate (to)   abogar por (ah-<u>b</u>oh-GAHR pohr)

aerodynamic / streamlined (adj.)   aerodinámico (ah-eh-roh-<u>d</u>ee-NAH-mee-koh)

aesthetics   *f.* estética (ehs-TEH-tee-kah) ◑(adj.) **aesthetic** -ico◐

affability / geniality   *f.* afabilidad (ah-fah-<u>b</u>ee-lee-<u>D</u>AH<u>D</u>)

affable / gracious (adj.)   afable (ah-FAH-<u>b</u>leh) 💣

affect (*have influence upon*) (to)   afectar (ah-fehk-TAR)

affectation   *f.* afectación (ah-fehk-tah-SYOHN)

affected / mannered / stilted (adj.)   afectado (ah-fehk-TAH-<u>d</u>oh)

affection   *f.* afecto (ah-FEHK-toh) / cariño (kah-REE-NYOH)

affectionate (adj.)   afectuoso (ah-fehk-TWOH-soh) / cariñoso (kah-ree-NYOH-soh)

affinity (adj.)   afinidad (ah-fee-nee-<u>D</u>AH<u>D</u>)

affix (to)   fijar (fee-HAHR) 💣

afflict / distress (to)   afligir (ah-flee-HEER)

affliction / trouble / grief   *f.* aflicción (ah-fleek-SYOHN)
   ① Closely related: (to) **mourn**—afligirse (ah-flee-HEER-seh)

agency   *f.* agencia (ah-HEN-syah)

agent (*representative*)   *m.* agente (ah-HEHN-teh)

aggravate (to)   agravar (ah-grah-<u>B</u>AHR)

aggression / attack / assault   *f.* agresión (ah-greh-SYOHN)

aggressive (adj.)   agresivo (ah-greh-SEE-<u>b</u>oh)

agile / nimble / limber (adj.)   ágil (AH-heel)

agility / nimbleness   *f.* agilidad (ah-hee-lee-<u>D</u>AH<u>D</u>)

agitate / shake / ruffle / stir / wave (to)   agitar (ah-hee-TAHR)

agitation (*physical*) / restlessness   *f.* agitación (ah-hee-tah-SYOHN)

agony   *f.* agonía (ah-goh-NEE-ah)

agreeable / nice / pleasant / pleasing (adj.)   agradable (ah-grah-<u>D</u>AH-<u>b</u>leh)

agriculture / farming   *f.* agricultura (ah-gree-kool-TOO-rah)

aid / assistance / help   *f.* ayuda (ah-YOO-<u>d</u>ah)
   ① **aide / helper**—*m. & f.* ayudante (ah-yoo-<u>D</u>AHN-teh)

air   *m.* aire (EYE-reh)

air conditioning   *f.* acondicionamiento del aire (ah-kohn-dee-syoh-nah-MYEHN-toh dehl EYE-reh)

airline   *f.* aereolínea (ah-eh-reh-oh-LEE-neh-ah)

airplane / plane   *m.* aeroplano (ah-eh-roh-PLAH-noh)

airport   *m.* aeropuerto (ah-eh-roh-PWEHR-toh)

alarm (*warning or device*) / fear   *f.* alarma (ah-LAHR-mah)

album   *m.* álbum (AHL-boom)

alcohol   *m.* alcohol (ahl-koh-OHL)

alcoholic   *m.* alcohólico (ahl-koh-OH-lee-koh) ↻*f.* -ca↻ ↻(adj.) ☐↻

alert / alarm / warning   *f.* alerta (ah-LEHR-tah)

alert / watchful / intelligent / quick / brisk (adj.)   alerto (ah-LEHR-toh)

alert / give warning (to)   alertar (ah-lehr-TAHR)

alien (*strange*) (adj.)   ajeno (ah-HEH-noh)

allegation   *m.* alegato (ah-leh-GAH-toh) 💣

allege (to)   alegar (ah-leh-GAHR) 💣

allergic (adj.)   alérgico (ah-LEHR-hee-koh) 💣

allergy   *f.* alergia (ah-LEHR-hyah) 💣

alleviate / ease / relieve (to)   aliviar (ah-lee-<u>B</u>YAHR) 💣

alleviation / relief   *m.* alivio (ah-LEE-<u>b</u>yoh) 💣

alliance   *f.* alianza (ah-LYAHN-sah) 💣

allusion   *f.* alusión (ah-loo-SYOHN) 💣

almanac   *m.* almanaque (ahl-mah-NAH-keh)

alphabet   *m.* alfabeto (ahl-fah-<u>B</u>EH-toh) / *m.* abecedario (ah-<u>b</u>eh-seh-<u>D</u>AH-ryoh)

alphabetic / alphabetical (adj.)   alfabético (ahl-fah-<u>B</u>EH-tee-koh)
  ① Importantly related and logical, although noncognate: **literacy**— *m.* alfabetismo (ahl-fah-<u>b</u>eh-TEEZ-moh)

altar   *m.* altar (ahl-TAHR)

alter (*make different*) / change (to)   alterar (ahl-teh-RAHR)

alter (*become different*) / change (to)   alterarse (ahl-teh-RAHR-seh)

alteration   *f.* alteración (ahl-teh-rah-SYOHN)

altercation / fracas / quarrel / run-in   *m.* altercado (ahl-tehr-KAH-<u>d</u>oh)

alternate / stagger (to)   alternar (ahl-tehr-NAHR) ↻(adj.) -no↻

alternative   *f.* alternativa (ahl-tehr-nah-TEE-<u>b</u>ah) ↻(adj.) -vo↻

altitude   *f.* altitud (ahl-tee-TOO<u>D</u>)

aluminum   *m.* aluminio (ah-loo-MEE-nyoh)

amass (to)   amasar (ah-mah-SAHR)

ambassador   *m.* embajador (ehm-bah-hah-<u>D</u>OHR) ↻*f.* -ra↻ 💣

amber   *m.* ámbar (AHM-bahr)

ambience / surroundings   *m.* ambiente (ahm-BYEHN-teh)

ambiguity   *f.* ambigüedad (ahm-bee-gweh-<u>D</u>AH<u>D</u>)

ambiguous (adj.)   ambiguo (ahm-BEE-gwoh)

ambition   *f.* ambición (ahm-bee-SYOHN)

ambitious (adj.)   ambicioso (ahm-bee-SYOH-soh)

ambulance   *f.* ambulancia (ahm-boo-LAHN-syah)

amend / correct (to)   enmendar (ehn-mehn-<u>D</u>AHR) 💣

amendment   *f.* enmienda (ehn-MYEHN-dah) 💣

amenity   *f.* amenidad (ah-meh-nee-<u>D</u>AH<u>D</u>)

amiability / friendliness / niceness   *f.* amabilidad (ah-mah-<u>b</u>ee-lee-<u>D</u>AH<u>D</u>)

amiable / friendly / kind (adj.)   amable (ah-MAH-<u>b</u>leh)

amorous (adj.)   enamoradizo (eh-nah-moh-rah-<u>D</u>EE-soh) 💣

amount / sum / total / value   *f.* monta (MOHN-tah) 💣

amount to (to)   montar a (mohn-TAHR ah) 💣

ample / full (adj.)   amplio (AHM-plyoh)

amplify / enlarge / magnify (to)   amplificar (ahm-plee-fee-KAHR)

amulet / charm   *m.* amuleto (ah-moo-LEH-toh)

anal (adj.)   anal (ah-NAHL)

analgesic / painkiller   *m.* analgésico (ah-nahl-HEH-see-koh)

analogy   *f.* analogía (ah-nah-loh-HEE-ah)

analysis / review   *m.* análisis (ah-NAH-lee-sees)

analyst   *m. & f.* analista (ah-nah-LEES-tah)

analytic / analytical (adj.)   analítico (ah-nah-LEE-tee-koh)

analyze (to)   analizar (ah-nah-lee-SAHR)

anatomy   *f.* anatomía (ah-nah-toh-MEE-ah)

ancestor   *m.* antecesor (ahn-teh-seh-SOHR) ↻*f.* -ra↻

ancestral (adj.)   ancestral (ahn-sehs-TRAHL)

anecdote   *f.* anécdota (ah-NEHK-<u>d</u>oh-tah)

anemia   *f.* anemia (ah-NEH-myah)

anemic (adj.)   anémico (ah-NEH-mee-koh)

anesthetic   *m.* anestésico (ah-nehs-TEH-see-koh) ↻(adj.) ☐↻

anesthetist   *m. & f.* anestesista (ah-nehs-teh-SEES-tah)

anesthetize (to)   anestesiar (ah-nehs-teh-SYAHR)

angel   *m.* ángel (AHN-hehl)

angelic (adj.)   angélico (ahn-HEH-lee-koh)

angle (*geometric*)   *m.* ángulo (AHN-goo-loh)

anguish   *f.* angustia (ahn-GOOS-tyah)

angular (adj.) angular (ahn-goo-LAHR)

animal   *m.* animal (ah-nee-MAHL) ↻(adj.) ☐↻

animate / enliven / liven / pep up (to)   animar (ah-nee-MAHR)

animated / lively / spirited / vivacious (adj.)   animado (ah-nee-MAH-<u>d</u>oh)

animation / liveliness / excitement   *f.* animación (ah-nee-mah-SYOHN)

animosity / ill will   *f.* animosidad (ah-nee-moh-see-<u>D</u>AH<u>D</u>)

annex / (structural) addition   *m.* anexo (ah-NEHG-soh)

anniversary   *m.* aniversario (ah-nee-<u>b</u>ehr-SAH-ryoh)

annotate / record / write down (to)   anotar (ah-noh-TAHR)

annotation / notation / entry   *f.* anotación (ah-noh-tah-SYOHN)

announce / herald / advertise (!) (to)   anunciar (ah-noon-SYAHR)

announcement / advertisement   *m.* anuncio (ah-NOON-syoh)

annual / yearbook   *m.* anuario (ah-NWAH-ryoh)

annual / yearly (adj.)   anual (ah-NWAHL)

annul / nullify / quash (to)   anular (ah-noo-LAHR)

annulment / nullification   *f.* anulación (ah-noo-lah-SYOHN)

anodyne / dull / insipid / nondescript (adj.)   anodino (ah-noh-<u>D</u>EE-noh)

anomaly   *f.* anomalía (ah-noh-mah-LEE-ah)

anonymity   *m.* anonimato (ah-noh-nee-MAH-toh)

anonymous / faceless / nameless (adj.)   anónimo (ah-NOH-nee-moh)

antagonism   *m.* antagonismo (ahn-tah-goh-NEEZ-moh)

antagonize (to)   antagonizar (ahn-tah-goh-nee-SAHR)

anthology   *f.* antología (ahn-toh-loh-HEE-ah)

anthropology   *f.* antropología (ahn-troh-poh-loh-HEE-ah)

anticipate (to)   anticipar (ahn-tee-see-PAHR)

anticipation   *f.* anticipación (ahn-tee-see-pah-SYOHN)

antidote   *m.* antídoto (ahn-TEE-<u>d</u>oh-toh)

antipathy / dislike   *f.* antipatía (ahn-tee-pah-TEE-ah)

antiperspirant   *m.* antitranspirante (ahn-tee-trahns-pee-RAHN-teh)

antiquated / outdated / outmoded (adj.)   anticuado (ahn-tee-KWAH-<u>d</u>oh)

antique (*old object*)   *f.* antigüedad (ahn-tee-gweh-<u>D</u>AH<u>D</u>)

antique / ancient / very old (adj.)   antiguo (ahn-TEE-gwoh)

antiquity   *f.* antigüedad (ahn-tee-gweh-<u>D</u>AH<u>D</u>)

antiseptic   *m.* antiséptico (ahn-tee-SEHP-tee-koh) ↻(adj.) ▢↻

antisocial (adj.)   antisocial (ahn-tee-soh-SYAHL)

anxiety / worry / tension   *f.* ansiedad (ahn-syeh-<u>D</u>AH<u>D</u>)

anxious / worried / eager / keen (adj.)   ansioso (ahn-SYOH-soh)

anxiousness / apprehension   *f.* ansia (AHN-syah)

apart / separate / separated / aside (adj.)   aparte (ah-PAHR-teh)

apartment   *m.* apartamento (ah-pahr-tah-MEHN-toh) 💣

apathetic / torpid (adj.)   apático (ah-PAH-tee-koh)

apathy / torpor   *f.* apatía (ah-pah-TEE-ah)

aperture / opening / slit   *f.* abertura (ah-<u>b</u>ehr-TOO-rah)
   ① Related to this noun are the very important noncognate terms: (to)
   open—abrir (ah-<u>B</u>REER) and (adj.) **open**—abierto (ah-<u>B</u>YEHR-toh).

aphrodisiac   *m.* afrodisíaco (ah-froh-<u>d</u>ee-SEE-ah-koh)

aplomb / composure / poise   *m.* aplombo (ah-PLOHM-boh)

apparatus / contraption / gadget   *m.* aparato (ah-pah-RAH-toh) 💣

apparent / seeming (adj.)   aparente (ah-pah-REHN-teh) 💣

appeal for / beg reconsideration (to)   apelar (ah-peh-LAHR) 💣

appear (*come into view*) (to)   aparecer (ah-pah-reh-SEHR) 💣

appear / seem (to)   parecer (pah-reh-SEHR) 💣

appearance / semblance   *f.* apariencia (ah-pah-RYEHN-syah) 💣

appendage / appendix (!)   *f.* apéndice (ah-PEHN-dee-seh) 💣

appendicitis   *f.* apendicitis (ah-pehn-dee-SEE-tees) 💣

appetite   *m.* apetito (ah-peh-TEE-toh) 💣

applaud / clap / cheer (to)   aplaudir (ah-plaow-<u>D</u>EER) 💣

applause   *m.* aplauso (ah-PLAOW-soh) 💣

applicable (adj.)   aplicable (ah-plee-KAH-<u>b</u>leh) 💣

apply (*put to use*) (to)   aplicar (ah-plee-KAHR) 💣

apply oneself / to be apt / to be fitting (to)   aplicarse (ah-plee-
   KAHR-seh) 💣

appreciate (*cherish / value / prize*) (to)   apreciar (ah-preh-SYAHR) 💣

appreciation (*valuing*)   *f.* apreciación (ah-preh-syah-SYOHN) 💣

apprehension / alarm / fear   *f.* aprensión (ah-prehn-SYOHN) 🔊

approbation / approval / acceptance   *f.* aprobación (ah-proh-<u>b</u>ah-SYOHN) 🔊

appropriate / proper / suitable (adj.)   apropiado (ah-proh-PYAH-<u>d</u>oh) 🔊

appropriate (to)   apropiarse (ah-proh-PYAHR-seh) 🔊

appropriation   *f.* apropiación (ah-proh-pyah-SYOHN) 🔊

approve / sanction / think well of (to)   aprobar (ah-proh-<u>B</u>AHR) 🔊
   ① Related: (to) **disapprove**—desaprobar (deh-sah-proh-<u>B</u>AHR)

approximate (to)   aproximarse (ah-prohk-see-MAHR-seh) 🔊

approximate (adj.)   aproximado (ah-prohk-see-MAH-<u>d</u>oh) 🔊

approximation   *f.* aproximación (ah-prohk-see-mah-SYOHN) 🔊

apt (adj.)   apto (AHP-toh)

aptitude   *f.* aptitud (ahp-tee-TOO<u>D</u>)

aquarium   *m.* acuario (ah-KWAH-ryoh) 🔊

aquatic (adj.)   acuático (ah-KWAH-tee-koh) 🔊

Arab   *m. & f.* árabe (AH-rah-<u>b</u>eh) ↺(adj.) **Arabic** []↺

arbiter / umpire   *m.* árbitro (AHR-<u>b</u>ee-troh) ↺*f.* -ra↺

arbitrary / high-handed (adj.)   arbitrario (ahr-<u>b</u>ee-TRAH-ryoh)

arbitrate / officiate (in sports) / referee (to)   arbitrar (ahr-<u>b</u>ee-TRAHR)

arbitration   *m.* arbitraje (ahr-<u>b</u>ee-TRAH-heh)

arbitrator / referee   *m.* árbitro (AHR-<u>b</u>ee-troh) ↺*f.* -ra↺

arc / arch   *m.* arco (AHR-koh)
   ① This word is easy to confuse with: **ark**—*f.* arca. 🔊

arcane (adj.)   arcano (ahr-KAH-noh)

archaeological (adj.)   arqueológico (ahr-keh-oh-LOH-hee-koh)

archaeologist   *m.* arqueólogo (ahr-keh-OH-loh-goh) ↺*f.* -ga↺

archaeology   *f.* arqueología (ahr-keh-oh-loh-HEE-ah)

archaic (adj.)   arcaico (ahr-KEYE-koh)

archetype   *m.* arquetipo (ahr-keh-TEE-poh) 🔊

architect   *m.* arquitecto (ahr-kee-TEHK-toh) ↺*f.* -ta↺ 🔊

architectural (adj.)   arquitectónico (ahr-kee-tehk-TOH-nee-koh) 🔊

architecture *f.* arquitectura (ahr-kee-tehk-TOO-rah) 💣

archive(s) / file(s) *m.* archivo (ahr-CHEE-<u>b</u>oh)

ardent / fiery (adj.) ardiente (ahr-<u>D</u>YEHN-teh)

ardor *m.* ardor (ahr-<u>D</u>OHR)

arduous (adj.) arduo (AHR-<u>d</u>woh)

area (*extent or region*) *f.* área (AH-reh-ah)

arena / sand *f.* arena (ah-REH-nah)

argot / jargon / lingo / slang *m.* argot (ahr-GOHT)

argue (*posit a logical thesis, not "quarrel"*) (to) argüir (ahr-GWEER)
   ① The concept of arguing in a quarrelsome manner is embraced by
   the noncognates: **quarrel**—*m.* altercado (ahl-tehr-KAH-<u>d</u>oh); and
   (to) **quarrel**—altercar (ahl-tehr-KAHR).

argument *m.* argumento (ahr-goo-MEHN-toh)

arid (adj.) árido (AH-ree-<u>d</u>oh)

aristocracy / gentry *f.* aristocracia (ah-rees-toh-KRAH-syah)

aristocrat *m. & f.* aristócrata (ah-rees-TOH-krah-tah)

aristocratic (adj.) aristocrático (ah-rees-toh-KRAH-tee-koh)

arithmetic *f.* aritmética (ah-reet-MEH-tee-kah)

arm / weapon *f.* arma (AHR-mah)
   ① **gun**—*f.* arma de fuego (AHR-mah deh FWEH-goh)

arm (to) armar (ahr-MAHR)

armor *f.* armadura (ahr-mah-<u>D</u>OO-rah)

arms (*weaponry*) *f. pl.* armas (AHR-mahs)

aroma / scent *f.* aroma (ah-ROH-mah) ↻(adj.) **aromatic** -matico↻

arrest (*take into custody*) (to) arrestar (ah-rrehs-TAHR)

arrival *m.* arribo (ah-RREE-<u>b</u>oh)

arrive / get somewhere (to) arribar (ah-rree-<u>B</u>AHR)

arrogance *f.* arrogancia (ah-rroh-GAHN-syah)

arrogant / self-important (adj.) arrogante (ah-rroh-GAHN-teh)

art (*field of, act of making, or specific work* [*s*]) *m.* arte (AHR-teh)

artery *f.* arteria (ahr-TEH-ryah)

arthritic (adj.)   artrítico (ahr-TREE-tee-koh)

arthritis   *f.* artritis (ahr-TREE-tees)

article (*literary or physical*) / item   *m.* artícolo (ahr-TEE-koh-loh)
   ① **a physical thing**—*f.* una cosa (oo-nah KOH-sah)

articulate (*say aloud / utter*) (to)   articular (ahr-tee-koo-LAHR)

artifact   *m.* artefacto (ahr-teh-FAHK-toh)

artifice   *f.* artificio (ahr-tee-FEE-syoh)

artificial / man-made (adj.)   artificial (ahr-tee-fee-SYAHL)

artisan / craftsman   *m.* artesano (ahr-teh-SAH-noh) ◑*f.* -na◐

artisanship / craftsmanship   *f.* artesanía (ahr-teh-sah-NEE-ah)

artist / performer / entertainer   *m. & f.* artista (ahr-TEES-tah)

artistic (adj.)   artístico (ahr-TEES-tee-koh)

artistry   *m.* arte (AHR-teh)

ascend / promote (*in rank or position*) (to)   ascender (ahs-sehn-<u>D</u>EHR)
   ① Related: **elevator**—*m.* ascensor (ahs-sehn-SOHR)

ascendancy   *m.* ascendiente (ahs-sehn-DYEHN-teh)

ascent / ascension / climb   *m.* ascenso (ahs-SEHN-soh)

aspect / appearance of / regard   *m.* aspecto (ahs-PEHK-toh)

aspiration   *f.* aspiración (ahs-pee-rah-SYOHN)

aspire (to)   aspirar (ahs-pee-RAHR)

aspirin   *f.* aspirina (ahs-pee-REE-nah)

ass / jackass / donkey / burro   *m.* asno (AHS-noh)

assailant   *m. & f.* asaltante (ah-sahl-TAHN-teh)

assassin / killer / murderer   *m.* asesino (ah-seh-SEE-noh) ◑*f.* -na◐

assassinate / murder / slay (to)   asesinar (ah-seh-see-NAHR)

assassination / murder   *m.* asesinato (ah-seh-see-NAH-toh)

assault   *m.* asalto (ah-SAHL-toh)

assault / assail (to)   asaltar (ah-sahl-TAHR)

assent   *m.* asentimiento (ah-sehn-tee-MYEHN-toh)

assent / agree to (to)   asentir (ah-sehn-TEER)

assign (to)   asignar (ah-seeg-NAHR)

assimilate (to)   asimilar (ah-see-mee-LAHR)

assist (to)   asistir (ah-sees-TEER)

assistance   *f.* asistencia (ah-sees-TEHN-syah)

assistant   *m. & f.* asistente (ah-sees-TEHN-teh)

associate   *m.* asociado (ah-soh-SYAH-<u>d</u>oh) ↻*f.* -da↺

associate (to)   asociar (ah-soh-SYAHR)
    ① (to) **associate with / consort with**—asociarse (ah-soh-SYAHR-seh);
    (to) **join (*as member*)**—asociarse a

association (*group organization*)   *f.* asociación (ah-soh-syah-SYOHN)

asthma   *m.* asma (AHZ-mah)

astrology   *f.* astrología (ahs-troh-loh-HEE-ah)

astronaut   *m. & f.* astronauta (ahs-troh-NAOW-tah)

astronautics   *f.* astronáutica (ahs-troh-NAOW-tee-kah)

astronomer   *m.* astrónomo (ahs-TROH-noh-moh) ↻*f.* -na↺

astronomical (adj.)   astronómico (ahs-troh-NOH-mee-koh)

astronomy   *f.* astronomía (ahs-troh-noh-MEE-ah)

astute / cunning / shrewd / sly (adj.)   astuto (ahs-TOO-toh)

astuteness / cunning / guile   *f.* astucia (ahs-TOO-syah)

asylum (*refuge or institution*)   *m.* asilo (ah-SEE-loh)

asymmetric / lopsided (adj.)   asimétrico (ah-see-MEH-tree-koh)

asymmetry   *f.* asimetría (ah-see-meh-TREE-ah)

athlete   *m. & f.* atleta (aht-LEH-tah)

athletic (adj.)   atlético (aht-LEH-tee-koh)

athletics   *m.* atletismo (aht-leh-TEEZ-moh)

atlas   *m.* atlas (AHT-lahs)

atmosphere (*air*)   *f.* atmósfera (aht-MOHS-feh-rah)

atmospheric (adj.)   atmosférico (aht-mohs-FEH-ree-koh)

atom   *m.* átomo (AH-toh-moh)

atomic (adj.)   atómico (ah-TOH-mee-koh)

atrocious (adj.)   atroz (ah-TROHS)

atrocity   *f.* atrocidad (ah-troh-see-<u>D</u>AH<u>D</u>)

attach (to)   atar (ah-TAHR) 💣

attack   *m.* ataque (ah-TAH-keh) / *m.* asalto (ah-SAHL-toh)

attack (to)   atacar (ah-tah-KAHR) 💣

attacker / assailant—*m.* atacador (ah-tah-kah-DOHR) ↺*f.* -ra↻ ↺(adj.) ☐↻

attempt   *f.* tentativa (tehn-tah-TEE-<u>b</u>ah) 💣

attempt / try (to)   intentar (een-tehn-TAHR) 💣

attend (to)   atender (ah-tehn-DEHR) 💣

attention / notice / heed   *f.* atención (ah-tehn-SYOHN) 💣

attentive / engrossed (adj.)   atento (ah-TEHN-toh) 💣

attenuate (to)   atenuar (ah-teh-NWAHR)

attest (to)   atestar (ah-tehs-TAHR)

attitude   *f.* actitud (ahk-tee-TOO<u>D</u>) 💣

attract / lure (to)   atraer (ah-trah-EHR) 💣

attraction   *f.* atracción (ah-trahk-SYOHN) 💣

attractive / glamorous (adj.)   atractivo (ah-trahk-TEE-<u>b</u>oh) 💣

attractiveness / glamor   *m.* atractivo (ah-trahk-TEE-<u>b</u>oh) 💣

attribute   *m.* atributo (ah-tree-<u>B</u>OO-toh) 💣

attribute / ascribe (to)   atribuir (ah-tree-<u>B</u>WEER) 💣

audible (adj.)   audible (aow-<u>D</u>EE-<u>b</u>leh)

audience (*meeting with or observers*)   *f.* audiencia (aow-<u>D</u>YEHN-syah)

audit (to)   auditar (aow-<u>d</u>ee-TAHR)

audition   *f.* audición (aow-<u>d</u>ee-SYOHN)

auditor   *m.* auditor (aow-<u>d</u>ee-TOHR) ↺*f.* -ra↻

auditorium   *m.* auditorio (aow-<u>d</u>ee-TOH-ryoh)

augment / increase (to)   aumentar (aow-mehn-TAHR) 💣

august / imposing (adj.)   augusto (aow-GOOS-toh)

augury / omen   *m.* augurio (aow-GOO-ryoh)

aura *f.* aura (AOW-rah)

austere / severe (adj.) austero (aows-TEH-roh)

austerity *f.* austeridad (aows-teh-ree-<u>D</u>AH<u>D</u>)

authentic (adj.) auténtico (aow-TEHN-tee-koh)

authenticity *f.* autenticidad (aow-tehn-tee-see-<u>D</u>AH<u>D</u>)

author *m.* autor (aow-TOHR) ↻*f.* -ra↻

authoritative (adj.) autorizado (aow-toh-ree-SAH-<u>d</u>oh)

authority (*expert or power*) *f.* autoridad (aow-toh-ree-<u>D</u>AH<u>D</u>)

authorization *f.* autorización (aow-toh-ree-sah-SYOHN)

authorize (to) autorizare (aow-toh-ree-SAHR)

autobiographical (adj.) autobiográfico (aow-toh-<u>b</u>yoh-GRAH-fee-koh)

autobiography *f.* autobiografia (aow-toh-<u>b</u>yoh-grah-FEE-ah)

automatic (adj.) automático (aow-toh-MAH-tee-koh)

automobile *m.* automóvil (aow-toh-MOH-<u>b</u>eel) / auto (AOW-toh)

automotive (adj.) automotor (aow-toh-moh-TOHR)

autonomy *f.* autonomía (aow-toh-noh-MEE-ah)

autopsy / postmortem *f.* autopsia (aow-TOHP-syah)

autumn / fall *m.* otoño (oh-TOH-nyoh) ⬥

avarice / greed *f.* avaricia (ah-<u>b</u>ah-REE-syah)

avaricious / greedy (adj.) avaricioso (ah-<u>b</u>ah-ree-SYOH-soh)
    ① Related noncognates: **miser / tightwad**—*m.* avaro (ah-<u>B</u>AH-roh) ↻(adj.)
    miserly / stingy ▢↻

aversion / dislike *f.* aversión (ah-<u>b</u>ehr-SYOHN)

aviation *f.* aviación (ah-<u>b</u>yah-SYOHN)

aviator / flier *m.* aviador (ah-<u>b</u>yah-<u>D</u>OHR) ↻*f.* -ra↻

avid / eager / enthusiastic (adj.) ávido (AH-<u>b</u>ee-<u>d</u>oh)

baby / infant *m.* bebé (beh-<u>B</u>EH)
    ① This direct-from-English import is becoming increasingly common in
    larger urban centers, in conversation with English speakers. Among Spanish
    speakers themselves, however, the terms *niño / niña* and *infante* remain the
    norm. Related: **babyhood / childhood**—*f.* niñez (nee-NYEHS); and
    babysitter—*f.* niñera (nee-NYEH-rah).

—B—

bacteria (*pl. of* **bacterium,** *used as sing. noun*)   *f.* bacteria (bahk-TEH-ryah)

bacterial (adj.)   bacteriano (bahk-teh-RYAH-noh)

bacteriologist   *m.* bacteriólogo (bahk-teh-ree-OH-loh-goh) ○*f.* -ga○

bacteriology   *f.* bacteriología (bahk-teh-ryoh-loh-HEE-ah)

balance (*weighing device*)   *f.* balanza (bah-LAHN-sah)

balcony   *m.* balcón (bahl-KOHN)

ball / dance (*rhythmic movement*)   *m.* baile (BYE-leh)
　① (to) **dance**—bailar (bye-LAHR); **dancer**—*m.* bailarín (bye-lah-REEN) ○*f.* -rina○

ball (*sphere*)   *f.* bola (BOH-lah)

ballad   *f.* balada (bah-LAH-dah)

ballet   (*French*) *m.* ballet (bah-LEH)

banal (adj.)   banal (bah-NAHL) ○*f.* **banality** -lidad○

banana   *m.* banana (bah-NAH-nah)

band (*strip or group*) **/ gang**   *f.* banda (BAHN-dah)

bank (*financial*) **/ treasury**   *m.* banco (BAHN-koh)

banker   *m.* banquero (bahn-KEH-roh) ○*f.* -ra○

banking   *f.* banca (BAHN-kah)

banner / flag   *f.* bandera (bahn-DEH-rah)

banquet   *m.* banquete (bahn-KEH-teh)

baptism / christening   *m.* bautismo (baow-TEEZ-moh)

baptize / christen (to)   bautizar (bawo-tee-SAHR)

bar / barroom / saloon / tavern   *m.* bar (BAHR)

bar / rod   *f.* barra (BAH-rrah)

barbarian   *m.* bárbaro (BAHR-bah-roh) ○*f.* -ra○

barbarous / merciless (adj.)   bárbaro (BAHR-bah-roh)

barbarity / barbarism   *f.* barbaridad (bahr-bah-ree-DAHD)

barbecue   *f.* barbacoa (bahr-bah-KOH-ah)

barber *m.* barbero (bahr-<u>BEH</u>-roh) ○*f.* -ra○

   ⓘ Related: **beard / chin** (!)—*f.* barba (BAHR-<u>b</u>ah); (adj.) **bearded**—barbudo (bahr-<u>B</u>OO-<u>d</u>oh)

barometer *m.* barómetro (bah-ROH-meh-troh)

barometric (adj.) barométrico (bah-roh-MEH-tree-koh)

baroque (adj.) barroco (bah-RROH-koh)

barrel / keg *m.* barril (bah-RREEL)

barricade *f.* barricada (bah-rree-KAH-<u>d</u>ah)

barrier / tollgate *f.* barrera (bah-RREH-rah)

base / basis / foundation *f.* base (BAH-seh)

base / ground (to) basar (bah-SAHR)

basic / rudimentary / staple (adj.) básico (BAH-see-koh)

bastard *m.* bastardo (bahs-TAHR-<u>d</u>oh) ○*f.* -da○ ○(adj.) □○

bastion / stronghold *m.* bastión (bahs-TYOHN)

bat / club / cudgel *m.* bate (BAH-teh)

battalion *m.* batallón (bah-tah-YOHN)

battery (*military or electrical*) *f.* batería (bah-teh-REE-ah)

battle *f.* batalla (bah-TAH-yah)

battlefield *m.* campo de batalla (KAHM-poh deh bah-TAH-yah)

bawl / bleat (to) balar (bah-LAHR)

bay / inlet *f.* bahía (bah-EE-ah)

bazaar *m.* bazar (bah-SAHR)

beast *f.* bestia (BEHS-tyah)

beefsteak / steak *m.* bistec (bees-TEHK)

belligerence *f.* beligerancia (beh-lee-heh-RAHN-syah)

belligerent *m. & f.* beligerante (beh-lee-heh-RAHN-teh) ○(adj.) □○

bench / pew *m.* banco (BAHN-koh)

benediction / blessing *f.* bendición (behn-dee-SYOHN)

benefactor *m.* benefactor (beh-neh-fahk-TOHR) ○*f.* -ra (beh-neh-fahk-TOH-rah)○

beneficence *f.* beneficencia (beh-neh-fee-SEHN-syah)

beneficent (adj.)   benéfico (beh-NEH-fee-koh)

beneficial (adj.)   beneficioso (beh-neh-fee-SYOH-soh)

beneficiary   *m.* beneficiario (beh-neh-fee-SYAH-ryoh) ⟳*f.* –ia⟳
⟳(adj.) ☐⟳

benefit (to)   beneficiar (beh-neh-fee-SYAHR)

benefit   *m.* beneficio (beh-neh-FEE-syoh)

benevolence   *f.* benevolencia (beh-neh-boh-LEHN-syah)

benevolent / benign (adj.)   benévolo (beh-NEH-boh-loh)

beverage / drink   *f.* bebida (beh-BEE-dah)
➀ (to) **drink**—beber (beh-BEHR)

bias (*has to do with sewing*)   *m.* bies (BYEHS)
➀ **on the bias**—al bies (ahl BYEHS)

Bible   *f.* Biblia (BEE-blyah)

biblical / scriptural (adj.)   bíblico (BEE-blee-koh)

bibliography   *f.* bibliografía (bee-blyoh-grah-FEE-ah)

bicarbonate   *m.* bicarbonato (bee-kahr-boh-NAH-toh)

biceps   *m.* bíceps (BEE-sehps)

bicycle / bike   *f.* bicicleta (bee-see-KLEH-tah)

bicyclist / cyclist   *m. & f.* ciclista (see-KLEES-tah) ♠

bifocals   *m. pl.* bifocales (bee-foh-KAH-lehs)

bigamy   *f.* bigamia (bee-GAH-myah)

bikini   *m.* bikini (bee-KEE-nee)

bile   *f.* bilis (BEE-lees)

bilingual (adj.)   bilingüe (bee-LEEN-gweh)

bill (*currency*) **/ banknote**   *m.* billete (bee-YEH-teh)

billfold   *f.* billetera (bee-yeh-TEH-rah)

billiards   *m.* billar (bee-YAHR)

binoculars / field glasses   *m. pl.* binoculares (bee-noh-koo-LAH-rehs)

biochemistry   *f.* bioquímica (byoh-KEE-mee-kah)

biographer   *m.* biógrafo (BYOH-grah-foh) ⟳*f.* –fa⟳

biographical (adj.)   biográfico (byoh-GRAH-fee-koh)

biography *f.* biografía (byoh-grah-FEE-ah)

biology *f.* biología (byoh-loh-HEE-ah)

biologic / biological (adj.) biológico (byoh-LOH-hee-koh)

biologist *m.* biólogo (BYOH-loh-goh) ↻*f.* -ga↻

biscuit / sponge cake *m.* bizcocho (bees-KOH-cho)

blank / unmarked (adj.) en blanco (ehn BLAHN-koh)

blaspheme / curse / swear (to) blasfemar (blahs-feh-MAHR)

blasphemy / profanity *f.* blasfemia (blahs-FEH-myah)

block / hunk / chunk *m.* bloque (BLOH-keh)

blouse *f.* blusa (BLOO-sah)
   ① The related noncognate: **shirt**—*f.* camisa (kah-MEE-sah)

boat *m.* bote (BOH-teh)

bohemian *m.* bohemio (boh-EH-myoh) ↻*f.* -mia↻ ↻(adj.) □↻

bomb / pump *f.* bomba (BOHM-bah)

bomb / bombard / shell (to) bombardear (bohm-bahr-<u>d</u>eh-AHR)

bombastic (adj.) bombástico (bohm-BAHS-tee-koh)

bombardment *m.* bombardeo (bohm-bahr-<u>DEH</u>-oh)

bomber *m.* bombardero (bohm-bahr-<u>DEH</u>-roh)

boot *f.* bota (BOH-tah) ↻*f.* **(infant's) bootie** -tita↻

border / brink / brim / edge / rim *m.* borde (BOHR-<u>d</u>eh)

botanic /botanical (adj.) botánico (boh-TAH-nee-koh)

botanist *m.* botánico (boh-TAH-nee-koh) ↻*f.* -ca↻ / *m. & f.* botanista (boh-tah-NEES-tah)

botany *f.* botánica (boh-TAH-nee-kah)

bottle *f.* botella (boh-TEH-yah)

boutique (*French*) *f.* boutique (boo-TEEK)

box / fist fight (to) boxear (bohk-seh-AHR)

boxer / prizefighter *m.* boxeador (bohk-seh-ah-<u>D</u>OHR) ↻*f.* -ra↻

boycott *m.* boicot (bohy-KOHT)

boycott (to) boicotear (bohy-koh-teh-AHR)

bracelet   *m.* brazalete (brah-sah-LEH-teh)

brandish (to)   blandir (blahn-DEER) 💣

brandy   *m.* brandy (BRAHN-dee)

bravado   *f.* bravata (brah-BAH-tah)

brazier   *m.* brasero (brah-SEH-roh)

breeze   *f.* brisa (BREE-sah)

brevity   *f.* brevedad (breh-beh-DAHD)

brief / short / fleeting (adj.)   breve (BREH-beh)

brilliance   *m.* brillo (BREE-yoh) / brillantez (bree-YAHN-tehs)

brilliant / bright / shiny / remarkable (adj.)   brillante (bree-YAHN-teh)

brio / zest / zing   *m.* brío (BREE-oh)

British (adj.)   británico (bree-TAH-nee-koh)

bronze   *m.* bronce (BROHN-seh)

brooch   *m.* broche (BROH-cheh)

brusque / curt / gruff / short (*in expression*) (adj.)   brusco (BROOS-koh)

brusqueness / curtness   *f.* brusquedad (broos-keh-DAHD)

brutal / brutish (adj.)   brutal (broo-TAHL)

brutality   *f.* brutalidad (broo-tah-lee-DAHD)

brutalize (to)   brutalizar (broo-tah-lee-SAHR)

brute (*large animal or brutal man*)   *m.* bruto (BROO-toh) ↻(adj.) ☐↻

Buddha   *m.* Buda (BOO-dah)

Buddhism   *m.* budismo (boo-DEEZ-moh)

Buddhist   *m. & f.* budista (boo-DEES-tah) ↻(adj.) ☐↻

buffoon / jester   *m.* bufón (boo-FOHN) ↻*f.* -fona↻

bulb (*botanical*)   *m.* bulbo (BOOL-boh)
   ① An **electric light bulb** is: *f.* bombilla (bohm-BEE-yah).

bulletin   *m.* boletín (boh-leh-TEEN)

buoy   *f.* boya (BOH-yah)

buoyant (adj.)   boyante (boh-YAHN-teh)

bureaucracy   *f.* burocracia (boo-roh-KRAH-syah)

bureaucrat   *m. & f.* burócrata (boo-ROH-krah-tah)

bureaucratic (adj.)   burocrático (boo-roh-KRAH-tee-koh)

bus   *m.* bus (BOOS) / *m.* autobús (aow-toh-BOOS) / *m.* camión (kah-MYOHN)

bust *(statue or chest area)*   *m.* busto (BOOS-toh)

button / (flower) bud   *m.* botón (boh-TOHN)

—C—

cabaret   *m.* cabaré (kah-bah-REH)

cabinet (*governmental*)   *m.* gabinete (gah-bee-NEH-teh) 💣

cable   *m.* cable (KAH-bleh)

cacophony   *f.* cacofonía (kah-koh-foh-NEE-ah)

cactus   *m.* cacto (KAHK-toh)

cadaver / corpse   *m.* cadáver (kah-DAH-behr)

cadence   *f.* cadencia (kah-DEHN-syah)

cafeteria   *f.* cafetería (kah-feh-teh-REE-ah)

caffeine   *f.* cafeína (kah-feh-EE-nah)

calamity   *f.* calamidad (kah-lah-mee-DAHD)

calcium   *m.* calcio (KAHL-syoh)

calculate / estimate (to)   calcular (kahl-koo-LAHR)

calculation / calculus   *m.* cálculo (KAHL-koo-loh)

calculator   *f.* calculadora (kahl-koo-lah-DOH-rah)

calibration   *f.* calibración (kah-lee-brah-SYOHN)

calligraphy / penmanship   *f.* caligrafía (kah-lee-grah-FEE-ah)

calm / quiet / lull   *f.* calma (KAHL-mah)

calm / still / composed (adj.)   calmo (KAHL-moh)

calm / lull / quiet / soothe (to)   calmar (kahl-MAHR)

calorie   *f.* caloría (kah-loh-REE-ah)

camera   *f.* cámera (KAH-meh-rah)

camp / campsite   *m.* campamento (kahm-pah-MEHN-toh)

campaign (*military*)   *f.* campaña (kahm-PAH-nyah)

camper (*person*)   *m. & f.* campista (kahm-PEES-tah)

camper (*vehicle*)   *m.* cámper (KAHM-pehr)

canal / channel   *m.* canal (kah-NAHL)

cancel / revoke (to)   cancelar (kahn-seh-LAHR)

cancer   *m.* cáncer (KAHN-sehr)

candidacy   *f.* candidatura (kahn-dee-<u>d</u>ah-TOO-rah)

candidate / nominee   *m.* candidato (kahn-dee-<u>D</u>AH-toh) ↻*f.* -ta↻

candle   *f.* candela (kahn-DEH-lah)

candlestick   *m.* candelero (kahn-deh-LEH-roh)

canine (*dog or tooth*)   *m.* canino (kah-NEE-noh) ↻(adj.) ☐↻

canoe   *f.* canoa (kah-NOH-ah)

capacity (*volume or ability*)   *f.* capacidad (kah-pah-see-<u>D</u>AH<u>D</u>)

cape (*garment*)   *f.* capa (KAH-pah)

cape / headland   *m.* cabo (KAH-<u>b</u>oh)

capillary   *m.* capilar (kah-pee-LAHR)

capital (*city*)   *f.* capital (kah-pee-TAHL) ↻*m. (money)* ☐↻

capitalism   *m.* capitalismo (kah-pee-tah-LEEZ-moh)

capitulate (to)   capitular (kah-pee-too-LAHR)

capitulation   *f.* capitulación (kah-pee-too-lah-SYOHN)

caprice / fancy / whim   *m.* capricho (kah-PREE-choh)

capricious / temperamental (adj.)   caprichoso (kah-pree-CHOH-soh)

capsule   *f.* cápsula (KAHP-soo-lah)

captain / skipper   *m.* capitán (kah-pee-TAHN) ↻*f.* -ana [*sans accent*]↻

captive   *m.* cautivo (kaow-TEE-<u>b</u>oh) ↻(adj.) ☐↻ ✦

capture / seizure   *f.* captura (kahp-TOO-rah)

capture / seize (to)   capturar (kahp-too-RAHR)

carafe / decanter   *f.* garrafa (gah-RRAH-fah) ✦

caramel   *m.* caramelo (kah-rah-MEH-loh)

caravan   *f.* caravana (kah-rah-<u>B</u>AH-nah)

carbohydrate   *m.* carbohidrato (kahr-<u>b</u>oh-hee-<u>D</u>RAH-toh)

carbonated (adj.)   carbonatado (kahr-<u>b</u>oh-nah-TAH-<u>d</u>oh)

carburetor   *m.* carburador (kahr-<u>b</u>oo-rah-<u>D</u>OHR)

carcinogen   *m.* carcinógeno (kahr-see-NOH-heh-noh)

carcinogenic (adj.)   carcinogénico (kahr-see-noh-HEH-nee-koh)

card / chart / letter   *f.* carta (KAHR-tah)

cardiac (adj.)   cardiaco (kahr-<u>D</u>YAH-koh)

care / affection / love   *m.* cariño (kah-REE-nyoh)

career   *f.* carrera (kah-RREH-rah)

caress   *f.* caricia (kah-REE-syah)

cargo / burden   *f.* carga (KAHR-gah)

caricature   *f.* caricatura (kah-ree-kah-TOO-rah)

caricaturist   *m. & f.* caricaturista (kah-ree-kah-too-REES-tah)

carillon   *m.* carillón (kah-ree-YOHN)

carnage   *f.* carnicería (kahr-nee-seh-REE-ah)

caring / loving (adj.)   cariñoso (kah-ree-NYOH-soh)

carnal (adj.)   carnal (kahr-NAHL)

carnival   *m.* carnaval (kahr-nah-<u>B</u>AHL)

carnivore   *m.* carnívoro (kahr-NEE-<u>b</u>oh-roh) ◖*f.* -ra◗
◖(adj.) **carnivorous** ▯◗

carousel   *m.* carrusel (kah-rroo-SEHL)

carpenter   *m.* carpintero (kahr-peen-TEH-roh)

carpentry   *f.* carpintería (kahr-peen-teh-REE-ah)

carriage (*vehicle*)   *m.* carruaje (kah-rroo-AH-heh)

cart   *f.* carreta (kah-RREH-tah) / *m.* carro (KAH-rroh)

cartilage / gristle   *m.* cartílago (kahr-TEE-lah-goh)

carton / cardboard (!)   *m.* cartón (kahr-TOHN)

cartographer   *m.* cartógrafo (kahr-TOH-grah-foh) ◖*f.* -fa◗

cartography   *f.* cartografía (kahr-toh-grah-FEE-ah)

cartridge *m.* cartucho (kahr–TOO–choh)

cascade / waterfall *f.* cascada (kahs–KAH–<u>d</u>ah)

case (*instance*) *m.* caso (KAH–soh)

cashmere *m.* cachemir (kah–cheh–MEER)

casino *m.* casino (kah–SEE–noh)

cassette *m. & f.* casete (kah–SEH–teh)

castigate / chastise / punish (to) castigar (kahs–tee–GAHR)

castigation / punishment *m.* castigo (kahs–TEE–goh)

castle *m.* castillo (kahs–TEE–yoh)

castrate / neuter (to) castrar (kahs–TRAHR)

casual / haphazard (adj.) casual (kah–SWAHL)

cataclysm *m.* cataclismo (kah–tah–KLEEZ–moh)

catalogue *m.* catálogo (kah–TAH–loh–goh)

catalyst *m.* catalizador (kah–tah–lee–sah–<u>D</u>OHR)

catapult (to) catapultar (kah–tah–pool–TAHR)

cataract *f.* catarata (kah–tah–RAH–tah)

catastrophe / disaster *f.* catástrofe (kah–TAHS–troh–feh)

catastrophic (adj.) catastrófico (kah–tahs–TROH–fee–koh)

catechism *m.* catecismo (kah–teh–KEEZ–moh)

category *f.* categoría (kah–teh–goh–REE–ah)

catharsis *f.* catarsis (kah–TAHR–sees)

cathedral *f.* catedral (kah–teh–<u>D</u>RAHL)
    ① Related noncognate: **church**—*f.* iglesia (ee–GLEH–syah)

(Roman) Catholic *m.* católico (kah–TOH–lee–koh) ↻*f.* –ca↻

Catholicism *m.* catolicismo (kah–toh–lee–SEEZ–moh)

cause *f.* causa (KAOW–sah)
    ① An important phrase: **because of**—a causa de (ah KAOW–sah deh)

cause / start (to) causar (kaow–SAHR)

caustic / acrimonious (adj.) cáustico (KAOWS–tee–koh)

cauterize (to) cauterizar (kaow–teh–ree–SAHR)

cautious / wary (adj.) cauteloso (kaow-teh-LOH-soh)

cavalier / knight *m.* caballero (kah-<u>b</u>ah-YEH-roh)

cavalry / chivalry *f.* caballería (kah-<u>b</u>ah-yeh-REE-ah)

cave *f.* cueva (KWEH-<u>b</u>ah)

cavern *f.* caverna (kah-<u>BEHR</u>-nah)

cavernous (adj.) cavernoso (kah-<u>b</u>ehr-NOH-soh)

caviar *m.* caviar (kah-<u>B</u>YAHR)

cavity *f.* cavidad (kah-<u>b</u>ee-<u>D</u>AH<u>D</u>)

cease / be at end (to) cesar (seh-SAHR)

cede / yield / surrender (to) ceder (seh-<u>D</u>EHR)

celebrant *m. & f.* celebrante (seh-leh-<u>BR</u>AHN-teh)

celebrate (to) celebrar (seh-leh-<u>BR</u>AHR)

celebrated / famous (adj.) célebre (SEH-leh-<u>b</u>reh)

celebration *f.* celebración (seh-leh-<u>b</u>rah-SYOHN)

celebrity (*person or fame / renown*) *f.* celebridad (seh-leh-<u>b</u>ree-<u>D</u>AH<u>D</u>)

celestial / heavenly (adj.) celestial (seh-lehs-TYAHL)

celibacy *m.* celibato (seh-lee-<u>B</u>AH-toh)

cell (*small room*) *f.* celda (SEHL-<u>d</u>ah)

cell (*biological*) *f.* célula (SEH-loo-lah)

cellist *m. & f.* violonchelista (<u>b</u>yoh-lohn-cheh-LEES-tah)

cello *m.* violonchelo (<u>b</u>yoh-lohn-CHEH-loh)

cellular (adj.) celular (seh-loo-LAHR)

cement (*glue*) *m.* cemento (seh-MEHN-toh)

cement (to) cementar (seh-mehn-TAHR)

cemetery / graveyard *m.* cementerio (seh-mehn-TEH-ryoh)

censor *m.* censor (sehn-SOHR) ◯*f.* -ra◯

censor / censure / decry (to) censurar (sehn-soo-RAHR)

censorship / stricture *f.* censura (sehn-SOO-rah)

census *m.* censo (SEHN-soh)

cent / penny *m.* centavo (sehn-TAH-<u>b</u>oh)

centennial *m.* centenario (sehn-teh-NAH-ryoh)

center / hub *m.* centro (SEHN-troh)

center (to) centrar (sehn-TRAHR)

centigrade (adj.) centígrado (sehn-TEE-grah-<u>d</u>oh)

centigram *m.* centigramo (sehn-tee-GRAH-moh)

centimeter *m.* centímetro (sehn-TEE-meh-troh)

central (adj.) central (sehn-TRAHL)

centralize (to) centralizar (sehn-tra-lee-SAHR)

ceramics / pottery *f.* cerámica (seh-RAH-mee-kah)

cereal (grain) *m.* cereal (seh-reh-AHL)

cerebral (adj.) cerebral (seh-REH-<u>b</u>rahl)

ceremony *f.* ceremonia (seh-reh-MOH-nyah)

certain (*true, sure of*) (adj.) cierto (SYEHR-toh)

certainty / certitude *f.* certeza (sehr-TEH-sah)

certificate *m.* certificado (sehr-tee-fee-KAH-<u>d</u>oh)

certification *f.* certificación (sehr-tee-fee-kah-SYOHN)

certified (adj.) certificado (seer-tee-fee-KAH-<u>d</u>oh)

certify (to) certificar (sehr-tee-fee-KAHR)

cervical (adj.) cervical (sehr-<u>b</u>ee-KAHL)

cessation *f.* cesación (seh-sah-SYOHN)

champagne *f.* champaña (cham-PAH-nyah)

champion *m.* campeón (kahm-peh-OHN) / paladín (pah-lah-DEEN)
   ① **runner-up**—*m.* subcampeón (soob-kahm-peh-OHN). For the feminine of the last three terms: drop the preceding accent and add -*a*.

championship *m.* campeonato (kahm-peh-oh-NAH-toh) 💣

chant / song *m.* canto (KAHN-toh) 💣

chant / sing (to) cantar (kahn-TAHR) 💣

chanter / singer *m. & f.* cantante (kahn-TAHN-teh)

chaos *m.* caos (KAH-ohs) 💣

chaotic (adj.) caótico (kah-OH-tee-koh)

chap / boy / young man *m.* chico (CHEE-koh)
   ⓘ Without derogatory implication, a **girl / lass / young woman** is often referred to as: *f.* chica.

chapel *f.* capilla (kah-PEE-yah) 💣

chaperon *m.* chaperón (chah-peh-ROHN) ↺*f.* –rona↺

chaplain *m.* capellán (kah-peh-YAHN) 💣

character (*alphabetic symbol or fictional person*) *m.* carácter (kah-RAHK-tehr) 💣

characteristic (*typical*) (adj.) característico (kah-rahk-teh-REES-tee-koh) 💣

characteristic (*trait*) *f.* característica (kah-rahk-teh-REES-tee-kah) 💣

characterization *f.* caracterización (kah-rahk-teh-ree-sah-SYOHN) 💣

characterize (to) caracterizar (kah-rahk-teh-ree-SAHR) 💣

charisma *m.* carisma (kah-REEZ-mah) 💣

charismatic (adj.) carismático (kah-reez-MAH-tee-koh) 💣

charitable (adj.) caritativo (kah-ree-tah-TEE-boh) 💣

charity *f.* caridad (kah-ree-DAHD) 💣

charlatan / phony *m.* charlatán (char-lah-TAHN) ↺*f.* –ana↺ 💣

chastity *f.* castidad (kahs-tee-DAHD) 💣

chauffeur / driver *m.* chofer (choh-FEHR)

chauvinism *m.* chauvinismo (chaow-bee-NEEZ-moh)

check (*bank draft*) *m.* cheque (CHEH-keh)

checkup (*physical or mechanical*) *m.* chequeo (che-KEH-oh)

chemical (adj.) químico (KEE-mee-koh) 💣

chemist *m.* químico (KEE-mee-koh) ↺*f.* –ca↺ 💣

chemistry *f.* química (KEE-mee-kah) 💣

chic / stylish / fashionable (adj.) (*French*) chic (SHEEK)

chili / chili pepper *m.* chile (CHEE-leh)

chimney / fireplace *f.* chimenea (chee-meh-NEH-ah)

chimpanzee *m.* chimpancé (cheem-pahn-SEH)

chiropractor *m.* quiropráctico (kee-roh-PRAHK-tee-koh) ⟲*f.* -ca⟲ 💣

choreographer *m.* coreógrafo (koh-reh-OH-grah-foh) ⟲*f.* -fa⟲ 💣

choreography *f.* coreografía (koh-reh-oh-grah-FEE-ah) 💣

chorus / choir *m.* coro (KOH-roh) 💣

Christ *m.* Cristo (KREES-toh)

Christendom *f.* cristiandad (krees-tyahn-DAH<u>D</u>)

Christian *m.* cristiano (krees-TYAH-noh) ⟲*f.* -na⟲ ⟲(adj.) ☐⟲ 💣

Christianization *f.* cristianización (krees-tyah-nee-sah-SYOHN)

Christianize (to) cristianizar (krees-tyah-nee-SAHR)

Christianity *m.* cristianismo (krees-tyah-NEEZ-moh) 💣

chrome *m.* cromo (KRHO-moh) 💣

chronic (adj.) crónico (KROH-nee-koh) 💣

chronicle *f.* crónica (KROH-nee-kah) / *f.* historia (ees-TOH-ryah) 💣

chronological (adj.) cronológico (kroh-noh-LOH-hee-koh) 💣

chronology *f.* cronología (kroh-noh-loh-HEE-ah) 💣

chronometer / timer *m.* cronómetro (kroh-NOH-meh-troh)
   ① Noncognate **clock / timepiece / watch / wristwatch**: *m.* reloj (reh-LOH)

cinematic (adj.) cinematográfico (see-neh-mah-toh-GRAH-fee-koh)

circle / ring *m.* círculo (SEER-koo-loh)

circuit *m.* circuito (seer-KWEE-toh)

circular *f.* circular (seer-koo-LAHR) ⟲(adj.) ☐⟲

circulate / mingle (to) circular (seer-koo-LAHR)

circulation *f.* circulación (seer-koo-lah-SYOHN)

circulatory (adj.) circulatorio (seer-koo-lah-TOH-ryoh)

circumference / girth *f.* circunferencia (seer-koon-feh-REHN-syah) 💣

circumstance *f.* circunstancia (seer-koons-TAHN-syah) 💣

circumstantial (adj.) circunstancial (seer-koons-tahn-SYAHL) 💣

circus *m.* circo (SEER-koh)

citation / subpoena / summons *f.* citación (see-tah-SYOHN)

cite / quote (to) citar (see-TAHR)

citizenry / citizenship *f.* ciudadanía (syoo-dah-dah-NEE-ah)

citrus (fruit) *m.* cítrico (SEE-tree-koh) ○(adj.) **citric** ▢○

civic (adj.) cívico (SEE-bee-koh)

civic center / downtown *m.* centro cívico (SEHN-troh SEE-bee-koh)

civil / civilized / polite / secular (adj.) civil (see-BEEL)

civilian *m. & f.* civil (see-BEEL) ○(adj.) ▢○

civilization *f.* civilización (see-bee-lee-sah-SYOHN)

civilize (to) civilizar (see-bee-lee-SAHR)

clairvoyance *f.* clarividencia (kla-ree-bee-DEHN-syah)

clairvoyant / psychic *m. & f.* clarividente (kla-ree-bee-DEHN-teh)
 ○(adj.) ▢○

clamor / outcry *m.* clamor (klah-MOHR)

clamor (to) clamar (klah-MAHR)

clamorous (adj.) clamoroso (klah-moh-ROH-soh)

clan *m.* clan (KLAHN)

clarification *f.* clarificación (klah-ree-fee-kah-SYOHN)

clarify (to) clarificar (klah-ree-fee-KAHR)

clarinet *m.* clarinete (klah-ree-NEH-teh)

clarity *f.* claridad (klah-ree-DAHD)

class (learning group) *f.* clase (KLAH-seh)
 ① **classroom**—*f.* sala de clase (SAH-lah deh KLAH-seh)

classic / classical (adj.) clásico (KLAH-see-koh)

classification *f.* clasificación (klah-see-fee-kah-SYOHN)

classify / categorize (to) clasificar (klah-see-fee-KAHR)

clause *f.* cláusula (KLAOW-soo-lah)

claustrophobia *f.* claustrofobia (klaows-troh-FOH-byah)

clear / bright / plain (adj.) claro (KLAH-roh)

clemency / mercy *f.* clemencia (kleh-MEHN-syah)

clement / mild (adj.)   clemente (kleh-MEHN-teh)

clergy   *m.* clero (KLEH-roh)

clergyman / parson / pastor   *m.* clérigo (KLEH-ree-goh) ↻*f.* -ga↺

clerical (adj.)   clerical (kleh-ree-KAHL)

client / customer / buyer   *m.* cliente (KLYEHN-teh) ↻*f.* -ta↺

clientele   *f.* clientela (klyehn-TEH-lah)

climate   *m.* clima (KLEE-mah)

clinic   *f.* clínica (KLEE-nee-kah) ↻(adj.) **clinical** -co↺

cloister   *m.* claustro (KLAOWS-troh)

clone   *m.* clon (KLOHN)

closure   *f.* clausura (klaow-SOO-rah)

club (*association*)   *m.* club (KLOOB)

coach / carriage   *m.* coche (KOH-cheh)

coalition   *f.* coalición (koh-ah-lee-SYOHN)

coast / coastline / shore   *f.* costa (KOHS-tah)

coastal (adj.)   costero (kohs-TEH-roh)

cocaine   *f.* cocaína (koh-kah-EE-nah)

cocktail   *m.* coctel (kohk-TEHL)

cocoa   *m.* cacao (kah-KAH-oh)

coconut   *m.* coco (KOH-koh)

code (*law*)   *m.* código (KOH-dee-goh)

coexistence   *f.* coexistencia (koh-ehg-sees-TEHN-syah)

cognac   *m.* coñac (koh-NYAHK)

cognition   *f.* cognición (kohg-nee-SYOHN)

coherence   *f.* coherencia (koh-eh-REHN-syah)

coherent (adj.)   coherente (koh-eh-REHN-teh)

cohesion   *f.* cohesión (koh-eh-SYOHN) ↻(adj.) **cohesive** -ivo↺

coincide (to)   coincidir (kohyn-see-<u>D</u>EER)

coincidence   *f.* coincidencia (kohyn-see-<u>D</u>EHN-syah)

coincident (adj.)   coincidente (kohyn-see-<u>D</u>EHN-teh)

collaborate (to)   colaborar (koh-lah-boh-RAHR) 💣

collaboration   *f.* colaboración (koh-lah-boh-rah-SYOHN)

collaborator   *m.* colaborador (koh-lah-boh-rah-DOHR) ↻ *f.* -ra↻ 💣

colander / strainer   *m.* colador (koh-lah-DOHR)

collar / necklace (!)   *m.* cuello (KWEH-yoh)

colleague   *m. & f.* colega (koh-LEH-gah) 💣

collect (to)   coleccionar (koh-lehk-syoh-NAHR) 💣

collection   *f.* colección (koh-lehk-SYOHN) 💣

collector   *m. & f.* coleccionista (koh-lehk-syoh-NEES-tah) 💣

college   *m.* colegio (koh-YEH-hyoh)

collide (to)   colisionar (koh-lee-syoh-NAHR) 💣

colloquial (adj.)   coloquial (koh-loh-KYAHL) 💣

collusion   *f.* colusión (koh-loo-SYOHN) 💣

colonial (adj.)   colonial (koh-loh-NYAHL)

colonial / settler   *m.* colono (koh-LOH-noh) ↻ *f.* -na↻

colonization   *f.* colonización (koh-loh-nee-sah-SYOHN)

colonize (to)   colonizar (koh-loh-nee-SAHR)

colony / settlement   *f.* colonia (koh-LOH-nyah)

color / hue   *m.* color (koh-LOHR)

color (to)   colorar (koh-loh-RAHR)

coloration / coloring   *f.* coloración (koh-loh-rah-SYOHN)

colossal (adj.)   colosal (koh-loh-SAHL)

column / pillar   *f.* columna (koh-LOOM-nah)

combat / fight   *m.* combate (kohm-BAH-teh)

combat / fight (to)   combatir (kohm-bah-TEER)

combatant / fighter / soldier   *m. & f.* combatiente (kohm-bah-TYEHN-teh) ↻(adj.) **combatant / fighting**↻

combination   *f.* combinación (kohm-bee-nah-SYOHN)

combine / merge (to)   combinar (kohm-bee-NAHR)

combustible (adj.)   combustible (kohm-boos-TEE-bleh)

combustion *f.* combustión (kohm-boos-TYOHN)

comedy *f.* comedia (koh-MEH-dyah)

comestibles / groceries *m.* comestibles (koh-mehs-TEE-blehs)

comet *f.* cometa (koh-MEH-tah)

comfort *m.* confort (kohn-FOHRT) 🔖

comfort (to) confortar (kohn-fohr-TAHR) 🔖

comfortable (adj.) confortable (kohn-fohr-TAH-bleh) 🔖

comforter / consoler *m.* confortador (kohn-fohr-tah-DOHR) ↻*f.* –ra↻ 🔖

comic / comic strip *m.* cómico (KOH-mee-koh) ↻*f.* –ca↻

comic / comical / droll / funny (adj.) cómico (KOH-mee-koh)

(printed) comics *f.* tiras cómicas (TEE-rahs KOH-mee-kahs)

command *m.* mando (MAHN-doh) 🔖

command (to) comandar (koh-mahn-DAHR) 🔖

commander *m.* comandante (koh-mahn-DAHN-teh)

commandment *m.* mandamiento (mahn-dah-MYEHN-toh) 🔖

commemorate / memorialize (to) conmemorar (kohn-meh-moh-RAHR) 🔖

commemoration *f.* conmemoración (kohn-meh-moh-rah-SYOHN) 🔖

commence / begin / start / set in (to) comenzar (koh-mehn-SAHR) 🔖

commencement / beginning *m.* comienzo (koh-MYEHN-soh) 🔖

comment / remark (to) comentar (koh-mehn-TAHR) 🔖

commentary / remark (!) *m.* comentario (koh-mehn-TAH-ryoh) 🔖

commentator *m. & f.* comentarista (koh-mehn-tah-REES-tah) 🔖

commerce / trade *m.* comercio (koh-MEHR-syoh) 🔖
   ① Closely related noncognates are: **merchant / trader**—*m.* comerciante (koh-mehr-SYAHN-teh); (to) **trade**—comerciar (koh-mehr-SYAHR).

commercial (*broadcast ad*) *m.* comercial (koh-mehr-SYAHL) ↻(adj.) ☐↻ 🔖

commercialize / market (to) comercializar (koh-mehr-syah-lee-SAHR) 🔖

commission (*fee or official body*) *f.* comisión (koh-mee-SYOHN) 🔖

commission (to)   comisionar (koh-mee-syoh-NAHR) 💣

commissioner   *m.* comisario (koh-mee-SAH-ryoh) ↻ *f.* -ria↻ 💣

commit / perpetrate (to)   cometer (koh-meh-TEHR) 💣

committee   *m.* comité (koh-mee-TEH) 💣

commode / chest of drawers   *f.* cómoda (KOH-moh-<u>d</u>ah) 💣

common (adj.)   común (koh-MOON) 💣

commotion / stir   *f.* conmoción (kohn-moh-SYOHN) 💣

commune   *f.* comuna (koh-MOO-nah) 💣

communicate / convey (to)   comunicar (koh-moo-nee-KAHR) 💣

communication (*message or act*)   *f.* comunicación (koh-moo-nee-kah-SYOHN) 💣

communicative (adj.)   comunicativo (koh-moo-nee-kah-TEE-<u>b</u>oh) 💣

communion   *f.* comunión (koh-moo-NYOHN) 💣

Communism   *m.* comunismo (koh-moo-NEEZ-moh) 💣

community   *f.* comunidad (koh-moo-nee-<u>D</u>AH<u>D</u>) 💣

compact (adj.)   compacto (kohm-PAHK-toh)

compact disk   *m.* disco compacto (dees-koh kohm-PAHK-toh)
   ① The acronym is also increasingly familiar: **CD** (SEH-DEH).

(social) companion / escort   *m. & f.* acompañante (ah-kohm-pah-NYAHN-teh)

company (*commercial or military*)   *f.* compañía (kohm-pah-NYEE-ah)

comparable (adj.)   comparable (kohm-pah-RAH-<u>b</u>leh)

comparative (adj.)   comparativo (kohm-pah-rah-TEE-<u>b</u>oh)

compare / liken (to)   comparar (kohm-pah-RAHR)

comparison   *f.* comparación (kohm-pah-rah-SYOHN)

compartment   *m.* compartimiento (kohm-pahr-tee-MYEHN-toh)

compass (*drawing instrument*)   *m.* compás (kohm-PAHS)
   ① A **magnetic, directional compass**: *f.* brújula (BROO-hoo-lah)

compassion / sympathy / pity   *f.* compasión (kohm-pah-SYOHN)

(be) compassionate / pity (to)   compadecer (kohm-pah-<u>d</u>eh-SEHR)

compassionate (adj.)   compasivo (kohm-pah-SEE-<u>b</u>oh)

compatibility   *f.* compatibilidad (kohm-pah-tee-<u>b</u>ee-lee-<u>D</u>AH<u>D</u>)

compatible (adj.)   compatibile (kohm-pah-TEE-<u>b</u>leh)

compatriot / countryman   *m. & f.* compatriota (kohm-pah-TRYOH-tah)

compel (to)   compeler (kohm-peh-LEHR)

compendium / digest / summary   *m.* compendio (kohm-PEHN-dyoh)

compensate (to)   compensar (kohm-pehn-SAHR)

compensation   *f.* compensación (kohm-pehn-sah-SYOHN)

compete (to)   competir (kohm-peh-TEER)

competence / competition (!)   *f.* competencia (kohm-peh-TEHN-syah)

competent / proficient (adj.)   competente (kohm-peh-TEHN-teh)

competitive (adj.)   competitivo (kohm-peh-tee-TEE-<u>b</u>oh)

competitor / contestant   *m.* competidor (kohm-peh-tee-<u>D</u>OHR) ◑*f.* -ra◐

compile (to)   compilar (kohm-pee-LAHR)

complete / full / entire / (adj.)   completo (kohm-PLEH-toh)

complete / finish (to)   completar (kohm-pleh-TAHR)

complement / enhancement   *m.* complemento (kohm-pleh-MEHN-toh)

complement (*complete*) (to)   complementar (kohm-pleh-mehn-TAHR)

complementary (*enhancing / balancing*) (adj.)   complementario (kohm-pleh-mehn-TAH-ryoh)

complex / involved (adj.)   complejo (kohm-PLEH-hoh)

complexity   *f.* complejidad (kohm-pleh-hee-<u>D</u>AH<u>D</u>)

complicate (to)   complicar (kohm-plee-KAHR)

complicated / involved (adj.)   complicado (kohm-plee-KAH-doh)

complication   *f.* complicación (kohm-plee-kah-SYOHN)

complicity   *f.* complicidad (kohm-plee-see-<u>D</u>AH<u>D</u>)

compliment (*admiration / praise*)   *m.* cumplido (koohm-PLEE-<u>d</u>oh)

comply / acquiesce (to)   complir (kohm-PLEER)

component   *m.* componente (kohm-poh-NEHN-teh) ◑(adj.) ▯◐

comport (*oneself*) / behave (to)   comportarse (kohm-pohr-TAHR-seh)

comportment / behavior   *m.* comportamiento (kohm-pohr-tah-MYEHN-toh)

compose (to)   componer (kohm-poh-NEHR)

composer   *m.* compositor (kohm-poh-see-TOHR) ⟲*f.* -ra⟲

composition / makeup (of)   *f.* composición (kohm-poh-see-SYOHN)

composure / aplomb   *f.* compostura (kohm-pohs-TOO-rah)

compote / jam / preserves   *f.* compota (kohm-POH-tah)

compound / mixture   *m.* compuesto (kohm-PWEHS-toh)

comprehend / understand (to)   comprender (kohm-prehn-DEHR)

comprehension / understanding   *f.* comprensión (kohm-prehn-SYOHN)

comprehensive (adj.)   comprensivo (kohm-prehn-SEE-<u>b</u>oh)

compress   *f.* compresa (kohm-PREH-sah)

compromise   *m.* compromiso (kohm-proh-MEE-soh)

compulsion (*urge*)   *f.* compulsión (kohm-pool-SYOHN)

compulsive (adj.)   compulsivo (kohm-pool-SEE-<u>b</u>oh)

compute (to)   computar (kohm-poo-TAHR)

computer (PC)   *f.* computadora (kohm-poo-tah-<u>D</u>OH-rah) / *m.* computador (kohm-poo-tah-<u>D</u>OHR)

comrade   *m. & f.* camarada (kah-mah-RAH-<u>d</u>ah)

concave (adj.)   cóncavo (KOHN-kah-<u>b</u>oh)

concede / bestow (to)   conceder (cohn-seh-<u>D</u>EHR)

conceivable (adj.)   concebible (kohn-seh-<u>B</u>EE-<u>b</u>leh)

conceive (to)   concebir (kohn-seh-<u>B</u>EER)

concentrate / focus (to)   concentrar (kohn-sehn-TRAHR)

concentrated / intent (adj.)   concentrado (kohn-sehn-TRAH-<u>d</u>oh)

concentration   *f.* concentración (kohn-sehn-tra-SYOHN)

concept / idea / notion   *m.* concepto (kohn-SEHP-toh)

conception (*beginning of life*)   *f.* concepción (kohn-sehp-SYOHN)

concert / concerto   *m.* concierto (kohn-SYEHR-toh)

conciliatory (adj.)   conciliatorio (kohn-see-lyah-TOH-ryoh)

concise / brief (adj.)   conciso (kohn-SEE-soh)

conclude / close / end (to)   concluir (kohn-KLWEER)

conclusion   *f.* conclusión (kohn-kloo-SYOHN)

conclusive (adj.)   concluyente (kohn-kloo-YEHN-teh)

concord / accord   *f.* concordia (kohn-KOHR-dyah)

concrete   *m.* concreto (kohn-KREH-toh) ↻(adj.) **concrete / real** □↻

concur (to)   concurrir (kohn-koo-RREER)

concurrent (adj.)   concurrente (kohn-koo-RREHN-teh)

condemn / censure (to)   condenar (kohn-deh-NAHR)

condemnation   *f.* condena (kohn-DEH-nah)

condense (to)   condensar (kohn-dehn-SAHR)

condescend (to)   condescender (kohn-dehs-sehn-DEHR)

condescension   *f.* condescendencia (kohn-dehs-sehn-DEHN-syah)

condiment / relish   *m.* condimento (kohn-dee-MEHN-toh)

condition (*state of, stipulation*)   *f.* condición (kohn-dee-SYOHN)

conditional (adj.)   condicional (kohn-dee-syoh-NAHL)

condolence   *f.* condolencia (kohn-doh-LEHN-syah)

condominium   *m.* condominio (kohn-doh-MEE-nyoh)

conduct / behavior / deportment   *f.* conducta (kohn-DOOK-tah)

conduct / lead / steer (to)   conducir (kohn-doo-SEER)

cone (*geometric or confection*)   *m.* cono (KOH-noh)

conical (adj.)   cónico (KOH-nee-koh)

confederation / confederacy   *f.* confederación (kohn-feh-deh-rah-SYOHN)

confer / bestow (to)   conferir (kohn-feh-REER)

conference / meeting   *f.* conferencia (kohn-feh-REHN-syah)

confess / admit to (to)   confesar (kohn-feh-SAHR)

confession   *f.* confesión (kohn-feh-SYOHN)

confidant   *m. & f.* confidente (kohn-fee-DEHN-teh)

confide / trust / be (to)   confiar (kohn-FYAHR)
    ① (to) **mistrust**—desconfiar de (dehs-kohn-FYAHR deh)

confidence / trust / reliance *f.* confianza (kohn-FYAHN-sah)
   ① **mistrust**—*f.* desconfianza (dehs-kohn-FYAHN-sah)

confident / self-confident (adj.) confiado (kohn-FYAH-<u>d</u>oh)

confidential / private (adj.) confidencial (kohn-fee-<u>d</u>ehn-SYAHL)

confine (to) confinar (kohn-fee-NAHR)

confines (*limits of*) *m.* confines (kohn-FEE-nehs)

confirm / substantiate / verify (to) confirmar (kohn-feer-MAHR)

confirmation *f.* confirmación (kohn-feer-mah-SYOHN)

confiscate (to) confiscar (kohn-fees-KAHR)

conflict / strife *m.* conflicto (kohn-FLEEK-toh)

conform (to) conformarse (kohn-fohr-MAHR-seh)

conformity / keeping *f.* conformidad (kohn-fohr-mee-<u>DAHD</u>)

confound / confuse (to) confundir (kohn-foon-DEER)

confront / meet (to) enfrentarse (ehn-frehn-TAHR-seh) 💣

confrontation *f.* confrontación (kohn-frohn-tah-SYOHN)

confused / addled (adj.) confuso (kohn-FOO-soh)

confusion / disorder *f.* confusión (kohn-foo-SYOHN)

congeal / freeze (to) congelar (kohn-heh-LAHR)

congestion *f.* congestión (kohn-hehs-TYOHN)

congratulate (to) congratular (kohn-grah-too-LAHR)

congregate (to) congregar (kohn-greh-GAHR)

congregation *f.* congregación (kohn-greh-gah-SYOHN)

congress / convention / meeting *m.* congreso (kohn-GREH-soh)

conjecture / guess / surmise *f.* conjetura (kohn-heh-TOO-rah)

conjecture / guess (to) conjeturar (kohn-heh-too-RAHR)

conjunction *f.* conjunción (kohn-hoon-SYOHN)

connect / link (to) conectar (koh-nehk-TAHR) 💣

connection / linkage *f.* conexión (koh-nehg-SYOHN) 💣

connoisseur *m.* conocedor (koh-noh-seh-<u>D</u>OHR) ↻*f.* -ra↻ 💣

connotation *f.* connotación (kohn-noh-tah-SYOHN)

connote (to)   connotar (kohn-noh-TAHR)

conscience / consciousness   *f.* conciencia (kohn-SYEHN-syah)

conscientious (adj.)   concienzudo (kohn-syehn-SOO-doh)

conscious / aware / mindful (adj.)   consciente (kohns-SYEHN-teh)

consecrate (to)   consagrar (kohn-sah-GRAHR)

consecutive (adj.)   consecutivo (kohn-seh-koo-TEE-boh)

consensus   *m.* consenso (kohn-SEHN-soh)

consent / acquiescence   *m.* consentimiento (kohn-sehn-tee-MYEHN-toh)

consent / acquiesce (to)   consentir (kohn-sehn-TEER)

consequence / outgrowth   *f.* consecuencia (kohn-seh-KWEHN-syah)

consequent / consequential (adj.)   consiguiente (kohn-see-GYEHN-teh)

conservation / preservation   *f.* conservación (kohn-sehr-bah-SYOHN)

conservationist   *m. & f.* conservacionista (kohn-sehr-bah-syoh-NEES-tah)

conservatism   *m.* conservadurismo (kohn-sehr-bah-doo-REEZ-moh)

conservative   *m.* conservador (kohn-sehr-bah-DOHR) ↻*f.* -ra↺

conservative / preservative (adj.)   conservador (kohn-sehr-bah-DOHR)

conservatory   *m.* conservatorio (kohn-sehr-bah-TOH-ryoh)

conserve / keep (to)   conservar (kohn-sehr-BAHR)

consider / ponder (to)   considerar (kohn-see-deh-RAHR)

considerable (*quantity*) (adj.)   considerable (kohn-see-deh-RAH-bleh)

considerate / thoughtful (adj.)   considerado (kohn-see-deh-RAH-doh)

consideration / thoughtfulness   *f.* consideración (kohn-see-deh-rah-SYOHN)

consist of (to)   consistir en (kohn-sees-TEER ehn)

consistency   *f.* consistencia (kohn-sees-TEHN-syah)

consolation / solace   *m.* consuelo (kohn-SWEH-loh)

console (to)   consolar (kohn-soh-LAHR)

consolidate (to)   consolidar (kohn-soh-lee-DAHR)

conspiracy   *f.* conspiración (kohns-pee-rah-SYOHN)

conspirator   *m.* conspirador (kohns-pee-rah-DOHR) ↻*f.* -ra↺

conspire (to)   conspirar (kohns-pee-RAHR)

constancy   *f.* constancia (kohns-TAHN-syah)

constant / continual (adj.)   constante (kohns-TAHN-teh)

constellation   *f.* constelación (kohns-teh-lah-SYOHN)

consternate / dismay (to)   consternar (kohns-tehr-NAHR)

consternation / dismay   *f.* consternación (kohns-tehr-nah-SYOHN)

constitute (to)   constituir (kohns-tee-TWEER)

constitution (*law; physical makeup of something or someone*)   *f.* constitución (kohns-tee-too-SYOHN)

constitutional (adj.)   constitucional (kohns-tee-too-syoh-NAHL)

construct (to)   construir (kohns-troo-EER)

construction   *f.* construcción (kohns-trook-SYOHN)

constructive (adj.)   constructivo (kohns-trook-TEE-boh)

constructor / builder   *m.* constructor (kohns-trook-TOHR) ☾*f.* -ra☽

consul   *m. & f.* cónsul (KOHN-sool)

consular (adj.)   consular (kohn-soo-LAHR)

consulate   *m.* consulado (kohn-soo-LAH-doh)

consult (to)   consultar (kohn-sool-TAHR)

consultant   *m.* consultor (kohn-sool-TOHR) ☾*f.* -ra☽

consultation   *f.* consulta (kohn-SOOL-tah)

consume (to)   consumir (kohn-soo-MEER)

consumer   *m.* consumidor (kohn-soo-mee-DOHR) ☾*f.* -ra☽

contact   *m.* contacto (kohn-TAHK-toh)

contact (to)   contactar (kohn-tahk-TAHR)

contagious / communicable (adj.)   contagioso (kohn-tah-HYOH-soh)

contain (*hold*) (to)   contener (kohn-teh-NEHR)

contain / restrain oneself (to)   contenerse (kohn-teh-NEHR-seh)

contaminant / pollutant   *m.* contaminante (kohn-tah-mee-NAHN-teh)

contaminate / pollute / taint (to)   contaminar (kohn-tah-mee-NAHR)

contamination / pollution   *f.* contaminación (kohn-tah-mee-nah-SYOHN)

contemplate / ponder (to)   contemplar (kohn-tehm-PLAHR)

contemplation *f.*   contemplación (kohn-tehm-plah-SYOHN)

contemporary / modern (adj.)   contemporáneo (kohn-tehm-poh-RAH-neh-oh)

contend (*struggle*) (to)   contender (kohn-tehn-DEHR)

contender   *m. & f.* contendiente (kohn-tehn-DYEHN-teh)

content / contentment   *m.* contento (kohn-TEHN-toh) ↻(adj.) ▯↻

content / please (to)   contentar (kohn-tehn-TAHR)

content (*substance contained*) / contents (of) *m.*   contenido (kohn-teh-NEE-doh)

contest   *f.* contienda (kohn-TYEHN-dah)

context   *m.* contexto (kohn-TEHKS-toh)

continent / mainland   *m.* continente (kohn-tee-NEHN-teh)

continental (adj.)   continental (kohn-tee-nehn-TAHL)

contingency   *f.* contingencia (kohn-teen-HEHN-syah)

contingent (adj.)   contingente (kohn-teen-HEHN-teh)

continuous / continual (adj.)   continuo (kohn-TEE-nwoh)

continuation   *f.* continuación (kohn-tee-nwah-SYOHN)

continue (to)   continuar (kohn-tee-NWAHR)

continuity   *f.* continuidad (kohn-tee-nwee-DAHD)

contortion   *f.* contorsión (kohn-tohr-SYOHN)

contour   *m.* contorno (kohn-TOHR-noh)

contraband   *m.* contrabando (kohn-trah-BAHN-doh)
　　① **smuggler**—*m. & f.* contrabandista (kohn-trah-bahn-DEES-tah); (to) **smuggle**—contrabandear (kohn-trah-bahn-deh-AHR)

contraception   *f.* contracepción (kohn-trah-sehp-SYOHN)

contraceptive   *m.* contraceptivo (kohn-trah-sehp-TEE-boh) ↻(adj.) ▯↻

contract   *m.* contrato (kohn-TRAH-toh)

contract (*formally agree*) (to)   contraer (kohn-trah-EHR)

contraction   *f.* contracción (kohn-trahk-SYOHN)

contractor   *m. & f.* contratista (kohn-trah-TEES-tah)

contradict (to)   contradecir (kohn-trah-<u>d</u>eh-SEER)

contradiction   *f.* contradicción (kohn-trah-deek-SYOHN)

contradictory (adj.)   contradictorio (kohn-trah-deek-TOH-ryoh)

contrary / opposite   *m.* contrario (kohn-TRAH-ryoh) ↻(adj.) ☐↻

contrary to / against   contra (KOHN-trah)

contrast   *m.* contraste (kohn-TRAHS-teh)

contrast (to)   contrastar (kohn-trahs-TAHR)

contribute (to)   contribuir (kohn-tree-<u>B</u>WEER)

contribution   *f.* contribución (kohn-tree-<u>b</u>oo-SYOHN)

contributor   *m.* contribuidor (kohn-tree-<u>b</u>wee-<u>D</u>OHR) ↻*f.* -ra↻

contrition   *f.* contrición (kohn-tree-SYOHN)

control (to)   controlar (kohn-troh-LAHR)

controllable (adj.)   controlable (kohn-troh-LAH-<u>b</u>leh)

controller   *m.* controlador (kohn-troh-lah-<u>D</u>OHR) ↻*f.* -ra↻

controversial (adj.)   controvertido (kohn-troh-<u>b</u>ehr-TEE-<u>d</u>oh)

controversy   *f.* controversia (kohn-troh-<u>B</u>EHR-syah)

convalesce (to)   convalecer (kohn-bah-leh-SEHR)

convalescence   *f.* convalecencia (kohn-bah-leh-SEHN-syah)

convenience   *f.* conveniencia (kohn-beh-NYEHN-syah)

convenient / expedient (adj.)   conveniente (kohn-beh-NYEHN-teh)

convent   *m.* convento (kohn-BEHN-toh)

convention (*tradition or meeting*)   *f.* convención (kohn-behn-SYOHN)

conventional (adj.)   convencional (kohn-behn-syoh-NAHL)

converge (to)   converger (kohn-behr-HEHR)

convergence   *f.* convergencia (kohn-behr-HEHN-syah)

conversant with (adj.)   versado con (behr-SAH-<u>d</u>oh kohn) 💣

conversation / talk / discourse   *f.* conversación (kohn-behr-sah-SYOHN)

converse / talk (to)   conversar (kohn-behr-SAHR)

conversion   *f.* conversión (kohn-behr-SYOHN)

convert (to)   convertir (kohn-behr-TEER)

convertible   *m.* convertible (kohn-behr-TEE-_b_leh) ○(adj.) ☐○

conviction / belief   *f.* convicción (kohn-beek-SYOHN)

convince (to)   convencer (kohn-behn-SEHR)

convincing (adj.)   convincente (kohn-been-SEHN-teh)

cooperate (to)   cooperar (koh-oh-peh-RAHR)

cooperation / teamwork   *f.* cooperación (koh-oh-peh-rah-SYOHN)

cooperative   *f.* cooperativa (koh-oh-peh-rah-TEE-_b_ah) ○(adj.) -vo○

coordinate / mesh with (to)   coordinar (koh-ohr-_d_ee-NAHR)

coordination   *f.* coordinación (koh-ohr-_d_ee-nah-SYOHN)

coordinator   *m.* coordinador (koh-ohr-_d_ee-nah-_D_OHR) ○*f.* -ra○

copier / photocopier   *f.* copiadora (koh-pyah-_D_OH-rah)

copious (adj.)   copioso (koh-PYOH-soh)

copulate / mate (to)   copular (koh-poo-LAHR)

copulation   *f.* cópula (KOH-poo-lah) / *f. pl.* relaciones (reh-lah-SYOH-nehs)

copy / duplicate   *f.* copia (KOH-pyah)

copy (imitate) (to)   copiar (koh-PYAHR)

cord / rope   *f.* cuerda (KWEHR-_d_ah)

cordial / genial (adj.)   cordial (kohr-_D_YAHL)

cordiality / geniality   *f.* cordialidad (kohr-_d_yah-lee-_D_AH_D_)

cordon off / rope off (to)   acordonar (ah-kohr-_d_oh-NAHR) ☕

cornea   *f.* córnea (KOHR-neh-ah)

corollary   *m.* corolario (koh-roh-LAH-ryoh)

corona   *f.* corona (koh-ROH-nah)

corporal / physical / bodily (adj.)   corporal (kohr-poh-RAHL)

corporate (adj.)   corporativo (kohr-poh-rah-TEE-_b_oh)

corporation   *f.* corporación (kohr-poh-rah-SYOHN)

corpse / body   *m.* cuerpo (KWEHR-poh)

corpulent / portly / stout (adj.)   corpulento (kohr-poo-LEHN-toh)

corral / corner (to)   acorralar (ah-koh-rrah-LAHR)

correct / right / proper (adj.)   correcto (koh-RREHK-toh)

correct (to)   corregir (koh-rreh-HEER)

correction   *f.* corrección (koh-rrehk-SYOHN)

corrective / remedial (adj.)   correctivo (koh-rrehk-TEE-<u>b</u>oh)

correlation   *f.* correlación (koh-rreh-lah-SYOHN)

correspond / fit / match (to)   corresponder (koh-rrehs-pohn-DEHR)

correspond (*exchange letters*) with (to)   corresponderse con (koh-rrehs-pohn-DEHR-seh kohn)

correspondence (*written interchange*)   *f.* correspondencia (koh-rrehs-pohn-DEHN-syah)

correspondent   *m. & f.* corresponsal (koh-rrehs-pohn-SAHL)

corridor / hall / hallway   *m.* corredor (koh-rreh-<u>D</u>OHR)

corroborate (to)   corroborar (koh-rroh-<u>b</u>oh-RAHR)

corroboration   *f.* corroboración (koh-rroh-<u>b</u>oh-rah-SYOHN)

corrosion   *f.* corrosión (koh-rroh-SYOHN)

corrosive (adj.)   corrosivo (koh-rroh-SEE-<u>b</u>oh)

corrupt (adj.)   corrupto (koh-RROOP-toh)

corrupt (to)   corromper (koh-rrohm-PEHR)

corruption   *f.* corrupción (koh-rroop-SYOHN)

corsair / privateer   *m.* corsario (kohr-SAH-ryoh)

corset / girdle   *m.* corsé (kohr-SEH)

cosmetic   *m.* cosmético (kohz-MEH-tee-koh) ↻(adj.) ▯↻

cosmic (adj.)   cósmico (KOHZ-mee-koh)

cosmopolitan   *m. & f.* cosmopolita (kohz-moh-poh-LEE-tah) ↻(adj.) ▯↻

cosmos   *m.* cosmos (KOHZ-mohs)

cost / price   *m.* costo (KOHS-toh)

cost (to)   costar (kohs-TAHR)

costly / expensive (adj.)   costoso (kohs-TOH-soh)

cot   *m.* catre (KAH-treh)

counsel / council / advice   *m.* consejo (kohn-SEH-hoh)

counsel / advise (to)   aconsejar (ah-kohn-seh-HAR) ●

counselor / councilman   *m.* concejal (kohn-seh-HAHL) ↻*f.* -la↻

count / countdown　*f.* cuenta (KWEHN-tah)

count (to)　contar (kohn-TAHR)

count on / rely upon (to)　contar con (kohn-TAHR kohn)

counter / against (adj.)　contrario (kohn-TRAH-ryoh)

countermand (to)　contramandar (kohn-trah-mahn-DAHR)

counterpart　*f.* contraparte (kohn-trah-PAHR-teh)

counterproductive (adj.)　contraproducente (kohn-trah-proh-<u>d</u>oo-SEHN-teh)

countless (adj.)　incontable (een-kohn-TAH-<u>b</u>leh) 💣※

coupon　*m.* cupón (koo-POHN)

courage / spunk　*m.* coraje (koh-RAH-heh)

courageous / spunky (adj.)　corajudo (koh-rah-HOO-<u>d</u>oh)

court (*royal or legal*)　*f.* corte (KOHR-teh)

court / woo (to)　cortejar (kohr-teh-HAHR)

courteous / genteel (adj.)　cortés (kohr-TEHS)

courtesy / gentility　*f.* cortesía (kohr-teh-SEE-ah)

courtship　*m.* cortejo (kohr-TEH-hoh)

cover / lid / shelter　*f.* cubierta (koo-<u>B</u>YEHR-tah)

cover (to)　cubrir (koo-<u>B</u>REER)

coverage　*f.* cobertura (koh-<u>b</u>ehr-TOO-rah)

coward　*m. & f.* cobarde (koh-<u>B</u>AHR-<u>d</u>eh) ↻(adj.) **cowardly / craven** ◻↻ 💣※

cowardice　*f.* cobardía (koh-<u>b</u>ahr-<u>D</u>EE-ah) 💣※

crater　*m.* cráter (KRAH-tehr)

crayon　*m.* crayón (krah-YOHN)

cream　*f.* crema (KREH-mah) ↻(adj.) **creamy** -moso↻

create (to)　crear (kreh-AHR)

creation　*f.* creación (kreh-ah-SYOHN) ↻(adj.) **creative** -ativo↻

creator / originator　*m.* creador (kreh-ah-<u>D</u>OHR) ↻*f.* -ra↻

creativity　*f.* creatividad (kreh-ah-tee-<u>b</u>ee-<u>D</u>AHD)

creature　*f.* criatura (kryah-TOO-rah)

credentials *f. pl.* credenciales (kreh-<u>d</u>ehn-SYAH-lehs)

credibility / plausibility *f.* credibilidad (kreh-<u>d</u>ee-<u>b</u>ee-lee-<u>D</u>AH<u>D</u>)

credible / believable (adj.) creíble (kreh-EE-<u>b</u>leh)

credit / credence *m.* crédito (KREH-<u>d</u>ee-toh)

credit / believe / accept (to) creer (kreh-EHR)
   ① **believer**—*m. & f.* creyente (kreh-YEHN-teh)

creditor *m.* acreedor (ah-kreh-eh-<u>D</u>HOR) ↺*f.* -ra↺ 💣

credulity *f.* credulidad (kreh-<u>d</u>oo-lee-<u>D</u>AH<u>D</u>)

credulous / gullible (adj.) crédulo (KREH-<u>d</u>oo-loh)

creed / faith *m.* credo (KREH-<u>d</u>oh)

cremation *f.* cremación (kreh-mah-SYOHN)

crescendo *m.* crescendo (krehs-SEHN-doh)

crescent *m.* creciente (kreh-SYEHN-teh)

crest *f.* cresta (KREHS-tah)

crime *m.* crimen (KREE-mehn)

criminal / felon *m.* criminal (kree-mee-NAHL) ↺(adj.) ☐↺

crisis *f.* crisis (KREE-sees)

criterion / standard *m.* criterio (kree-TEH-ryoh)

critic / reviewer *m.* crítico (KREE-tee-koh) ↺*f.* -ca↺

critical / judgmental (adj.) crítico (KREE-tee-koh)

criticism / critique *f.* crítica (KREE-tee-kah)

criticize (to) criticar (kree-tee-KAHR)

cross (*a street*) (to) cruzar (kroo-SAHR)

crossroads / crossing / junction *m.* cruce (KROO-seh)

crown (to) coronar (koh-roh-NAHR)

crucial (adj.) crucial (kroo-SYAHL)

crucifix *m.* crucifijo (kro-see-FEE-hoh)

crucify (to) crucificar (kroo-see-fee-KAHR)

crude / unrefined / raw (adj.) crudo (KROO-<u>d</u>oh)

cruel / mean (adj.) cruel (kroo-EHL)

cruelty / meanness   *f.* crueldad (kroo-ehl-<u>DAHD</u>)

crystal   *m.* cristal (krees-TAHL) ↻(adj.) **crystalline** –lino↻

cube   *m.* cubo (KOO-<u>b</u>oh) ↻(adj.) **cubic** –bico↻

cubicle   *m.* cubículo (koo-<u>BEE</u>-koo-loh)

cuisine / kitchen   *f.* cocina (koh-SEE-nah)

culinary (adj.)   culinario (koo-lee-NAH-ryoh)

culminate / climax (to)   culminar (kool-mee-NAHR)

culmination   *f.* culminación (kool-mee-nah-SYOHN)

culpability / fault / guilt / blame   *f.* culpabilidad (kool-pah-<u>b</u>ee-lee-<u>DAHD</u>)
   ① Related: (to) **blame**—culpar (kool-PAHR)

culprit   *m. & f.* culpable (kool-PAH-<u>b</u>leh) ↻(adj.) **culpable / guilty** []↻

cult   *m.* culto (KOOL-toh)

cultivate / farm / grow (to)   cultivar (kool-tee-<u>B</u>AHR)

cultivated (farmed / refined) (adj.)   cultivado (kool-tee-<u>B</u>AH-<u>d</u>oh)

cultivation / farming / crop (!)   *m.* cultivo (kool-tee-<u>b</u>oh)

cultivator / grower   *m.* cultivador (kool-tee-<u>b</u>ah-<u>DOHR</u>) ↻*f.* -ra↻

cultural (adj.)   cultural (kool-too-RAHL)

culture (*arts or prevailing ethos*)   *f.* cultura (kool-TOO-rah)

cultured / refined (adj.)   culto (KOOL-toh)

cumulative (adj.)   acumulativo (ah-koo-moo-lah-TEE-<u>b</u>oh) 💣

cupola / dome   *f.* cúpula (KOO-poo-lah)

cure / remedy / age meat   *f.* cura (KOO-rah)

cure / heal (to)   curar (koo-RAHR)

curiosity / inquisitiveness   *f.* curiosidad (koo-ryoh-see-<u>DAHD</u>)

curious (*inquisitive or odd*) (adj.)   curioso (koo-RYOH-soh)

(be) curious / pry (to)   curiosear (koo-ryoh-seh-AHR)

current / flow   *f.* corriente (koh-RRYEHN-teh)

current / contemporary (adj.)   corriente (koh-RRYEHN-teh)

curriculum   *m.* currículum (koo-RREE-koo-loom)

cursor   *m.* cursor (KOOR-sohr)

curtail (to)   acortar (ah-kohr-TAHR) 💣

curtain / drape / window shade   *f.* cortina (kohr-TEE-nah)

curvaceous / rounded / shapely (adj.)   curvilíneo (koor-<u>b</u>ee-LEE-neh-oh)

curvature   *f.* curvatura (koor-<u>b</u>ah-TOO-rah)

curve   *f.* curva (KOOHR-<u>b</u>ah)

curved / bent (adj.)   encorvado (ehn-kohr-<u>B</u>AH-<u>d</u>oh) 💣

cushion   *m.* cojín (koh-HEEN)

cusp   *f.* cúspide (KOOS-pee-<u>d</u>eh)

custodian   *m.* custodio (koos-TOH-<u>d</u>yoh) ↻*f.* -ia↻

custody   *f.* custodia (koos-TOH-<u>d</u>yah)

(have) custody of / guard (to)   custodiar (koos-toh-<u>D</u>YAHR)

custom / manner   *f.* costumbre (kohs-TOOM-<u>b</u>reh)

cut (to)   cortar (kohr-TAHR)

cycle   *m.* ciclo (SEE-kloh)

cyclone   *m.* ciclón (see-KLOHN)

cylinder   *m.* cilindro (see-LEEN-droh)

cylindrical (adj.)   cilíndrico (see-LEEN-dree-koh)

cynic   *m.* cínico (SEE-nee-koh) ↻*f.* -ca↻ ↻(adj.) **cynic / cynical** []↻

cynicism   *m.* cinismo (see-NEEZ-moh)

—D—

damage / injury / mischief   *m.* daño (DAH-nyoh)

damage / harm / injure / spoil (to)   dañar (dah-NYAHR)

data   *m.* datos (DAH-tohs)

deacon   *m.* diácono (DYAH-koh-noh)

debacle   *m.* debacle (deh-<u>B</u>AH-kleh)

debate   *m.* debate (deh-<u>B</u>AH-teh)

debate (to)   debatir (deh-<u>b</u>ah-TEER)

debilitate / sap / weaken (to)   debilitar (deh-<u>b</u>ee-lee-TAHR)

debilitated / fragile / weak (adj.)   débil (DEH-_b_eel)

debilitation   *m.* debilitamiento (deh-_b_ee-lee-tah-MYEHN-toh)

debility / weakness / foible   *f.* debilidad (deh-_b_ee-lee-_D_AH_D_)

debit   *m.* débito (DEH-_b_ee-toh)

debut   *m.* debut (deh-_B_OOT)

debut (to)   debutar (deh-_b_oo-TAHR)

decadence / decay / deterioration / decline   *f.* decadencia (deh-kah-_D_EHN-syah)

decadent (adj.)   decadente (deh-kah-_D_EHN-teh)

decency / propriety   *f.* decencia (deh-SEHN-syah)

decent (*respectable*) (adj.)   decente (deh-SEHN-teh)

decide / determine / make up one's mind (to)   decidir (deh-see-_D_EER)

decision   *f.* decisión (deh-see-SYOHN)

decisive (adj.)   decisivo (deh-see-SEE-_b_oh)

declaration / pronouncement   *f.* declaración (deh-klah-rah-SYOHN)

declare / aver / pronounce / state (to)   declarar (deh-klah-RAHR)

decline (turn down) (to)   declinar (deh-klee-NAHR)

decompose / rot (to)   descomponerse (dehs-kohm-poh-NEHR-seh)

decomposition / rot   *f.* descomposición (dehs-kohm-poh-see-SYOHN)

decorate / adorn (to)   decorar (deh-koh-RAHR)

decoration / decor   *f.* decoración (deh-koh-rah-SYOHN)

decoration / scenery   *m.* decorado (deh-koh-RAH-_d_oh)

decorative (adj.)   decorativo (deh-koh-rah-TEE-_b_oh)

decorator   *m.* decorador (deh-koh-rah-_D_OHR) ⟳*f.* -ra⟳

decorum / propriety   *m.* decoro (deh-KOH-roh)

decrease (to)   decrecer (deh-kreh-SEHR)

decree / ordain (to)   decretar (deh-kreh-TAHR)

decrepit (adj.)   decrépito (deh-KREH-pee-toh)

dedicate / invest (to)   dedicar (deh-_d_ee-KAHR)

dedication   *f.* dedicación (deh-_d_ee-kah-SYOHN)

deduce / deduct (to)   deducir (deh-<u>d</u>oo-SEER)

deductable (adj.)   deducible (deh-<u>d</u>oo-SEE-<u>b</u>leh)

deduction   *f.* deducción (deh-<u>d</u>ook-SYOHN)

defamation / libel / slander   *f.* difamación (dee-fah-mah-SYOHN) 💣

defamatory / slanderous (adj.)   difamatorio (dee-fah-mah-TOH-ryoh) 💣

defame / libel / slander (to)   difamar (dee-fah-MAHR) 💣

defect / flaw   *m.* defecto (deh-FEHK-toh)

defective (adj.)   defectuoso (deh-fehk-TWOH-soh)

defend (to)   defender (deh-fehn-DEHR)

defender   *m.* defensor (deh-fehn-SOHR) ↻*f.* -ra↻ / *f.* defensa (deh-FEHN-sah)

defending / defensive (adj.)   defensor (deh-fehn-SOHR)

defense   *f.* defensa (deh-FEHN-sah)

defenseless (adj.)   indefenso (een-deh-FEHN-soh) 💣

defensive (adj.)   defensivo (deh-fehn-SEE-<u>b</u>oh)

defer / postpone (to)   deferir (deh-feh-REER)

deference   *f.* deferencia (deh-feh-REHN-syah)

deficiency   *f.* deficiencia (deh-fee-SYEHN-syah)

deficient / wanting (adj.)   deficiente (dee-fee-SYEHN-teh)

deficit   *m.* déficit (DEH-fee-seet)

define (to)   definir (deh-fee-NEER) ↻(adj.) **definite** -nido↻ 💣

definition   *f.* definición (deh-fee-nee-SYOHN)

definitive (adj.)   definitivo (deh-fee-nee-TEE-<u>b</u>oh)

deformed / misshapen (adj.)   deforme (deh-FOHR-meh)

deformity   *f.* deformidad (deh-fohr-mee-<u>D</u>AH<u>D</u>)

defraud / cheat (to)   defraudar (deh-fraow-<u>D</u>AHR)

defunct / deceased (!) (adj.)   difunto (dee-FOON-toh)

degenerate (to)   degenerar (deh-heh-neh-RAHR)

degeneration   *f.* degeneración (deh-heh-neh-rah-SYOHN)

degradation / demotion (!)   *f.* degradación (deh-grah-<u>d</u>ah-SYOHN)

degrade / cheapen (to)　degradar (deh-grah-_D_AHR)

deify (to)　deificar (day-fee-KAHR)

deity　_f._ deidad (day-_D_AH_D_)

delegate　_m._ delegado (deh-leh-GAH-_d_oh) ◑_f._ -da◐

delegate (to)　delegar (deh-leh-GAHR)

delegation　_f._ delegación (deh-leh-gah-SYOHN)

deliberate / intentional (adj.)　deliberado (deh-lee-_b_eh-RAH-_d_oh)

deliberate (to)　deliberar (deh-lee-_b_eh-RAHR)

deliberation　_f._ deliberación (deh-lee-_b_eh-rah-SYOHN)

delicacy / kindness (!)　_f._ delicadeza (deh-lee-kah-_D_EH-sah)

delicate / fragile / subtle / (adj.)　delicado (deh-lee-KAH-_d_oh)

delicious / delectable / delightful (adj.)　delicioso (deh-lee-SYOH-soh)

delight　_m._ deleite (deh-LAY-teh)

delight / give pleasure to (to)　deleitar (deh-lay-TAHR)

delightful (adj.)　deleitoso (deh-lay-TOH-soh)

delinquency　_f._ delincuencia (deh-leen-KWEHN-syah)

delirious (adj.)　delirante (deh-lee-RAHN-teh)

delirium　_m._ delirio (deh-LEE-ryoh)
　　① A related noncognate: (to) **rave**—delirar (deh-lee-RAHR)

deluxe (adj.)　de lujo (deh LOO-hoh)

demand　_f._ demanda (deh-MAHN-dah)

demand / sue (!) (to)　demandar (deh-mahn-DAHR)

demarcation　_f._ demarcación (deh-mahr-kah-SYOHN)

demented / insane (adj.)　demente (deh-MEHN-teh)

dementia / insanity　_f._ demencia (deh-MEHN-syah)

(sufferer of) dementia / madman　_m. & f._ demente (deh-MEHN-teh)

democracy　_f._ democracia (deh-moh-KRAH-syah)

democrat　_m. & f._ demócrata (deh-MOH-crah-tah)

democratic (adj.)　democrático (deh-moh-KRAH-tee-koh)

demolish / raze (to)　demoler (deh-moh-LEHR)

demolition *f.* demolición (deh-moh-lee-SYOHN)

demon / fiend *m.* demonio (deh-MOH-nyoh)

demonstrate / prove (to)   demostrar (deh-mohs-TRAHR) 💣

demonstration *f.* demostración (deh-mohs-trah-SYOHN) 💣

demonstrative (adj.)   demostrativo (deh-mohs-trah-TEE-boh) 💣

demonstrator *m.* demostrador (deh-mohs-trah-DOHR) ↻*f.* -ra↻ 💣

demoralize (to)   desmoralizar (dehz-moh-rah-lee-SAHR) 💣

denigrate / disparage / belittle (to)   denigrar (deh-nee-GRAHR)

denomination (value) *f.* denominación (deh-noh-mee-nah-SYOHN)

denote (to)   denotar (deh-noh-TAHR)

denounce (to)   denunciar (deh-noon-SYAHR)

dense (adj.)   denso (DEHN-soh)

density *f.* densidad (dehn-see-DAHD)

dental (adj.)   dental (dehn-TAHL)

dentist *m. & f.* dentista (dehn-TEES-tah)

denude / disrobe (to)   desnudar (dehz-noo-DAHR)

denuded / naked (adj.)   desnudo (dehz-NOO-doh)
   ① **nudity / nakedness**—*f.* desnudez (dehz-noo-DEHS)

denunciation *f.* denuncia (deh-NOON-syah)

deodorant *m.* desodorante (deh-soh-doh-RAHN-teh) 💣

depart / leave / (to)   partir (pahr-TEER) 💣

department *m.* departamento (deh-pahr-tah-MEHN-toh)

departmental (adj.)   departamental (deh-pahr-tah-mehn-TAHL)

departure *f.* partida (pahr-TEE-dah) 💣

depend on / be contingent upon (to)   depender de (deh-pehn-DEHR deh)

dependence / reliance *f.* dependencia (deh-pehn-DEHN-syah)

dependent / reliant (adj.)   dependiente (deh-pehn-DYEHN-teh)

deplorable (adj.)   deplorable (deh-ploh-RAH-bleh)

deplore (to)   deplorar (deh-ploh-RAHR)

deport (to)   deportar (deh-pohr-TAHR)

deportation *f.* deportación (deh-pohr-tah-SYOHN)

deposit / depository *m.* depósito (deh-POH-see-toh)

deposit (to) depositar (deh-poh-see-TAHR)

depositor *m.* depositador (deh-poh-see-tah-<u>D</u>OHR) ♻*f.* -ra♻ /
  m. & f. depositante (deh-poh-see-TAHN-teh) ♻(adj.) ☐♻

depravity *f.* depravación (deh-prah-<u>b</u>ah-SYOHN)

deprecate / scorn (to) despreciar (dehs-preh-SYAHR)

deprecation / scorn *f.* desprecio (dehs-PREH-syoh)

depreciate / devalue (to) depreciar (deh-preh-SYAHR)

depression *f.* depresión (deh-preh-SYOHN)

deprive (to) privar (pree-<u>B</u>AHR) ♦⁂

descend / drop / fall / sink (to) descender (dehs-sehn-DEHR)

descendant *m. & f.* descendiente (dehs-sehn-DYEHN-teh)

descent / decline / slide *m.* descenso (dehs-SEHN-soh)

describe (to) describir (dehs-kree-<u>B</u>EER)

description / depiction *f.* descripción (dehs-kreep-SYOHN)

descriptive (adj.) descriptivo (dehs-kreep-TEE-<u>b</u>oh)

desert / wasteland *m.* desierto (deh-SYEHR-toh)

desert / defect (to) desertar (deh-sehr-TAHR)

deserter / defector *m.* desertor (deh-sehr-TOHR) ♻*f.* -ra♻

desertion / defection *f.* deserción (deh-sehr-SYOHN)

design / pattern *m.* diseño (dee-SEH-nyoh)

design (to) diseñar (dee-seh-NYAHR) ♦⁂

designate (to) designar (deh-seeg-NAHR)

designation *f.* designación (deh-seeg-nah-SYOHN)

designer *m.* diseñador (dee-seh-nyah-<u>D</u>OHR) ♻*f.* -ra♻ ♦⁂

desirable (adj.) deseable (deh-seh-AH-<u>b</u>leh)

desire / want *m.* deseo (deh-SEH-oh)

desire / wish for (to) desear (deh-seh-AHR)

desolate / forlorn (adj.) desolado (deh-soh-LAH-<u>d</u>oh)

desolation *f.* desolación (deh-soh-lah-SYOHN)

despair (to) desesperar (deh-sehs-peh-RAHR)

desperate / hopeless (adj.) desesperado (deh-sehs-peh-RAH-doh) ●͏
    ① Transformed from adjective to noun and respelled, this word has been
    imported into English as: **dangerous criminal / bold outlaw—**
    m. desperado (dehs-peh-RAH-doh).

desperation / despair *f.* desesperación (deh-sehs-peh-rah-SYOHN) ●͏

destination *f.* destinación (dehs-tee-nah-SYOHN)

destiny / fate *m.* destino (dehs-TEE-noh)

destroy / ruin / wreck (to) destruir (dehs-troo-EER)

destruction *f.* destrucción (dehs-trook-SYOHN)

destructive (adj.) destructivo (dehs-trook-TEE-boh)

detail *m.* detalle (deh-TAH-yeh)

detail / itemize (to) detallar (deh-tah-YAHR)

detailed (adj.) detallado (deh-tah-YAH-doh)

detain / halt / stop / arrest (to) detener (deh-teh-NEHR)

detect (to) detectar (deh-tehk-TAHR)

detective / sleuth *m. & f.* detective (deh-tehk-TEE-beh)

detention *f.* detención (deh-tehn-SYOHN)

detergent *m.* detergente (deh-tehr-HEHN-teh)

deteriorate (to) deteriorarse (deh-teh-ryoh-RAHR-seh)

deterioration *m.* deterioro (deh-teh-RYOH-roh) / *f.* deterioración (deh-teh-
    ryoh-rah-SYOHN)

determination *f.* determinación (deh-tehr-mee-nah-SYOHN)

determine / ascertain (to) determinar (deh-tehr-mee-NAHR)

determined / purposeful (adj.) determinado (deh-tehr-mee-NAH-doh)

detest / hate (to) detestar (deh-tehs-TAHR)

detestable / odious / hateful (adj.) detestable (deh-tehs-TAH-bleh)

detriment *m.* detrimento (deh-tree-MEHN-toh)

devastate / desolate / ravage (to) devastar (deh-bahs-TAHR)

devastation *f.* devastación (deh-bahs-tah-SYOHN)

deviation / diversion (from)   *f.* desviación (dehz-<u>b</u>yah-SYOHN)

devotee   *m.* devoto (deh-<u>B</u>OH-toh) ◑*f.* -ta◑

devotion (*dedication to*)   *f.* devoción (deh-<u>b</u>oh-SYOHN)

devour / eat (to)   devorar (deh-<u>b</u>oh-RAHR)

devout (adj.)   devoto (deh-<u>B</u>OH-toh)

diabolical / diabolic (adj.)   diabólico (dyah-<u>B</u>OH-lee-koh) ⬤⃛

diagnose (to)   diagnosticar (dyahg-nohs-tee-KAHR)

diagnosis   *m.* diagnóstico (dyahg-NOHS-tee-koh) ◑(adj.) **diagnostic** ☐◑

diagonal   *f.* diagonal (dyah-goh-NAHL) ◑(adj.) ☐◑

diagram   *m.* diagrama (dyah-GRAH-mah)

dialect   *m.* dialecto (dyah-LEHK-toh)

dialogue   *m.* diálogo (DYAH-loh-goh)

diameter   *m.* diámetro (DYAH-meh-troh)

diamond   *m.* diamante (dyah-MAHN-teh)

diaphanous / filmy (adj.)   diáfano (DYAH-fah-noh)

diarrhea   *f.* diarrea (dyah-RREH-ah)

diary / journal   *m.* diario (DYAH-ryoh)

diatribe / tirade   *f.* diatriba (dyah-TREE-<u>b</u>ah)

dictate (to)   dictar (deek-TAHR)

dictation   *m.* dictado (deek-TAH-<u>d</u>oh)

dictator   *m.* dictador (deek-tah-<u>D</u>OHR) ◑*f.* -ra◑

dictatorship   *f.* dictadura (deek-tah-<u>D</u>OO-rah)

diction   *f.* dicción (deek-SYOHN)

dictionary   *m.* diccionario (deek-syoh-NAH-ryoh)

diet (*food restriction*)   *f.* dieta (DYEH-tah)

dietary (adj.)   dietético (dyeh-TEH-tee-koh)

differ (to)   diferir (dee-feh-REER)

difference (*dissimilarity*)   *f.* diferencia (dee-feh-REHN-syah)

differenciate (to)   diferenciar (dee-feh-rehn-SYAHR)

differenciation   *f.* diferenciación (dee-feh-rehn-syah-SYOHN)

different (adj.)   diferente (dee-feh-REHN-teh)

difficult / hard (adj.)   difícil (dee-FEE-seel)

difficulty / hardship   *f.* dificultad (dee-fee-kool-TAH<u>D</u>)

diffuse / widespread (adj.)   difuso (dee-FOO-soh)

digest (to)   digerir (dee-heh-REER)

digestible (adj.)   digerible (dee-heh-REE-<u>b</u>leh)

digestion   *f.* digestión (dee-hehs-TYOHN)

digit (*numeral*)   *m.* dígito (DEE-hee-toh)

digital (adj.)   digital (dee-hee-TAHL)

dignified (adj.)   digno (DEEG-noh)

dignify (to)   dignificar (deeg-nee-fee-KAHR)

dignity   *f.* dignidad (deeg-nee-<u>D</u>AH<u>D</u>)

digress (to)   divagar (dee-<u>b</u>ah-GAHR)

digression   *f.* digresión (dee-greh-SYOHN)

dilate / expand (to)   dilatar (dee-lah-TAHR)

dilemma / quandary   *m.* dilema (dee-LEH-mah)

diligence   *f.* diligencia (dee-lee-HEHN-syah) ↻(adj.) **diligent** -nte↻

dilute (to)   diluir (dee-LWEER)

dimension   *f.* dimensión (dee-mehn-SYOHN)

diminish / decrease (to)   disminuir (deez-mee-NWEER) ◆⁕

diminutive / miniature (adj.)   diminuto (dee-mee-NOO-toh)

diploma   *m.* diploma (dee-PLOH-mah)

diplomacy   *f.* diplomacia (dee-ploh-MAH-syah)

diplomat   *m.* diplomático (dee-ploh-MAH-tee-koh) ↻*f.* -ca↻

diplomatic / politic (adj.)   diplomático (dee-ploh-MAH-tee-koh)

direct (adj.)   directo (dee-REHK-toh)

direct / administer (to)   dirigir (dee-ree-HEER)

direction (*line of sight or leadership*)   *f.* dirección (dee-rehk-SYOHN)

director / manager / conductor   *m.* director (dee-rehk-TOHR) ↻*f.* -ra↻

directory   *m.* directorio (dee-rehk-TOH-ryoh)

disadvantage / drawback *f.* desventaja (dehs-_b_ehn-TAH-hah) 💣

disagreeable / unpleasant (adj.) desagradable (deh-sah-grah-_D_AH-_b_leh) 💣

disappear (to) desaparecer (deh-sah-pah-reh-SEHR) 💣

disappearance *f.* desaparición (deh-sah-pah-ree-SYOHN) 💣

disaster *m.* desastre (deh-SAHS-treh) 💣

disastrous (adj.) desastroso (deh-sahs-TROH-soh) 💣

discern (to) discernir (dees-sehr-NEER)

discernment / judgment *m.* discernimiento (dees-sehr-nee-MYEHN-toh)

discharge (to) descargar (dehs-kahr-GAHR) 💣

disciple / pupil *m.* discípulo (dees-SEE-poo-loh) ↺*f.* -la↺

discipline (*field of work*) *f.* disciplina (dees-see-PLEE-nah)

discipline (*control*) (to) disciplinar (dees-see-plee-NAHR)

discolor / fade (to) descolorar (dehs-koh-loh-RAHR) 💣

discoloration *f.* descoloración (dehs-koh-loh-rah-SYOHN) 💣

disconnect (to) desconectar (dehs-koh-nehk-TAHR) 💣
   ① The noncognate adjective: **disconnected**—inconexo (een-koh-NEHK-soh)

discontent / dissatisfaction *m.* descontento (dehs-kohn-TEHN-toh) 💣

discontented / dissatisfied (adj.) descontento (dehs-kohn-TEHN-toh) 💣

discontinue (to) discontinuar (dees-kohn-tee-NWAHR) 💣

discord *f.* discordia (dees-KOHR-dyah)

discount *m.* descuento (dehs-KWEHN-toh) 💣

discount / deduct (to) descontar (dehs-kohn-TAHR) 💣

discourse / formal speech *m.* discurso (dees-KOOR-soh)

discourteous / impolite (adj.) descortés (dehs-kohr-TEHS)

discourtesy / rudeness *f.* descortesía (dehs-kohr-teh-SEE-ah)

discover / detect (to) descubrir (dehs-koo-_B_REER) 💣

discoverer *m.* descubridor (dehs-koo-_b_ree-_D_OHR) ↺*f.* -ra↺ 💣

discovery / detection *m.* descubrimiento (dehs-koo-_b_ree-MYEHN-toh) 💣

discredit / disrepute *m.* descrédito (dehs-KREH-dee-toh) 💣

discredit / debunk (to) desacreditar (deh-sah-kreh-dee-TAHR) 💣

discreet / tactful (adj.) discreto (dees-KREH-toh)

discrepancy *f.* discrepancia (dees-kreh-PAHN-syah)

discretion / tact *f.* discreción (dees-kreh-SYOHN) / *m.* tacto (TAHK-toh)

discriminate (to) discriminar (dees-kree-mee-NAHR)

discrimination *f.* discriminación (dees-kree-mee-nah-SYOHN)

discuss (to) discutir (dees-koo-TEER)

discussion *f.* discusión (dees-koo-SYOHN)

disdain *m.* desdén (dehz-DEHN) 💣

disdain (to) desdeñar (dehz-deh-NYAHR)

disenchant (to) desencantar (deh-sehn-kahn-TAHR) 💣

disenchantment *m.* desencanto (deh-sehn-KAHN-toh) 💣

disfigure / deface (to) desfigurar (dehs-fee-goo-RAHR) 💣

disfigurement / defacement *f.* desfiguración (dehs-fee-goo-rah-SYOHN)

disgrace *f.* desgracia (dehz-GRAH-syah) 💣

dishonest (adj.) deshonesto (dehs-oh-NEHS-toh) 💣

dishonesty / deceit *f.* deshonestidad (dehs-oh-nehs-tee-DAHD) 💣

dishonor / disrepute *f.* deshonra (dehs-OHN-rah) 💣

dishonor / disgrace (to) deshonrar (dehs-ohn-RAHR) 💣

dishonorable / disgraceful (adj.) deshonroso (dehs-ohn-ROH-soh) 💣

disillusion (to) desilusionar (deh-see-loo-syoh-NAHR) 💣

disillusion / disillusionment *f.* desilusión (deh-see-loo-SYOHN) 💣

disinfect (to) desinfectar (deh-seen-fehk-TAHR) 💣

disintegrate (to) desintegrar (deh-seen-teh-GRAHR) 💣

disintegration *f.* desintegración (deh-seen-teh-grah-SYOHN) 💣

disk / disc *m.* disco (DEES-koh)

dislocate (to) dislocar (dees-loh-KAHR)

dislodge (to) desalojar (deh-sah-loh-HAHR) 💣

disloyal / faithless (adj.) desleal (dehz-leh-AHL) 💣

disloyalty / faithlessness *f.* deslealtad (dehz-leh-ahl-TAH<u>D</u>) 💣

disobedience *f.* desobediencia (deh-soh-<u>b</u>eh-<u>D</u>YEHN-syah) 💣

disobedient (adj.) desobediente (deh-soh-<u>b</u>eh-<u>D</u>YEHN-teh) 💣

disobey / defy (to) desobedecer (deh-soh-<u>b</u>eh-<u>d</u>eh-SEHR) 💣

disorder / disarray / clutter *m.* desorden (deh-SOHR-<u>d</u>ehn) 💣

disorderly / messy / untidy (adj.) desordenado (deh-sohr-<u>d</u>eh-NAH-<u>d</u>oh) 💣

disorganization *f.* desorganización (deh-sohr-gah-nee-sah-SYOHN) 💣

dispenser (*person or machine*) *m.* dispensador (dees-pehn-sah-<u>D</u>OHR)

disperse (*give out*) (to) dispersar (dees-pehr-SAHR)

disperse / disband (to) dispersarse (dees-pehr-SAHR-seh)

dispersion / dispersal *f.* dispersión (dees-pehr-SYOHN)

displace (to) desplazar (dehs-plah-SAHR) 💣

displacement *m.* desplazamiento (dehs-plah-sah-MYEHN-toh)

disposition / status of *f.* disposición (dees-poh-see-SYOHN) 💣
① As temperament: **disposition**—*m.* genio (HEH-nyoh)

disproportion *f.* desproporción (dehs-proh-pohr-SYOHN) 💣

disproportionate (adj.) desproporcionado (dehs-proh-pohr-syoh-NAH-<u>d</u>oh) 💣

disputable (adj.) disputable (dees-poo-TAH-<u>b</u>leh)

dispute / argument *f.* disputa (dees-POO-tah)

dispute / contest / quarrel (to) disputar (dees-poo-TAHR)

disqualification *f.* descalificación (dehs-kah-lee-fee-kah-SYOHN) 💣

disqualify (to) descalificar (dehs-kah-lee-fee-KAHR) 💣

disquiet / disturb / worry / harass (to) inquietar (een-kyeh-TAHR)
① (to) **be unquiet / disturbed / worried / upset**—inquietarse (een-kyeh-TAHR-seh)

disquietude / disquiet / uneasiness *f.* inquietud (een-kyeh-TOO<u>D</u>)

disquieting / disturbing / worrying / alarming (adj.) inquietante (een-kyeh-THAN-teh)

dissect (to) disecar (dee-seh-KAHR) 💣

disseminate (to)   diseminar (dee-seh-mee-NAHR) 💣

dissemination   f. diseminación (dee-seh-mee-nah-SYOHN) 💣

dissension / dissent   f. disensión (dee-sehn-SYOHN) 💣

dissent / disagree (to)   disentir (dee-sehn-TEER) 💣

dissimilar / unlike (adj.)   disímil (dee-SEE-meel) 💣

dissipate (to)   disipar (dee-see-PAHR) 💣

dissolve / melt (to)   disolver (dee-sohl-_B_EHR) 💣

dissonance   f. disonancia (dee-soh-NAHN-syah) 💣

distance   f. distancia (dees-TAHN-syah) ↻(adj.) **distant** -ante↻

distinct (*different***)** (adj.)   distinto (dees-TEEN-toh)

distinction (*difference***)**   f. distinción (dees-teen-SYOHN)

distinctive (adj.)   distintivo (dees-teen-TEE-_b_oh)

distinguish / differentiate (to)   distinguir (dees-teen-GHEER)

distinguished / honored / notable (adj.)   distinguido (dees-teen-
GHEE-_d_oh)

distort / misrepresent (to)   distorcionar (dees-tohr-syoh-NAHR)

distortion   f. distorción (dees-tohr-SYOHN)

distract / sidetrack (to)   distraer (dees-trah-EHR)

distracted / absentminded (adj.)   distraído (dees-trah-EE-doh)

distraction / inattention   f. distracción (dees-trahk-SYOHN)

distribute / apportion / allot / mete (to)   distribuir (dees-tree-_B_WEER)

distribution   f. distribución (dees-stree-_b_oo-SYOHN)

district / precinct   _m._ distrito (dees-TREE-toh)

disturbance   _m._ disturbio (dees-TOOR-_b_yoh)

divan / davenport / sofa   _m._ diván (dee-_B_AHN)

diverge / deviate from (to)   divergir (dee-_b_ehr-HEER)

divergence   f. divergencia (dee-_b_ehr-HEHN-syah)

divergent / differing (adj.)   divergente (dee-_b_ehr-HEHN-teh)

diverse / manifold (adj.)   diverso (dee-_B_EHR-soh)

diversion (*amusement***) / distraction / fun**   f. diversión (dee-_b_ehr-SYOHN)

diversity *f.* diversidad (dee-<u>b</u>ehr-see-<u>DAHD</u>)

divide / split / part (to)   dividir (dee-<u>b</u>ee-<u>DEER</u>)

dividend *m.* dividendo (dee-<u>b</u>ee-<u>DEHN</u>-doh)

divine / guess (to)   adivinar (ah-<u>d</u>ee-<u>b</u>ee-NAHR) 💣

divine / godlike (adj.)   divino (dee-<u>BEE</u>-noh)

divinity *f.* divinidad (dee-<u>b</u>ee-nee-<u>DAHD</u>)

division (*portion or math operation*)   *f.* división (dee-<u>b</u>ee-SYOHN)

divorce *m.* divorcio (dee-<u>BOHR</u>-syoh)

divorce (to)   divorciar (dee-<u>b</u>ohr-SYAHR)

divulge (to)   divulgar (dee-<u>b</u>ool-GAHR)

docile / meek (adj.)   dócil (DOH-seel)

docility / meekness *f.* docilidad (doh-see-lee-<u>DAHD</u>)

doctor (*scholastic*) *m.* doctor (dohk-TOHR) ⟳*f.* -ra⟳
    ① **doctor (*medical*) / physician**—*m.* médico (MEH-dee-koh) ⟳*f.* -ca⟳

doctrine *f.* doctrina (dohk-TREE-nah)

document *m.* documento (doh-koo-MEHN-toh)

documentary *m.* documental (doh-koo-mehn-TAHL) ⟳(adj.) ▯⟳

documentation *f.* documentación (doh-koo-mehn-tah-SYOHN)

dogma *m.* dogma (DOHG-mah)

dogmatic / opinionated (adj.)   dogmático (dohg-MAH-tee-koh)

dogmatism *m.* dogmatismo (dohg-mah-TEEZ-moh)

dollar *m.* dólar (DOH-lahr) 💣

dolphin *m.* delfín (dehl-FEEN)

domestic / local (adj.)   doméstico (doh-MEHS-tee-koh)

domestic (*household worker*) *m.* doméstico (doh-MEHS-tee-koh)
    ⟳*f.* -ca⟳

domesticate / tame (to)   domesticar (doh-mehs-tee-KAHR)

domesticated / tame (adj.)   domesticado (doh-mehs-tee-KAH-<u>d</u>oh)

dominant (adj.)   dominante (doh-mee-NAHN-teh)

dominate / control (to)   dominar (doh-mee-NAHR)

domination / dominance *f.* dominación (doh-mee-nah-SYOHN)

dominion / domain *m.* dominio (doh-MEE-nyoh)

donate (to) donar (doh-NAHR)

donation *f.* donación (doh-nah-SYOHN)

donor *m.* donador (doh-nah-<u>D</u>OHR) ↻*f.* -ra↻

dormitory / bedroom (!) *m.* dormitorio (dohr-mee-TOH-ryoh)

dose / dosage *f.* dosis (DOH-sees)

double / dual (adj.) doble (DOH-<u>b</u>leh)

double / fold over / bend (to) doblar (doh-<u>B</u>LAHR)

doubt *f.* duda (DOO-<u>d</u>ah)

doubt / be uncertain (to) dudar (doo-<u>D</u>AHR)

doubtful / dubious (adj.) dudoso (doo-<u>D</u>OH-soh)
    ① (adj.) **doubtless / certain**—indudable (een-doo-<u>D</u>AH-<u>b</u>leh) / cierto (SYEHR-toh); (adv.) **doubtless(ly) / without any doubt / certainly**—sin duda (seen DOO-<u>d</u>ah) / indudablemente (een-doo-<u>d</u>ah-<u>b</u>leh-MEHN-teh) / ciertamente (syehr-tah-MEHN-teh)

drain (to) drenar (dreh-NAHR)

drama *m.* drama (DRAH-mah) / teatro (teh-AH-troh)
    ① (a theatrical) play—*f.* representación (reh-preh-sehn-tah-SYOHN)

dramatic / theatrical (adj.) dramático (drah-MAH-tee-koh)

dramatist / playwright *m.* dramaturgo (drah-mah-TOOR-goh)

dramatization *f.* dramatización (drah-mah-tee-sah-SYOHN)

dramatize (to) dramatizar (drah-mah-tee-SAHR)

drastic (adj.) drástico (DRAHS-tee-koh)

drug *f.* droga (DROH-gah)

duel *m.* duelo (DWEH-loh)

duo / duet *m.* dúo (DOO-oh)

duplicate / copy of *m.* duplicado (doo-plee-KAH-<u>d</u>oh) ↻(adj.) ▢↻

duplicate / copy (to) duplicar (doo-plee-KAHR)

duplication *f.* duplicación (doo-plee-kah-SYOHN)

durability / toughness *f.* durabilidad (doo-rah-<u>b</u>ee-lee-<u>D</u>AH<u>D</u>)

durable / hard (adj.)   duradero (doo-rah-<u>D</u>EH-roh)
   ① Shortened, this becomes: (adj.) **hard / tough / resistant**—duro (DOO-roh)

duration   *f.* duración (doo-rah-SYOHN)

during   durante (doo-RAHN-teh)

dynamic (adj.)   dinámico (dee-NAH-mee-koh)

dynasty   *f.* dinastía (dee-nahs-TEE-ah)

—E—

east   *m.* este (EHS-teh) ◑(adj.) *f*◐

eccentric / oddball   *m.* excéntrico (ehs-SEHN-tree-koh) ◑*f.* -ca◐

eccentric / odd (adj.)   excéntrico (ehs-SEHN-tree-koh) ♦

eccentricity   *f.* excentricidad (ehs-sehn-tree-see-<u>D</u>AH<u>D</u>) ♦

echo   *m.* eco (EH-koh)

eclipse   *m.* eclipse (eh-KLEEP-seh)

ecological (adj.)   ecológico (eh-koh-LOH-hee-koh)

ecologist / environmentalist   *m. & f.* ecologista (eh-koh-loh-HEES-tah)

ecology   *f.* ecología (eh-koh-loh-HEE-ah)

economic / thrifty (adj.)   económico (eh-koh-NOH-mee-koh)

economist   *m. & f.* economista (eh-koh-noh-MEES-tah)

economize (to)   economizar (eh-koh-noh-mee-SAHR)

economy / thrift   *f.* economía (eh-koh-noh-MEE-ah)

ecosystem   *m.* ecosistema (eh-koh-sees-TEH-mah)

ecstasy / rapture   *m.* éxtasis (EHS-stah-sees) ♦

ecstatic / rapturous (adj.)   extático (ehs-STAH-tee-koh) ♦

edict   *m.* edicto (eh-deek-toh)

edification   *f.* edificación (eh-<u>d</u>ee-fee-kah-SYOHN)

edifice / building / structure   *m.* edificio (eh-<u>d</u>ee-FEE-syoh)

edify (to)   edificar (eh-<u>d</u>ee-fee-KAHR)
   ① This same term also translates as: (to) **build (!)**

edition   *f.* edición (eh-<u>d</u>ee-SYOHN)

editorial   *m.* editorial (eh-<u>d</u>ee-toh-RYAHL) ↻(adj.) ☐↻
   ① **editor**—*m.* redactor (reh-<u>d</u>ahk-TOHR) ↻*f.* -ra↻; **publisher**—*m.* editor
    (eh-<u>d</u>ee-TOHR) ↻*f.* -ra↻; **publishing house**—*f.* casa editorial (KAH-sah
    eh-<u>d</u>ee-toh-RYAHL) / *f.* casa editora (KAH-sah eh-<u>d</u>ee-TOH-rah)

educate (to)   educar (eh-<u>d</u>oo-KAHR)

educated (adj.)   educado (eh-<u>d</u>oo-KAH-<u>d</u>oh)
   ① (adj.) **ill-mannered / rude**—maleducado (mah-leh-<u>d</u>oo-KAH-<u>d</u>oh)

education / upbringing   *f.* educación (eh-<u>d</u>oo-kah-SYOHN)

educational (adj.)   educativo (eh-<u>d</u>oo-kah-TEE-<u>b</u>oh)

educator   *m.* educador (eh-<u>d</u>oo-kah-<u>D</u>OHR) ↻*f.* -ra↻

effect (*result or influence*)   *m.* efecto (eh-FEHK-toh)

effect (*carry out*) (to)   efectuar (eh-fehk-TWAHR)

effective / effectual (adj.)   efectivo (eh-fehk-TEE-<u>b</u>oh)
   ① Coloquially, this same word is used as a masculine noun to mean **cash
   money.**

effectiveness / efficacy   *f.* eficacia (eh-fee-KAH-syah)

effeminate (adj.)   afeminado (ah-feh-mee-NAH-<u>d</u>oh) ●

effervescence / fizz   *f.* efervescencia (eh-fehr-<u>b</u>ehs-SEHN-syah)

efficiency   *f.* eficiencia (eh-fee-SYEHN-syah)

efficient (adj.)   eficiente (eh-fee-SYEHN-teh)

ego (*self, not self-esteem*)   *m.* ego (EH-goh)

egocentric / self-centered (adj.)   egocéntrico (eh-goh-SEHN-tree-koh)

egoism / egotism / selfishness   *m.* egoísmo (eh-goh-EEZ-moh)

egoist / egotist   *m. & f.* egoísta (eh-goh-EES-tah)

egoistic / selfish (adj.)   egoísta (eh-goh-EES-tah)

elaborate (to)   elaborar (eh-lah-<u>b</u>oh-RAHR)

elaborate / fancy (adj.)   elaborado (eh-lah-<u>b</u>oh-RAH-<u>d</u>oh)

elaboration   *f.* elaboración (eh-lah-<u>b</u>oh-rah-SYOHN)

elastic (adj.)   elástico (eh-LAHS-tee-koh)

elasticity / resilience   *f.* elasticidad (eh-lahs-tee-see-<u>D</u>AH<u>D</u>)

elect (to)   elegir (eh-leh-HEER)

elect (adj.)   electo (eh-LEHK-toh)

election   *f.* elección (eh-lehk-SYOHN)

elective (adj.)   electivo (eh-lehk-TEE-<u>b</u>oh)

elector / voter   *m.* elector (eh-lehk-TOHR) ◐*f.* -ra◐

electoral (adj.)   electoral (eh-lehk-toh-RAHL)

electorate / electoral body   *m.* electorado (eh-lehk-toh-RAH-<u>d</u>oh)

electric / electrical (adj.)   eléctrico (eh-LEHK-tree-koh)

electrician   *m. & f.* electricista (eh-lehk-tree-SEES-tah)

electricity   *f.* electricidad (eh-lehk-tree-see-<u>DAHD</u>)

electrification   *f.* electrificación (eh-lehk-tree-fee-kah-SYOHN)

electrify (to)   electrificar (eh-lehk-tree-fee-KAHR)

electron   *m.* electrón (eh-lehk-TROHN)

electronic (adj.)   electrónico (eh-lehk-TROH-nee-koh)

electronics   *f.* electrónica (eh-lehk-TROH-nee-kah)

elegance / smartness   *f.* elegancia (eh-leh-GAHN-syah)

elegant / chic / posh (adj.)   elegante (eh-leh-GAHN-teh)

element   *m.* elemento (eh-leh-MEHN-toh)

elementary / elemental (adj.)   elemental (eh-leh-mehn-TAHL)

elevate / lift up (to)   elevar (eh-leh-<u>B</u>AHR)

elevation   *f.* elevación (eh-leh-<u>b</u>ah-SYOHN)

elevator   *m.* elevador (eh-leh-<u>b</u>ah-<u>D</u>OHR)

(become) elevated / rise (to)   elevarse (eh-leh-<u>B</u>AHR-seh)

elf / pixie   *m.* elfo (EHL-foh)

eligibility   *f.* elegibilidad (eh-leh-hee-<u>b</u>ee-lee-<u>DAHD</u>)

eligible (adj.)   elegible (eh-leh-HEE-<u>b</u>leh)

eliminate / remove (to)   eliminar (eh-lee-mee-NAHR)

elimination / removal   *f.* eliminación (eh-lee-mee-nah-SYOHN)

elite   *f.* elite (eh-LEE-teh)

elitism   *m.* elitismo (eh-lee-TEEZ-moh)

elitist   *m. & f.* elitista (eh-lee-TEES-tah) ◐(adj.) □◐

eloquence *f.* elocuencia (eh-loh-KWEHN-syah)

eloquent (adj.) elocuente (eh-loh-KWEHN-teh)

elude / dodge (to) eludir (eh-loo-<u>D</u>EER)

emanation *f.* emanación (eh-mah-nah-SYOHN)

emasculate (to) emascular (eh-mahs-koo-LAHR)

embargo *m.* embargo (ehm-BAHR-goh)

embark / board (to) embarcarse (ehm-bahr-KAHR-seh)

embarrassing (adj.) embarazoso (ehm-bah-rah-SOH-soh)

embassy *f.* embajada (ehm-bah-HAH-<u>d</u>ah)

embellish (to) embellecer (ehm-beh-yeh-SEHR)

emblem *m.* emblema (ehm-BLEH-mah)

embroil (to) embrollar (ehm-broh-YAHR)

emerge (to) emerger (eh-mehr-HEHR)

emergency *f.* emergencia (eh-mehr-HEHN-syah)

emigrant *m. & f.* emigrante (eh-mee-GRAHN-teh) ↻(adj.) ☐↻

emigrate (to) emigrar (eh-mee-GRAHR)

emigration *f.* emigración (eh-mee-grah-SYOHN)

eminence *f.* eminencia (eh-mee-NEHN-syah)

eminent / noted (adj.) eminente (eh-mee-NEHN-teh)

emission *f.* emisión (eh-mee-SYOHN)

emit (to) emitir (eh-mee-TEER)

emotion / thrill *f.* emoción (eh-moh-SYOHN)

emotional (*filled with emotion*) (adj.) emocional (eh-moh-syoh-NAHL)

emotional (*touching*) / thrilling (adj.) emocionante (eh-moh-syoh-NAHN-teh)
   ① (to) **move / touch**—emocionar (eh-moh-syoh-NAHR); (to) **be moved or touched / become emotional**—emocionarse (eh-moh-syoh NAHR-seh)

emphasis / stress *m.* énfasis (EHN-fah-sees) 💣

emphasize / stress (to) enfatizar (ehn-fah-tee-SAHR) 💣

emphatic (adj.) enfático (ehn-FAH-tee-koh) 💣

empire *m.* imperio (eem-PEH-ryoh) 💣

employ / engage / hire (to) emplear (ehm-pleh-AHR)

employee *m.* empleado (ehm-pleh-AH-<u>d</u>oh) ◑*f.* -da◑

employment / job *m.* empleo (ehm-PLEH-oh)
    ① The antonym: **unemployment**— *m.* desempleo (deh-sehm-PLEH-oh)

emulate (to) emular (eh-moo-LAHR)

enamor (to) enamorar (eh-nah-moh-RAHR)

enchant / charm / delight (to) encantar (ehn-kahn-TAHR)

enchanting / charming (adj.) encantador (ehn-kahn-tah-<u>D</u>OHR)

enchantment / charm / attraction *m.* encanto (ehn-KAHN-toh)

encircle / enclose (to) cercar (sehr-KAHR)

encounter *m.* encuentro (ehn-KWEHN-troh)

encounter / meet (to) encontrar (ehn-kohn-TRAHR)

encyclopedia *f.* enciclopedia (ehn-see-kloh-PEH-<u>d</u>yah)

encyclopedic (adj.) enciclopédico (ehn-see-kloh-PEH-<u>d</u>ee-koh)

endorse (*sign*) (to) endosar (ehn-doh-SAHR)

endorsement (*signature*) *m.* endoso (ehn-DOH-soh)

endure / last (to) durar (doo-RAHR)

enduring / lasting (adj.) duradero (doo-rah-<u>D</u>EH-roh)

enemy / foe *m.* enemigo (eh-neh-MEE-goh) ◑*f.* -ga◑

energetic / lively / spirited (adj.) enérgico (eh-NEHR-hee-koh)

energy / pep *f.* energía (eh-nehr-HEE-ah)

engineer (*technical, not railway*) *m.* ingeniero (een-heh-NYEH-roh)
    ◑*f.* -ra◑ 💣

engineering *f.* ingeniería (een-heh-nyeh-REE-ah) 💣

enigma *m.* enigma (eh-NEEG-mah)

enigmatic (adj.) enigmático (eh-neeg-MAH-tee-koh)

enormity *f.* enormidad (eh-nohr-mee-<u>D</u>AH<u>D</u>)

enormous / huge (adj.) enorme (eh-NOHR-meh)

enrich (to) enriquecer (ehn-ree-keh-SEHR)

enrichment   *m.* enriquecimiento (ehn-ree-keh-see-MYEHN-toh)

enter / go into (to)   entrar en (ehn-TRAHR ehn)

entertainment   *m.* entretenimiento (ehn-treh-teh-nee-MYEHN-toh)

enthusiasm / eagerness   *m.* entusiasmo (ehn-too-SYAHZ-moh)

enthusiast   *m. & f.* entusiasta (ehn-too-SYAHS-tah)
    ◑(adj.) **enthusiastic** ☐◑

entire / whole (adj.)   entero (ehn-TEH-roh)

entity   *f.* entidad (ehn-tee-<u>D</u>AH<u>D</u>)

entrance / admission to   *f.* entrada (ehn-TRAH-<u>d</u>ah)
    ① The related noncognate: **exit / outlet**—*f.* salida (sah-LEE-<u>d</u>ah)

entry / notation   *f.* entrada (ehn-TRAH-<u>d</u>ah)

enumerate (to)   enumerar (eh-noo-meh-RAHR)

enunciate (to)   enunciar (eh-noon-SYAHR)

enunciation   *f.* enunciación (eh-noon-syah-SYOHN)

enviable (adj.)   envidiable (ehn-<u>b</u>ee-<u>D</u>YAH-<u>b</u>leh)

envious / jealous (adj.)   envidioso (ehn-<u>b</u>ee-<u>D</u>YOH-soh)

envy   *f.* envidia (ehn-<u>B</u>EE-<u>d</u>yah)

envy (to)   envidiar (ehn-<u>b</u>ee-<u>D</u>YAHR)

ephemeral / short–lived (adj.)   efímero (eh-FEE-meh-roh)

epic (*poem, novel, or film*)   *f.* epopeya (eh-poh-PEH-yah)

epic (adj.)   épico (EH-pee-koh)

epidemic   *f.* epidemia (eh-pee-<u>D</u>HEH-myah)

epidemic (adj.)   epidémico (eh-pee-<u>D</u>EH-mee-koh)

episode   *m.* episodio (eh-pee-SOH-<u>d</u>yoh)

epitaph   *m.* epitafio (eh-pee-TAH-fyoh)

epithet   *m.* epíteto (eh-PEE-teh-toh)

epoch   *f.* época (EH-poh-kah)

equal / peer   *m. & f.* igual (ee-GWAHL) 💣

equal / alike / same (adj.)   igual (ee-GWAHL) 💣
    ① The antonym: (adj.) **unequal**—desigual (deh-see-GWAHL)

equal / match (to)   igualar (ee-gwah-LAHR) 💣

equality *f.* igualdad (ee-gwahl-DAHD) 💣

equalize (to)   igualar (ee-gwah-LAHR) 💣

equation *f.* ecuación (eh-kwah-SYOHN) 💣

equator *m.* ecuador (eh-kwah-DOHR) 💣

equatorial (adj.)   ecuatorial (eh-kwah-toh-RYAHL) 💣

equilibrium / balance *m.* equilibrio (eh-kee-LEE-bryoh)

equip / outfit (to)   equipar (eh-kee-PAHR)

equipage / baggage *m.* equipaje (eh-kee-PAH-heh)

equipment / outfit / tackle (!) *m.* equipo (eh-KEE-poh)

equity *f.* equidad (eh-kee-DAHD)

equivalence *f.* equivalencia (eh-kee-bah-LEHN-syah)

equivalent / tantamount (adj.)   equivalente (eh-kee-bah-LEHN-teh)

equivocal (adj.)   equívoco (eh-KEE-boh-koh)

era *f.* era (EH-rah)

eradicate (to)   erradicar (eh-rrah-dee-KAHR) 💣

erect (adj.)   erecto (eh-REHK-toh)

erect (to)   erigir (eh-ree-HEER)

erection *f.* erección (eh-rehk-SYOHN)

erosion *f.* erosión (eh-roh-SYOHN)

erotic (adj.)   erótico (eh-ROH-tee-koh)

eroticism *m.* erotismo (eh-roh-TEEZ-moh)

err / miss / (*morally*) stray (to)   errar (eh-RRAHR)

errant (adj.)   errante (eh-RRAHN-teh)

erratic (adj.)   errático (eh-RRAH-tee-koh)

erroneous / incorrect (adj.)   erróneo (eh-RROH-neh-oh)

error / blunder *m.* error (eh-RROHR)

erudite / learned / scholarly (adj.)   erudito (eh-roo-DEE-toh)

eruption (*volcanic or skin rash*) *f.* erupción (eh-roop-SYOHN)

escalation *f.* escalada (ehs-kah-LAH-dah)

escalator / staircase *f.* escalera (ehs-kah-LEH-rah)

escape / getaway / leak *m.* escape (ehs-KAH-peh)

escape clause / loophole *f.* escapatoria (ehs-kah-pah-TOH-ryah)

escape (to) escapar (ehs-kah-PAHR)

esoteric (adj.) esotérico (eh-soh-TEH-ree-koh)

espionage *m.* espionaje (ehs-pyoh-NAH-heh)

essay *m.* ensayo (ehn-SAH-yoh) 💣

essence / soul *f.* esencia (eh-SEHN-syah)

essential / prerequisite (adj.) esencial (eh-sehn-SYAHL)

establish (to) establecer (ehs-tah-<u>b</u>leh-SEHR)

establishment *m.* establecimiento (ehs-tah-<u>b</u>leh-see-MYEHN-toh)

esteem / respect / regard *f.* estima (ehs-TEE-mah)

estimation / estimate *f.* estimación (ehs-tee-mah-SYOHN)

estimate / gauge (to) estimar (ehs-tee-MAHR)

eternal / everlasting / timeless (adj.) eterno (eh-TEHR-noh)

eternity *f.* eternidad (eh-tehr-nee-<u>DAHD</u>)

ethereal (adj.) etéreo (eh-TEH-reh-oh)

ethics *f.* ética (EH-tee-kah) ◯(adj.) **ethical** –co◯

etiquette / manners *f.* etiqueta (eh-tee-KEH-tah)

evacuate (to) evacuar (eh-<u>b</u>ah-KWAHR)

evacuation *f.* evacuación (eh-<u>b</u>ah-kwah-SYOHN)

evade / circumvent (to) evadir (eh-<u>b</u>ah-DEER)

evaluate / test (to) evaluar (eh-<u>b</u>ah-LWAHR)

evaluation / rating *f.* evaluación (eh-<u>b</u>ah-lwah-SYOHN)

evangelical (adj.) evangélico (eh-<u>b</u>ahn-HEH-lee-koh)

evangelism *m.* evangelismo (eh-<u>b</u>ahn-heh-LEEZ-moh)

evangelist *m. & f.* evangelista (eh-<u>b</u>ahn-heh-LEES-tah) ◯(adj.) ▢◯ / *m.*
    evangelizador (eh-<u>b</u>ahn-heh-lee-sah-DOHR) ◯*f.* –ra◯ ◯(adj.) ▢◯

evangelization *f.* evangelización (eh-<u>b</u>ahn-heh-lee-sah-SYOHN)

evangelize (to) evangelizar (eh-<u>b</u>ahn-heh-lee-SAHR)

evaporate (to)   evaporarse (eh-<u>b</u>ah-poh-RAHR-seh)

evaporation   *f.* evaporación (eh-<u>b</u>ah-poh-rah-SYOHN)

evasion / circumvention   *f.* evasión (eh-<u>b</u>ah-SYOHN)

evasive / elusive / (adj.)   evasivo (eh-<u>b</u>ah-SEE-<u>b</u>oh)

evidence (*proof*)   *f.* evidencia (eh-<u>b</u>ee-<u>D</u>EHN-syah)

evident / noticeable (adj.)   evidente (eh-<u>b</u>ee-<u>D</u>EHN-teh)

evolution   *f.* evolución (eh-<u>b</u>oh-loo-SYOHN)

evolutionary (adj.)   evolutivo (eh-<u>b</u>oh-loo-TEE-<u>b</u>oh)

evolve (to)   evolucionar (eh-<u>b</u>oh-loo-syoh-NAHR)

exact / accurate / precise (adj.)   exacto (ehg-SAHK-toh)

exactitude / accuracy   *f.* exactitud (ehg-sahk-tee-TOO<u>D</u>)

exaggerate / magnify / overstate (to)   exagerar (ehg-sah-heh-RAHR)

exaggerated (adj.)   exagerado (ehg-sah-heh-RAH-<u>d</u>oh)

exaggeration   *f.* exageración (ehg-sah-heh-rah-SYOHN)

examination / exam / quiz   *m.* examen (ehg-SAH-mehn)

examine / review / test (to)   examinar (ehg-sah-mee-NAHR)

example / illustration / instance   *m.* ejemplo (eh-HEHM-ploh) 💣

exasperating / infuriating (adj.)   exasperante (ehg-sahs-peh-RAHN-teh)

exasperation   *f.* exasperación (ehg-sahs-peh-rah-SYOHN)

excavation   *f.* excavación (ehs-skah-<u>b</u>ah-SYOHN)

exceed (to)   exceder (ehs-seh-<u>D</u>EHR)

excellence   *f.* excelencia (ehs-seh-LEHN-syah)

excellent / prime (adj.)   excelente (ehs-seh-LEHN-teh)

except / exclude / leave out (to)   exceptuar (ehs-sehp-TWAHR)

exception   *f.* excepción (ehs-sehp-SYOHN)

exceptional / outstanding (adj.)   excepcional (ehs-sehp-syoh-NAHL)

excess / glut   *m.* exceso (ehs-SEH-soh)

excess / excessive / (adj.)   excesivo (ehs-seh-SEE-<u>b</u>oh)

excitability *f.* excitabilidad (ehs-see-tah-<u>b</u>ee-lee-<u>D</u>AH<u>D</u>)

excite / arouse (to)   excitar (ehs-see-TAHR) ◐(adj.) **excited** -ado◐

excitement *f.* excitación (ehs-see-tah-SYOHN) 💣

exciting / heady (adj.)   excitante (ehs-see-TAHN-teh) 💣

exclaim (to)   exclamar (ehs-sklah-MAHR)

exclamation *f.* exclamación (ehs-sklah-mah-SYOHN)

exclude (to)   excluir (ehs-SKLWEER)

exclusion *f.* exclusión (ehs-skloo-SYOHN)

exclusive (adj.)   exclusivo (ehs-skloo-SEE-<u>b</u>oh)

exclusiveness *f.* exclusividad (ehs-skloo-see-<u>b</u>ee-<u>D</u>AH<u>D</u>)

excursion / jaunt *f.* excursión (ehs-skoor-SYOHN)

excuse *f.* excusa (ehs-SKOO-sah)

excuse / pardon (to)   excusar (ehs-skoo-SAHR)

execute / perform (to)   ejecutar (eh-heh-koo-TAHR) 💣

execution / performance *f.* ejecución (eh-heh-koo-SYOHN) 💣

executive *m.* ejecutivo (eh-heh-koo-TEE-<u>b</u>oh) ◐*f.* -va◐
◐(adj.) ▯◐ 💣

exemplify / illustrate (to)   ejemplificar (eh-hehm-plee-fee-KAHR) 💣

exempt (to)   eximir (ehg-see-MEER)

exemption *f.* exención (ehg-sehn-SYOHN) 💣

exercise / exertion *m.* ejercicio (eh-hehr-SEE-syoh) 💣

exercise (to)   ejercitar (eh-hehr-see-TAHR) 💣

exhaustive (adj.)   exhaustivo (ehg-saows-TEE-<u>b</u>oh)

exhibit / display (to)   exhibir (ehg-see-<u>B</u>EER)

exhibition / exhibit / display *f.* exhibición (ehg-see-<u>b</u>ee-SYOHN)

exile / banishment *m.* exilio (ehg-SEE-lyoh)

exile / outcast *m.* exiliado (ehg-see-LYAH-<u>d</u>oh) ◐*f.* -da◐

exist / be (to)   existir (ehg-sees-TEER)

existence *f.* existencia (ehg-sees-TEHN-syah)

exodus *m.* éxodo (EHG-soh-<u>d</u>oh)

exonerate (to)   exonerar (ehg-soh-neh-RAHR)

exoneration   *f.* exoneración (ehg-soh-neh-rah-SYOHN)

exorbitant / outrageous (adj.)   exorbitante (ehg-sohr-<u>b</u>ee-TAHN-teh)

exorcism   *m.* exorcismo (ehg-sohr-SEEZ-moh)

exotic (adj.)   exótico (ehg-SOH-tee-koh)

expand (to)   expandir (ehs-spahn-<u>D</u>EER)

expansion / enlargement   *f.* expansión (ehs-spahn-SYOHN)

expansive (adj.)   expansivo (ehs-spahn-SEE-<u>b</u>oh)

expatriate   *m.* expatriado (ehs-spah-TRYAH-<u>d</u>oh) ○*f.* -da○ ○(adj.) ☐○

expect (*anticipate or count on*) (to)   esperar (ehs-peh-RAHR) ●

expectancy / prospect   *f.* expectativa (ehs-spehk-tah-TEE-<u>b</u>ah)

expectant (adj.)   expectante (ehs-spehk-TAHN-teh)

expectation   *f.* expectación (ehs-spehk-tah-SYOHN)

expedient   *m.* expediente (ehs-speh-<u>D</u>YEHN-teh)

expedition   *f.* expedición (ehs-speh-<u>d</u>ee-SYOHN)

expel / eject (to)   expeler (ehs-speh-LEHR)

experience   *f.* experiencia (ehs-speh-RYEHN-syah)

experiment   *m.* experimento (ehs-speh-ree-MEHN-toh)

experiment / experience (!) (to)   experimentar (ehs-speh-ree-mehn-TAHR)

experimental (adj.)   experimental (ehs-speh-ree-mehn-TAHL)

experimentation   *f.* experimentación (ehs-speh-ree-mehn-tah-SYOHN)

expert / master   *m.* experto (ehs-SPEHR-toh) ○*f.* -ta○ ○(adj.) **expert / skilled** ☐○

explicate / explain (to)   explicar (ehs-splee-KAHR)

explanation / rationale   *f.* explicación (ehs-splee-kah-SYOHN)

explicit (adj.)   explícito (ehs-SPLEE-see-toh)

exploit / explode (!) (to)   explotar (ehs-sploh-TAHR)

exploitation   *f.* explotación (ehs-sploh-tah-SYOHN)

exploration   *f.* exploración (ehs-sploh-rah-SYOHN)

exploratory (adj.)   exploratorio (ehs-sploh-rah-TOH-ryoh)

explore (to)   explorar (ehs-sploh-RAHR)

explorer / lookout   *m.* explorador (ehs-sploh-rah-<u>D</u>OHR) ↻*f.* -ra↻

explosion   *f.* explosión (ehs-sploh-SYOHN)

explosive   *m.* explosivo (ehs-sploh-SEE-<u>b</u>oh) ↻(adj.) □↻

export (to)   exportar (ehs-spohr-TAHR)

exportation   *f.* exportación (ehs-spohr-tah-SYOHN)

exporter   *m.* exportador (ehs-spohr-tah-<u>D</u>OHR) ↻*f.* -ra↻

expound / set forth (to)   exponer (ehs-spoh-NEHR)

express (adj.)   expreso (ehs-SPREH-soh)

express / say (to)   expresar (ehs-spreh-SAHR)

expression / utterance   *f.* expresión (ehs-spreh-SYOHN)

expressive (adj.)   expresivo (ehs-spreh-SEE-<u>b</u>oh)

expulsion / ejection   *f.* expulsión (ehs-spool-SYOHN)

exquisite (adj.)   exquisito (ehs-skee-SEE-toh)

extend / enlarge / lengthen (to)   extender (ehs-stehn-DEHR)

extension / extent   *f.* extensión (ehs-stehn-SYOHN)

extensive / sweeping (adj.)   extenso (ehs-STEHN-soh)

exterior / outside   *m.* exterior (ehs-steh-RYOHR) ↻(adj.) □↻

external / outer (adj.)   externo (ehs-STEHR-noh)

extinction   *f.* extinción (ehs-steen-SYOHN)

extinguish (to)   extinguir (ehs-steen-GHEER)

extinguisher   *m.* extinguidor (ehs-steen-ghee-<u>D</u>OHR)

extortion   *f.* extorsión (ehs-stohr-SYOHN)

extra   *m.* extra (EHS-strah) ↻(adj.) □↻

extract   *m.* extracto (ehs-STRAHK-toh)

extract / mine / remove (to)   extraer (ehs-strah-EHR)

extraction / removal   *f.* extracción (ehs-strahk-SYOHN)

extraordinary / remarkable (adj.)   extraordinario (ehs-strah-ohr-<u>d</u>ee-NAH-ryoh)

extravagance   *f.* extravagancia (ehs-strah-<u>b</u>ah-GAHN-syah)

extravagant (adj.)   extravagante (ehs-strah-<u>b</u>ah-GAHN-teh)

extreme / utmost   *m.* extremo (ehs-STREH-moh) ◓(adj.) **extreme / intense** ☐◓

extrovert   *m.* extrovertido (ehs-stroh-<u>b</u>ehr-TEE-<u>d</u>oh) ◓*f.* -da◓

exuberance / flamboyance   *f.* exuberancia (ehg-soo-<u>b</u>eh-RAHN-syah)

exuberant / flamboyant (adj.)   exuberante (ehg-soo-<u>b</u>eh-RAHN-teh)

exude (to)   exudar (ehg-soo-<u>D</u>AHR)

exult / glory (to)   exultar (ehg-sool-TAHR)

exultation   *f.* exultación (ehg-sool-tah-SYOHN)

—F—

fable   *f.* fábula (FAH-<u>b</u>oo-lah)

fabled / fabulous (adj.)   fabuloso (fah-<u>b</u>oo-LOH-soh)

fabricate / manufacture (to)   fabricar (fah-<u>b</u>ree-KAHR)
   ① Related: **factory / plant**—*f.* fábrica (FAH-<u>b</u>ree-kah)

fabricator / manufacturer   *m. & f.* fabricante (fah-<u>b</u>ree-KAHN-teh)

facet   *f.* faceta (fah-SEH-tah)

facial   *m.* tratamiento facial (trah-tah-MYEHN-toh fah-SYAHL)

facial (adj.)   facial (fah-SYAHL)

facile / easy (adj.)   fácil (FAH-seel)

facilitate (to)   facilitar (fah-see-lee-TAHR)

facility (*ease*) / knack   *f.* facilidad (fah-see-lee-<u>D</u>AH<u>D</u>)

facsimile / fax   *m.* facsímile (fahk-SEE-mee-leh) / fax (FAHKS)

faction   *f.* facción (fahk-SYOHN)

factor   *m.* factor (fahk-TOHR)

faculty (*ability or talent*)   *f.* facultad (fah-kool-TAH<u>D</u>)

fail (to)   fallar (fah-YAHR)

fair   *f.* feria (FEH-ryah)

faith (*belief in*) *f.* fe (FEH)

fallacy *f.* falacia (fah-LAH-syah)

false / deceitful / counterfeit (adj.) falso (FAHL-soh)

falsehood / lie *f.* falsedad (fahl-seh-<u>D</u>AH<u>D</u>)

falsifier / counterfeiter *m.* falsificador (fahl-see-fee-kah-<u>D</u>OHR)
○*f.* –ra○

falsify / forge / fake (to) falsificar (fahl-see-fee-KAHR)
① **forged / counterfeited / fake**—(adj.) falsificado (fahl-see-fee-KAH-<u>d</u>oh)

falsification / forgery *f.* falsificación (fahl-see-fee-kah-SYOHN)

fame / renown *f.* fama (FAH-mah)

familiar (*intimate, acquainted*) (adj.) familiar (fah-mee-LYAHR)

familiarity / intimacy *f.* familiaridad (fah-mee-lyah-ree-<u>D</u>AH<u>D</u>)

familiarize (to) familiarizar (fah-mee-lyah-ree-SAHR)

family / household *f.* familia (fah-MEE-lyah)

famine / hunger *f.* hambre (AHM-breh)
① (to) **be famished / hungry**—tener hambre (teh-NEHR AHM-breh);
(to) **famish**—hacer morir / padecer de hambre (ah-SEHR moh-REER /
pah-deh-SEHR deh AHM-breh); (adj.) **hungry**—hambriento (ahm-
BRYEHN-toh)

famished (adj.) famélico / muerto de hambre (fah-MEH-lee-koh /
MWEHR-toh deh AHM-breh)

famous / renowned (adj.) famoso (fah-MOH-soh)

fanatic / zealot *m.* fanático (fah-NAH-tee-koh) ○*f.* –ca○

fanatical (adj.) fanático (fah-NAH-tee-koh)

fanaticism *m.* fanatismo (fah-nah-TEEZ-moh)

fanfare *f.* fanfarria (fahn-FAH-rryah)

fantastic / fanciful (adj.) fantástico (fahn-TAHS-tee-koh)

fantasy *f.* fantasía (fahn-tah-SEE-ah)

farce *f.* farsa (FAHR-sah)

fascinate (to) fascinar (fahs-see-NAHR)

fascinating (adj.) fascinante (fahs-see-NAHN-teh)

fascination *f.* fascinación (fahs-see-nah-SYOHN)

fatal / deadly (adj.)   fatal (fah-TAHL)

fatalist   *m. & f.* fatalista (fah-tah-LEES-tah)

fatality   *f.* fatalidad (fah-tah-lee-<u>D</u>AH<u>D</u>)

fatigue / weariness   *f.* fatiga (fah-TEE-gah)

fatigue / tire (to)   fatigar (fah-tee-GAHR)

fatigued / tired (adj.)   fatigado (fah-tee-GAH-<u>d</u>oh)

fault (*defect or deficiency*)   *f.* falta (FAHL-tah)

favor / kindness   *m.* favor (fah-<u>B</u>OHR)

favorable (adj.)   favorable (fah-<u>b</u>oh-RAH-<u>b</u>leh)

favorite   *m.* favorito (fah-<u>b</u>oh-REE-toh) ↻*f.* -ta↺

favoritism   *m.* favoritismo (fah-<u>b</u>oh-ree-TEEZ-moh)

feasibility   *f.* factibilidad (fahk-tee-<u>b</u>ee-lee-<u>D</u>AH<u>D</u>) 💣

feast   *m.* festín (fehs-TEEN)

feast (to)   festejar (fehs-teh-HAHR)

federal (adj.)   federal (feh-<u>d</u>eh-RAHL)

federation   *f.* federación (feh-<u>d</u>eh-rah-SYOHN)

felicity / happiness   *f.* felicidad (feh-lee-see-<u>D</u>AH<u>D</u>)
   ① Closely related noncognates are: (adj.) **happy / joyful / joyous**—feliz (feh-LEES); and **unhappy**—infeliz (een-feh-LEES).

female / feminine (adj.)   femenino (feh-meh-NEE-noh) / femenil (feh-meh-NEEL)

femininity   *f.* feminidad (feh-mee-nee-<u>D</u>AH<u>D</u>)

feminism   *m.* feminismo (feh-mee-NEEZ-moh)

feminist   *m. & f.* feminista (feh-mee-NEES-tah) ↻(adj.) ☐↺

femur / thighbone   *m.* fémur (FEH-moor)

ferment (*social / political unrest*)   *m.* fermento (fehr-MEHN-toh)

ferocious / fierce (adj.)   feroz (feh-ROHS)

ferocity / savagery   *f.* ferocidad (feh-roh-see-<u>D</u>AH<u>D</u>)

fertile (adj.)   fértil (FEHR-teel)

fertility   *f.* fertilidad (fehr-tee-lee-<u>D</u>AH<u>D</u>)

fervor / zeal   *m.* fervor (fehr-<u>B</u>OHR)

fervent / zealous (adj.)   ferviente (fehr-<u>B</u>YEHN-teh)

festive (adj.)   festivo (fehs-TEE-<u>b</u>oh)

festivity   *f.* festividad (fehs-tee-<u>b</u>ee-<u>D</u>AH<u>D</u>)

fetish   *m.* fetiche (feh-TEE-cheh)

fever / temperature   *f.* fiebre (FYEH-<u>b</u>reh)

fiasco / failure   *m.* fiasco (FYAHS-koh)
   ① (to) **fail / fall through / fall apart** *(all in reference to projects / plans)*—
   fracasar (frah-kah-SAHR)

fiber / roughage   *f.* fibra (FEE-<u>b</u>rah)

fibrous / sinewy / stringy (adj.)   fibroso (fee-<u>B</u>ROH-soh)

fiction   *f.* ficción (feek-SYOHN)

fictional / fictitious (adj.)   ficticio (feek-TEE-syoh)

fidelity / faithfulness   *f.* fidelidad (fee-<u>d</u>eh-lee-<u>D</u>AH<u>D</u>)

figure (*shape, outline, or personage*)   *f.* figura (fee-GOO-rah)

figure of speech   *f.* figura retórica (fee-GOO-rah reh-TOH-ree-kah)

file (*row of people or things*)   *f.* fila (FEE-lah)

film / movie   *m.* film (FEELM) / *m.* filme (FEEL-meh)
   ① More commonly: **movie**—*f.* película (peh-LEE-koo-lah)

film (to)   filmar (feel-MAHR)

filter   *m.* filtro (FEEL-troh)

filter (to)   filtrar (feel-TRAHR)

final / eventual / last (adj.)   final (fee-NAHL)

final / ending   *m.* final (fee-NAHL) ↻*f.* **finals / finale** *(sports)* ▯↻

finalist   *m. & f.* finalista (fee-nah-LEES-tah)

finality   *f.* finalidad (fee-nah-lee-<u>D</u>AH<u>D</u>)

finalize (to)   finalizar (fee-nah-lee-SAHR)

finance / fund (to)   financiar (fee-nahn-SYAHR)

finance / finances   *f. pl.* finanzas (feh-NAHN-sahs)

financial (adj.)   financiero (fee-nahn-SYEH-roh)

financier   *m. & f.* financista (fee-nahn-SEES-tah)

financing / funding   *f.* financiación (fee-nahn-syah-SYOHN)

fine (*very small or thin*) / flimsy (adj.)   fino (FEE-noh)

finish / end   *m.* fin (FEEN)

firm / steady / secure (adj.)   firme (FEER-meh)

(commercial) firm / company   *f.* firma (FEER-mah)

firmness   *f.* firmeza (feer-MEH-sah)

first-class (adj.)   primera clase (pree-MEH-rah KLAH-seh)

first-rate / top quality (adj.)   de primera clase (deh pree-MEH-rah KLAH-seh)

fiscal (adj.)   fiscal (fees-KAHL)

fix (*attach or establish*) (to)   fijar (fee-HAHR)

fixed / set / steady (adj.)   fijo (FEE-hoh)

flaccid / limp (adj.)   flácido (FLAH-see-doh)

flagrant (adj.)   flagrante (flah-GRAHN-teh)

flatulent (adj.)   flatulento (flah-too-LEHN-toh)

fleet   *f.* flota (FLOH-tah)

flirt (to)   flirtear (fleer-teh-AHR)

float (to)   flotar (floh-TAHR)

flora   *f.* flora (FLOH-rah)

floral (adj.)   floral (floh-RAHL)

florid / flowered (adj.)   florido (floh-REE-doh)

florist   *m. & f.* florista (floh-REES-tah)

flourish / flower / bloom (to)   florecer (floh-reh-SEHR)

flourishing / flowering (adj.)   floreciente (floh-reh-SYEHN-teh)

flow / flux   *m.* flujo (FLOO-hoh)

flow (to)   fluir (FLWEER)

fluctuate / waver (to)   fluctuar (flook-TWAHR)

fluctuation   *f.* fluctuación (flook-twah-SYOHN)

fluid / flowing / fluent (!) (adj.)   flúido (FLOO-ee-doh)

fluidity / fluency (!)   *f.* fluidez (flwee-DEHS)

flute (*instrument*)   *f.* flauta (FLAOW-tah)

focal (adj.)   focal (foh-KAHL)

focus   *m.* foco (FOH-koh)

foliage   *m.* follaje (foh-YAH-heh)

folio   *m.* folio (FOH-lyoh)

folklore   *m.* folklore (fohlk-LOH-reh)

football   *m.* fútbol americano (FOOT-bohl ah-meh-ree-KAH-noh)

for   por (POHR) / para (PAH-rah)

force / power / strength   *f.* fuerza (FWEHR-sah)

force (to)   forzar (fohr-SAHR)

forced (adj.)   forzado (fohr-SAH-doh)

forcible (adj.)   forzoso (fohr-SOH-soh)

forge (*create and shape*) (to)   forjar (fohr-HAHR)

form / formation / contour   *f.* forma (FOHR-mah)
   ① (adj.) **shapeless**—informe (een-FOHR-meh)

form / shape / mold (to)   formar (fohr-MAHR)

formal (adj.)   formal (forh-MAHL)

formality   *f.* formalidad (fohr-mah-lee-DHAD)

format   *m.* formato (fohr-MAH-toh)

formation   *f.* formación (fohr-mah-SYOHN)

formative (adj.)   formativo (fohr-mah-TEE-boh)

formidable (adj.)   formidable (fohr-mee-DAH-bleh)

formula   *f.* fórmula (FOHR-moo-lah)

fornicate (to)   fornicar (fohr-nee-KAHR)

fornication   *f.* fornicación (fohr-nee-kah-SYOHN)

fort   *m.* fuerte (FWEHR-teh)

fortification   *f.* fortificación (fohr-tee-fee-kah-SYOHN)

fortitude / fortress (!)   *f.* fortaleza (fohr-tah-LEH-sah)

fortuitous (adj.)   fortuito (fohr-TWEE-toh)

fortunate / lucky (adj.)   afortunado (ah-fohr-too-NAH-doh) 💣

fortune (*luck or wealth*)   *f.* fortuna (fohr-TOO-nah)

forum *m.* foro (FOH-roh)

fossil *m.* fósil (FOH-seel)

foul (*in sports*) *m.* foul (FAOWL)

found / establish (to) fundar (foon-DAHR)

foundation / base *m.* fundamento (foon-dah-MEHN-toh)

foundation (*institution or process*) *f.* fundación (foon-dah-SYOHN) / fundamento (foon-dah-MEHN-toh)

founder *m.* fundador (foon-dah-DOHR) ↻*f.* -ra↻

fount (*source*) / fountain *f.* fuente (FWEHN-teh)

fraction *f.* fracción (frahk-SYOHN)

fracture / break *f.* fractura (frahk-TOO-rah)

fracture (to) fracturar (frahk-too-RAHR)

fragile / brittle (adj.) frágil (FRAH-heel)

fragility *f.* fragilidad (frah-hee-lee-DAHD)

fragment / shard *m.* fragmento (frahg-MEHN-toh)

fragment (to) fragmentar (frahg-mehn-TAHR)

fragrance *f.* fragancia (frah-GAHN-syah) ↻(adj.) **fragrant** -nte↻ 💣

frank / candid / forthcoming (adj.) franco (FRAHN-koh)

frankly / candidly con franqueza (kohn frahn-KEH-sah)

frankness / candor *f.* franqueza (frahn-KEH-sah)

fraternal (adj.) fraterno (frah-TEHR-noh)

fraternity / brotherhood *f.* fraternidad (frah-tehr-nee-DAHD)

fraternization *f.* fraternización (frah-tehr-nee-sah-SYOHN)

fraternize (to) fraternizar (frah-tehr-nee-SAHR)

fraud *m.* fraude (FRAOW-deh)

fraudulent (adj.) fraudulento (fraow-doo-LEHN-toh)

frenzy *m.* frenesí (freh-neh-SEE)

frequency *f.* frecuencia (freh-KWEHN-syah)

frequent (adj.) frecuente (freh-KWEHN-teh)

frequent / haunt (to) frecuentar (freh-kwehn-TAHR)

fresh / refreshed (adj.)   fresco (FREHS-koh)

freshness / impudence   *f.* frescura (frehs-KOO-rah)

friction   *f.* fricción (freek-SYOHN)

frivolity   *f.* frivolidad (free-<u>b</u>oh-lee-<u>D</u>AH<u>D</u>)

frivolous / flighty / flippant (adj.)   frívolo (FREE-<u>b</u>oh-loh)

front / forehead / forward part   *f.* frente (FREHN-teh)

frontier / (geographical) border   *f.* frontera (frohn-TEH-rah)

frugal (adj.)   frugal (froo-GAHL)

frugality / thrift   *f.* frugalidad (froo-gah-lee-<u>D</u>AH<u>D</u>)

fruit   *f.* fruta (FROO-tah)

fruits (*of labor, etc.*)   *m. pl.* frutos (FROO-tohs)

fruitful / fructiferous / fruit bearing (adj.)   fructífero (frook-TEE-feh-roh)

frustrate / defeat / foil / thwart (to)   frustrar (froos-TRAHR)

frustrating (adj.)   frustrante (froos-TRAHN-teh)

frustration   *f.* frustración (froos-trah-SYOHN)

fry (to)   freír (freh-EER)

fugitive / escapee   *m.* fugitivo (foo-hee-TEE-<u>b</u>oh) ↻*f.* -va↻ ↻(adj.) ▯↻

fume / smoke   *m.* humo (OO-moh) 💣

fume / smoke / use tobacco (to)   humear (oo-meh-AHR) 💣

fumigate (to)   fumigar (foo-mee-GAHR)

function   *f.* función (foon-SYOHN)

function / run (to)   funcionar (foon-syoh-NAHR)

functional (adj.)   funcional (foon-syoh-NAHL)

functionary / official / civil servant   *m.* funcionario (foon-syoh-NAH-ryoh) ↻*f.* -ia↻

fund / bottom (!)   *m.* fondo (FOHN-doh)

fundamental   *m.* fundamento (foon-dah-MEHN-toh)

fundamental / basic / pivotal (adj.)   fundamental (foon-dah-mehn-TAHL)

funds / wherewithal   *m. pl.* fondos (FOHN-dohs)

funeral   *m. pl.* funerales (foo-neh-RAH-lehs)

funeral home / mortuary *f.* funeraria (foo-neh-RAH-ryah)

furious / livid / irate (adj.) furioso (foo-RYOH-soh)

furtive / stealthy (adj.) furtivo (foor-TEE-<u>b</u>oh)

fury / rage / temper *f.* furia (FOO-ryah)

fuse / merge (to) fusionarse (foo-syoh-NAHR-seh)

fusion / merger (!) *f.* fusión (foo-SYOHN)

future *m.* futuro (foo-TOO-roh) ○(adj.) ▯○

—G—

gain / get / earn (to) ganar (gah-NAHR)

gala *f.* gala (GAH-lah) ○(adj.) **de gala** (deh GAH-lah)○

galactic (adj.) galáctico (gah-LAHK-tee-koh)

gallant (adj.) galante (gah-LAHN-teh)

gallon *m.* galón (gah-LOHN)

gallop (to) galopar (gah-loh-PAHR)

gambit *m.* gambito (gahm-BEE-toh)

gamut *f.* gama (GAH-mah)

gangster *m. & f.* gángster (GAHNG-stehr)

garage *m.* garaje (gah-RAH-heh)

garden *m.* jardín (hahr-<u>D</u>EEN) ♠

gardener *m.* jardinero (har-<u>d</u>ee-NEH-roh) ○*f.* -ra○ ♠

garnish (to) guarnecer (gwahr-neh-SEHR)

gas (*oxygen, helium*) *m.* gas (GAHS)

gasoline *f.* gasolina (gah-zoh-LEE-nah)

gastronomic (adj.) gastronómico (gahs-troh-NOH-mee-koh)

gastronomy *f.* gastronomía (gahs-troh-noh-MEE-ah)
    ① Closely related: **gourmet**—*m.* gastrónomo (gahs-TROH-noh-moh)
    ○*f.* -ma○ / epicúreo (eh-pee-KOO-reh-oh) ○*f.* -a○

gauze *f.* gasa (GAH-zah)

gazette *f.* gaceta (gah-SEH-tah)

gem   *f.* gema (HEH-mah)

gender (*linguistic*) / genre   *m.* género (HEH-neh-roh)

gene   *m.* gen (HEHN) / gene (HEH-neh)

genealogical (adj.)   genealógico (heh-neh-ah-LOH-hee-koh)
   ① **genealogical tree / family tree**—arból genealógico (AHR-<u>b</u>ohl heh-neh-ah-LOH-hee-koh)

genealogy (*academic study*)   *f.* genealogía (heh-neh-ah-loh-HEE-ah)

general   *m.* general (heh-neh-RAHL) ↻(adj.) ▯↻

generality   *f.* generalidad (heh-neh-rah-lee-<u>D</u>AH<u>D</u>)

generalization   *f.* generalización (heh-neh-rah-lee-sah-SYOHN)

generalize (to)   generalizar (heh-neh-rah-lee-SAHR)

generate (to)   generar (heh-neh-RAHR)

generation (*measure of time*)   *f.* generación (heh-neh-rah-SYOHN)

generic (adj.)   genérico (heh-NEH-ree-koh)

generosity / largess   *f.* generosidad (heh-neh-roh-see-<u>D</u>AH<u>D</u>)

generous (adj.)   generoso (heh-neh-ROH-soh)

genetic (adj.)   genético (heh-NEH-tee-koh)

genetics   *f.* genética (heh-NEH-tee-kah)

genital (adj.)   genital (heh-nee-TAHL)

genitals   *m. pl.* genitales (heh-nee-TAH-lehs)

genius   *m.* genio (HEH-nyoh)

genocide   *m.* genocidio (heh-noh-SEE-<u>d</u>yoh)

genuine (adj.)   genuino (heh-NWEE-noh)

geographic / geographical (adj.)   geográfico (heh-oh-GRAH-fee-koh)

geography   *f.* geografía (heh-oh-grah-FEE-ah)

geologic / geological (adj.)   geológico (heh-oh-LOH-hee-koh)

geology   *f.* geología (heh-oh-loh-HEE-ah)

geometric (adj.)   geométrico (heh-oh-MEH-tree-koh)

geometry   *f.* geometría (heh-oh-meh-TREE-ah)

geriatric (adj.)   geriátrico (heh-RYAH-tree-koh)

germ *m.* germen (HEHR-mehn)

germinate (to) germinar (hehr-mee-NAHR)

gesture / gesticulate (to) gesticular (hehs-tee-koo-LAHR)

gesture (*movement or token*) *m.* gesto (HEHS-toh)

ghetto *m.* gueto (GEH-toh)

giant *m.* gigante (hee-GAHN-teh)

gigantic / jumbo (adj.) gigantesco (hee-gahn-TEHS-koh)

gladiator *m.* gladiador (glah-dyah-DOHR)

global (adj.) global (gloh-BAHL)

globe / sphere / ball / balloon *m.* globo (GLOH-boh)

glorification *f.* glorificación (gloh-ree-fee-kah-SYOHN)

glorify (to) glorificar (gloh-ree-fee-KAHR)

glorious / resplendent (adj.) glorioso (gloh-RYOH-soh)

glory / praise *f.* gloria (GLOH-ryah)

glossary *m.* glosario (gloh-SAH-ryoh)

glutton / wolverine (!) *m.* glotón (gloh-TOHN)

gluttony *f.* glotonería (gloh-toh-neh-REE-ah)

goal (*soccer score*) *m.* gol (GOHL)

golf *m.* golf (GOHLF)

golfer *m. & f.* golfista (gohl-FEES-tah)

govern / rule (to) gobernar (goh-behr-NAHR)

government *m.* gobierno (goh-BYEHR-noh)

governmental (adj.) gubernamental (goo-behr-nah-mehn-TAHL) 💣

governor *m.* gobernador (goh-behr-nah-DOHR) ↻*f.* -ra↺

grace *f.* gracia (GRAH-syah)

graceful (adj.) gracioso (grah-SYOH-soh) / lleno de gracia (YEH-noh deh GRAH-syah)

gracefulness *f.* gracia (GRAH-syah)

gracile (adj.) grácil (GRAH-seel)

gracileness / gracility *f.* gracilidad (grah-see-lee-DAHD)

gradation *f.* gradación (grah-<u>d</u>ah-SYOHN)

grade / degree / rank *m.* grado (GRAH-<u>d</u>oh)

gradual (adj.) gradual (grah-<u>D</u>WAHL)

graduate *m.* graduado (grah-<u>D</u>WAH-doh) ↻*f.* -da↺

graduate (to) graduarse (grah-<u>D</u>WAHR-seh)

graduation (adj.) graduación (grah-<u>d</u>wah-SYOHN)

graffiti *m.* graffiti (grahf-FEE-tee)

grain (*cereal grass*) / kernel *m.* grano (GRAH-noh)

gram *m.* gramo (GRAH-moh)

grammar *f.* gramática (grah-MAH-tee-kah)

grammatical (adj.) gramatical (grah-mah-tee-KAHL)

grandeur *f.* grandiosidad (grahn-dyoh-see-<u>D</u>AH<u>D</u>)

grandiose / imposing (adj.) grandioso (grahn-<u>D</u>YOH-soh)

granite *m.* granito (grah-NEE-toh)

graph *m.* gráfico (GRAH-fee-koh) ↻(adj.) **graphic** □↺

gratification / indulgence *f.* gratificación (grah-tee-fee-kah-SYOHN)

gratify / indulge (to) gratificar (grah-tee-fee-KAHR)

gratis / cost-free (adj.) gratis (GRAH-tees)
    ① Also frequently heard / seen: (adj.) **complimentary (*without cost*)**—de cortesía (deh kohr-teh-SEE-ah) / gratuito (grah-TWEE-toh)

gratitude / gratefulness *f.* gratitud (grah-tee-TOO<u>D</u>)

gratuitous (adj.) gratuito (grah-TWEE-toh)
    ① An important related noncognate: **gratuity**—*f.* propina (proh-PEE-nah)

grave / serious / solemn / deep (adj.) grave (GRAH-<u>b</u>eh)

gravitate (to) gravitar (grah-<u>b</u>ee-TAHR)

gravity (*physical force or seriousness*) *f.* gravedad (grah-<u>b</u>eh-<u>D</u>AH<u>D</u>)

grease / fat *f.* grasa (GRAH-sah)

greasy (adj.) grasoso (grah-SOH-soh)

greatness *f.* grandeza (grahn-DEH-sah)

gregarious (adj.) gregario (greh-GAH-ryoh)

grievous (adj.) gravoso (grah-<u>B</u>OH-soh)

gross / rude / vulgar (adj.)   grosero (groh-SEH-roh)

grotesque (adj.)   grotesco (groh-TEHS-koh)

group / cluster   *m.* grupo (GROO-poh)

group / cluster (to)   agrupar (ah-groo-PAHR) 💣

guarantee / warranty   *f.* garantía (gah-rahn-TEE-ah)

guarantee (to)   garantizar (gah-rahn-tee-SAHR)

guard / watchman   *m. & f.* guarda (GWAHR-dah)

guard / look at / tend to (to)   guardar (gwahr-DAHR)

guardian / watchman   *m.* guardián (gwahr-DYAHN) ↺*f.* -diana↻

guerilla (*group of hit-and-hide warriors*)   *f.* guerrilla (geh-RREE-yah)

guerilla / guerilla fighter / partisan   *m.* guerrillero (geh-rree-YEH-roh) ↺*f.* -a↻

guide / guidebook / tour leader   *f.* guía (GHEE-ah)

guide / steer (to)   guiar (ghee-AHR)

guitar   *f.* guitarra (ghee-TAH-rrah)

gulf (*of water*)   *m.* golfo (GOHL-foh)

gum (*material*)   *f.* goma (GOH-mah)

gymnasium / gym   *m.* gimnasio (heem-NAH-syoh)

gymnast   *m. & f.* gimnasta (heem-NAHS-tah) ↺(adj.) **gymnastic** -nástico↻

gymnastics   *f.* gimnasia (heem-NAH-syah)

gyrate / revolve / rotate / spin / turn (to)   girar (hee-RAHR)

gyration   *m.* giro (HEE-roh)

gyroscope   *m.* giroscopio (hee-rohs-KOH-pyoh)

—H—

habit   *m.* hábito (AH-bee-toh)

habitable / inhabitable (adj.)   habitable (ah-bee-TAH-bleh)

habitat   *m.* hábitat (AH-bee-taht)

habitation / room (!) / bedroom (!)   *f.* habitación (ah-bee-tah-SYOHN)

habitual (adj.)   habitual (ah-bee-TWAHL)

hallucinate (to)   alucinar (ah-loo-see-NAHR) 💣

hallucination   *f.* alucinación (ah-loo-see-nah-SYOHN) 💣

halo   *m.* halo (AH-loh)

hamburger   *f.* hamburguesa (ahm-boor-GEH-sah)

hammock   *f.* hamaca (ah-MAH-kah)

harmonic (adj.)   armónico (ahr-MOH-nee-koh) 💣

harmonica   *f.* armónica (ahr-MOH-nee-kah) 💣

harmonious / sweet-sounding (adj.)   armonioso (ahr-moh-NYOH-soh) 💣

harmonize (to)   armonizar (ahr-moh-nee-SAHR) 💣

harmony   *f.* armonía (ahr-moh-NEE-ah) 💣

hatchet / axe   *f.* hacha (AH-chah) 💣

heir / inheritor   *m.* heredero (eh-reh-<u>D</u>EH-roh) ◑*f.* **heiress** -ra◑

helicopter   *m.* helicóptero (eh-lee-KOHP-teh-roh)

helmet   *m.* yelmo (YEHL-moh) / casco (KAHS-koh)

hemisphere   *m.* hemisferio (eh-mees-FEH-ryoh)

hemispheric / hemispherical (adj.)   hemisférico (eh-mees-FEH-ree-koh)

hemophilia   *f.* hemofilia (eh-moh-FEE-lyah)

hemorrhage   *f.* hemorragia (eh-moh-RRAH-hyah)

herb / grass   *f.* hierba (YEHR-<u>b</u>ah)

herbal (adj.)   herbario (ehr-<u>B</u>AH-ryoh)

hereditary (adj.)   hereditario (eh-reh-<u>d</u>ee-TAH-ryoh)

heredity (*biology*)   *f.* herencia (eh-REHN-syah)

heresy   *f.* herejía (eh-reh-HEE-ah)

hermetic / tight (adj.)   hermético (ehr-MEH-tee-koh)

hermit / recluse   *m.* eremitaño (eh-reh-mee-TAH-nyoh) ◑*f.* -ña◑ 💣

hero   *m.* héroe (eh-ROH-eh)

heroic / heroical (adj.)   heroico (eh-ROHY-koh)

heroine   *f.* heroína (eh-roh-EE-nah)

heroism   *m.* heroísmo (eh-roh-EEZ-moh) / *f.* heroicidad (eh-roh-ee-see-<u>D</u>AH<u>D</u>)

① **heroic times**—tiempos heroicos (TYEM-pohs eh-ROHY-kohs)

heterosexual   *m. & f.* heterosexual (eh-teh-roh-sehg-SWAHL) ◓(adj.) □◕

hexagon   *m.* hexágono (ehg-SAH-goh-noh)

Hey!   ¡eh! (EH) / ¡oye! (OH-yeh) 💣

hiatus   *m.* hiato (YAH-toh)

hierarchy   *f.* jerarquía (heh-rahr-KEE-ah) 💣

hilarious (adj.)   hilarante (ee-lah-RAHN-teh)

hilarity   *f.* hilaridad (ee-lah-ree-<u>D</u>AH<u>D</u>)

hippie   *m. & f.* hippie (HEEP-pee)

Hindu (*religion*)   *m. & f.* hindú ◓(adj.) □◕

Hinduism   *m.* hinduismo (een-DWEEZ-moh)

historian   *m.* historiador (ees-toh-ryah-<u>D</u>OHR) ◓*f.* -ra◕

historic / historical (adj.)   histórico (ees-TOH-ree-koh)

history   *f.* historia (ees-TOH-ryah)

holistic (adj.)   holístico (oh-LEES-tee-koh)

holocaust   *m.* holocausto (oh-loh-KAOWS-toh)

homage   *m.* homenaje (oh-meh-NAH-heh)

homicidal / murderous (adj.)   homicida (oh-mee-SEE-<u>d</u>ah)

homicide / murder   *m.* homicidio (oh-mee-SEE-<u>d</u>yoh)

homogeneous (adj.)   homogéneo (oh-moh-HEH-neh-oh)

homosexual   *m. & f.* homosexual (oh-moh-sehg-SWAHL) ◓(adj.) □◕

homosexuality   *f.* homosexualidad (oh-moh-sehg-swah-lee-<u>D</u>AH<u>D</u>)

honest / forthright / straight (adj.)   honesto (oh-NEHS-toh)

honesty   *f.* honestidad (ho-nehs-tee-<u>D</u>AH<u>D</u>)

honor   *m.* honor (oh-NOHR)

honor (to)   honrar (ohn-RAHR)

honorable (adj.)   honorable (oh-noh-RAH-<u>b</u>leh)

honorableness / hostesy   *f.* honorabilidad (oh-noh-rah-<u>b</u>ee-lee-<u>D</u>AH<u>D</u>) / honradez (ohn-rah-<u>D</u>EHS)

honorary (adj.)   honorario (oh-noh-RAH-ryoh)

honorarium (*pl.* honoraria *or* honorariums)   *m. pl.* honorarios (oh-noh-RAH-ryohs)

horizon / skyline   *m.* horizonte (oh-ree-SOHN-teh)

horizontal / level (adj.)   horizontal (oh-ree-sohn-TAHL)

horoscope   *m.* horóscopo (oh-ROHS-koh-poh)

horrendous / dreadful (adj.)   horrendo (oh-RREHN-doh)

horrible / ghastly (adj.)   horrible (oh-RREE-bleh)

horrid / hellish / hideous (adj.)   horroroso (oh-rroh-ROH-soh)

horrify (to)   horrorizar (oh-rroh-ree-SAHR)

horror   *m.* horror (oh-RROHR)

hospice   *m.* hospicio (ohs-PEE-syoh)

hospitable (adj.)   hospitalario (ohs-pee-tah-LAH-ryoh)

hospital   *m.* hospital (ohs-pee-TAHL)

hospitality   *f.* hospitalidad (ohs-pee-tah-lee-DAHD)

hospitalization   *f.* hospitalización (ohs-pee-tah-lee-sah-SYOHN)

hospitalize (to)   hospitalizar (ohs-pee-tah-lee-SAHR)

hostile / antagonistic (adj.)   hostil (ohs-TEEL)

hostility / antagonism   *f.* hostilidad (ohs-tee-lee-DAHD)

hotel   *m.* hotel (oh-TEHL)

hour / time   *f.* hora (OH-rah)

human   *m.* humano (oo-MAH-noh) ↻(adj.) ▢↻

humanism   *m.* humanismo (oo-mah-NEEZ-moh)

humanist   *m. & f.* humanista (oo-mah-NEES-tah)

humanitarian   *m.* humanitario (oo-mah-nee-TAH-ryoh) ↻*f.* –ia↻

humanitarian / humane (adj.)   humanitario (oo-mah-nee-TAH-ryoh)

humanity / mankind   *f.* humanidad (oo-mah-nee-DAHD)

humble / lowly (adj.)   humilde (oo-MEEL-deh)

humble (to)   humillar (oo-mee-YAHR)

humble oneself (to)   humillarse (oo-mee-YAHR-seh)

humid / damp / moist (adj.)   húmedo (OO-meh-<u>d</u>oh)

humidifier   *m.* humedificador (oo-meh-<u>d</u>ee-fee-kah-<u>D</u>OHR)

humidify / dampen (to)   humedificar (oo-meh-<u>d</u>ee-fee-KAHR)

humidity / moisture / damp   *f.* humedad (oo-meh-<u>D</u>AH<u>D</u>)

humiliate / abase (to)   humillar (oo-mee-YAHR)

humiliate (*oneself*) **/ grovel** (to)   humillarse (oo-mee-YAHR-seh)

humiliating (adj.)   humillante (oo-mee-YAHN-teh)

humiliation   *f.* humillación (oo-mee-yah-SYOHN)

humility   *f.* humildad (oo-meel-DAH<u>D</u>)

humor (*temper / mood or comedy*)   *m.* humor (oo-MOHR)

humorist   *m. & f.* humorista (oo-moh-REES-tah)

humorous / jocular (adj.)   humorístico (oo-moh-REES-tee-koh)

hurricane   *m.* huracán (oo-rah-KAHN)

hygiene   *f.* higiene (ee-HYEH-neh) 💣

hymn   *m.* himno (EEM-noh) 💣

hyperactive / overactive (adj.)   hiperactivo (ee-peh-rahk-TEE-<u>b</u>oh) 💣

hyperactivity   *f.* hiperactividad (ee-peh-rahk-TEE-<u>b</u>ee-<u>D</u>AH<u>D</u>) 💣

hyperbole   *f.* hipérbole (ee-PEHR-<u>b</u>oh-leh) 💣

hyperbolic (adj.)   hyperbólico (ee-pehr-<u>B</u>OH-lee-koh) 💣

hypersensitive (adj.)   hipersensible (ee-pehr-sehn-SEE-<u>b</u>leh) 💣

hypersensitivity   *f.* hipersensibilidad (ee-pehr-sehn-see-<u>b</u>ee-lee-<u>D</u>AH<u>D</u>) 💣

hypertension   *f.* hipertensión (ee-pehr-tehn-SYOHN) 💣

hypnosis   *f.* hipnosis (eep-NOH-sees) 💣

hypnotic (adj.)   hipnótico (eep-NOH-tee-koh) 💣

hypnotize / mesmerize (to)   hipnotizar (eep-noh-tee-SAHR) 💣

hypocrisy   *f.* hipocresía (ee-poh-kreh-SEE-ah) 💣

hypocrite   *m. & f.* hipócrita (ee-POH-kree-tah) ↺(adj.) **hypocritical** ▢↺ 💣

hypothesis   *f.* hipótesis (ee-POH-teh-sees) 💣

hypothetical (adj.)   hipotético (ee-poh-TEH-tee-koh) 💣

hysteria *f.* histeria (ees-TEH-ryah) 💣

hysterical (adj.) histérico (ees-TEH-ree-koh) 💣

hysterics *m.* histerismo (ees-teh-REEZ-moh) 💣

icon *m.* icono (ee-KOH-noh)

iconoclast *m. & f.* iconoclasta (ee-koh-noh-KLAHS-tah)

idea / thought / notion *f.* idea (ee-DEH-ah)

ideal *m.* ideal (ee-deh-AHL) ↻(adj.) ☐↻

idealism *m.* idealismo (ee-deh-ah-LEEZ-moh)

idealist *m. & f.* idealista (ee-deh-ah-LEES-tah) ↻(adj.) **idealistic** ☐↻

idealize (to) idealizar (ee-deh-ah-lee-SAHR)

identical (adj.) idéntico (ee-DEHN-tee-koh)

identicalness / sameness *f.* identidad (ee-dehn-tee-DAHD)

identifiable (adj.) identificable (ee-dehn-tee-fee-KAH-bleh)

identification *f.* identificación (ee-dehn-tee-fee-kah-SYOHN)

identify (to) identificar (ee-dehn-tee-fee-KAHR)

identity *f.* identidad (ee-dehn-tee-DAHD)

idiocy *f.* idiotez (ee-dyoh-TEHS)

idiomatic (adj.) idiomático (ee-dyoh-MAH-tee-koh)

    ① **idiomatic expression**—expresión idiomática (ehs-spreh-SYOHN ee-dyoh-MAH-tee-kah)

idiot /fool *m. & f.* idiota (ee-DYOH-tah)

idiotic / idiotical / foolish (adj.) idiota (ee-DYOH-tah)

idiotism (*idiocy*) *m.* idiotismo (ee-dyoh-TEEZ-moh)

idiotism (*idiom*) *m.* idiotismo (ee-dyoh-TEEZ-moh) / modismo (moh-DEEZ-moh)

idiosyncrasy *f.* idiosincrasia (ee-dyoh-seen-KRAH-syah)

idolize (to) idolatrar (ee-doh-lah-TRAHR)

idyllic (adj.) idílico (ee-DEE-lee-koh)

ignominious (adj.)   ignominioso (eeg-noh-mee-NYOH-soh)

ignominy / disgrace / shame   *f.* ignominia (eeg-noh-MEE-nyah)

ignorance   *f.* ignorancia (eeg-noh-RAHN-syah)

ignorant (adj.)   ignorante (eeg-noh-RAHN-teh) ↻*m. & f.* **ignoramus** ☐↻

ignore / disregard (to)   ignorar (eeg-noh-RAHR)

illegal (adj.)   ilegal (ee-leh-GAHL) 💣

illegality   *f.* ilegalidad (ee-leh-gah-lee-DAHD) 💣

illegible (adj.)   ilegible (ee-leh-HEE-bleh) 💣

illegitimate (adj.)   ilegítimo (ee-leh-HEE-tee-moh) 💣

illicit (adj.)   ilícito (ee-LEE-see-toh) 💣

illogical (adj.)   ilógico (ee-LOH-hee-koh) 💣

illuminate / light / enlighten (to)   iluminar (ee-loo-mee-NAHR) 💣

illumination / lighting   *f.* iluminación (ee-loo-mee-nah-SYOHN) 💣

illusion / delusion   *f.* ilusión (ee-loo-SYOHN) 💣

illustrate (to)   ilustrar (ee-loos-TRAHR) 💣

illustration   *f.* ilustración (ee-loos-trah-SYOHN) 💣

illustrative (adj.)   ilustrativo (ee-loos-trah-TEE-boh) 💣

illustrator   *m.* ilustrador (ee-loos-trah-DOHR) ↻*f.* -ra↻ 💣

illustrious (adj.)   ilustre (ee-LOOS-treh) 💣

image   *f.* imagen (ee-MAH-hehn)

imagery   *f.* imaginería (ee-mah-hee-neh-REE-ah)

imaginary (adj.)   imaginario (ee-mah-hee-NAH-ryoh)

imagination   *f.* imaginación (ee-mah-hee-nah-SYOHN)

imaginative / fanciful (adj.)   imaginativo (ee-mah-hee-nah-TEE-boh)

imagine / envision / suspect (to)   imaginar (ee-mah-hee-NAHR)

imbecile / half-wit   *m. & f.* imbécil (eem-BEH-seel)

imbecile /imbecilic / foolish (adj.)   imbécil (eem-BEH-seel)

imbecility   *f.* imbecilidad (eem-beh-see-lee-DAHD)

imbibe / drink (to)   beber (beh-BEHR)

imbiber / drinker   *m.* bebedor (beh-beh-DOHR) ↻*f.* -ra↻

imitable (adj.)   imitable (ee-mee-TAH-<u>b</u>leh)

imitate / copy (to)   imitar (ee-mee-TAHR)

imitating / imitative (adj.)   imitador (ee-mee-tah-<u>D</u>OHR)

imitation / fake / mimicry   *f.* imitación (ee-mee-tah-SYOHN)

imitator / mimic   *m.* imitador (ee-mee-tah-<u>D</u>OHR) ↻*f.* -ra↻

immaculate (adj.)   inmaculado (een-mah-koo-LAH-<u>d</u>oh) 💣

immature (adj.)   inmaduro (een-mah-<u>D</u>OO-roh) 💣

immaturity   *f.* inmadurez (een-mah-<u>d</u>oo-REHS) 💣

immediate / summary (adj.)   inmediato (een-meh-<u>D</u>YAH-toh) 💣

immense / huge (adj.)   inmenso (een-MEHN-soh) 💣

immensity   *f.* inmensidad (een-mehn-see-<u>D</u>AH<u>D</u>) 💣

immigrant   *m. & f.* inmigrante (een-mee-GRAHN-teh) ↻(adj.) ▯↻ 💣

immigrate (to)   inmigrar (een-mee-GRAHR) 💣

immigration   *f.* inmigración (een-mee-grah-SYOHN) 💣

imminent (adj.)   inminente (een-mee-NEHN-teh) 💣

immobile (*motionless, still*) (adj.)   inmóvil (een-MOH-<u>b</u>eel) 💣

immobility   *f.* inmovilidad (een-moh-<u>b</u>ee-lee-<u>D</u>AH<u>D</u>) 💣

immoderate / intemperate (adj.)   inmoderado (een-moh-<u>d</u>eh-RAH-<u>d</u>oh) 💣

immodest (adj.)   inmodesto (een-moh-<u>D</u>EHS-toh) 💣

immodesty   *f.* inmodestia (een-moh-<u>D</u>EHS-tyah) 💣

immoral (adj.)   inmoral (een-moh-RAHL) 💣

immorality   *f.* inmoralidad (een-moh-rah-lee-<u>D</u>AH<u>D</u>) 💣

immortal / deathless (adj.)   inmortal (een-mohr-TAHL) 💣

immortality   *f.* inmortalidad (een-mohr-tah-lee-<u>D</u>AH<u>D</u>) 💣

immovable / immobile (*fixed*) (adj.)   inmovible (een-moh-<u>B</u>EE-<u>b</u>leh) / inmoble (een-MOH-<u>b</u>leh) / inmóvil (een-MOH-<u>b</u>eel) 💣

immune (adj.)   inmune (een-MOO-neh) 💣

immunity   *f.* inmunidad (een-moo-nee-<u>D</u>AH<u>D</u>) 💣

immutability   *f.* inmutabilidad (een-moo-tah-<u>b</u>ee-lee-<u>D</u>AH<u>D</u>)

immutable (adj.)   inmutable (een-moo-TAH-<u>b</u>leh) 💣

impact (to) impactar (eem-pahk-TAHR)

impact *m.* impacto (eem-PAHK-toh)

impart (to) impartir (eem-pahr-TEER)

impartial / fair / (adj.) imparcial (eem-pahr-SYAHL)

impartiality / fairness *f.* imparcialidad (eem-pahr-syah-lee-<u>D</u>AH<u>D</u>)

impasse / stalemate (*French*) *m.* impasse (eem-PAHS)

impatience *f.* impaciencia (eem-pah-SYEHN-syah)

impatient / restless (adj.) impaciente (eem-pah-SYEHN-teh)

impede / hinder / prevent / stop (to) impedir (eem-peh-<u>D</u>EER)

impeder *m.* impedidor (eem-peh-<u>d</u>ee-<u>D</u>OHR) ↻*f.* –ra↺ / *m.* obstructor (ohbs-truhk-TOHR) ↻*f.* –ra↺

impediment / hinderance *m.* impedimento (eem-peh-<u>d</u>ee-MEHN-toh) / obstrucción (oh<u>b</u>-struhk- SYOHN)

impeditive (adj.) impeditivo (eem-peh-<u>d</u>ee-TEE-<u>b</u>oh) / obstructivo (ohbs-truhk-TEE-<u>b</u>oh)

impenetrable (adj.) impenetrable (eem-peh-neh-TRAH-<u>b</u>leh)

imperative *m.* imperativo (eem-peh-rah-TEE-<u>b</u>oh) ↻(adj.) ☐↺

imperfect / faulty (adj.) imperfecto (eem-pehr-FEHK-toh)

imperfection / defect / flaw *f.* imperfección (eem-pehr-fehk-SYOHN)

imperial (adj.) imperial (eem-peh-RYAHL)

imperialism *m.* imperialismo (eem-peh-ryah-LEEZ-moh)

imperialist *m. & f.* imperialista (eem-peh-ryah-LEES-tah) ↻(adj.) ☐↺

imperious / overbearing (adj.) imperioso (eem-peh-RYOH-soh)

impermeable / waterproof (adj.) impermeable (eem-pehr-meh-AH-<u>b</u>leh)
  ① Used as a masculine noun, this word also means: **raincoat / slicker**.

impersonal (adj.) impersonal (eem-pehr-soh-NAHL)

impertinence *f.* impertinencia (eem-pehr-tee-NEHN-syah)

impertinent / sassy (adj.) impertinente (eem-pehr-tee-NEHN-teh)

imperturbable / impassive (adj.) imperturbable (eem-pehr-toor-<u>B</u>AH-<u>b</u>leh)

impetuosity / rashness *f.* impetuosidad (eem-peh-twoh-see-<u>D</u>AH<u>D</u>)

impetuous / dashing (adj.) impetuoso (eem-peh-TWOH-soh)

impetus   *m.* ímpetu (EEM-peh-too)

implacable / remorseless (adj.)   implacable (eem-plah-KAH-bleh)

implant   *m.* implante (eem-PLAHN-teh)

implant (to)   implantar (eem-plahn-TAHR)

implement   *m.* implemento (eem-pleh-MEHN-toh)

implement (to)   implementar (eem-pleh-mehn-TAHR)

implication   *f.* implicación (eem-plee-kah-SYOHN)

implicit / implied (adj.)   implícito (eem-PLEE-see-toh)

implore / plead (to)   implorar (eem-ploh-RAHR)

imponderability   *f.* imponderabilidad (eem-pohn-deh-ra-bee-lee-DAHD)

imponderable   *m.* imponderable (eem-pohn-deh-RAH-bleh)
   ↻(adj.) ☐↻

import (to)   importar (eem-pohr-TAHR)

importable (adj.)   importable (eem-pohr-TAH-bleh)

importer   *m.* importador (eem-pohr-tah-DOHR) ↻*f.* -ra↻ ↻(adj.) ☐↻

importance / import   *f.* importancia (eem-pohr-TAHN-syah)

important (adj.)   importante (eem-pohr-TAHN-teh)

(be) important / matter (to)   importar (eem-pohr-TAHR)

importation / import (*item*)   *f.* importación (eem-pohr-tah-SYOHN)

imposition / infliction   *f.* imposición (eem-poh-see-SYOHN)

impossibility   *f.* imposibilidad (eem-poh-see-bee-lee-DAHD)

impossible (adj.)   imposible (eem-poh-SEE-bleh)

impost / tax   *m.* impuesto (eem-PWEHS-toh)

impostor / faker   *m.* impostor (eem-pohs-TOHR) ↻*f.* -ra↻
   ↻(adj.) ☐↻

imposture   *f.* impostura (eem-pohs-TOO-rah)

impotence / helplessness   *f.* impotencia (eem-poh-TEHN-syah)

impotent / helpless (adj.)   impotente (eem-poh-TEHN-teh)

imprecise (adj.)   impreciso (eem-preh-SEE-soh)

impresario / entrepreneur (!)   *m.* empresario (eem-preh-SAH-ryoh)
   ↻*f.* –ia↻ ●※

impress (to) impresionar (eem-preh-syoh-NAHR)

impression / printing *f.* impresión (eem-preh-SYOHN)
  ① This word also denotes a printed reproduction; related is: **printer**—
  m. impresor (eem-preh-SOHR) ◑*f.* -ra◐.

impressive (adj.) impresionante (eem-preh-syoh-NAHN-teh)

improbability *f.* improbabilidad (eem-proh-<u>b</u>ah-<u>b</u>ee-lee-<u>D</u>AH<u>D</u>)

improbable / unlikely (adj.) improbable (eem-proh-<u>B</u>AH-<u>b</u>leh)

improper (adj.) impropio (eem-PROH-pyoh)

impropriety *f.* impropiedad (eem-proh-pyeh-<u>D</u>AH<u>D</u>)

improvisation *f.* improvisación (eem-proh-<u>b</u>ee-sah-SYOHN)

improvise (to) improvisar (eem-proh-<u>b</u>ee-SAHR

improviser *m.* improvisador (eem-proh-<u>b</u>ee-sah-DOHR) ◑*f.* -ra◐ ◐(adj.)
  improvisatorial / improvisatory ☐◐

improvised / impromptu / (adj.) improvisado (eem-proh-<u>b</u>ee-SAH-<u>d</u>oh)

imprudence / foolhardiness *f.* imprudencia (eem-proo-<u>D</u>EHN-syah)

imprudent / injudicious / rash (adj.) imprudente (eem-proo-<u>D</u>EHN-teh)

impulse *m.* impulso (eem-POOL-soh)

impulsive (adj.) impulsivo (eem-pool-SEE-<u>b</u>oh)

impulsiveness *f.* impulsividad (eem-pool-see-<u>b</u>ee-<u>D</u>AH<u>D</u>)

impunity *f.* impunidad (eem-poo-nee-<u>D</u>AH<u>D</u>)

impure (adj.) impuro (eem-POO-roh)

impurity / taint *f.* impureza (eem-poo-REH-sah)

in / into en (EHN)

inaccessible (adj.) inaccesible (een-ahk-seh-SEE-<u>b</u>leh)

inaction *f.* inacción (een-ahk-SYOHN)

inactive / dormant / idle (adj.) inactivo (een-ahk-TEE-<u>b</u>oh)

inactivity / idleness *f.* inactividad (een-ahk-tee-<u>b</u>ee-<u>D</u>AH<u>D</u>)

inadequate (adj.) inadecuado (een-ah-<u>d</u>eh-KWAH-<u>d</u>oh)

inapplicable (adj.) inaplicable (een-ah-plee-KAH-<u>b</u>leh) ◆

inappropriate / inapt (adj.) inapropiado (een-ah-proh-PYAH-<u>d</u>oh)

inaudible (adj.) inaudible (een-aow-<u>D</u>EE-<u>b</u>leh)

incalculable / immeasurable (adj.) incalculable (een-kahl-koo-LAH-bleh)

incapacitate (to) incapacitar (een-kah-pah-see-TAHR)

incapacitated / handicapped (adj.) incapacitado (een-kah-pah-see-TAH-doh) 💣

incapacity / inability / incapability *f.* incapacidad (een-kah-pah-see-DAHD)

incarcerate / imprison (to) encarcelar (ehn-kahr-seh-LAHR) 💣

incarceration / imprisonment *f.* encarcelación (ehn-kahr-seh-lah-SYOHN)

incarcerator *m.* encarcelador (ehn-kahr-seh-lah-DOHR) ↻*f.* -ra↻

incarnate (to) encarnar (ehn-kahr-NAHR) ↻(adj.) -nado↻

incarnation / embodiment *f.* encarnación (ehn-kahr-nah-SYOHN) 💣

incentive / inducement *m.* incentivo (een-sehn-TEE-boh)

incertitude *f.* incertitumbre (een-sehr-tee-TOOM-breh)

incessant / ceaseless / continual (adj.) incesante (een-seh-SAHN-teh)

incest *m.* incesto (een-SEHS-toh)

incestuous (adj) incestuoso (een-sehs-TWOH-soh)

incident *m.* incidente (een-see-DEHN-teh)

incidental (adj.) incidental (een-see-dehn-TAHL)

incisive (adj.) incisivo (een-see-SEE-boh)

incite / stir up (to) incitar (een-see-TAHR)

incitement *f.* incitación (een-see-tah-SYOHN)

inciter *m.* incitador (een-see-tah-DOHR) ↻*f.* -ra↻

inclemency *f.* inclemencia (een-kleh-MEHN-syah)

inclement (adj.) inclemente (een-kleh-MEHN-teh)

inclination / incline / tendency *f.* inclinación (een-klee-nah-SYOHN)

incline / slant / slope (to) inclinar (een-klee-NAHR)

include / enclose (to) incluir (een-KLWEER)

inclusion *f.* inclusión (een-kloo-SYOHN)

inclusive (adj.) inclusivo (een-kloo-SEE-boh)

incognito (adj.) de incógnito (deh een-KOHG-nee-toh)

incoherence _f._ incoherencia (een-koh-heh-REHN-syah)

incoherent / garbled (adj.)   incoherente (een-koh-eh-REHN-teh)

incombustibility _f._ incombustibilidad (een-kohm-boos-tee-<u>b</u>ee-lee-<u>D</u>AH<u>D</u>)

incombustible / fireproof (adj.)   incombustible (een-kohm-boos-TEE-<u>b</u>leh)

income _m. pl._ ingresos (een-GREH-sohs)

incommensurability _f._ inconmensurabilidad (een-kohn-mehn-soo-rah-<u>b</u>ee-lee-<u>D</u>AH<u>D</u>)

incommensurable / incommensurate (adj.)   inconmensurable (een-kohn-mehn-soo-RAH-<u>b</u>leh)

incomparable / peerless (adj.)   incomparable (een-kohm-pah-RAH-<u>b</u>leh)

incompatibility _f._ incompatibilidad (een-kohm-pah-tee-<u>b</u>ee-lee-<u>D</u>AH<u>D</u>)

incompatible (adj.)   incompatible (een-kohm-pah-TEE-<u>b</u>leh)

incompetence / ineptitude _f._ incompetencia (een-kohm-peh-TEHN-syah)

incompetent (adj.)   incompetente (een-kohm-peh-TEHN-teh)

incomplete / sketchy (adj.)   incompleto (een-kohm-PLEH-toh)

incomprehensible / garbled (adj.)   incomprensible (een-kohm-prehn-SEE-<u>b</u>leh)

incomprehension _f._ incomprensión (een-kohm-prehn-SYOHN)

inconceivable (adj.)   inconcebible (een-kohn-seh-<u>B</u>EE-<u>b</u>leh)

inconclusive (adj.)   inconcluyente (een-kohn-kloo-YEHN-teh)

incongruous (adj.)   incongruente (een-kohn-GRWEHN-teh)

inconsideration / thoughtlessness _f._ inconsideración (een-kohn-see-<u>d</u>eh-rah-SYOHN)

inconsiderate / thoughtless / rash (adj.)   inconsiderado (een-kohn-see-<u>d</u>eh-RAH-<u>d</u>oh) ⟳_n._ **inconsiderate person** ☐⟳ ◆

inconsistence / inconsistency _f._ inconsistencia (een-kohn-sees-TEHN-syah)

inconsistent (adj.)   inconsistente (een-kohn-sees-TEHN-teh)

inconstancy _f._ inconstancia (een-kohns-TAHN-syah)

inconstant / changeable / fickle (adj.)   inconstante (een-kohns-TAHN-teh)

incontinence _f._ incontinencia (een-kohn-tee-NEHN-syah)

incontinent (adj.)   incontinente (een-kohn-tee-NEHN-teh)

inconvenience *f.* inconveniencia (een-kohn-beh-NYEHN-syah)

inconvenient (adj.) inconveniente (een-kohn-beh-NYEHN-teh)

incorporate / include (to) incorporar (een-kohr-poh-RAHR)

incorrect / inaccurate (adj.) incorrecto (een-koh-RREHK-toh)

incorrectness *f.* incorrección (een-koh-rrehk-SYOHN)

incorrigibility *f.* incorregibilidad (een-koh-rreh-hee-bee-lee-_DAHD_)

incorregible (adj.) incorregible (een-koh-rreh-HEE-bleh)

incredible (adj.) incredible (een-kreh-_DEE_-bleh)

incredulity / disbelief *f.* incredulidad (een-kreh-doo-lee-_DAHD_)

incriminate (to) incriminar (een-kree-mee-NAHR)

inculcate / instill (to) inculcar (een-kool-KAHR)

incur (to) incurrir (een-koo-RREER)

incurable (adj.) incurable (een-koo-RAH-bleh)

indecency *f.* indecencia (een-deh-SEHN-syah)

indecent (adj.) indecente (een-deh-SEHN-teh)

indecipherable (adj.) indescifrable (een-deh-see-FRAH-bleh)

indecision / indecisiveness *f.* indecisión (een-deh-see-SYOHN)

indecisive / hesitant / (adj.) indeciso (een-deh-SEE-soh)

indefinite (adj.) indefinido (een-deh-fee-NEE-doh)

indelicate (adj.) indelicado (een-deh-lee-KAH-doh)

independence *f.* independencia (een-deh-pehn-DEHN-syah)

independent (adj.) independiente (een-deh-pehn-DYEHN-teh)

indescribable (adj.) indescriptible (een-dehs-kreep-TEE-bleh) 💣

indeterminate / indefinite (adj.) indeterminado (een-deh-tehr-mee-NAH-doh)

index / forefinger (!) *m.* índice (EEN-dee-seh)

Indian *m.* indio (EEN-dyoh) ↻*f.* -ia↺

indicate / suggest / signify (to) indicar (een-dee-KAHR)

indication / inkling / tip-off *f.* indicación (een-dee-kah-SYOHN)

indicative (adj.) indicativo (een-dee-kah-TEE-boh)

indicator *m.* indicador (een-dee-kah-_D_OHR)

indifference / detachment *f.* indiferencia (een-dee-feh-R EHN-syah)

indifferent / disinterested (adj.) indiferente (een-dee-feh-REHN-teh)

indigenous / native to (adj.) indígena (een-DEE-heh-nah)

indigent / pauper *m. & f.* indigente (een-dee-HEHN-teh) ↻(adj.) ▯↻ / *m.* necesitado (neh-seh-see-TAH-_d_oh) ↻(adj.) ▯↻ / *m. & f.* pobre (POH-_b_reh) ↻(adj.) ▯↻

　④ **the needy, the poor**—*m. & f.* los indigentes (lohs een-dee-HEHN-tehs)

indigestion *f.* indigestión (een-dee-hehs-TYOHN)

indignant (adj.) indignado (een-deeg-NAH-_d_oh)

indignation *f.* indignación (een-deeg-nah-SYOHN)

indignity *f.* indignidad (een-deeg-nee-_D_AH_D_)

indirect / roundabout (adj.) indirecto (een-dee-REHK-toh)

indiscreet / tactless (adj.) indiscreto (een-dees-KREH-toh)

indiscretion *f.* indiscreción (een-dees-kreh-SYOHN)

indiscriminate (adj.) indiscriminado (een-dees-kree-mee-NAH-_d_oh)

indispensable (adj.) indispensable (een-dees-pehn-SAH-_b_leh)

indisposed / unwell (adj.) indispuesto (een-dees-PWEHS-toh)

indisputable (adj.) indiscutible (een-dees-koo-TEE-_b_leh) ⬤

indistinct / shadowy / vague (adj.) indistinto (een-dees-TEEN-toh)

individual / person *m.* individuo (een-dee-_B_EE-_d_woh)

individual (adj.) individual (een-dee-_b_ee-_D_WAHL)

individualist *m. & f.* individualista (een-dee-_b_ee-_d_wah-LEES-tah)

individuality *f.* individualidad (een-dee-_b_ee-_d_wah-lee-_D_AH_D_)

indolence *f.* indolencia (een-doh-LEHN-syah)

indolent (adj.) indolente (een-doh-LEHN-teh)

indomitability / indomitableness *f.* indomabilidad (een-doh-mah-_b_ee-lee-_D_AH_D_)

indomitable (adj.) indomable (een-doh-MAH-_b_leh/ indómito (een-DOH-mee-toh)

induce (to) inducir (een-doo-SEER)

indulgent / forgiving / lenient (adj.)   indulgente (een-dool-HEHN-teh)

industrial (adj.)   industrial (een-doos-TRYAHL)

industrialism   *m.* industrialismo (een-doos-tryah-LEEZ-MOH)

industrialist   *m. & f.* industrialista (een-doos-tryah-LEES-tah)

industrialization   f. industrialización (een-doos-tryah-lee-sah-SYOHN)

industrialize (to)   industrializar (een-doos-tryah-lee-SAHR)

industrious (adj.)   industrioso (een-doos-TRYOH-soh)

industry   *f.* industria (een-DOOS-tryah)

ineffective / ineffectual (adj.)   ineficaz (ee-neh-fee-KAHS)

inefficiency   *f.* ineficiencia (ee-neh-fee-SYEHN-syah)

inefficient (adj.)   ineficiente (ee-neh-fee-SYEHN-teh)

ineligibility   *f.* inelegibilidad (ee-neh-leh-hee-<u>b</u>ee-lee-<u>D</u>AH<u>D</u>)

inept (adj.)   inepto (ee-NEHP-toh)

ineptitude   *f.* ineptitud (ee-nehp-tee-TOO<u>D</u>)

inestimable / priceless (adj.)   inestimable (ee-nehs-TEE-mah-<u>b</u>leh)

inevitability   *f.* inevitabilidad (ee-neh-<u>b</u>ee-tah-<u>b</u>ee-lee-<u>D</u>AH<u>D</u>)

inevitable / inescapable (adj.)   inevitable (ee-neh-<u>b</u>ee-TAH-<u>b</u>leh)

inexact / inaccurate (adj.)   inexacto (ee-nehg-SAHK-toh)

inexcusable / indefensible (adj.)   inexcusable (ee-nehs-skoo-SAH-<u>b</u>leh)

inexperience   *f.* inexperiencia (ee-nehs-speh-RYEHN-syah)

inexplicable (adj.)   inexplicable (ee-nehs-splee-KAH-<u>b</u>leh)

infallible / foolproof (adj.)   infalible (een-fah-LEE-<u>b</u>leh)

infamous (adj.)   infame (een-FAH-meh)

infamy   *f.* infamia (een-FAH-myah)

infancy / childhood   *f.* infancia (een-FAHN-syah)

infant / prince (!)   *m.* infante (een-FAHN-teh) / ○*f.* **infant / princess (!)** infanta (een-FAHN-tah)○

infantile / childlike (adj.)   infantil (een-fahn-TEEL)

infect (to)   infectar (een-fehk-AHR)

infected (adj.)   infecto (een-FEHK-toh)

infection   *f.* infección (een-fehk-SYOHN)

infectious (adj.)   infeccioso (een-fehk-SYOH-soh)

infecund (adj.)   infecundo (een-feh-KOON-doh)

infecundity   *f.* infecundidad (een-feh-koon-dee-<u>D</u>AH<u>D</u>)

inference   *f.* inferencia (een-feh-REHN-syah)

inferior / lower / under (adj.)   inferior (een-feh-RYOHR)

inferior / subordinate   *m. & f.* inferior (een-feh-RYOHR)

inferiority   *f.* inferioridad (een-feh-ryoh-ree-<u>D</u>AH<u>D</u>)
    ① **inferiority complex**—*m.* complejo de inferioridad (kohm-pleh-HOdeh een-feh-ryoh-ree-<u>D</u>AH<u>D</u>)

infernal (adj.)   infernal (een-fehr-NAHL)

inferno / hell   *m.* infierno (een-FYEHR-noh)

infidelity   *f.* infidelidad (een-fee-<u>d</u>eh-lee-<u>D</u>AH<u>D</u>)

infinite / infinity   *m.* infinito (een-fee-NEE-toh)

infinite / endless / limitless (adj.)   infinito (een-fee-NEE-toh)

infirm / ailing / diseased (adj.)   enfermo (ehn-FEHR-moh) 💣
    ① Closely related: **nurse / medical assistant**—*f.* enfermera (ehn-fehr-MEH-rah)

infirmity / illness / disease   *f.* enfermedad (ehn-fehr-meh-<u>D</u>AH<u>D</u>) 💣

inflame / provoke (to)   inflamar (een-flah-MAHR)

inflammable (adj.)   inflamable (een-flah-MAH-<u>b</u>leh)

inflammation   *f.* inflamación (een-flah-mah-SYOHN)

inflammatory (adj.)   inflamatorio (een-flah-mah-TOH-ryoh)

inflated / puffy (adj.)   inflado (een-FLAH-<u>d</u>oh)

inflation   *f.* inflación (een-flah-SYOHN)

inflict (to)   infligir (een-flee-HEER)

influence / affect / leverage   *f.* influencia (een-FLWEHN-syah)

influence / affect / sway (to)   influenciar (een- flwehn-SYAHR)

influential (adj.)   influyente (een-floo-YEHN-teh)

influenza   *f.* influenza (een-FLWEHN-sah)

inform / apprise (to)   informar (een-fohr-MAHR)

informal (adj.)   informal (een-fohr-MAHL)

informality   f. informalidad (een-fohr-mah-lee-DAHD)

informant / informer   m. & f. informante (een-fohr-MAHN-teh)

information / data   f. información (een-fohr-mah-SYOHN)

informative (adj.)   informativo (een-fohr-mah-TEE-boh)

informed / knowledgeable (adj.)   informado (een-fohr-MAH-doh)

infrastructure   f. infraestructura (een-frah-ehs-trook-TOO-rah)

infrequent (adj.)   infrecuente (een-freh-KWEHN-teh)

infuriate / enrage (to)   enfurecer (ehn-foo-reh-SEHR) 💣

infuriated / enraged (adj.)   enfurecido (ehn-foo-reh-SEE-doh) 💣

ingratitude   f. ingratitud (een-grah-tee-TOOD)

ingredient   m. ingrediente (een-greh-DYEHN-teh)

inhabit (to)   habitar (ah-bee-TAHR) 💣

inhabitant   m. & f. habitante (ah-bee-TAHN-teh) 💣

inhalant   m. inhalante (een-ah-LAHN-teh)

inhale (to)   inhalar (een-ah-LAHR)

inhaler   m. inhalador (een-ah-lah-DOHR)

inherent / intrinsic (adj.)   inherente (een-eh-REHN-teh)

inherit (to)   heredar (eh-reh-DAHR) 💣

inheritance / heritage   f. herencia (eh-REHN-syah) 💣

inhibit (to)   inhibir (een-ee-BEER)

inhibition   f. inhibición (een-ee-bee-SYOHN)

inhuman / inhumane (adj.)   inhumano (een-oo-MAH-noh)

inhumanity   f. inhumanidad (een-oo-mah-nee-DAHD)

initial (*alphabetic symbol*)   f. inicial (ee-nee-SYAHL)

initial / first (adj.)   inicial (ee-nee-SYAHL)

initiate (*begin*) (to)   iniciar (ee-nee-SYAHR)

initiation / start / beginning   f. iniciación (ee-nee-syah-SYOHN)

initiative   f. iniciativa (ee-nee-syah-TEE-bah)

inject (to)   inyectar (een-yehk-TAHR) 💣

injection   *f.* inyección (een-yehk-SYOHN)

injustice / (*moral-ethical*) wrong   *f.* injusticia (een-hoos-TEE-syah)

innate / inborn (adj.)   innato (een-NAH-toh)

inner / interior / inside (adj.)   interior (een-teh-RYOHR)

innocence   *f.* inocencia (ee-noh-SEHN-syah)

innocent / simpleton   *m. &. f.* inocente (ee-noh-SEHN-teh)

innocent / guileless / naïve (adj.)   inocente (ee-noh-SEHN-teh)

innocuous / inoffensive (adj.)   inocuo (ee-NOH-kwoh)

innovate (to)   innovar (een-noh-<u>B</u>AHR)

innovation   *f.* innovación (een-noh-<u>b</u>ah-SYOHN)

innovative / innovatory (adj.)   innovador (een-noh-<u>b</u>ah-<u>D</u>OHR)

innovator   *m.* innovador (een-noh-<u>b</u>ah-<u>D</u>OHR) ◯*f.* -ra◯

innumerable / countless (adj.)   innumerable (een-noo-meh-RAH-<u>b</u>leh)

inoculate (to)   inocular (ee-noh-koo-LAHR)

inoculation   *f.* inoculación (ee-noh-koo-lah-SYOHN)

inoffensive (adj.)   inofensivo (ee-noh-fehn-SEE-<u>b</u>oh)

inoperable (adj.)   inoperable (ee-noh-peh-RAH-<u>b</u>leh)

inopportune (adj.)   inoportuno (ee-noh-pohr-TOO-noh)

inquisitive (adj.)   inquisitivo (een-kee-see-TEE-<u>b</u>oh)

insatiable (adj.)   insaciable (een-sah-SYAH-<u>b</u>leh)

inscribe (to)   inscribir (eens-kree-<u>B</u>EER)
   ① Related, very basic but noncognate: (to) **write**—escribir (ehs-kree-<u>B</u>EER)

inscription   *f.* inscripción (eens-kreep-SYOHN)

insect   *m.* insecto (een-SEHK-toh)

insecticide   *m.* insecticida (een-sehk-tee-SEE-<u>d</u>ah) ◯(adj.) **insecticidal** ▢◯

insecure (adj.)   inseguro (een-seh-GOO-roh)

insecurity   *f.* inseguridad (een-seh-goo-ree-<u>D</u>AH<u>D</u>)

inseminate (to)   inseminar (een-seh-mee-NAHR)

insemination   *f* inseminación (een-seh-mee-nah-SYOHN)

inseminator   *m.* inseminador (een-seh-mee-nah-DOHR) ↻*f.* -ra↺

insensibility / insensitivity (adj.)   insensibilidad (een-sehn-see-<u>b</u>ee-lee-<u>D</u>AH<u>D</u>)

insensible / impervious (adj.)   insensible (een-sehn-SEE-<u>b</u>leh)

inseparability   *f.* inseparabilidad (een-seh-pah-rah-<u>b</u>ee-lee-<u>D</u>AH<u>D</u>)

inseparable (adj.)   inseparable (een-seh-pah-RAH-<u>b</u>leh)

insert (to)   insertar (een-sehr-TAHR)

insertion / insert   *f.* inserción (een-sehr-SYOHN)

insidious (adj.)   insidioso (een-see-<u>D</u>YOH-soh)

insignificance   *f.* insignificancia (een-seeg-nee-fee-KAHN-syah)

insignificant / negligible (adj.)   insignificante (een-seeg-nee-fee-KAHN-teh)

insincere (adj.)   insincero (een-seen-SEH-roh)

insincerity   *f.* insinceridad (een-seen-seh-ree-<u>D</u>AH<u>D</u>)

insinuate / intimate / imply (to)   insinuar (een-see-NWHAR)

insinuating / suggestive (adj.)   insinuante (een-see-NWAHN-teh)

insinuation / innuendo / hint   *f.* insinuación (een-see-nwah-SYOHN)

insist / harp on (to)   insistir (een-sees-TEER)

insistence   *f.* insistencia (een-sees-TEHN-syah)

insistent (adj.)   insistente (een-sees-TEHN-teh)

insolence / impudence   *f.* insolencia (een-soh-LEHN-syah)

insolent / impudent (adj.)   insolente (een-soh-LEHN-teh)

insolvency   *f.* insolvencia (een-sohl-<u>B</u>EHN-syah)

insolvent (adj.)   insolvente (een-sohl-<u>B</u>EHN-teh)

insomnia   *m.* insomnio (een-SOHM-nyoh)

inspect (to)   inspeccionar (eens-pehk-syoh-NAHR)

inspection   *f.* inspección (eens-pehk-SYOHN)

inspector   *m.* inspector (eens-pehk-TOHR) ↻*f.* -ra↺

inspiration   *f.* inspiración (eens-pee-rah-SYOHN)

inspire (to)   inspirar (eens-pee-RAHR)

install (to)   instalar (eens-tah-LAHR)

installation *f.* instalación (eens-tah-lah-SYOHN)

instance *f.* instancia (eens-TAHN-syah)

instant / instantaneous (adj.) instantáneo (eens-tahn-TAH-neh-oh)

instigate (to) instigar (eens-tee-GAHR)

instigation *f.* incitación (een-see-tah-SYOHN) ♠※

instigator *m.* instigador (eens-tee-gah-<u>D</u>OHR) ↺*f.* -ra↺

instinct *m.* instinto (eens-TEEN-toh)

institute (to) instituir (eens-tee-TWEER)

institution *f.* institución (eens-tee-too-SYOHN)

instruct / teach (to) instruir (eens-TRWEER)

instruction / teaching *f.* instrucción (eens-trook-SYOHN)

instructive / instructional (adj.) instructivo (eens-trook-TEE-<u>b</u>oh)

instructor *m.* instructor (eens-trook-TOHR) ↺*f.* -ra↺

instrument *m.* instrumento (eens-troo-MEHN-toh)

instrumental (adj.) instrumental (eens-troo-mehn-TAHL)

instrumentalist *m. & f.* instrumentalista (eens-troo-mehn-tah-LEES-tah)

insubstantial (adj.) insustancial (een-soos-tahn-SYAHL) ♠※

insufferable / intolerable (adj.) insufrible (een-soo-FREE-<u>b</u>leh)

insufficient (adj.) insuficiente (een-soo-fee-SYEHN-teh)

insult *m.* insulto (een-SOOL-toh)

insult / revile (to) insultar (een-sool-TAHR)

insulting (adj.) insultante (een-sool-TAHN-teh)

intact (adj.) intacto (een-TAHK-toh)

intangible (adj.) intangible (een-tahn-HEE-<u>b</u>leh)

integrate (to) integrar (een-teh-GRAHR)

integrity *f.* integridad (een-teh-gree-<u>D</u>AH<u>D</u>)

intellect *m.* intelecto (een-teh-LEHK-toh)

intellectual / highbrow *m. & f.* intelectual (een-teh-lehk-TWAHL)
  ↺(adj.) ☐↺

intelligence / wit *f.* inteligencia (een-teh-lee-HEHN-syah)

intelligent / smart (adj.)   inteligente (een-teh-lee-HEHN-teh)

intelligible (adj.)   inteligible (een-teh-lee-HEE-bleh)

intense (adj.)   intenso (een-TEHN-soh)

intenseness / intensity   *f.* intensidad (een-tehn-see-DAHD)

intensification   *f.* intensificación (een-tehn-see-fee-kah-SYOHN)

intensify (to)   intensificar (een-tehn-see-fee-KAHR)

intention / intent   *f.* intención (een-tehn-SYOHN)

intentional (adj.)   intencional (een-tehn-syoh-NAHL)

interact (to)   interactuar (een-teh-rahk-TWAHR)

interaction / interplay   *f.* interacción (een-teh-rahk-SYOHN)

interactive (adj.)   interactivo (een-teh-rahk-TEE-boh)

intercept (to)   interceptar (een-tehr-sehp-TAHR)

interception   *f.* intercepción (een-tehr-sehp-SYOHN)

intercontinental (adj.)   intercontinental (een-tehr-kohn-tee-nehn-TAHL)

interdependent (adj.)   interdependiente (een-tehr-deh-pehn-DYEHN-teh)

interest (*beneficial or financial*)   *m.* interés (een-teh-REHS)

interest (to)   interesar (een-teh-reh-SAHR)

interesting / engaging (adj.)   interesante (een-teh-reh-SAHN-teh)

interference   *f.* interferencia (een-tehr-feh-REHN-syah)

interim / meantime   *m.* ínterin (EEN-teh-reen) 💣

interim / meantime (adj.)   interino (een-teh-REE-noh)

interior / inside   *m.* interior (een-teh-RYOHR) ↻(adj.) ☐↻

interjection   *f.* interjección (een-tehr-hehk-SYOHN)

interlude   *m.* interludio (een-tehr-LOO-dyoh)

intermediary   *m.* intermediario ↻*f.* -ria↻ ↻(adj.) ☐↻

intermediate / mediate (to)   intermediar (een-tehr-meh-DYAHR)

intermediate / medium / intervening (!) (adj.)   intermedio (een-tehr-MEH-dyoh)

interminable / endless (adj.)   interminable (een-tehr-mee-NAH-bleh)

intermission   *f.* intermisión (een-tehr-mee-SYOHN)

intermittent / fitful / occasional (adj.)   intermitente (een-tehr-mee-TEHN-teh)

intern / interne   *m.* interno (een-TEHR-noh) ↻*f.* –na↺

internal (adj.)   interno (een-TEHR-noh)

international (adj.)   internacional (een-tehr-nah-syoh-NAHL)

interpret / construe (to)   interpretar (een-tehr-preh-TAHR)

interpretation / rendition   *f.* interpretación (een-tehr-preh-tah-SYOHN)

interpreter   *m. & f.* intérprete (een-TEHR-preh-teh)

interrelate (to)   interrelacionar (een-teh-rreh-lah-syoh-NAHR)

interrelationship   *f.* interrelación (een-teh-rreh-lah-SYOHN)

interrogate / question (to)   interrogar (een-teh-rroh-GAHR)

interrogation   *f.* interrogación (een-teh-rroh-gah-SYOHN)

interrogator   *m.* interrogador (een-teh-rroh-gah-<u>D</u>OHR) ↻*f.* –ra↺

interrupt / intrude (to)   interrumpir (een-teh-rroom-PEER)

interruption   *f.* interrupción (een-teh-rroop-SYOHN)

intersect (to)   intersecarse (een-tehr-seh-KAHR-seh)

intersection   *f.* intersección (een-tehr-sehk-SYOHN)

interval   *m.* intervalo (een-tehr-<u>B</u>AH-loh)

intervene / meddle (!) (to)   intervenir (een-tehr-<u>b</u>eh-NEER)

intervention / audit (!)   *f.* intervención (een-tehr-<u>b</u>ehn-SYOHN)

intimacy   *f.* intimidad (een-tee-mee-<u>D</u>AH<u>D</u>)

intimate / (personally) close (adj.)   íntimo (EEN-tee-moh)

intimidate (to)   intimidar (een-tee-mee-<u>D</u>AHR)

intimidation   *f.* intimidación (een-tee-mee-<u>d</u>ah-SYOHN)

intolerable (adj.)   intolerable (een-toh-leh-RAH-<u>b</u>leh)

intolerance / bigotry   *f.* intolerancia (een-toh-leh-RAHN-syah)

intolerant / bigoted (adj.)   intolerante (een-toh-leh-RAHN-teh) ↻*n.* **bigot** []↺

intransigence   *f.* intransigencia (een-trahn-see-HEHN-syah)

intrepid / fearless / dauntless (adj.)   intrépido (een-TREH-pee-<u>d</u>oh)

intrepidity / fearlessness *f.* intrepidez (een-treh-pee-<u>D</u>EHS)

intricate (adj.) intricado (een-tree-KAH-<u>d</u>oh)

intrigue / conspiracy / plot *f.* intriga (een-TREE-gah)

intrigue / conspire / plot (to) intrigar (een-tree-GAHR)

intriguer/ intrigant *m. & f.* intrigante (een-tree-GAHN-teh)

intriguing (adj.) intrigante (een-tree-GAHN-teh)

introduce (*bring in*) (to) introducir (een-troh-<u>d</u>oo-SEER)

introduction (*of book*) *f.* introducción (een-troh-<u>d</u>ook-SYOHN)

introductory (adj.) introductorio (een-troh-<u>d</u>ook-TOH-ryoh)

introspection *f.* introspección (een-trohs-pehk-SYOHN)

introvert *m.* introvertido (een-troh-<u>b</u>erh-TEE-<u>d</u>oh) ○*f.* -da○

intrusion *f.* intrusión (een-troo-SYOHN)

intruder / interloper *m.* intruso (een-TROO-soh) ○*f.* -sa○

intrusional / intrusive (adj.) intruso (een-TROO-soh) / entremetido (ehn-treh-meh-TEE-<u>d</u>oh)

intuit / sense (to) intuir (een-TWEER)

intuition *f.* intuición (een-twee-SYOHN)

intuitive (adj.) intuitivo (een-twee-TEE-<u>b</u>oh)

inundate / deluge / swamp (to) inundar (ee-noon-DAHR)

inundated / awash / flooded (adj.) inundado (ee-noon-DAH-<u>d</u>oh)

inundation / deluge / flood / glut *f.* inundación (ee-noon-dah-SYOHN)

invade / raid (to) invadir (een-bah-<u>D</u>EER)

invader / raider *m.* invasor (een-bah-SOHR) ○*f.* -ra○

invalid / shut-in *m.* inválido (een-BAH-lee-<u>d</u>oh) ○*f.* -da○ ○(adj.) □○

invalidate / nullify (to) invalidar (een-bah-lee-<u>D</u>AHR)

invalidity *f.* invalidez (een-<u>b</u>ah-lee-<u>D</u>EHS)

invaluable (adj.) invalorable (een-bah-loh-RAH-<u>b</u>leh)

invariable (adj.) invariable (een-bah-RYAH-<u>b</u>leh)

invasion / raid *f.* invasión (een-bah-SYOHN)

invasive (adj.) invasivo (een-bah-SEE-<u>b</u>oh)

invent / make up (to)   inventar (een-behn-TAHR)

invention   *f.* invención (een-behn-SYOHN)

inventive (adj.)   inventivo (een-behn-TEE-<u>b</u>oh)

inventor / originator   *m.* inventor (een-behn-TOHR) ↻*f.* -ra↺

inventory   *m.* inventario (een-behn-TAH-ryoh)

inversion / reversal   *f.* inversión (een-behr-SYOHN)

invert / reverse (*order or direction*) (to)   invertir (een-behr-TEER)

inverse / reverse (adj.)   inverso (een-BEHR-soh)

investigate / research (to)   investigar (een-behs-tee-GAHR)

investigation / research   *f.* investigación (een-behs-tee-gah-SYOHN)

investigator / researcher   *m.* investigador (een-behs-tee-gah-<u>D</u>OHR) ↻*f.* -ra↺

invigorate (to)   vigorizar (bee-goh-ree-SAHR) ♦※

invigorating (adj.)   vigorizante (bee-goh-ree-SAHN-teh) ♦※

invisibility   *f.* invisibilidad (een-bee-see-<u>b</u>ee-lee-<u>D</u>AH<u>D</u>)

invisible (adj.)   invisible (een-bee-SEE-<u>b</u>leh)

invitation   *f.* invitación (een-bee-tah-SYOHN)

invite (to)   invitar (een-bee-TAHR)

invitee / guest   *m.* invitado (een-bee-TAH-<u>d</u>oh) ↻*f.* -da↺

involve / wrap (!) (to)   envolver (ehn-bohl-<u>B</u>EHR) ♦※

invulnerable (adj.)   invulnerable (een-bool-neh-RAH-<u>b</u>leh)

irate (adj.)   airado (eye-RAH-<u>d</u>oh) ♦※

ire / anger   *f.* ira (EE-rah)

ironic (adj.)   irónico (ee-ROH-nee-koh)

irony   *f.* ironía (ee-roh-NEE-ah)

irrational (adj.)   irracional (ee-rrah-syoh-NAHL)

irrationality   *f.* irracionalidad (ee-rrah-syoh-nah-lee-<u>D</u>AH<u>D</u>)

irrefutable (adj.)   irrefutable (ee-rreh-foo-TAH-<u>b</u>leh)

irregular / fitful / ragged (adj.)   irregular (ee-rreh-goo-LAHR)

irregularity   *f.* irregularidad (ee-rreh-goo-lah-ree-<u>D</u>AH<u>D</u>)

irrelevance *f.* irrelevancia (ee-rreh-leh-<u>B</u>AHN-syah)

irrelevant / immaterial (adj.) irrelevante (ee-rreh-leh-<u>B</u>AHN-teh)

irreplaceable (adj.) irreemplazable (ee-rreh-ehm-plah-SAH-<u>b</u>leh)

irresistible (adj.) irresistible (ee-rreh-sees-TEE-<u>b</u>leh)

irresponsibility *f.* irresponsabilidad (ee-rrehs-pohn-sah-<u>b</u>ee-lee-<u>D</u>AH<u>D</u>)

irresponsible / feckless (adj.) irresponsable (ee-rrehs-pohn-SAH-<u>b</u>leh)

irreverence *f.* irreverencia (ee-rreh-<u>b</u>eh-REHN-syah)

irreverent (adj.) irreverente (ee-rreh-<u>b</u>eh-REHN-teh)

irrevocable (adj.) irrevocable (ee-rreh-<u>b</u>oh-KAH-<u>b</u>leh)

irritable / petulant (!) (adj.) irritable (ee-rree-TAH-<u>b</u>leh)

irritant *m.* irritante (ee-rree-TAHN-teh) ↻(adj.) **irritating / irksome** ☐↻

irritate / irk / peeve (to) irritar (ee-rree-TAHR)
    ① (to) **get angry / lose one's temper (with / for)**—irritarse (con / por) (ee-rree-TAHR-seh [kohn / pohr])

irritation *f.* irritación (ee-rree-tah-SYOHN)

isle / islet *m.* islote (ees-LOH-teh)

isolate / insulate (to) aislar (eyes-LAHR)

isolated (adj.) aislado (eyes-LAH-<u>d</u>oh)

isolation *m.* aislamiento (eyes-lah-MYEHN-toh)

itinerant (adj.) itinerante (ee-tee-neh-RAHN-teh)

itinerary *m.* itinerario (ee-tee-neh-RAH-ryoh)

—J—

jacket *f.* chaqueta (chah-KEH-tah)

jade *m.* jade (HAH-deh)

jar *f.* jarra (HAH-rrah)
    ① A larger vessel changes gender: **jug / pitcher**—*m.* jarro (HAH-rroh).

jazz *m.* jazz (JAHS)

jealous (adj.) celoso (seh-LOH-soh)

jeans *m.* jeans (JEENS)

jeep *m.* jeep (JEEP)

jelly *f.* jalea (hah-LEH-ah)

jersey *m.* jersey (HEHR-say)

Jesus *m.* Jesús (heh-SOOS)

jockey *m. & f.* jockey (HOH-kee)

jocular (adj.) jocoso (hoh-KOH-soh)

jocularity *f.* jocosidad (hoh-koh-see-<u>D</u>AH<u>D</u>)

jovial / cheerful (adj.) jovial (hoh-<u>B</u>YAHL)

joviality / cheerfulness *f.* jovialidad (hoh-<u>b</u>yah-lee-<u>D</u>AH<u>D</u>)

jubilant (adj.) jubiloso (hoo-<u>b</u>ee-LOH-soh)

jubilation / glee *m.* júbilo (HOO-<u>b</u>ee-loh)
    ① Notable noncognates: (to) **retire** (*from work*)—jubilarse (hoo-<u>b</u>ee-LAHR-seh); **retirement**—*f.* jubilación (hoo-<u>b</u>ee-lah-SYOHN)

jubilee *m.* jubileo (hoo-<u>b</u>ee-LEH-oh)

Judaism *m.* judaísmo (hoo-<u>d</u>ah-EEZ-moh)

judge *m. & f.* juez (HWEHS)

judge / adjudicate (to) juzgar (hoos-GAHR) 💣

judicial (adj.) judicial (hoo-<u>d</u>ee-SYAHL)

judiciary *f.* judicatura (hoo-<u>d</u>ee-kah-TOO-rah)

judicious (adj.) juicioso (hwee-SYOH-soh) 💣

judo *m.* judo (HOO-<u>d</u>oh)

juice *m.* jugo (HOO-goh)

juicy (adj.) jugoso (hoo-GOH-soh)

juncture *f.* juntura (hoon-TOO-rah)

jungle *f.* jungla (HOON-glah)

jurisdiction *f.* jurisdicción (hoo-reez-<u>d</u>eek-SYOHN)

jurisprudence *f.* jurisprudencia (hoo-rees-proo-<u>D</u>EHN-syah)

jurist *m. & f.* jurista (hoo-REES-tah)

juror / jury *m.* jurado (hoo-RAH-<u>d</u>oh) ○*f.* -da○

just / fair / impartial (adj.) justo (HOOS-toh)

justice *f.* justicia (hoos-TEE-syah)

justification *f.* justificación (hoos-tee-fee-kah-SYOHN)

justify (*defend or warrant*) (to)   justificar (hoos-tee-fee-KAHR)

juvenile (adj.)   juvenil (hoo-<u>b</u>eh-NEEL)

    ① **juvenile**—*m. & f.* menor (meh-NOHR); (adj.) **young**—joven (HOH-behn); **young person / young man or woman / youth**— *m. & f.* joven (HOH-<u>b</u>ehn)

juxtapose (to)   yuxtaponer (yook-stah-poh-NEHR) 💣

juxtaposition (to)   yuxtaposición (yook-stah-poh-see-SYOHN) 💣

—K—

kaki (*tree*) / kaki (*fruit—Japanese persimmon*)   *m.* caqui (KAH-kee)

keel   *f.* quilla (KEE-yah) 💣

khaki (*color*) / khaki (*cloth and color*)   *m.* caqui (KAH-kee) 💣

kilo   *m.* kilo (KEE-loh)

kilocycle   *m.* kilociclo (kee-loh-SEE-kloh)

kilogram   *m.* kilogramo (kee-loh-GRAH-moh)

kilometer   *m.* kilómetro (kee-LOH-meh-troh)

kindergarten   *m.* kindergarten (keen-dehr-GAHR-tehn)

kitchen / stove (!)   *f.* cocina (koh-SEE-nah) 💣

—L—

labor (*specific task*)   *f.* labor (la-<u>B</u>OHR)

laboratory   *m.* laboratorio (la-<u>b</u>oh-rah-TOH-ryoh)

laborious (adj.)   laborioso (lah-<u>b</u>oh-RYOH-soh)

laboriousness   *f.* laboriosidad (lah-<u>b</u>oh-ryoh-see-<u>D</u>AH<u>D</u>)

labyrinth   *m.* laberinto (lah-<u>b</u>eh-REEN-toh)

lacerate (to)   lacerar (lah-seh-RAHR)

laceration   *f.* laceración (lah-seh-rah-SYOHN)

lackey   *m.* lacayo (lah-KAH-yoh)

laconic / terse (adj.)   lacónico (lah-KOH-nee-koh)

lagoon   *f.* laguna (lah-GOO-nah)

lake *m.* lago (LAH-goh)

lament / cry / groan / wail *m.* lamento (lah-MEHN-toh)

lament / grieve / mourn (to) lamentar (lah-mehn-TAHR)

lamentable / pitiful / (adj.) lamentable (lah-mehn-TAH-<u>b</u>leh)

lamp *f.* lámpara (LAHM-pah-rah)

language *m.* lenguaje (lehn-GWAH-heh)

languid / listless (adj.) lánguido (LAHN-ghee-<u>d</u>oh)

languish (to) languidecer (lahn-ghee-<u>d</u>eh-SEHR)

lantern *f.* linterna (leen-TEHR-nah)

lapidate (to) lapidar (lah-pee-DAHR)

lapidation *f.* lapidación (lah-pee-dah-SYOHN)

lapse *m.* lapso (LAHP-soh)

laptop computer *f.* laptop (LAHP-tohp)

lascivious / lecherous / lewd (adj.) lascivo (lahs-SEE-<u>b</u>oh)

lasciviousness / lechery / lewdness *f.* lascivia (lahs-SEE-<u>b</u>yah)

laser *m.* láser (LAH-sehr)

lassitude *f.* lasitud (lah-see-TOO<u>D</u>) 💣

lasso / noose *m.* lazo (LAH-soh)

latent (adj.) latente (lah-TEHN-teh)

lateral (adj.) lateral (lah-teh-RAHL)

latex (*botany*) *m.* látex (LAH-teks)

latitude *f.* latitud (lah-tee-TOO<u>D</u>)

laundry (*cleaning establishment*) *f.* lavandería (lah-<u>b</u>ahn-deh-REE-ah)

laureate *m.* laureado (laow-reh-AH-<u>d</u>oh) ↻*f.* -da↻

layman (*noncleric*) *m.* laico (LEYE-koh) ↻*f.* -ca↻ ↻(adj.) **lay** ☐↻

league (*class, category*) *f.* liga (LEE-gah)

league (*unit of measure*) *f.* legua (LEH-gwah)

legacy / bequest *m.* legado (leh-GAH-<u>d</u>oh)

legal / lawful / licit (adj.) legal (leh-GAHL)

legality *f.* legalidad (leh-gah-lee-<u>D</u>AH<u>D</u>)

legalize (to)   legalizar (leh-gah-lee-SAHR)

legend (*story or inscription*)   *f.* leyenda (leh-YEHN-dah)

legendary (adj.)   legendario (leh-hehn-DAH-ryoh)

legibility   *f.* legibilidad (leh-hee-bee-lee-DAHD)

legible (adj.)   legible (leh-HEE-bleh)

legislate (to)   legislar (leh-hees-LAHR)

legislation   *f.* legislación (leh-hees-lah-SYOHN)

legislative (adj.)   legislativo (leh-hees-lah-TEE-boh)

legislator   *m.* legislador (leh-hees-lah-DOHR) ↻*f.* -ra↺

legitimacy   *f.* legitimidad (leh-hee-tee-mee-DAHD)

legitimate / lawful (adj.)   legítimo (leh-HEE-tee-moh)

legume / vegetable   *f.* legumbre (leh-GOOM-breh)

lemon   *m.* limón (lee-MOHN) ↻(adj.) **lemon / lemon-yellow** ☐↺

leniency   *f.* lenidad (leh-nee-DAHD)

lens   *m. & f.* lente (LEHN-teh)

lesion   *f.* lesión (leh-SYOHN)

lesson   *f.* lección (lehk-SYOHN)

lethal (adj.)   letal (leh-TAHL)

lethargic (adj.)   letárgico (leh-TAHR-hee-koh)

lethargy   *m.* letargo (leh-TAHR-goh)

letter (*alphabetic character*)   *f.* letra (LEH-trah)

liberal   *m. & f.* liberal (lee-beh-RAHL) ↻(adj.) ☐↺

liberalism   *m.* liberalismo (lee-beh-rah-LEEZ-moh)

liberalize (to)   liberalizar (lee-beh-rah-lee-SAHR)

liberate / extricate / free (to)   liberar (lee-beh-RAHR)

liberated / free / independent (adj.)   libre (LEE-breh)

liberating (adj.)   liberador (lee-beh-rah-DOHR)

liberation / deliverance   *f.* liberación (lee-beh-rah-SYOHN)

liberation (*from*) **/ riddance**   *m.* libramiento (lee-brah-MYEHN-toh)

liberator / rescuer   *m.* libertador (lee-behr-tah-DOHR) ↻*f.* -ra↺

libertarian   *m.* libertario (lee-<u>b</u>ehr-TAH-ryoh) ◐*f.* -ria◑
   ◐(adj.) ☐◑

libertinage   *m.* libertinaje (lee-<u>b</u>ehr-tee-NAH-heh)

libertine / rake   *m.* libertino (lee-<u>b</u>ehr-TEE-noh) ◐*f.* -na◑
   ◐(adj.) ☐◑

liberty / freedom   *f.* libertad (lee-<u>b</u>ehr-TAH<u>D</u>)

license / permit   *f.* licencia (lee-SEHN-syah)

licentious / wanton (adj.)   licencioso (lee-sehn-SYOH-soh)

lieutenant   *m. & f.* teniente (teh-NYEHN-teh) ◕

limbo   *m.* limbo (LEEM-boh)

lime   *f.* lima (LEE-mah) / *m.* limón verde (lee-MOHN BEHR-<u>d</u>eh)

limit / boundary   *m.* límite (LEE-mee-teh)

limit / confine (to)   limitar (lee-mee-TAHR)

limitation   *f.* limitación (lee-mee-tah-SYOHN)

limited / restricted (adj.)   limitado (lee-mee-TAH-<u>d</u>oh)

limousine   *f.* limusina (lee-moo-SEE-nah)

line (*course or graphical mark*)   *f.* línea (LEE-neh-ah)
   ① **line** (*row of people or things*)—*f.* fila (FEE-lah)

lineage / parentage   *m.* linaje (lee-NAH-heh)

linear (adj.)   lineal (lee-neh-AHL)

linen / flax   *m.* lino (LEE-noh)

linguist   *m. & f.* lingüista (leen-GWEES-tah)

linguistic (adj.)   lingüístico (leen-GWEES-tee-koh)

linguistics   *f.* lingüística (leen-GWEES-tee-kah)

liniment   *m.* linimento (lee-nee-MEHN-toh)

liquid / fluid   *m.* líquido (LEE-kee-<u>d</u>oh) ◐(adj.) ☐◑

liquidate (to)   liquidar (lee-kee-<u>D</u>AHR)

liquidation   *f.* liquidación (lee-kee-<u>d</u>ah-SYOHN)

liquidity   *f.* liquidez (lee-kee-<u>D</u>EHS)

liquor / liqueur   *m.* licor (lee-KOHR)

list / roster   *f.* lista (LEES-tah)

list / itemize (to)   listar (lees-TAHR)
   ① (to) **list / make a list**—hacer una lista (ah-SEHR OO-nah LEES-tah)

liter / litre   *m.* litro (LEE-troh)

literal (adj.)   literal (lee-teh-RAHL)

literary (adj.)   literario (lee-teh-RAH-ryoh)

literature   *f.* literatura (lee-teh-rah-TOO-rah)

litigant   *m. & f.* litigante (lee-tee-GAHN-teh) ↻(adj.) ☐↻

litigate (to)   litigar (lee-tee-GAHR)

litigation / lawsuit   *f.* litigación (lee-tee-gah-SYOHN)

local / regional (adj.)   local (loh-KAHL)

locale / locality   *f.* localidad (loh-kah-lee-D̲AHD̲)

locate (*find*) (to)   localizar (loh-kah-lee-SAHR)

lodge (*Masonic*)   *f.* logia (LOH-hyah)

lodging (*act of*)   *m.* alojamiento (ah-loh-hah-MYEHN-toh) 💣

logic   *f.* lógica (LOH-hee-kah) ↻(adj.) **logical** –co ☐↻

logistics   *f.* logística (loh-HEES-tee-kah)

longevity   *f.* longevidad (lohn-heh-b̲ee-D̲AHD̲)

longitude / length (!)   *f.* longitud (lohn-hee-TOO D̲)

loquacious / talkative (adj.)   locuaz (loh-KWAHS)

lot (*land parcel*)   *m.* lote (LOH-teh)

lotion   *f.* loción (loh-SYOHN)

loupe / magnifying glass   *f.* lupa (LOO-pah)

lottery   *f.* lotería (loh-teh-REE-ah)

loyal (adj.)   leal (leh-AHL)

loyalty / allegiance   *f.* lealtad (leh-ahl-TAHD̲)

lubricant   *m.* lubricante (loo-b̲ree-KAHN-teh)

lubricate / oil / grease (to)   lubricar (loo-b̲ree-KAHR)

lucid (adj.)   lúcido (LOO-see-d̲oh)

lucidity   *f.* lucidez (loo-see-D̲EHS)

lucrative (adj.)   lucrativo (loo-krah-TEE-b̲oh)

luminous / shining (adj.)   luminoso (loo-mee-NOH-soh)

lunar (adj.)   lunar (loo-NAHR)

lunatic   *m.* lunático (loo-NAH-tee-koh) ↻*f.* -ca↻ ↻(adj.) ☐↻

luster / sheen / polish   *m.* lustre (LOOS-treh)

lustrous / shiny / glossy (adj.)   lustroso (loos-TROH-soh)

luxurious / lush (adj.)   lujoso (loo-HOH-soh)

luxury   *m.* lujo (LOO-hoh)

lyric / lyrical (adj.)   lírico (LEE-ree-koh)

—M—

macabre (adj.)   macabro (mah-KAH-<u>b</u>roh)

machine   *f.* máquina (MAH-kee-nah)

machinery   *f.* maquinaria (mah-kee-NAH-ryah)

machinist   *m.* maquinista (mah-kee-NEES-tah)

magic   *f.* magia (MAH-hyah) / mágica (MAH-hee-kah)

magic / magical (adj.)   mágico (MAH-hee-koh)

magician   *m.* mago (MAH-goh) ↻*f.* -a↻

magnetic (adj.)   magnético (mahg-NEH-tee-koh)

magnetism   *m.* magnetismo (mahg-neh-TEEZ-moh)
   ① The associated noun is not at all cognate: **magnet**—*m.* imán (ee-MAHN).

magnificence   *f.* magnificencia (mahg-nee-fee-SEHN-syah)

magnificent (adj.)   magnífico (mahg-NEE-fee-koh)

magnitude   *f.* magnitud (mahg-nee-TOO<u>D</u>)

maintain (*assert*) (to)   mantener (mahn-teh-NEHR)

maintenance   *m.* mantenimiento (mahn-teh-nee-MYEHN-toh)

majestic / stately (adj.)   majestuoso (mah-hehs-TWOH-soh)

majesty / splendor / stateliness   *f.* majestuosidad (mah-hehs-twoh-see-<u>D</u>AH<u>D</u>)

major (*important, greater*) (adj.)   mayor (mah-YOHR)

majority   *f.* mayoría (mah-yoh-REE-ah)

malediction / curse   *f.* maldición (mahl-dee-SYOHN)

malefactor   *m.* malhechor (mahl-eh-CHOHR) ○*f.* -ra○

malevolence / wickedness   *f.* malevolencia (mah-leh-<u>b</u>oh-LEHN-syah)

malevolent / wicked (adj.)   malévolo (mah-LEH-<u>b</u>oh-loh)

malformation (*medicine*)   *f.* malformación (mahl-fohr-mah-SYOHN)

malformed (adj.)   mal formado (MAHL fohr-MAH-<u>d</u>oh) / malhecho (mahl-HEH-choh)

malfunction (to)   funcionar mal (foon-syoh-NAHR MAHL)

malice / wickedness   *f.* malicia (mah-LEE-syah)

malicious / mean (adj.)   maléfico (mah-LEH-fee-koh)

malignant / malign (adj.)   maligno (mah-LEEG-noh)

mama / mamma / mom   *f.* mamá (mah-MAH)

manage / handle (to)   manejar (mah-neh-HAHR)

manageable (adj.)   manejable (mah-neh-HAH-<u>b</u>leh)

management (*handling*)   *m.* manejo (mah-NEH-hoh)

mandate / command / commission   *m.* mandado (mahn-DAH-<u>d</u>oh)

(authority to) mandate / command   *m.* mando (MAHN-doh)

mandate / command / dictate (to)   mandar (mahn-DAHR)

maneuver   *f.* maniobra (mah-NYOH-<u>b</u>rah)

maneuver / manipulate (to)   maniobrar (mah-nyoh-<u>B</u>RAHR)

mania / craze / fad   *f.* manía (mah-NEE-ah)

maniac   *m.* maníaco (mah-NEE-ah-koh) ○*f.* -ca○ ○(adj.) **maniac / maniacal** □○

manicure   *f.* manicura (mah-nee-KOO-rah)

manicurist   *m.* manicuro (mah-nee-KOO-roh) ○*f.* -ra○

manifest / evident (adj.)   manifesto (mah-nee-FEHS-toh)

manifest / show (to)   manifestar (mah-nee-fehs-TAHR)

manifestation   *f.* manifestación (mah-nee-fehs-tah-SYOHN)

manifesto   *m.* manifesto (mah-nee-FEHS-toh)

manipulate (to)   manipular (mah-nee-pooh-LAHR)

manipulation   *f.* manipulación (mah-nee-pooh-lah-SYOHN)

manipulator   *m.* manipulador (mah-nee-pooh-lah-<u>D</u>OHR) ◐*f.* -ra◑
◑(adj.) **manipulative** ▢◑

manner / way   *f.* manera (mah-NEH-rah) / modo (MOH-<u>d</u>oh)

mansion   *f.* mansión (mahn-SYOHN)

manual / handbook   *m.* manual (mah-NWAHL)

manual (*by hand*) (adj.)   manual (mah-NWAHL)

manufacture   *f.* manufactura (mah-noo-fahk-TOO-rah)

manufacture (to)   manufacturar (mah-noo-fahk-too-RAHR)

manufacturer   *m.* manufacturero (mah-noo-fahk-too-REH-roh) ◐*f.* -ra◑

manuscript   *m.* manuscrito (mah-noos-KREE-toh)

map   *m.* mapa (MAH-pah)

marathon   *m.* (*sometimes f.*) maratón (mah-rah-TOHN)

marble   *m.* mármol (MAHR-mohl)

march   *f.* marcha (MAHR-chah)

march (to)   marchar (mahr-CHAHR)

margin / edge   *m.* margen (MAHR-hehn)

marginal (adj.)   marginal (mahr-hee-NAHL)

marine (*military sailor*)   *m.* marino (mah-REE-noh)

marine / oceanic (adj.)   marino (mah-REE-noh)

mariner / sailor   *m.* marinero (mah-ree-NEH-roh)

mark / blemish   *f.* marca (MAHR-kah)

mark / score / scratch (to)   marcar (mahr-KAHR)

marked / notable (adj.)   marcado (mahr-KAH-<u>d</u>oh)

marker   *m.* marcador (mahr-kah-<u>D</u>OHR) ◐*f.* -ra◑ ◑(adj.) **marking** ▢◑

market / marketplace   *m.* mercado (mehr-KAH-<u>d</u>oh) 💣

martyr   *m. & f.* mártir (MAHR-teer)

marvel / wonder   *f.* maravilla (mah-rah-<u>B</u>EE-yah)

marvelous / wondrous (adj.)   maravilloso (mah-rah-<u>b</u>ee-YOH-soh)

masculine (adj.)   masculino (mahs-koo-LEE-noh)

masculinity   *f.* masculinidad (mahs-koo-lee-nee-<u>DAHD</u>)

mask   *f.* máscara (MAHS-kah-rah)

mask (to)   enmascarar (ehn-mahs-kah-RAHR) 💣

masochist   *m. & f.* masoquista (mah-soh-KEES-tah) ↻(adj.) ▢↻

masquerade   *f.* mascarada (mahs-kah-RAH-<u>d</u>ah)

mass (*religious service*)   *f.* misa (MEE-sah)
   ① (to) **attend / hear mass**—oír misa (oh-eer MEE-sah); (to) **say mass**—celebrar misa (seh-leh-<u>B</u>RAHR MEE-sah)

mass (*matter*)   *f.* masa (MAH-sah)

massacre / slaughter   *m.* masacre (mah-SAH-kreh)

massacre (to)   masacrar (mah-sah-KRAHR)

massage   *m.* masaje (mah-SAH-heh)

massage (to)   masajear (mah-sah-heh-AHR)

masseur / masseuse   *m. & f.* masajista (mah-sah-HEES-tah)

massive (adj.)   masivo (mah-SEE-<u>b</u>oh)

master / teacher   *m.* maestro (mah-EHS-troh)

masterly (adj.)   magistral (mah-hees-TRAHL)

mastery / master's degree   *f.* maestría (mah-ehs-TREE-ah)

masterpiece / masterwork   *f.* obra maestra (OH-brah mah-EHS-trah) 💣

masticate / chew (to)   masticar (mahs-tee-KAHR)
   ① **chewing gum**—*f.* goma de mascar (GOH-mah deh mahs-KAHR)

material (*in general, not cloth*)   *m.* material (mah-teh-RYAHL) ↻(adj.) ▢↻

materialism   *m.* materialismo (mah-teh-ryah-LEEZ-moh)

materialist   *m. & f.* materialista (mah-teh-ryah-LEES-tah)

materialist / materialistic (adj.)   materialista (mah-teh-ryah-LEES-tah)

maternal / motherly (adj.)   maternal (mah-tehr-NAHL)

maternity / motherhood   *f.* maternidad (mah-tehr-nee-<u>DAHD</u>)

mathematical (adj.)   matemático (mah-teh-MAH-tee-koh)

mathematician   *m.* matemático (mah-teh-MAH-tee-koh) ↻*f.* -ca↻

mathematics   *f. sing.* matemática (mah-teh-MAH-tee-kah) / *f. pl.* matemáticas (mah-teh-MAH-tee-kahs)

matinée _f._ matinée (mah-tee-NEH)

matriarch _f._ matriarca (mah-TRYAHR-kah)

matriculate / enroll (to) matricular (mah-tree-koo-LAHR)

matrimonial / marital (adj.) matrimonial (mah-tree-moh-NYAHL)

matrimony / marriage _m._ matrimonio (mah-tree-MOH-nyoh)

matron _f._ matrona (mah-TROH-nah)

matter (_substance_) _f._ materia (mah-TEH-ryah)

mature / grown (adj.) maduro (mah-DOO-roh)

mature / ripen (to) madurar (mah-doo-RAHR)

maturity _f._ madurez (mah-doo-REHS)

mausoleum _m._ mausoleo (maow-soh-LEH-oh)

mayonnaise _f._ mayonesa (mah-yoh-NEH-sah)

meager (adj.) magro (MAH-groh) 💣

mechanic _m._ mecánico (meh-KAH-nee-koh) ↻(adj.) **mechanical** ▯↻

mechanism _m._ mecanismo (meh-kah-NEEZ-moh)

medallion _m._ medallón (meh-dah-YOHN)

mediate (to) mediar (meh-DYAHR)

mediation _f._ mediación (meh-dyah-SYOHN)

mediator / peacemaker _m._ mediador (meh-dyah-DOHR) ↻_f._ -ra↻

medic / doctor _m._ médico (MEH-dee-koh) ↻_f._ -ca↻ ↻(adj.) **medical** ▯↻

medical treatment _m._ medicamento (meh-dee-kah-MEHN-toh)

medicate (to) medicar (meh-dee-KAHR)

medication _f._ medicación (meh-dee-kah-SYOHN)

medicinal (adj.) medicinal (meh-dee-see-NAHL)

medicine (_science of; healing compound_) _f._ medicina (meh-dee-SEE-nah)

medieval (adj.) medieval (meh-dyeh-BAHL)

mediocre / second-rate (adj.) mediocre (meh-DYOH-kreh)

mediocrity _f._ mediocridad (meh-dyoh-kree-DAHD)

meditate / muse (to) meditar (meh-dee-TAHR)

meditation / thought _f._ meditación (meh-dee-tah-SYOHN)

medium (*means, instrumentality*)   *m.* medio (MEH-<u>d</u>yoh)

medium / average (adj.)   mediano (meh-<u>D</u>YAH-noh)

melancholia / melancholy / gloom   *f.* melancolía (meh-lahn-koh-LEE-ah)

melancholiac / melancholic / melancholy / blue / depressed (adj.)   melancólico (meh-lahn-KOH-lee-koh)

melodic (adj.)   melódico (meh-LOH-<u>d</u>ee-koh)

melodious / tuneful (adj.)   melodioso (meh-loh-<u>D</u>YOH-soh)

melodrama   *m.* melodrama (meh-loh-<u>D</u>RAH-mah)

melodramatic (adj.)   melodramático (meh-loh-<u>d</u>rah-MAH-tee-koh)

melody / tune   *f.* melodía (meh-loh-<u>D</u>EE-ah)

member   *m.* miembro (MYEHM-broh)

memoir   *f. pl.* (*used in the plural only*) memorias (meh-MOH-ryahs)

memorable (adj.)   memorable (meh-moh-RAH-<u>b</u>leh)

memorandum / memo   *m.* memorándum (meh-moh-RAHN-doom)

memory   *f.* memoria (meh-MOH-ryah)

mend / repair (to)   remendar (reh-mehn-DAHR) 💣

mental (adj.)   mental (mehn-TAHL)

mentality   *f.* mentalidad (mehn-tah-lee-<u>D</u>AH<u>D</u>)

mention   *f.* mención (mehn-SYOHN)

mention (to)   mencionar (mehn-syoh-NAHR)

mentor   *m.* mentor (mehn-TOHR)

menu   *m.* menú (meh-NOO) / *f.* carta (KAHR-tah)

merchandise / wares / goods   *f. pl.* mercancías (mehr-kahn-SEE-ahs) / *f. pl.* (*Americanism*) mercaderías (mehr-kah-deh-REE-ahs)
   ① **article / commodity**—*f.* mercancía (mehr-kahn-SEE-ah) / *f.* mercadería (mehr-kah-deh-REE-ah)

merchant   *m. & f.* comerciante (koh-mehr-SYAHN-teh) 💣

mere (adj.)   mero (MEH-roh)

merit   *m.* mérito (MEH-ree-toh)

merit / deserve (to)   merecer (meh-reh-SEHR)

meritorious / deserving (adj.)   meritorio (meh-ree-TOH-ryoh)

message   *m.* mensaje (mehn-SAH-heh) 💣

messenger / courier   *m.* mensajero (mehn-sah-HEH-roh) ↻*f.* -ra↻ 💣

metal   *m.* metal (meh-TAHL)

metallic (adj.)   metálico (meh-TAH-lee-koh)

metamorphosis   *f.* metamorfosis (meh-tah-mohr-FOH-sees)

metaphor   *f.* metáfora (meh-TAH-foh-rah)

meteor   *m.* meteoro (meh-teh-OH-roh)

meteoric (adj.)   meteórico (meh-teh-OH-ree-koh)

meter (*metric, literary or musical*)   *m.* metro (MEH-troh)

meter (*measuring device*)   *m.* medidor (meh-dee-DOHR)

method   *m.* método (MEH-toh-doh)

methodical (adj.)   metódico (meh-TOH-dee-koh)

meticulous / thorough (adj.)   meticuloso (meh-tee-koo-LOH-soh)

metric (adj.)   métrico (MEH-tree-koh)

metropolis   *f.* metrópoli (meh-TROH-poh-lee)

metropolitan (adj.)   metropolitano (meh-troh-poh-lee-TAH-noh)

microbe / germ   *m.* microbio (mee-KROH-byoh)

microphone   *m.* micrófono (mee-KROH-foh-noh)

microscope   *m.* microscopio (mee-krohs-KOH-pyoh)

microscopic / micro (adj.)   microscópico (mee-krohs-KOH-pee-koh)

mid (adj.)   medio (MEH-dyoh) 💣

middle / midst   *m.* medio (MEH-dyoh) 💣

middle / average (adj.)   medio (MEH-dyoh) / mediano (meh-DYAH-noh) 💣

middle class   *f.* clase media (KLAH-seh MEH-dyah) 💣

middle class (adj.)   de la clase media (deh lah KLAH-seh MEH-dyah)

midpoint   *m.* punto medio (POON-toh MEH-dyoh) 💣

migration   *f.* migración (mee-grah-SYOHN)

migratory (adj.)   migratorio (mee-grah-TOH-ryoh)

mile   *f.* milla (MEE-yah)

militant   *m. & f.* militante (mee-lee-TAHN-teh) ↻(adj.) ▢↻

military (adj.)   militar (mee-lee-TAHR)

military (man) / soldier   *m.* militar (mee-lee-TAHR)

militia   *f.* milicia (mee-LEE-syah)

milligram   *m.* miligramo (mee-lee-GRAH-moh) 💣

milliliter / millilitre   *m.* mililitro (mee-lee-LEE-troh) 💣

millimeter / millimetre   *m.* milímetro (mee-LEE-meh-troh) 💣

millionaire   *m.* millonario (mee-yoh-NAH-ryoh) ↻*f.* -ia↻

mime   *m.* mimo (MEE-moh)

mind   *f.* mente (MEHN-teh) 💣

mine (*diggings or explosive device*)   *f.* mina (MEE-nah)

miner   *m.* minero (mee-NEH-roh)

mineral / ore   *m.* mineral (mee-neh-RAHL)

miniature   *f.* miniatura (mee-nyah-TOO-rah)

miniature (adj.)   en miniatura (ehn mee-nyah-TOO-rah)

minimize (to)   minimizar (mee-nee-mee-SAHR)

minimum / least   *m.* mínimo (MEE-nee-moh) / *m.* mínimum
   (MEE-nee-moom)

minimum / minimal (adj.)   mínimo (MEE-nee-moh)

miniscule / tiny / wee (adj.)   minúscolo (mee-NOOS-koh-loh)

minister (*governmental*)   *m.* ministro (mee-NEES-troh) ↻*f.* -tra↻

ministry (*governmental*)   *m.* ministerio (mee-nees-TEH-ryoh)

minivan   *f.* minivan (mee-NEE-bahn)

minor / juvenile   *m. & f.* menor (meh-NOHR) 💣

minor / lesser / junior / younger (adj.)   menor (meh-NOHR)

minority   *f.* minoría (mee-noh-REE-ah)

minute / very small (*in scale*) (adj.)   menudo (meh-NOO-doh) 💣

minus   menos (MEH-nohs) 💣

misanthrope / misanthropist   *m.* misántropo (mee-SAHN-toh-poh)

misanthropic (adj.)   misantrópico (mee-sahn-TROH-pee-koh)

misanthropy *f.* misantropía (mee-sahn-trop-PEE-ah)

miscellaneous (adj.) misceláneo (mees-seh-LAH-neh-oh)

miscellany *f.* miscelánea (mees-seh-LAH-neh-ah)

miserable person / wretch *m. & f.* miserable (mee-seh-RAH-<u>b</u>leh)

miserable / wretched (adj.) miserable (mee-seh-RAH-<u>b</u>leh)

misery *f.* miseria (mee-SEH-ryah)

misfortune *m.* infortunio (een-fohr-TOO-nyoh) 💣

missal (*religion*) *m.* misal (mee-SAHL)

mission *f.* misión (mee-SYOHN)

missionary *m.* misionero (mee-syoh-NEH-roh) ◖*f.* -ra◗
◖(adj.) ▯◗

missive / letter *f.* misiva (mee-SEE-<u>b</u>ah)

mitigate / cushion / relieve (to) mitigar (mee-tee-GAHR)

mix / mixture / blend *f.* mezcla (MEHS-klah)

mix / blend / mingle (to) mezclar (mehs-KLAHR)

mobile / movable (adj.) móvil (MOH-<u>b</u>eel)

mobility *f.* movilidad (moh-<u>b</u>ee-lee-<u>DAHD</u>)

mobilization *f.* movilización (moh-<u>b</u>ee-lee-sah-SYOHN)

mobilize (to) movilizar (moh-<u>b</u>ee-lee-SAHR)

mode *m.* modo (MOH-doh)

model (*pattern or small copy*) *m.* modelo (moh-<u>D</u>EH-loh)

model / ideal (adj.) modelo (moh-<u>D</u>EH-loh)

model (to) modelar (moh-<u>d</u>eh-LAHR)

modem *m.* módem (MOH-<u>d</u>ehm)

(political) moderate *m.* moderado (moh-<u>d</u>eh-RAH-<u>d</u>oh) ◖*f.* -da◗
◖(adj.) ▯◗

moderate (*sentiments*) (to) moderar (moh-<u>d</u>eh-RAHR)
① (to) **become less extreme**—moderarse (moh-<u>d</u>eh-RAHR-seh)

moderation *f.* moderación (moh-<u>d</u>ehr-rah-SYOHN)

moderator *m.* moderador (moh-<u>d</u>eh-rah-<u>D</u>OHR) ◖*f.* -ra◗ / *m.* mediador (meh-<u>d</u>yah-<u>D</u>OHR) ◖*f.* -ra◗

modern (adj.) moderno (moh-DEHR-noh)

modernity *f.* modernidad (moh-dehr-nee-DAHD)

modernization *f.* modernización (moh-dehr-nee-sah-SYOHN)

modernize (to) modernizar (moh-dehr-nee-SAHR)

modest / humble (adj.) modesto (moh-DEHS-toh)

modesty *f.* modestia (moh-DEHS-tyah)

modification *f.* modificación (moh-dee-fee-kah-SYOHN)

modify (to) modificar (moh-dee-fee-KAHR)

mold (to) moldear (mohl-deh-AHR)

molest / annoy / bother (to) molestar (moh-lehs-TAHR)
    ① Note that this term does not carry the same implication of sexual violence as in English! Also: *f.* **nuisance / pest**—molestia (moh-LEHS-tyah).

momentary (adj.) momentáneo (moh-mehn-TAH-neh-oh)

momentum (*physics*) *m.* momento (moh-MEHN-toh)

monastery *m.* monasterio (moh-nahs-TEH-ryoh)

monetary (adj.) monetario (moh-neh-TAH-ryoh)

money (*coinage*) *f.* moneda (moh-NEH-dah)
    ① **Currency (bills)**—*f.* moneda corriente (moh-NEH-dah koh-RRYEHN-teh); **money in general**—*m.* dinero (dee-NEH-roh)

monitor (to) monitorear (moh-nee-toh-reh-AHR)

monitor (*watching / listening device*) *m.* monitor (moh-nee-TOHR)
    ◐*f.* -ra◑

monk *m.* monje (MOHN-heh) ◐*f.* **nun** -ja◑

monogamous (adj.) monógamo (moh-NOH-gah-moh)

monogamy *f.* monogamia (moh-noh-GAH-myah)

monologue *m.* monólogo (moh-NOH-loh-goh)

monopolize (to) monopolizar (moh-noh-poh-lee-SAHR)

monotone *f.* monotonía (moh-noh-toh-NEE-ah)

monotoneous / humdrum (adj.) monótono (moh-NOH-toh-noh)

monotony / dullness *f.* monotonía (moh-noh-toh-NEE-ah)

monster *m.* monstruo (MOHNS-trwoh)

monstrosity *f.* monstruosidad (mohns-trwoh-see-<u>D</u>AH<u>D</u>)

monstrous (adj.) monstruoso (mohns-TRWOH-soh)

monument *m.* monumento (moh-noo-MEHN-toh)

monumental (adj.) monumental (moh-noo-mehn-TAHL)

moral / morals (*personal ethics / morale*) *f.* moral (moh-RAHL)

moral (adj.) moral (moh-RAHL)

morality *f.* moralidad (moh-rah-lee-<u>D</u>AH<u>D</u>)

morbid (adj.) mórbido (MOHR-<u>b</u>ee-<u>d</u>oh)

more más (MAHS)

morgue *f.* morgue (MOHR-gweh)

mortal *m. & f.* mortal (mohr-TAHL) ↺(adj.) **mortal / deadly / fatal** ☐↺

mortality *f.* mortalidad (mohr-tah-lee-<u>D</u>AH<u>D</u>)

mortify (to) mortificar (mohr-tee-fee-KAHR)

mosaic *m.* mosaico (moh-SEYE-koh)

mosque *f.* mezquita (mehs-KEE-tah)

mosquito *m.* mosquito (mohs-KEE-toh)
    ① A potentially confusing noncognate: (adj.) **petty**—mezquino (mehs-KEE-noh)

mote / speck / blemish *f.* mota (MOH-tah)

motel *m.* motel (moh-TEHL)

mother–of–pearl *f.* madreperla (mah-<u>d</u>reh-PEHR-lah)

motion (*parliamentary proposal*) *m.* moción (moh-SYOHN)

motivate (to) motivar (moh-tee-<u>B</u>AHR)

motivation *f.* motivación (moh-tee-<u>b</u>ah-SYOHN)

motive / motif (!) *m.* motivo (moh-TEE-<u>b</u>oh)

motor / engine *m.* motor (moh-TOHR)

motorcycle / motorbike *f.* motocicleta (moh-toh-see-KLEH-tah)

motorcyclist *m. & f.* motociclista (moh-toh-see-KLEES-tah)

motorist *m. & f.* motorista (moh-toh-REES-tah)

movable / removable (adj.) movible (moh-<u>B</u>EE-<u>b</u>leh)

move (*something*) / shift the position of (to)   mover (moh-<u>B</u>EHR)

move (*oneself*) / shift position (to)   moverse (moh-<u>B</u>EHR-seh)

movement / motion   *m.* movimiento (moh-<u>b</u>ee-MYEHN-toh)

mule   *m.* mulo (MOO-loh) ↻*f.* -a↻

multiple (adj.)   múltiple (MOOL-tee-pleh)

multiplication   *f.* multiplicación (mool-tee-plee-kah-SYOHN)

multiplicity   *f.* multiplicidad (mool-tee-plee-see-<u>D</u>AH<u>D</u>)

multiply (*math operation*) (to)   multiplicar (mool-tee-plee-KAHR)

multiply (*grow numerous*) (to)   multiplicarse (mool-tee-plee-KAHR-seh)

multitude / crowd   *f.* multitud (mool-tee-TOO<u>D</u>)

multiuse / multipurpose (adj.)   multiuso (mool-tee-OO-soh) [Ok?]

municipal (adj.)   municipal (moo-nee-see-PAHL)

municipality / township   *m.* municipio (moo-nee-SEE-pyoh)

munitions   *f. pl.* municiones (moo-nee-SYOH-nehs)

mural   *m.* mural (moo-RAHL)

murmur / mutter (to)   murmurar (moor-moo-RAHR)

muscle   *m.* músculo (MOOS-koo-loh)

muscular (adj.)   muscular (moos-koo-LAHR)

muse   *f.* musa (MOO-sah)

museum   *m.* museo (moo-SEH-oh)

music   *f.* música (MOO-see-kah)

musical (adj.)   musical (moo-see-KAHL)

musician   *m.* músico (MOO-see-koh) ↻*f.* -ca↻

mustard   *f.* mostaza (mohs-TAH-sah)

mutant (*biology*)   *m.* mutante (moo-TAHN-teh) ↻(adj.) ☐↻

mutate (*genetic reference only*) (to)   mutar (moo-TAHR)

mutation   *f.* mutación (moo-tah-SYOHN)

mute (*person*)   *m.* mudo (MOO-<u>d</u>oh) ↻*f.* -da↻

mute / dumb / silent / (adj.)   mudo (MOO-<u>d</u>oh)

mutilate / maim (to)   mutilar (moo-tee-LAHR)

mutilation   *f.* mutilación (moo-tee-lah-SYOHN)

mutual (adj.)   mutuo (MOO-twoh)

my (adj.)   *sing.* mi (MEE) / *pl.* mis (MEES)

myself   me (MEH) / yo mismo (YOH MEEZ-moh) ○*f.* -ma○

mysterious (adj.)   misterioso (mees-teh-RYOH-soh)

mystery   *m.* misterio (mees-TEH-ryoh)

mystic   *m.* místico (MEES-tee-koh) ○*f.* -ca○

mystic / mystical (adj.)   místico (MEES-tee-koh)

mysticism   *m.* misticismo (mees-tee-SEEZ-moh)

myth   *m.* mito (MEE-toh)

mythical (adj.)   mítico (MEE-tee-koh)

mythological (adj.)   mitológico (mee-toh-LOH-hee-koh)

mythology   *f.* mitología (mee-toh-loh-HEE-ah)

—N—

nadir   *m.* nadir (nah-DEER)

name to / appoint (to)   nombrar (nohm-BRAHR)

narcissism   *m.* narcisismo (nahr-see-SEEZ-moh)

narcissist   *m. & f.* narcisista (nahr-see-SEES-tah) ○(adj.) **narcissistic** []○

narcotic   *m.* narcótico (nahr-KOH-tee-koh) ○(adj.) []○

narrate / recount (to)   narrar (nah-RRAHR)

narration   *f.* narración (nah-rrah-SYOHN)

narrative (*account of*)   *f.* narrativa (nah-rrah-TEE-bah) ○(adj.) -vo○

narrator   *m.* narrador (nah-rrah-DOHR) ○*f.* -ra○

nasal (adj.)   nasal (nah-SAHL)

natal (adj.)   natal (nah-TAHL)

nation   *f.* nación (nah-SYOHN)

national (adj.)   nacional (nah-syoh-NAHL)

nationalism *m.* nacionalismo (nah-syoh-nah-LEEZ-moh) 💣

nationalist *m. & f.* nacionalista (nah-syoh-nah-LEES-tah) ○(adj.) **-tic** ▢○

nationality *f.* nacionalidad (nah-syoh-nah-lee-DAHD)

nationalization *f.* nacionalización (nah-syoh-nah-lee-sah-SYOHN)

nationalize (to) nacionalizar (nah-syoh-nah-lee-SAHR)

native / indigenous person *m. & f.* natural (nah-too-RAHL)

native (adj.) natal (nah-TAHL)

Nativity (*religion*) *f.* Natividad (nah-tee-bee-DAHD)

natural (adj.) natural (nah-too-RAHL)

naturalist *m. & f.* naturalista (nah-too-rah-LEES-tah)

naturalness *f.* naturalidad (nah-too-rah-lee-DAHD)

nature (*character of, physical realm*) *f.* naturaleza (nah-too-rah-LEH-sah)

nauseating (adj.) nauseabundo (naow-seh-ah-BOON-doh)

nautical (adj.) náutico (NAOW-tee-koh)

naval (adj.) naval (nah-BAHL)

navigable (adj.) navegable (nah-beh-GAH-bleh)

navigate / sail (to) navegar (nah-beh-GAHR)

navigation / seafaring *f.* navegación (nah-beh-gah-SYOHN)

navigator *m. & f.* navegante (nah-beh-GAHN-teh)

navy *f.* marina de guerra (mah-REE-nah deh GEH-rrah) 💣

nebulous / hazy / misty (adj.) nebuloso (neh-boo-LOH-soh)

necessary / essential (adj.) necesario (neh-seh-SAH-ryoh) 💣

necessitate (to) necesitar (neh-seh-see-TAHR) 💣

necessity / requirement *f.* necesidad (neh-seh-see-DAHD)

nectar *m.* néctar (NEHK-tahr)

need / require (to) necesitar (neh-seh-see-TAHR)

needy (adj.) necesitado (neh-seh-see-TAH-doh)

nefarious (adj.) nefario (neh-FAH-ryoh)

negate / deny (to) negar (neh-GAHR)

negation / denial *f.* negación (neh-gah-SYOHN)

negative (*reply or value*) / **denial** *f.* negativa (neh-gah-TEE-<u>b</u>ah) ↺(adj.) -vo↺
   ① **(photographic) negative**—*m.* negativo (neh-gah-TEE-<u>b</u>oh)

negligee *m.* negligé (neh-glee-HEH)

negligence / **neglect** *f.* negligencia (neh-glee-HEHN-syah)

negligent / **remiss** (adj.) negligente (neh-glee-HEHN-teh)

negotiable (adj.) negociable (neh-goh-SYAH-<u>b</u>leh)

negotiate / **bargain** (to) negociar (neh-goh-SYAHR)

negotiation / **parley** *f.* negociación (neh-goh-syah-SYOHN)

negotiator *m.* negociador (neh-goh-syah-<u>D</u>OHR) ↺*f.* -ra↺

neon (*gas*) *m.* neón (neh-OHN)

neon (*gas*) (adj.) de neon (deh neh-OHN)

neophyte *m.* neófito (neh-OH-fee-toh) ↺*f.* -ta↺

nepotism *m.* nepotismo (neh-poh-TEEZ-moh)

nerve (*anatomical*) *m.* nervio (NEHR-<u>b</u>yoh)

nerves / **jitters** *m.* nervios (NEHR-<u>b</u>yohs)

nervous / **jumpy** (adj.) nervioso (nehr-<u>B</u>YOH-soh)

nervousness *m.* nerviosismo (nehr-<u>b</u>yoh-SEEZ-moh)

net (*of calculation*) (adj.) neto (NEH-toh)

neurological *f.* neurológico (nehoo-roh-LOH-hee-koh)

neurologist *m.* neurólogo (nehoo-ROH-loh-goh) ↺*f.* -ga↺

neurology *f.* neurología (nehoo-roh-loh-HEE-ah)

neurosis *f.* neurosis (nehoo-ROH-sees)

neurotic / **fretful** (adj.) neurótico (nehoo-ROH-tee-koh)

neutral / **impartial** / **nonpartisan** (adj.) neutral (nehoo-TRAHL)

neutrality *f.* neutralidad (nehoo-trah-lee-<u>D</u>AH<u>D</u>)

neutralize (to) neutralizar (nehoo-trah-lee-SAHR)

new to / **inexperienced** (adj.) novato (noh-<u>B</u>AH-toh)

newlywed / **groom** *m.* novio (NOH-<u>b</u>yoh) ↺*f.* **bride** -via↺
   ① This oddly all-purpose word regarding various forms of "new" love can
   also be used to denote **boyfriend** / **girlfriend**, **sweetheart**, and **fiancé** /
   fiancée.

news   *f.* noticias (noh-TEE-syahs)

niche   *m.* nicho (NEE-choh) ·

nightclub   *m.* club nocturno (kloob nohk-TOOR-noh)

no   no (NOH)

nobility / peerage   *f.* nobleza (noh-BLEH-sah)

noble / illustrous (adj.)   noble (NOH-bleh)

nobleman / noblewomam   *m. & f.* noble (NOH-bleh)

nocturnal / night (adj.)   nocturno (nohk-TOOR-noh)

nocturne   *m.* nocturno (nohk-TOOR-noh)

node   *m.* nudo (NOO-doh)

nodule   *m.* nódulo (NOH-doo-loh)

nomenclature   *f.* nomenclatura (noh-mehn-klah-TOO-rah)

nominal (adj.)   nominal (noh-mee-NAHL)

nominalism   *m.* nominalismo (noh-mee-nah-LEEZ-moh)

nominative (*grammar*)   *m.* nominativo (noh-mee-nah-TEE-boh) ↻(adj.) ☐↻

nonaligned (adj.)   no alineado (noh ah-lee-neh-AH-doh) 💣

noncombatant   *m. & f.* no combatiente (noh kohm-bah-TYEHN-teh) ↻(adj.) ☐↻ 💣

nonconformist / maverick   *m. & f.* inconformista (een-kohn-fohr-MEES-tah) 💣

nonconformity   *f.* inconformidad (een-kohn-fohr-mee-DAHD) 💣

noncontagious (adj.)   no contagioso (noh kohn-tah-HYOH-soh) 💣

nondiscriminatory (adj.)   no discriminatorio (noh dis-kree-mee-nah-TOH-ryoh) 💣

nonessential (adj.)   no esencial (noh eh-sehn-SYAHL) 💣

nonexistence   *f.* inexistencia (een-ehg-sees-TEHN-syah)

inexistent (adj.)   inexistente (een-ehg-sees-TEHN-teh)

nonflammable (adj.)   no inflamable (noh een-flah-MAH-bleh) 💣

nonintervention   *f.* no intervención (noh een-tehr-behn-SYOHN) 💣

nonnegotiable (adj.)   no negociable (noh neh-goh-SYAH-bleh) 💣

nonproductive (adj.)   improductivo (eem-proh-dook-TEE-boh) 💣

nonresident   *m. & f.* no residente (noh reh-see-<u>D</u>EHN-teh) ↻(adj.) ☐↻ 🔥

nonsectarian / nondenominational (adj.)   no sectario (noh sehk-TAH-ryoh) 🔥

nonstandard (adj.)   no estándar (noh ehs-TAHN-dahr) 🔥

nonviolence   *f.* no violencia (no <u>b</u>yoh-LEHN-syah) 🔥

nonviolent (adj.)   no violento (noh <u>b</u>yoh-LEHN-toh) 🔥

norm / standard   *f.* norma (NOHR-mah)

normal / average / standard (adj.)   normal (nohr-MAHL)

normalcy / normality   *f.* normalidad (nohr-mah-lee-<u>D</u>AH<u>D</u>)

normalize (to)   normalizar (nohr-mah-lee-SAHR)

north   *m.* norte (NOHR-teh)

north / northern (adj.)   norte (NOHR-teh) / del norte (dehl NOHR-teh)

northeast   *m.* nordeste (nohr-<u>D</u>EHS-teh) / *m.* noreste (noh-REHS-teh)

northeast / northeastern (adj.)   nordeste (nohr-<u>D</u>EHS-teh) / del nordeste (dehl nohr-<u>D</u>EHS-te)

northwest   *m.* noroeste (noh-roh-EHS-teh)

northwest / northwestern (adj.)   noroeste (noh-roh-EHS-teh) / del noroeste (dehl noh-roh-EHS-teh)

nose   *f.* nariz (nah-REES)

nostalgia / homesickness   *f.* nostalgia (nohs-TAHL-hyah)

nostalgic / homesick (adj.)   nostálgico (nohs-TAHL-hee-koh)

not   no (NOH)

notable / noteworthy (adj.)   notable (noh-TAH-<u>b</u>leh)

notable (*person of note*) / notability (*person and quality of person*   *f.* notabilidad (noh-tah-<u>b</u>ee-lee-<u>D</u>AH<u>D</u>)

notary   *m.* notario (noh-TAH-ryoh)

note (*musical or correspondence*)   *f.* nota (NOH-tah)
  ① As commonly, a brief written communication is: *f.* **cartita** (kahr-TEE-tah).

note (*mention or perceive*) / notice (to)   notar (noh-TAHR)

notification / notice   *f.* notificación (noh-tee-fee-kah-SYOHN)

notify (to)   notificar (noh-tee-fee-KAHR)

notion / idea *f.* noción (noh-SYOHN)

notoriety *f.* notoriedad (noh-toh-ryeh-<u>DAHD</u>)

notorious (adj.) notorio (noh-TOH-ryoh)

novel (*book*) *f.* novela (noh-<u>B</u>EH-lah)

novel / original (adj.) novel (noh-<u>B</u>EHL) / (*Americanism*) novedoso (noh-<u>b</u>eh-<u>D</u>OH-soh)

novelist *m. & f.* novelista (noh-<u>b</u>eh-LEES-tah)

novelty / newness *f.* novedad (noh-<u>b</u>eh-<u>D</u>AHD)

novice / beginner *m.* novato (noh-<u>B</u>AH-toh) ◐*f.* -ta◐

novice (*religious*) *m.* novicio (noh-<u>B</u>EE-syoh) ◐*f.* -ia◐

nuclear (adj.) nuclear (noo-kleh-AHR)

nucleus *m.* núcleo (NOO-kleh-oh)

nude / naked / (adj.) desnudo (dehs-NOO-<u>d</u>oh) 💣

nudism *m.* nudismo (noo-DEEZ-moh)

nudist *m. & f.* nudista (noo-DEES-tah)

nudity *f.* desnudez (dehs-noo-<u>D</u>EHS) 💣

null / void / zero (adj.) nulo (NOO-loh)

numeric / numerical (adj.) numérico (noo-MEH-ree-koh)

numerous (adj.) numeroso (noo-meh-ROH-soh)

nuptial (adj.) nupcial (noop-SYAHL)

nuptials / wedding *f. pl.* nupcias (NOOP-syahs)

nutrient (adj.) nutriente (noo-TRYEHN-teh)
    ① **nutrient / nutriment**—*m.* alimento nutritivo (ah-lee-MEHN-toh noo-tree-TEE-<u>b</u>oh); **nourishment** (*food*)—*m.* alimento (ah-lee-MEHN-toh); **nourishment** (*feeding*)—*f.* alimentación (ah-lee-mehn-tah-SYOHN) / *f.* nutrición (noo-tree-SYOHN)

nutrify / nourish / nurture (to) nutrir (noo-TREER)

nutrition / nourishment *m.* nutrición (noo-tree-SYOHN)

nutritious (adj.) nutritivo (noo-tree-TEE-<u>b</u>oh)

nylon *m.* nilón (nee-LOHN)

—O—

oasis   *m.* oasis (oh-AH-sees)

obedience   *f.* obediencia (oh-<u>b</u>eh-<u>D</u>YEHN-syah)

obedient (adj.)   obediente (oh-<u>b</u>eh-<u>D</u>YEHN-teh)

obelisk   *m.* obelisco (oh-<u>b</u>eh-LEES-koh)

obese (adj.)   obeso (oh-<u>B</u>EH-soh) / gordo (GOHR-<u>d</u>oh)

obesity   *f.* obesidad (oh-<u>b</u>eh-see-<u>D</u>AH<u>D</u>) / gordura (gohr-<u>D</u>OO-rah)

obey (to)   obedecer (oh-<u>b</u>eh-<u>d</u>eh-SEHR)

obfuscate (to)   ofuscar (oh-foos-KAHR) 💣

obituary   *m.* obituario (oh-<u>b</u>ee-TWAH-ryoh)

object   *m.* objeto (oh<u>b</u>-HEH-toh)

object (to)   objetar (oh<u>b</u>-heh-TAHR)

objection   *f.* objeción (oh<u>b</u>-heh-SYOHN)

objective / aim / target   *m.* objetivo (oh<u>b</u>-heh-TEE-<u>b</u>oh)

objective / impartial (adj.)   objetivo (oh<u>b</u>-heh-TEE-<u>b</u>oh)

objectivity   *f.* objetividad (oh<u>b</u>-heh-tee-<u>b</u>ee-<u>D</u>AH<u>D</u>)

obligate / oblige / compel (to)   obligar (oh-<u>b</u>lee-GAHR)

obligation / duty   *f.* obligación (oh-<u>b</u>lee-gah-SYOHN)

obligatory / mandatory (adj.)   obligatorio (oh-<u>b</u>lee-gah-TOH-ryoh)

oblique (*slanting*) (adj.)   oblicuo (oh-<u>B</u>LEE-kwoh)

obliterate (to)   obliterar (oh-<u>b</u>lee-teh-RAHR)

obliteration   *f.* obliteración (oh-<u>b</u>lee-teh-rah-SYOHN)

oblong (adj.)   oblongo (oh-BLOHN-goh)

obscene (adj.)   obsceno (oh<u>bs</u>-SEH-noh)

obscenity / profanity   *f.* obscenidad (oh<u>bs</u>-seh-nee-<u>D</u>AH<u>D</u>)

obscure / dim / murky (adj.)   oscuro (ohs-KOO-roh) 💣

obscure / cloud / darken (to)   oscurecer (ohs-koo-reh-SEHR) 💣

obscurity / murkiness   *f.* oscuridad (ohs-koo-ree-<u>D</u>AH<u>D</u>) 💣

observance   *f.* observancia (oh<u>b</u>-sehr-<u>B</u>AHN-syah)

observant (adj.)   observador (oh<u>b</u>-sehr-<u>b</u>ah-<u>D</u>OHR)

observation (*sighting or remark*)   *f.* observación (oh<u>b</u>-sehr-<u>b</u>ah-SYOHN)

observatory   *m.* observatorio (oh<u>b</u>-sehr-<u>b</u>ah-TOH-ryoh)

observe (to)   observar (oh<u>b</u>-sehr-<u>B</u>AHR)

observer   *m.* observador (oh<u>b</u>-sehr-<u>b</u>ah-<u>D</u>OHR) ↻*f.* -ra↺

obsess (to)   obsesionar (oh<u>b</u>-seh-syoh-NAHR)

obsession   *f.* obsesión (oh<u>b</u>-seh-SYOHN)

obsessive (adj.)   obsesivo (oh<u>b</u>-seh-SEE-<u>b</u>oh)

obsolescence   *f.* obsolescencia (oh<u>b</u>-soh-lehs-SEHN-syah)

obsolescent (adj.)   obsolescente (oh<u>b</u>-soh-lehs-SEHN-teh)

obsolete (adj.)   obsolento (oh<u>b</u>-soh-LEHN-toh)

obstacle / difficulty   *f.* obstáculo (oh<u>b</u>s-TAH-koo-loh)

obstetrics   *f.* obstetricia (ohbs-teh-TREE-syah)

obstinate / headstrong (adj.)   obstinado (oh<u>b</u>s-tee-NAH-<u>d</u>oh)

obstruct / bar / block (to)   obstruir (oh<u>b</u>s-TRWEER)

obstruction   *f.* obstrucción (oh<u>b</u>s-troohk-SYOHN)

obtain / procure (to)   obtener (oh<u>b</u>-teh-NEHR)

obvious (adj.)   obvio (OH<u>B</u>-<u>b</u>yoh)

occasion   *f.* ocasión (oh-kah-SYOHN) 💣

occasional (adj.)   ocasional (oh-kah-syoh-NAHL) 💣

occult / hidden (adj.)   oculto (oh-KOOL-toh) 💣

occupant   *m. & f.* ocupante (oh-koo-PAHN-teh)

occupation (*vocation*) / occupancy   *f.* ocupación (oh-koo-pah-SYOHN) 💣

occupy (*be in, live in, or make busy*) (to)   ocupar (oh-koo-PAHR)

occur / happen (to)   ocurrir (oh-koo-RREER)

occurrence   *f.* ocurrencia (oh-koo-RREHN-syah)

ocean   *m.* océano (oh-SEH-ah-noh)

oceanography   *f.* oceanografía (oh-seh-ah-noh-grah-FEE-ah)

octagon   *m.* octágono (ohk-TAH-goh-noh) ↻(adj.) **octagonal** -nal↺

octave *f.* octava (ohk-TAH-<u>b</u>ah)

ocular (adj.)   ocular (oh-koo-LAHR)

ode *f.* oda (OH-<u>d</u>ah)

odious / obnoxious / hateful (adj.)   odioso (oh-<u>D</u>YOH-soh)

odium / hatred *m.* odio (OH-<u>d</u>yoh)
    ① (to) **hate**—odiar (oh-<u>D</u>YAHR)

odor / scent / smell *m.* olor (oh-LOHR) 💣

offend (*feelings or propriety*) (to)   ofender (oh-fehn-<u>D</u>EHR) 💣

offense (*insult or transgression*) *f.* ofensa (oh-FEHN-sah) 💣

(take) offense (to)   ofenderse (oh-fehn-<u>D</u>EHR-seh) 💣

offensive (*military or sport status*) *f.* ofensiva (oh-fehn-SEE-<u>b</u>ah) 💣

offensive / objectionable (adj.)   ofensivo (oh-fehn-SEE-<u>b</u>oh) 💣

offer *f.* oferta (oh-FEHR-tah) 💣

offer (to)   ofrecer (oh-freh-SEHR) 💣

office (*business quarters*) / **bureau** *f.* oficina (oh-fee-SEE-nah) 💣

office (*position*) / **trade** *m.* oficio (oh-FEE-syoh) 💣

officer (*military or corporate*) *m.* oficial (oh-fee-SYAHL) 💣

official *m. & f.* oficial (oh-fee-SYAHL) ↻(adj.) ▯↻ 💣
    ① Related noncognate: **official**—*m.* funcionario (foon-syoh-NAH-ryoh)

officiate (to)   oficiar (oh-fee-SYAHR)

officious (adj.)   oficioso (oh-fee-SYOH-soh)

ogre *m.* ogro (OH-groh)

oil *m.* óleo (OH-leh-oh)

olfactory (adj.)   olfatorio (ohl-fah-TOH-ryoh) / olfativo (ohl-fah-TEE-<u>b</u>oh)

olive *f.* oliva (oh-LEE-<u>b</u>ah)

ominous (adj.)   ominoso (oh-mee-NOH-soh)

omission *f.* omisión (oh-mee-SYOHN)

omit (to)   omitir (oh-mee-TEEHR)

omnipotence *f.* omnipotencia (ohm-nee-poh-TEHN-syah)

omniscient (adj.)   omnisciente (ohm-nees-SYEHN-teh)

onerous (adj.)   oneroso (oh–neh–ROH–soh)

onyx   *m.* ónix (OH–neeks)

opal   *m.* ópalo (OH–pah–loh)

opaque (adj.)   opaco (oh–PAH–koh)

opera   *f.* ópera (OH–peh–rah)

operate (*medically or functionally*) (to)   operar (oh–peh–RAHR)

operation (*surgery*)   *f.* operación (oh–peh–rah–SYOHN)

operational (adj.)   operacional (oh–peh–rah–syoh–NAHL)

operative (adj.)   operativo (oh–peh–rah–TEE–<u>b</u>oh)

operator   *m.* operador (oh–peh–rah–<u>D</u>OHR) ↻*f.* –ra↻

operetta   *f.* opereta (oh–peh–REH–tah) M

opinion / belief / judgment   *f.* opinión (oh–pee–NYOHN)

opium   *m.* opio (OH–pyoh)

opponent   *m. & f.* oponente (oh–poh–NEHN–teh) 💣

opportune / timely (adj.)   oportuno (oh–pohr–TOO–noh) 💣

opportunist   *m. & f.* oportunista (oh–pohr–too–NEES–tah) 💣

opportunity   *f.* oportunidad (oh–pohr–too–nee–<u>D</u>AH<u>D</u>) 💣

oppose (to)   oponerse a (oh–poh–NEHR–seh ah) 💣

opposite (adj.)   opuesto (oh–PWEHS–toh) 💣

opposition   *f.* oposición (oh–poh–see–SYOHN) 💣

oppression   *f.* opresión (oh–preh–SYOHN) 💣

oppressive / harsh (adj.)   opresivo (oh–preh–SEE–<u>b</u>oh) 💣

oppressor   *m.* opresor (oh–preh–SOHR) ↻*f.* –ra↻ 💣

opt (to)   optar (ohp–TAHR)

optic / optical (adj.)   óptico (OHP–tee–koh)

optician   *m.* óptico (OHP–tee–koh) ↻*f.* –ca↻ 💣

optics   *f.* óptica (OHP–tee–kah)

optimal (adj.)   óptimo (OHP–tee–moh)

optimism   *m.* optimismo (ohp–tee–MEEZ–moh)

optimist   *m. & f.* optimista (ohp–tee–MEES–tah) ↻(adj.) **optimistic** ☐↻

option   *f.* opción (ohp-SYOHN)

optional (adj.)   optativo (ohp-tah-TEE-<u>b</u>oh)

opulence   *f.* opulencia (oh-poo-LEHN-syah)

opulent (adj.)   opulento (oh-poo-LEHN-toh)

opus   *m.* opus (OH-poos)

or   o (OH)

oral (adj.)   oral (oh-RAHL)

oration / prayer (!)   *f.* oración (oh-rah-SYOHN)

orator   *m.* orador (oh-rah-<u>D</u>OHR) ↻*f.* -ra↻

oratory (*art of speech*)   *f.* oratoria (oh-rah-TOH-ryah) / (*religion*) oratorio (oh-rah-TOH-ryoh)

orbit   *f.* órbita (OHR-<u>b</u>ee-tah)

orbit (to)   orbitar (ohr-<u>b</u>ee-TAHR)

orbital (adj.)   orbital (ohr-<u>b</u>ee-TAHL)

orchestra   *f.* orquesta (ohr-KEHS-tah) ↻(adj.) orchestral -al↻ 💣

orchestrate (to)   orquestar (ohr-kehs-TAHR) 💣

orchestration   *f.* orquestación (ohr-kehs-tah-SYOHN) 💣

orchid   *f.* orquídea (ohr-KEE-<u>d</u>eh-ah)

ordain (to)   ordenar (ohr-<u>d</u>eh-NAHR)

order / command   *f.* orden (OHR-<u>d</u>ehn)

order (*neatness or sequence*)   *m.* orden (OHR-<u>d</u>ehn)

order (*command*) / straighten up (to)   ordenar (ohr-<u>d</u>eh-NAHR)

orderly / neat (adj.)   ordenado (ohr-<u>d</u>eh-NAH-<u>d</u>oh)

ordinance   *f.* ordenanza (ohr-<u>d</u>eh-NAHN-sah)

ordinary / commonplace (adj.)   ordinario (ohr-<u>d</u>ee-NAH-ryoh)

organ (*musical or anatomical*)   *m.* órgano (OHR-gah-noh)

organic (adj.)   orgánico (ohr-GAH-nee-koh)

organism   *m.* organismo (ohr-gah-NEEZ-moh)

organist   *m. & f.* organista (ohr-gah-NEES-tah)

organization (*formal body*)   *f.* organización (ohr-gah-nee-sah-SYOHN)

organize (to)   organizar (ohr-gah-nee-SAHR)

orgasm   *m.* orgasmo (ohr-GAHZ-moh)

orgy   *f.* orgía (ohr-HEE-ah)

orient (to)   orientar (oh-ryehn-TAHR)

Orient / (the) East (*global region*)   *m.* Oriente (oh-RHYEN-teh)

Oriental / Eastern (*Asian*) (adj.)   oriental (oh-ryehn-TAHL)

orientation   *f.* orientación (oh-ryehn-tah-SYOHN)

orifice   *m.* orificio (oh-ree-FEE-syoh)

origin / fount / source   *m.* origen (oh-ree-HEHN)

original   *m.* original (oh-ree-hee-NAHL) ↻(adj.) ☐↻

originality   *f.* originalidad (oh-ree-hee-nah-lee-<u>D</u>AH<u>D</u>)

originate (to)   originar (oh-ree-hee-NAHR)

ornament   *m.* ornamento (ohr-nah-MEHN-toh)

ornament (to)   ornamentar (ohr-nah-mehn-TAHR)

ornamental (adj.)   ornamental (ohr-nah-mehn-TAHL)

ornamentation   *f.* ornamentación (ohr-nah-mehn-tah-SYOHN)

orphan   *m.* huérfano (WHER-fah-noh) ●※

orphanage   *m.* orfanato (ohr-fah-NAH-toh)

orthodoxy   *f.* ortodoxia (ohr-toh-DOHG-sya) ↻(adj.) **orthodox** -xo↻

orthopedic (adj.)   ortopédico (ohr-toh-PEH-<u>d</u>ee-koh)

oscillate / swing (to)   oscilar (ohs-see-LAHR)

oscillation   *f.* oscilación (ohs-see-lah-SYOHN)

osmosis   *f.* ósmosis (OHS-moh-sees)

ostensible (adj.)   ostensible (ohs-tehn-SEE-<u>b</u>leh)

ostentation / flashiness   *f.* ostentación (ohs-tehn-tah-SYOHN)

ostentatious / showy (adj.)   ostentoso (ohs-tehn-TOH-soh)

ostracism   *m.* ostracismo (ohs-trah-SEEZ-moh)

oval   *m.* óvalo (OH-<u>b</u>ah-loh)

oval (adj.)   oval (oh-<u>B</u>AHL) / ovalado (oh-<u>b</u>ah-LAH-<u>d</u>oh)

ovation   *f.* ovación (oh-<u>b</u>ah-SYOHN)

overture *f.* obertura (oh-<u>b</u>ehr-TOO-rah) 💣

ovulate (to) ovular (oh-<u>b</u>oo-LAHR)

ovulation *f.* ovulación (oh-<u>b</u>oo-lah-SYOHN)

ovum *m.* óvulo (OH-<u>b</u>oo-loh)

oxidation / rust *f.* oxidación (ohk-see-<u>d</u>ah-SYOHN)

oxidize / rust (to) oxidar (ohk-see-<u>D</u>AHR)

oxidized / rusty (adj.) oxidado (ohk-see-<u>D</u>AH-<u>d</u>oh)

oxygen *m.* oxígeno (ohk-SEE-heh-noh)

oyster *f.* ostra (OHS-trah)

ozone *m.* ozono (oh-SOH-noh)

—P—

pace (*speed or step / stride*) *m.* paso (PAH-soh)

pacific / peaceful / peaceable (adj.) pacífico (pah-SEE-fee-koh)

pacifism *m.* pacifismo (pah-see-FEEZ-moh)

pacifist *m. & f.* pacifista (pah-see-FEES-tah)

pacify / calm / still (to) pacificar (pah-see-fee-KAHR)

pack (to) empacar (ehm-pah-KAHR)

packet / package *m.* paquete (pah-KEH-teh)
 ① Related: **parcel post**—*m.* paquete postal (pah-KEH-teh pos-TAHL)

pact *m.* pacto (PAHK-toh)

pagan / heathen *m.* pagano (pah-GAH-noh) ⊃*f.* -na⊃ ⊃ (adj.) ☐⊃

paganism *m.* paganismo (pah-gah-NEEZ-moh)

page (*book leaf*) *f.* página (PAH-hee-nah)

paint (*mixture to paint with*) *f.* pintura (peen-TOO-rah)

paint (*artistically or practically*) (to) pintar (peen-TAHR)

painter (*of artistic pieces or houses*) *m.* pintor (peen-TOHR) ⊃*f.* -ra⊃

painting (*piece of art*) *f.* pintura (peen-TOO-rah)

pair (*of objects*) *m.* par (PAHR)

pair (*of people or animals*) / **couple** *f.* pareja (pah-REH-hah)

pajamas *m.* pijama (pee-HAH-mah)

palace / mansion *m.* palacio (pah-LAH-syoh)

palate (*sense of taste*) *m.* paladar (pah-lah-<u>D</u>AHR)

palette *f.* paleta (pah-LEH-tah)

palliative (adj.) paliativo (pah-lyah-TEE-<u>b</u>oh) 🔥

pallid / pale / pasty / wan (adj.) pálido (PAH-lee-<u>d</u>oh) 🔥

palm (*of hand*) *f.* palma (PAHL-mah)

palm tree *f.* palmera (pahl-MEH-rah)

palpable (adj.) palpable (pahl-PAH-<u>b</u>leh)

palpitate / pulsate / throb (to) palpitar (pahl-pee-TAHR)

palpitation *f.* palpitación (pahl-pee-tah-SYOHN)

pamphlet *m.* panfleto (pahn-FLEH-toh) 🔥

panacea *f.* panacea (pah-nah-SEH-ah)

pancake (*Americanism*) *m.* panqueque (pahn-KEH-keh)

pandemonium *m.* pandemonio (pahn-deh-MOH-nyoh)

panel (*enlisted group*) *m.* panel (pah-NEHL)

paneling (*of wall*) *m. pl.* paneles (pah-NEH-lehs)

panic *m.* pánico (PAH-nee-koh)

panorama / prospect / view *m.* panorama (pah-noh-RAH-mah)

panoramic (adj.) panorámico (pah-noh-RAH-mee-koh)

pantomime *f.* pantomima (pahn-toh-MEE-mah)

pants / trousers *m. pl.* pantalones (pahn-tah-LOH-nehs)

pap *f.* papilla (pah-PEE-yah)

papal (adj.) papal (pah-PAHL)

paper (*material or specific document*) *m.* papel (pah-PEHL)

paradise *m.* paraíso (pah-rah-EE-soh)

paradox *m.* paradoja (pah-rah-<u>D</u>OH-hah)

paradoxical (adj.) paradójico (pah-rah-<u>D</u>OH-hee-koh)

paraffin *f.* parafina (pah-rah-FEE-nah) 🔥

paragraph *m.* párrafo (PAH-rrah-foh)

parakeet   *m.* periquito (peh-ree-KEE-toh)

parallel   *m.* paralelo (pah-rah-LEH-loh) ◑(adj.) ▢◑ ◆

paralysis   *f.* parálisis (pah-RAH-lee-sees)

paralyze (to)   paralizar (pah-rah-lee-SAHR)

parameter   *m.* parámetro (pah-RAH-meh-troh)

paranoia   *f.* paranoia (pah-rah-NOH-yah) ◑(adj.) **paranoid** -ico◑

parapet   *m.* parapeto (pah-rah-PEH-toh)

paraphernalia   *f.* parafernalia (pah-rah-fehr-NAH-lyah) ◆

paraphrase   *f.* paráfrasis (pah-RAH-frah-sees)

paraphrase (to)   parafrasear (pah-rah-frah-seh-AHR)

paraplegic   *m.* parapléjico (pah-rah-PLEH-hee-koh) ◑*f.* -ca◑ ◑(adj.) ▢◑

parasite   *m.* parásito (pah-RAH-see-toh)

parasitic / parasitical (adj.)   parásito (pah-RAH-see-toh) / parasitario (pah-rah-see-TAH-ryoh)

pardon / forgiveness   *m.* perdón (pehr-DOHN)

pardon / forgive (to)   perdonar (pehr-doh-NAHR)

parenthesis   *m.* paréntesis (pah-REHN-teh-sees)

parenthetic (adj.)   parentético (pah-rehn-TEH-tee-koh)

pariah / outcast   *m. & f.* paria (PAH-ryah)

parity   *f.* paridad (pah-ree-<u>D</u>AH<u>D</u>)

park   *m.* parque (PAHR-keh)

park (to)   parquear (pahr-keh-AHR)

parka   *f.* parka (PAHR-kah)

parliament   *m.* parlamento (pahr-lah-MEHN-toh)

parliamentary (adj.)   parlamentario (pahr-lah-mehn-TAH-ryoh)

parochial (adj.)   parroquial (pah-rroh-KYAHL)
   ① Related: **parish**—*f.* parroquia (pah-RROH-kyah)

parody / spoof   *f.* parodia (pah-ROH-<u>d</u>yah)

parody (to)   parodiar (pah-roh-<u>D</u>YAHR)

parquet   *m.* parqué (pahr-KEH)

part (*portion / segment*)   *f.* parte (PAHR-teh)
   ① **(in) part / partly**—en parte (ehn PAHR-teh)

partial to / biased / incomplete (adj.)   parcial (pahr-SYAHL)

partiality   *f.* parcialidad (pahr-see-ah-lee-<u>D</u>AH<u>D</u>)

participant   *m. & f.* participante (pahr-tee-see-PAHN-teh)

participate (to)   participar (pahr-tee-see-PAHR)

participation   *f.* participación (pahr-tee-see-pah-SYOHN)

particle   *f.* partícula (pahr-TEE-koo-lah)

particular (adj.)   particular (pahr-tee-koo-LAHR)

parting / leaving   *f.* partida (pahr-TEE-<u>d</u>ah)

partisan   *m.* partisano (pahr-tee-SAH-noh) ↻*f.* -na↻

party (*political, not social*)   *m.* partido (pahr-TEE-<u>d</u>oh)

pass (*permitting document*)   *m.* pase (PAH-seh) 💣

pass (to)   pasar (pah-SAHR) 💣
   ① Two closely related noncognates are: (to) **walk**—pasear (pah-seh-AHR);
   and **walk / stroll**—*m.* paseo (pah-SEH-oh).

passable (*adequate / acceptable*) (adj.)   pasable (pah-SAH-<u>b</u>leh) 💣

passage (*of music / literature*) **/ passageway**   *m.* pasaje (pah-SAH-heh) 💣
   ① **aisle / corridor / hallway / (interior) passageway**—*m.* pasillo (pah-SEE-yoh) 💣

passenger   *m.* pasajero (pah-sah-HEH-roh) ↻*f.* -ra↻ 💣

passion   *f.* pasión (pah-SYOHN) 💣

passionate / ardent (adj.)   apasionado (ah-pah-syoh-NAH-<u>d</u>oh) 💣

passive (adj.)   pasivo (pah-SEE-<u>b</u>oh) 💣

passport   *m.* pasaporte (pah-sah-POHR-teh) 💣

past   *m.* pasado (pah-SAH-<u>d</u>oh) ↻(adj.) ☐ ↻

paste / pasta / dough (!)   *f.* pasta (PAHS-tah)

pastime / avocation   *m.* pasatiempo (pah-sah-TYEHM-poh)

pastor (*religion*) **/ minister / shepherd** (!)   *m.* pastor (pahs-TOHR)

pasture   *f.* pastura (pahs-TOO-rah) **/** *m.* pasto (PAHS-toh)

patch   *m.* parche (PAHR-cheh) 💣

patent *f.* patente (pah-TEHN-teh)

patent (to) patentar (pah-tehn-TAHR)

paternal / fatherly (adj.) paternal (pah-tehr-NAHL)

paternity / parenthood / fatherhood *f.* paternidad (pah-tehr-nee-<u>D</u>AH<u>D</u>)

pathetic (adj.) patético (pah-TEH-tee-koh)

pathological (adj.) patológico (pah-toh-LOH-hee-koh)

pathologist *m.* patólogo (pah-TOH-loh-goh) ↻*f.* -ga↻

pathology *f.* patología (pah-toh-loh-HEE-ah)

pathos *m.* patetismo (pah-teh-TEEZ-moh)

patience / forbearance *f.* paciencia (pah-SYEHN-syah)

patient / forbearing (adj.) paciente (pah-SYEHN-teh)

patient (*medical client*) *m. & f.* paciente (pah-SYEHN-teh)

patriarch *m.* patriarca (pah-TRYAHR-kah)

patrimony *f.* patrimonio (pah-tree-MOH-nyoh)

patriot *m. & f.* patriota (pah-TRYOH-tah)
    ① A related noncognate: **homeland / native land**—*f.* patria (PAH-tryah)

patriotic (adj.) patriótico (pah-TRYOH-tee-koh)

patriotism *m.* patriotismo (pah-tryoh-TEEZ-moh)

patrol *f.* patrulla (pah-TROO-yah)

patrol / police (*an area*) (to) patrullar (pah-troo-YAHR)

patron (*underwriter*) **/ sponsor** *m.* padrino (pah-<u>D</u>REE-noh) ↻*f.* madrina (mah-<u>D</u>REE-nah)↻

patronage (*sponsorship*) *m.* patrocinio (pah-troh-SEE-nyoh)

paunch / belly *f.* panza (PAHN-sah)

pause (to) pausar (paow-SAHR)

pause / lull *f.* pausa (PAOW-sah)

pave (to) pavimentar (pah-<u>b</u>ee-mehn-TAHR)

pavement *m.* pavimento (pah-<u>b</u>ee-MEHN-toh)

pavilion *m.* pabellon (pah-<u>b</u>eh-YOHN) 💣

pay / wages *f.* paga (PAH-gah) 💣

pay / repay (to)   pagar (pah-GAHR) 💣

payable / due (adj.)   pagadero (pah-gah-<u>D</u>EH-roh) 💣

payment   *m.* pago (PAH-goh) 💣

PC (*personal computer*)   *m.* PC (PEE SEE)

pear   *f.* pera (PEH-rah)

pearl   *f.* perla (PEHR-lah)

pecan (*botany*)   *f.* pacana (pah-KAH-nah)

peccadillo   *m.* pecadillo (peh-kah-<u>D</u>EE-yoh) 💣

peck (to)   picar (pee-KAHR)

peculiar (adj.)   peculiar (peh-koo-LYAHR)

peculiarity / quirk   *f.* peculiaridad (peh-koo-lyah-ree-<u>D</u>AH<u>D</u>)

pedal   *m.* pedal (peh-<u>D</u>AHL)

pedal (to)   pedalear (peh-<u>d</u>ah-leh-AHR)

pedant   *m. & f.* pedante (peh-<u>D</u>AHN-teh) ↻(adj.) **pedantic /
pedantical** *f*↻

pedestal   *m.* pedestal (peh-<u>d</u>ehs-TAHL)

pediatric (adj.)   pediátrico (peh-<u>D</u>YAH-tree-koh)

pedigree (*for animals*)   *m.* pedigrí (peh-<u>d</u>ee-GREE)

peel (to)   pelar (peh-LAHR)

peer / equal   *m.* par (PAHR) / igual (ee-GWAHL)

pejorative (adj.)   peyorativo (peh-yoh-rah-TEE-<u>b</u>oh)

penal (adj.)   penal (peh-NAHL)

penalize (to)   penalizar (peh-nah-lee-SAHR)

penalty   *f.* penalidad (peh-nah-lee-<u>D</u>AH<u>D</u>)

pending (adj.)   pendiente (pehn-<u>D</u>YEHN-teh)

pendulum   *m.* péndulo (PEHN-<u>d</u>oo-loh)

penetrate / permeate / pierce (to)   penetrar (peh-neh-TRAHR)

penetrating / pervasive (adj.)   penetrante (peh-neh-TRAHN-teh)

penetration (*physical or mental*)   *f.* penetración (peh-neh-trah-SYOHN)

peninsula   *f.* península (peh-NEEN-soo-lah)

penis *m.* pene (PEH-neh)

penitence / penance *f.* penitencia (peh-nee-TEHN-syah)

penitent *m. & f.* penitente (peh-nee-TEHN-teh) ○(adj.) ☐○

penitentiary *f.* penitenciaría (peh-nee-tehn-syah-REE-ah)

(be) pensive / think (to) pensar (pehn-SAHR)
    ① **thinker**—*m.* pensador (pehn-sah-<u>D</u>OHR) ○*f.* –ra○

pensive / thoughtful (adj.) pensativo (pehn-sah-TEE-<u>b</u>oh)

pensiveness / cognition *m.* pensamiento (pehn-sah-MYEHN-toh)

people *m.* pueblo (PWEH-<u>b</u>loh)

per (*for each*) **/ for / via** por (POHR)

per capita (adj.) per cápita (pehr KAH-pee-tah) / por cabeza (pohr kah-BEH-sah)

perceive (to) percibir (pehr-see-<u>B</u>EER)

percent *m.* por ciento (pohr SYEHN-toh) ○(adj.) ☐○

percentage *m.* porcentaje (pohr-sehn-TAH-heh)

perceptible (adj.) perceptible (pehr-sehp-TEE-<u>b</u>leh)

perception *f.* percepción (pehr-sehp-SYOHN)

perch (*roost or fish*) *f.* percha (PEHR-chah)

percussion *f.* percusión (pehr-koo-SYOHN)

perdition / damnation / doom *f.* perdición (pehr-<u>d</u>ee-SYOHN)

perennial / recurrent (adj.) perenne (peh-REHN-neh)

perfect / flawless (adj.) perfecto (pehr-FEHK-toh)

perfect (to) perfeccionar (pehr-fehk-syoh-NAHR)

perfection *f.* perfección (pehr-fehk-SYOHN)

perfectionist *m. & f.* perfeccionista (pehr-fehk-syoh-NEES-tah)

perfume / fragrance *m.* perfume (pehr-FOO-meh)

perfume (to) perfumar (pehr-foo-MAHR)

perfumed / scented (adj.) perfumado (pehr-foo-MAH-<u>d</u>oh)

perfumery *f.* perfumería (pehr-foo-meh-REE-ah)

perimeter *m.* perímetro (peh-REE-meh-troh)

period (*of time*) / stint   *m.* período (peh-REE-oh-<u>d</u>oh)

periodic / periodical (adj.)   periódico (peh-RYOH-<u>d</u>ee-koh)

peripheral (adj.)   periférico (peh-ree-FEH-ree-koh)

periphery   *f.* periferia (peh-ree-FEH-ryah)

perish (to)   perecer (peh-reh-SEHR)

perjury   *m.* perjurio (pehr-HOO-ryoh)

permanence   *f.* permanencia (pehr-mah-NEHN-syah)

permanent (*hair treatment*)   *f.* permanente (pehr-mah-NEHN-teh)

permanent (adj.)   permanente (pehr-mah-NEHN-teh)

permeability   *f.* permeabilidad (pehr-meh-ah-<u>b</u>ee-lee-<u>D</u>AH<u>D</u>)

permeable (adj.)   permeable (pehr-meh-AH-<u>b</u>leh)

permissible (adj.)   permisible (pehr-mee-SEE-<u>b</u>leh) ♦

permission / consent   *m.* permiso (pehr-MEE-soh) ♦

permissive (adj.)   permisivo (pehr-mee-SEE-<u>b</u>oh) ♦

permit   *m.* permiso (pehr-MEE-soh) / licencia (lee-SEHN-syah)

permit / allow (to)   permitir (pehr-mee-TEER)

perpendicular   *f.* perpendicular (pehr-pehn-dee-koo-LAHR) ↻(adj.) ▯↻

perpetrate (to)   perpetrar (pehr-peh-TRAHR)

perpetual (adj.)   perpetuo (pehr-PEH-twoh)

perpetuate (to)   perpetuar (pehr-peh-TWAHR)

perpetuity   *f.* perpetuidad (pehr-peh-twee-<u>D</u>AH<u>D</u>)

perplexed (adj.)   perplejo (pehr-PLEH-hoh)

perplexity / quandary   *f.* perplejidad (pehr-pleh-hee-<u>D</u>AH<u>D</u>)

persecute / chase (!) / pursue (!) (to)   perseguir (pehr-seh-GHEER)

persecution / pursuit (!)   *f.* persecución (pehr-seh-koo-SYOHN) / perseguimiento (pehr-seh-ghee-MYEHN-toh)

perseverance   *f.* perseverancia (pehr-seh-<u>b</u>eh-RAHN-syah)

persevere (to)   perseverar (pehr-seh-<u>b</u>eh-RAHR)

persist / remain (*continue unchanged*) (to)   persistir (pehr-sees-TEER)

persistent (adj.)   persistente (pehr-sees-TEHN-teh)

person *f.* persona (pehr-SOH-nah)

personal (adj.) personal (pehr-soh-NAHL)

personality *f.* personalidad (pehr-soh-nah-lee-_DAHD_)

personalize (to) personalizar (pehr-soh-nah-lee-SAHR)

personification / epitome *f.* personificación (pehr-soh-nee-fee-kah-SYOHN)

personify / epitomize (to) personificar (pehr-soh-nee-fee-KAHR)

personnel / staff *m.* personal (pehr-soh-NAHL)

perspective / outlook *f.* perspectiva (pehrs-pehk-TEE-_b_ah)

perspicacious / perceptive (adj.) perspicaz (pehrs-pee-KAHS)

perspicacity / insight *f.* perspicacia (pehrs-pee-KAH-syah)

perspiration *f.* transpiración (trahns-pee-rah-SYOHN) 💣

perspire (to) transpirar (trahns-pee-RAHR) 💣

persuade / prevail upon (to) persuadir (pehr-swah-_D_EER)

persuasion / persuasiveness *f.* persuasión (pehr-swah-SYOHN)

persuasive (adj.) persuasivo (pehr-swah-SEE-_b_oh)

pertinence *f.* pertinencia (pehr-tee-NEHN-syah)

pertinent / relevant (adj.) pertinente (pehr-tee-NEHN-teh)

perturb / disturb (to) perturbar (pehr-toor-_B_AHR)

perverse (adj.) perverso (pehr-_B_EHR-soh)

perversion *f.* perversión (pehr-_b_ehr-SYOHN)

pervert (to) pervertir (pehr-_b_ehr-TEER)

pessimism *m.* pesimismo (peh-see-MEEZ-moh) 💣

pessimist *m. & f.* pesimista (peh-see-MEES-tah) ↻(adj.) **pessimistic** ☐↻ 💣

pest (*insect or animal*) *f.* peste (PEHS-teh)

pesticide *m.* pesticida (pehs-tee-SEE-dah)

pestilence *f.* pestilencia (pehs-tee-LEHN-syah)

petition (to) peticionar (peh-tee-syoh-NAHR)

petition / request *f.* petición (peh-tee-SYOHN)

petitioner *m.* peticionario (peh-tee-syoh-NAH-ryoh) ↻*f.* -ia↻

petrify (to)   petrificar (peh-tree-fee-KAHR)

petroleum   *m.* petróleo (peh-TROH-leh-oh)

phantasm / ghost   *m.* fantasma (fahn-TAHZ-mah) 💣

phantasmal / ghostly (adj.)   fantasmal (fahn-tahz-MAHL) 💣

pharaoh   *m.* faraón (fah-rah-OHN) 💣

pharmacist / druggist   *m.* farmacéutico (fahr-mah-SEHOO-tee-koh) ○*f.* -ca○ 💣

pharmacological (adj.)   farmacológico (fahr-mah-koh-LOH-hee-koh)

pharmacologist   *m.* farmacólogo (fahr-mah-KOH-loh-goh) ○*f.* -ga○ 💣

pharmacology   *f.* farmacología (fahr-mah-koh-loh-HEE-ah) 💣

pharmacy / drugstore   *f.* farmacia (fahr-MAH-syah) 💣

phase   *f.* fase (FAH-seh) 💣

phenomenal (adj.)   fenomenal (feh-noh-meh-NAHL) 💣

phenomenon   *m.* fenómeno (feh-NOH-meh-noh) 💣

philanthropic (adj.)   filantrópico (fee-lahn-TROH-pee-koh) 💣

philanthropist   *m.* filántropo (fee-LAHN-troh-poh) ○*f.* -pa○💣

philanthropy   *f.* filantropía (fee-lahn-troh-PEE-ah) 💣

philosopher   *m.* filósofo (fee-LOH-soh-foh) ○*f.* -fa○💣

philosophic / philosophical (adj.)   filosófico (fee-loh-SOH-fee-koh) 💣

philosophize (to)   filosofar (fee-loh-soh-FAHR) 💣

philosophy   *f.* filosofía (fee-loh-soh-FEE-ah) 💣

phlegm   *f.* flema (FLEH-mah) 💣

phobia   *f.* fobia (FOH-<u>b</u>yah) 💣

phonetics (*grammar*)   *f.* fonética (foh-NEH-tee-kah) ○(adj.) **phonetic** -co○ 💣

phosphorus / match (!)   *m.* fósforo (FOHS-foh-roh) 💣

photocopier   *f.* fotocopiadora (foh-toh-koh-pyah-<u>D</u>OH-rah) 💣

photocopy   *f.* fotocopia (foh-toh-KOH-pyah) 💣

photocopy (to)   fotocopiar (foh-toh-koh-PYAHR) 💣

photogenic (adj.)   fotogénico (foh-toh-HEH-nee-koh) 💣

photograph   *f.* fotografía (foh-toh-grah-FEE-ah) / foto (FOH-toh) 💣

photograph (to)   fotografiar (foh-toh-grah-FYAHR) 💣

photographer   *m.* fotógrafo (foh-TOH-grah-foh) ☉*f.* -fa☉💣

photographic (adj.)   fotográfico (foh-toh-GRAH-fee-koh) 💣

photography   *f.* fotografía (foh-toh-grah-FEE-ah) 💣

phrase / sentence   *f.* frase (FRAH-seh) 💣

physicist   *m.* físico (FEE-see-koh) ☉*f.* -ca☉ 💣

physics (*science of*)   *f.* física (FEE-see-kah) ☉(adj.) **physical** -co☉ 💣

physiologic / physiological (adj.)   fisiológico (fee-syoh-LOH-hee-koh) 💣

physiologist   *m.* fisiólogo (fee-SYOH-loh-goh) ☉*f.* -ga☉ 💣

physiology   *f.* fisiología (fee-syoh-loh-HEE-ah) 💣

physique   *m.* físico (FEE-see-koh) 💣

pianist   *m. & f.* pianista (pyah-NEES-tah)

piano   *m.* piano (PYAH-noh)

picnic   *m.* picnic (PEEK-neek)

pictorial (adj.)   pictórico (peek-TOH-ree-koh)

picturesque / scenic (adj.)   pintoresco (peen-toh-REHS-koh) 💣

piece   *f.* pieza (PYEH-sah)

piety   *f.* piedad (pyeh-<u>D</u>AH<u>D</u>)

pigment   *m.* pigmento (peeg-MEHN-toh)

pigmentation   *f.* pigmentación (peeg-mehn-tah-SYOHN)

pile / stack   *f.* pila (PEE-lah)

pill   *f.* píldora (PEEL-doh-rah)

pillar / mainstay   *m.* pilar (pee-LAHR)

pilot   *m.* piloto (pee-LOH-toh)

pilot (to)   pilotar (pee-loh-TAHR)

pine tree   *m.* pino (PEE-noh)

pinnacle   *m.* pináculo (pee-NAH-koo-loh)

pint   *f.* pinta (PEEN-tah)

pioneer   *m.* pionero (pyoh-NEH-roh) ☉*f.* -ra☉

pious (adj.)   piadoso (pyah-<u>D</u>OH-soh)

pipe (*for smoking*)   *f.* pipa (PEE-pah)

piracy   *f.* piratería (pee-rah-teh-REE-ah)

pirate   *m.* pirata (pee-RAH-tah)

pirouette   *f.* pirueta (pee-RWEH-tah)

pistachio   *m.* pistacho (pees-TAH-choh)

piston   *m.* pistón (pees-TOHN)

pituitary (adj.)   pituitario (pee-twee-TAH-ryoh)

pivot   *m.* pivote (pee-BOH-teh)

pizza   *f.* pizza (PEES-sah)

placate / appease (to)   aplacar (ah-plah-KAHR) 💣

placebo   *m.* placebo (plah-SEH-boh)

placenta   *f.* placenta (plah-SEHN-tah)

placid (adj.)   plácido (PLAH-see-doh)

plagiarism   *m.* plagio (PLAH-hyoh)

plagiarist   *m.* plagiario (plah-HYAH-ryoh) ◑*f.* –ria◒

plagiarize (to)   plagiar (plah-HYAHR)

plague   *f.* plaga (PLAH-gah)

plague / afflict (to)   plagar (plah-GAHR)

plan / scheme   *m.* plan (PLAHN)

plan / scheme / schedule (to)   planear (plah-neh-AHR)

plane (*flat-level surface*)   *m.* plano (PLAH-noh)

plane / smooth (to)   aplanar (ah-plah-NAHR) 💣

planet   *m.* planeta (plah-NEH-tah)

planetary   *m.* planetario (plah-neh-TAH-ryoh)

plankton   *m.* plancton (PLAHNK-tohn)

plant (*flora or factory*)   *f.* planta (PLAHN-tah)

plant / pot / sow (to)   plantar (plahn-TAHR)

plantation   *f.* plantación (plahn-tah-SYOHN)

plaque (*dental accretion or memorial tablet*)   *f.* placa (PLAH-kah)

plasma   *m.* plasma (PLAHZ-mah)

plastic *m.* plástico (PLAHS-tee-koh)

plastic / pliable / flexible (adj.) plástico (PLAHS-tee-koh)

plate (*dish or serving of food***)** *m.* plato (PLAH-toh)
    ① **saucer**—*m.* platillo (plah-TEE-yoh)

platform / dais *f.* plataforma (plah-tah-FOHR-mah)

platinum *m.* platino (plah-TEE-noh)

pleasure / enjoyment *m.* placer (plah-SEHR) / gusto (GOOS-toh)

plebeian (adj.) plebeyo (pleh-BEH-yoh)

plethora *f.* plétora (PLEH-toh-rah)

plot / conspiracy *m.* complot (kohm-PLOHT) / *f.* conspiración
(kohns-pee-rah-SYOHN) 💣

plumage *m.* plumaje (ploo-MAH-heh)

plumber *m.* plomero (ploh-MEH-roh) ↻*f.* -ra↻

plumbing *f.* plomería (ploh-meh-REE-ah)

plume / feather *f.* pluma (PLOO-mah)

plural *m.* plural (ploo-RAHL) ↻(adj.) *f*↻

plurality *f.* pluralidad (ploo-rah-lee-<u>D</u>AH<u>D</u>)

pluralize (to) pluralizar (ploo-rah-lee-SAHR)

pneumatic (adj.) neumático (nehoo-MAH-tee-koh) 💣
    ① As a masculine noun, this term also means **(vehicular) tire** and
jackhammer.

poem *m.* poema (poh-EH-mah)

poet *m.* poeta (poh-EH-tah)

poetess *f.* poetisa (poh-eh-TEE-sah)

poetic (adj.) poético (poh-EH-tee-koh)

poetry *f.* poesía (poh-eh-SEE-ah)

pogrom *m.* pogromo (poh-GROH-moh)

point (*detail***) / period (***punctuation***)** *m.* punto (POON-toh)

point (*sharp end***) / tip** *f.* punta (POON-tah)

point (*a weapon***)** (to) apuntar (ah-poon-TAHR)

point of view / standpoint *m.* punto de vista (POON-toh deh <u>B</u>EES-tah)

pointed (adj.)   puntiagudo (poon-tyah-GOO-<u>d</u>oh)

pointer (*device*)   *m.* puntero (poon-TEH-roh)

polar (adj.)   polar (poh-LAHR)

polarize (to)   polarizar (poh-lah-ree-SAHR)

pole (*geographic, magnetic, or electrical*)   *m.* polo (POH-loh)

pole (*rod*)   *m.* palo (PAH-loh) 💣

polemicist   *m. & f.* polemista (po-leh-MEES-tah)

polemicize (to)   polemizar (poh-leh-mee-SAHR)

polemics   *f.* polémica (poh-LEH-mee-kah) ↻(adj.) **polemic / polemical** -co↻

police / police force   *f.* policía (poh-lee-SEE-ah)

police officer   *m.* (agente de) policía ([ah-HEHN-teh deh] poh-lee-SEE-ah)

policy (*political / governmental*)   *f.* política (poh-LEE-tee-kah)

policy (*insurance contract*)   *f.* póliza (POH-lee-sah)

polish (to)   pulir (poo-LEER)

political science   *f.* ciencia política (SYEHN-syah poh-LEE-tee-kah)

politician   *m.* político (poh-LEE-tee-koh) ↻(adj.) **political** □↻

politics   *f.* política (poh-LEE-tee-kah)

pollen   *m.* polen (POH-lehn) 💣

pollinate (to)   polinizar (poh-lee-nee-SAHR) 💣

pollination   *f.* polinización (poh-lee-nee-sah-SYOHN) 💣

polo   *m.* polo (POH-loh)

polyester   *m.* poliéster (poh-LYEHS-tehr)

pomp / pageantry   *f.* pompa (POHM-pah)

pomposity   *f.* pomposidad (pohm-poh-see-<u>D</u>AH<u>D</u>)

pompous (adj.)   pomposo (pohm-POH-soh)

pontiff   *m.* pontífice (pohn-TEE-fee-seh)

pontificate (to)   pontificar (pohn-tee-fee-KAHR)

pontoon   *m.* pontón (pohn-TOHN)

pony   *m.* poni (POH-nee)

poor / unfortunate (adj.)   pobre (POH-<u>b</u>reh) 💣

pope   *m.* papa (PAH-pah)

popular (*well liked, prevalent*) / pop (adj.)   popular (poh-poo-LAHR)

popularity   *f.* popularidad (poh-poo-lah-ree-<u>D</u>AH<u>D</u>)

populate (to)   poblar (poh-<u>B</u>LAHR)

population   *f.* población (poh-<u>b</u>lah-SYOHN)

populous (adj.)   populoso (poh-poo-LOH-soh)

porcelain   *f.* porcelana (pohr-seh-LAH-nah)

porch   *m.* porche (POHR-cheh)

pore   *m.* poro (POH-roh)

pornographic (adj.)   pornográfico (pohr-noh-GRAH-fee-koh)

pornography   *f.* pornografía (pohr-noh-grah-FEE-ah)

porous (adj.)   poroso (poh-ROH-soh)

portable (adj.)   portátil (pohr-TAH-teel)

portal / doorway   *m.* portal (pohr-TAHL)
   ① **door / gate / gateway**—*f.* puerta (PWEHR-tah)

porter / doorman   *m.* portero (pohr-TEH-roh) ⟳*f.* -ra⟳

portico / porch   *m.* pórtico (POHR-tee-koh)

portion / share / serving   *f.* porción (pohr-SYOHN)

pose (*pretence*)   *f.* pose (POH-seh)

pose / posture (to)   posar (poh-SAHR)

position / location   *f.* posición (poh-see-SYOHN)

positive / affirmative (adj.)   positivo (poh-see-TEE-<u>b</u>oh)

possess / own (to)   poseer (poh-seh-EHR)

possession (*holding of*)   *f.* posesión (poh-seh-SYOHN)

possessive (adj.)   posesivo (poh-seh-SEE-<u>b</u>oh)

possessor / owner   *m.* poseedor (poh-seh-eh-<u>D</u>OHR) ⟳*f.* -ra⟳

possibility / chance   *f.* posibilidad (poh-see-<u>b</u>ee-lee-<u>D</u>AH<u>D</u>)

possible / prospective (adj.)   posible (poh-SEE-<u>b</u>leh)

post / (*large, thick*) pole   *m.* poste (POHS-teh)

post (*position*) *m.* puesto (PWEHS-toh)

postal (adj.) postal (pohs-TAHL)

postcard *f.* postal (pohs-TAHL)

poster / placard *m.* póster (POHS-tehr)

posterity *f.* posteridad (pohs- teh-ree-<u>D</u>AH<u>D</u>)

postgraduate *m.* postgraduado (pohst-grah-<u>D</u>WAH-<u>d</u>oh) ⟳*f.* -da⟳

posthumous (adj.) póstumo (POHS-too-moh)

postoperative (adj.) postoperatorio (pohs-toh-peh-rah-TOH-ryoh)

postpone / delay / put off (to) posponer (pohs-poh-NEHR)

postscript *f.* posdata (pohs-<u>D</u>AH-tah) / *m.* post scriptum (POHST SKREEP-toom)

postulate (to) postular (pohs-too-LAHR)

posture / stance (*on an issue*) *f.* postura (pohs-TOO-rah)

pot *m.* pote (POH-teh) / *f.* olla (OH-yah)

potable / drinkable (adj.) potable (poh-TAH-<u>b</u>leh)

potato (*Americanism*) *f.* papa (PAH-pah) / (*in Spain*) *f.* patata (pah-TAH-tah)

potency *f.* potencia (poh-TEHN-syah)

potent / mighty / powerful (adj.) potente (poh-TEHN-teh)

potential / prospective *m.* potencial (poh-tehn-SYAHL) ⟳(adj.) ⬚⟳

potion *f.* poción (poh-SYOHN)

potpourri / medley *m.* popurrí (poh-poo-RREE)

practicable (adj.) practicable (prahk-tee-KAH-<u>b</u>leh)

practical (adj.) práctico (PRAHK-tee-koh)

practice (*custom or training exercise*) *f.* práctica (PRAHK-tee-kah)

practice (*employ skill or train for*) (to) practicar (prahk-tee-KAHR)

pragmatic (adj.) pragmático (prahg-MAH-tee-koh)

pragmatism (adj.) pragmatismo (prahg-mah-TEEZ-moh)

precarious (adj.) precario (preh-KAH-ryoh)

precaution *f.* precaución (preh-kaow-SYOHN)

precede (to) preceder (preh-seh-<u>D</u>EHR)

precedence *f.* precedencia (preh-seh-DEHN-syah)

precedent *m.* precedente (preh-seh-DEHN-teh)

preceding / foregoing (adj.) precedente (preh-seh-DEHN-teh)

precept *m.* precepto (preh-SEHP-toh)

precious / costly / valuable (adj.) precioso (preh-SYOH-soh)

precipice / cliff *m.* precipicio (preh-see-PEE-syoh)

precipitate / abrupt / hasty (adj.) precipitado (preh-see-pee-TAH-doh)

precipitate / hasten (to) precipitar (preh-see-pee-TAHR)

precipitation / rainfall *f.* precipitación (preh-see-pee-tah-SYOHN)

precise / exact (adj.) preciso (preh-SEE-soh)

precision *f.* precisión (preh-see-SYOHN)

precocious (adj.) precoz (preh-KOHS)

precocity *f.* precocidad (preh-koh-see-DAHD)

preconceive (to) preconcebir (preh-kohn-seh-BEER)

precondition *f.* precondición (preh-kohn-dee-SYOHN)

precook (to) precocinar (preh-koh-see-NAHR)

precursor / forerunner *m.* precursor (preh-koor-SOHR) ◑*f.* -ra◐

precursory (adj.) precursor (preh-koor-SOHR)

predator *m.* depredador (deh-preh-dah-DOHR) ◑*f.* -ra◐

predatory (adj.) depredador (deh-preh-dah-DOHR)

predecessor *m.* predecesor (preh-deh-seh-SOHR) ◑*f.* -ra◐

predestination *f.* predestinación (preh-dehs-tee-nah-SYOHN)

predestine / foreordain (to) predestinar (preh-dehs-tee-NAHR)

predetermine (to) predeterminar (preh-deh-tehr-mee-NAHR)

predict / forecast (to) predecir (preh-deh-SEER)

prediction / forecast *f.* predicción (preh-deek-SYOHN)

predilection *f.* predilección (preh-dee-lehk-SYOHN)

predispose (to) predisponer (preh-dees-poh-NEHR)

predisposition *f.* predisposición (preh-dees-poh-see-SYOHN)

predominance *m.* predominio (preh-doh-MEE-nyoh)

predominant (adj.)   predominante (preh-ḏoh-mee-NAHN-teh)

predominate (to)   predominar (preh-ḏoh-mee-NAHR)

preeminence   *f.* preeminencia (preh-eh-mee-NEHN-syah)

preeminent (adj.)   preeminente (preh-eh-mee-NEHN-teh)

prefabricated (adj.)   prefabricado (preh-fah-bree-KAH-ḏoh)

preface   *m.* prefacio (preh-FAH-syoh)

prefer (to)   preferir (preh-feh-REER)

preferable (adj.)   preferible (preh-feh-REE-ḇleh)

preference   *f.* preferencia (preh-feh-REHN-syah)

preferential (adj.)   preferencial (preh-feh-rehn-SYAHL)

prefix   *m.* prefijo (preh-FEE-hoh)

prehensile (adj.)   prensil (prehn-SEEL)

prehistoric / prehistorical (adj.)   prehistórico (preh-ees-TOH-ree-koh)

prejudge (to)   prejuzgar (preh-hoos-GAHR)

prejudice / bias   *m.* prejuicio (preh-HWEE-syoh) 💣

prejudice (to)   perjudicar (pehr-hoo-ḏee-KAHR) 💣

preliminary / prefatory (adj.)   preliminar (preh-lee-mee-NAHR)

prelude / preliminary   *m.* preludio (preh-LOO-ḏyoh)

premarital (adj.)   prematrimonial (preh-mah-tree-MOH-nyahl)

premature (adj.)   prematuro (preh-mah-TOO-roh)

premeditate (to)   premeditar (preh-meh-ḏee-TAHR)

premeditation   *f.* premeditación (preh-meh-ḏee-tah-SYOHN)

premise   *f.* premisa (preh-MEE-sah)

premium / bonus   *f.* prima (PREE-mah)

premonition   *f.* premonición (preh-moh-nee-SYOHN)

preoccupation   *f.* preocupación (preh-oh-koo-pah-SYOHN) 💣

preoccupied (adj.)   preocupado (preh-oh-koo-PAH-ḏoh) 💣

preparation (*arrangement for*)   *f.* preparación (preh-pah-rah-SYOHN)

preparation (*mixture*)   *m.* preparado (preh-pah-RAH-ḏoh)

preparatory (adj.)   preparatorio (preh-pah-rah-TOH-ryoh)

prepare / prime / coach (to)   preparar (preh-pah-RAHR)

prepared / ready (adj.)   preparado (preh-pah-RAH-<u>d</u>oh)

preponderance   *f.* preponderancia (preh-pohn-deh-RAHN-syah)

preponderant (adj.)   preponderante (preh-pohn-deh-RAHN-teh)

prerogative   *f.* prerrogativa (preh-rroh-gah-TEE-<u>b</u>ah)

presage / portent   *m.* presagio (preh-SAH-hyoh)

presage / portend (to)   presagiar (preh-sah-HYAHR)

preschool (adj.)   preescolar (preh-ehs-koh-LAHR)

presence   *f.* presencia (preh-SEHN-syah)

present (*current time*)   *m.* presente (preh-SEHN-teh)

present (*in attendance*) (adj.)   presente (preh-SEHN-teh)

present / introduce / tender (to)   presentar (preh-sehn-TAHR)

presentation / introduction   *f.* presentación (preh-sehn-tah-SYOHN)

preservation   *f.* preservación (preh-sehr-<u>b</u>ah-SYOHN)

preserve / save (*for later use*) (to)   preservar (preh-sehr-<u>B</u>AHR)

preside (to)   presidir (preh-see-<u>D</u>EER)

presidency   *f.* presidencia (preh-see-DEHN-syah)

president / chairman   *m.* presidente (preh-see-<u>D</u>EHN-teh) ◑*f.* -ta◑

presidential (adj.)   presidencial (preh-see-<u>d</u>ehn-SYAHL)

pressure   *f.* presión (preh-SYOHN)

pressure (to)   presionar (preh-syoh-NAHR)

pressurize (to)   presurizar (preh-soo-ree-SAHR)

prestige / stature   *m.* prestigio (prehs-TEE-hyoh)

prestigious (adj.)   prestigioso (prehs-tee-HYOH-soh)

presume / assume (to)   presumir (preh-soo-MEER)

presumed / supposed / so-called (adj.)   presunto (preh-SOON-toh)

presumption   *f.* presunción (preh-soon-SYOHN)

presuppose (to)   presuponer (preh-soo-poh-NEHR)

pretention / pretense   *f.* pretensión (preh-tehn-SYOHN)

pretentious (adj.)   pretencioso (preh-tehn-SYOH-soh)

prevail / triumph (to)   prevalecer (preh-<u>b</u>ah-leh-SEHR)

prevent / forestall (to)   prevenir (preh-<u>b</u>eh-NEER)

prevention   *f.* prevención (preh-<u>b</u>ehn-SYOHN)

preventive / precautionary (adj.)   preventivo (preh-<u>b</u>ehn-TEE-<u>b</u>oh)

previous (adj.)   previo (PREH-<u>b</u>yoh)

price / cost of / charge for   *m.* precio (PREH-syoh)

primary / first (adj.)   primario (pree-MAH-ryoh)

primate (*bishop*)   *m.* primado (pree-MAH-<u>d</u>oh)

primate (*animal*)   *m.* primate (pree-MAH-teh)

prime / first (adj.)   primero (pree-MEH-roh)

prime minister   *m.* primer ministro (pree-MEHR mee-NEES-troh)

primitive / primeval (adj.)   primitivo (pree-mee-TEE-<u>b</u>oh)

primordial (adj.)   primordial (pree-mohr-DYAHL)

prince   *m.* príncipe (PREEN-see-peh)

princess   *f.* princesa (preen-SEH-sah)

principal / capital / chief / (adj.)   principal (preen-see-PAHL)

principle (*basic tenet or ethic*)   *m.* principio (preen-SEE-pyoh)

print / print out (*via computer*) (to)   imprimir (eem-pree-MEER) 💣

priority   *f.* prioridad (pree-oh-ree-<u>D</u>AH<u>D</u>)

prism   *m.* prisma (PREEZ-mah)

prison   *f.* prisión (pree-SYOHN)

prisoner   *m.* prisionero (pree-syoh-NEH-roh) ↻*f.* -ra↻

pristine (adj.)   pristino (prees-TEE-noh)

privacy   *f.* privacidad (pree-<u>b</u>ah-see-<u>D</u>AH<u>D</u>)

private (adj.)   privado (pree-<u>B</u>AH-<u>d</u>oh)

privation / deprivation   *f.* privación (pree-<u>b</u>ah-SYOHN)

privilege   *m.* privilegio (pree-<u>b</u>ee-LEH-hyoh)

privileged (adj.)   privilegiado (pree-<u>b</u>ee-leh-HYAH-<u>d</u>oh)

prize / award   *m.* premio (PREH-myoh)

prize (adj.)   premiado (preh-MYAH-<u>d</u>oh)

pro / for *m.* pro (PROH)

probability / likelihood / odds *f.* probabilidad (proh-<u>b</u>ah-<u>b</u>ee-lee-<u>D</u>AH<u>D</u>)

probable / likely (adj.)   probable (proh-<u>B</u>AH-<u>b</u>leh)

problem / snag *m.* problema (proh-<u>B</u>LEH-mah)

problematic / problematical (adj.)   problemático (proh-<u>b</u>leh-MAH-tee-koh)

procedure *m.* procedimiento (proh-seh-<u>d</u>ee-MYEHN-toh)

proceed (to)   proceder (proh-seh-<u>D</u>EHR)

process / method / (*legal*) trial (!) *m.* proceso (proh-SEH-soh) 💣

process (to)   procesar (proh-seh-SAHR) 💣

procession *f.* procesión (proh-seh-SYOHN) 💣

proclaim / herald (to)   proclamar (proh-klah-MAHR)

proclamation *f.* proclamación (proh-kla-mah-SYOHN)

proclivity *f.* proclividad (proh-klee-<u>b</u>ee-<u>D</u>AH<u>D</u>)

procreate (to)   procrear (proh-kreh-AHR)

procreation *f.* procreación (proh-kreh-ah-SYOHN)

procure (to)   procurar (proh-koo-RAHR)

prodigal / lavish (adj.)   pródigo (PROH-<u>d</u>ee-goh)

prodigious (adj.)   prodigioso (proh-<u>d</u>ee-HYOH-soh)

prodigy *m.* prodigio (proh-<u>D</u>EE-hyoh)

produce / yield (to)   producir (proh-<u>d</u>oo-SEER)

producer *m.* productor (proh-<u>d</u>ook-TOHR) ↻*f.* -ra↻

product *m.* producto (proh-<u>D</u>OOK-toh)

production / output *f.* producción (proh-<u>d</u>ook-SYOHN)

productive (adj.)   productivo (proh-<u>d</u>ook-TEE-<u>b</u>oh)

productivity *f.* productividad (proh-<u>d</u>ook-tee-<u>b</u>ee-<u>D</u>AH<u>D</u>)

profane (adj.)   profano (proh-FAH-noh)

profane / desecrate (to)   profanar (proh-fah-NAHR)

profess (to)   profesar (proh-feh-SAHR) 💣

profession (*occupation*) *f.* profesión (proh-feh-SYOHN) 💣

professional / practitioner *m. & f.* profesional (proh-feh-syoh-NAHL) 💣

professional (adj.) profesional (proh-feh-syoh-NAHL) 💣

professionalism *m.* profesionalismo (proh-feh-syoh-nah-LEEZ-moh) 💣

professor *m.* profesor (proh-feh-SOHR) ↻ *f.* -ra↻ 💣

profile *m.* perfil (pehr-FEEL)

profound / deep (adj.) profundo (proh-FOON-doh)
① This term embraces both physical and conceptual depth: e.g., a deep lake or a deep thought. The word **deep**—hondo (OHN-doh) is used at least as often in reference to physical depth. The antonym is direct and comparative: (adj.) **shallow**—poco profundo (poh-koh proh-FOON-doh)—literally, "little deep."

profundity / depth *f.* profundidad (proh-foon-dee-<u>D</u>AH<u>D</u>)

profuse (adj.) profuso (proh-FOO-soh)

profusion *f.* profusión (proh-foo-SYOHN)

prognosticate / forecast (to) pronosticar (proh-nohs-tee-KAHR) 💣

prognostication / (medical) prognosis *m.* pronóstico (proh-NOHS-tee-koh) 💣

program / plan / schedule / syllabus *m.* programa (proh-GRAH-mah)

program (to) programar (proh-grah-MAHR)

programmer *m.* programador (proh-grah-mah-<u>D</u>OHR) ↻ *f.* -ra↻

progress *m.* progreso (proh-GREH-soh) 💣

progress (to) progresar (proh-greh-SAHR) 💣

progressive (adj.) progresivo (proh-greh-SEE-<u>b</u>oh)

prohibit / ban (to) prohibir (proh-ee-<u>B</u>EER)

prohibited / banned / forbidden (adj.) prohibido (proh-ee-<u>B</u>EE-<u>d</u>oh)

prohibition / ban *f.* prohibición (proh-ee-<u>b</u>ee-SYOHN)

prohibitive (adj.) prohibitivo (proh-ee-<u>b</u>ee-TEE-<u>b</u>oh)

project *m.* proyecto (proh-YEHK-toh) 💣

project (*plan or envision*) (to) proyectar (proh-yehk-TAHR) 💣

projectile *m.* proyectil (proh-yehk-TEEL)

projection *f.* proyección (proh-yehk-SYOHN) 💣

projector *m.* proyector (proh-yehk-TOHR)

proliferate (to) proliferar (proh-lee-feh-RAHR)

proliferation *f.* proliferación (proh-lee-feh-rah-SYOHN)

prolific (adj.) prolífico (proh-LEE-fee-koh)

prologue / foreword *m.* prólogo (PROH-loh-goh)

prolong / protract (to) prolongar (proh-lohn-GAHR)

prominence (*projection*) *f.* prominencia (proh-mee-NEHN-syah)

prominent (*jutting*) (adj.) prominente (proh-mee-NEHN-teh)

promiscuity *f.* promiscuidad (proh-mees-kwee-DAHD)

promiscuous (adj.) promiscuo (proh-MEES-kwoh)

promise / pledge / vow *f.* promesa (proh-MEH-sah)

promise (to) prometer (proh-meh-TEHR)

promising / rosy (adj.) prometedor (proh-meh-teh-DOHR)

promiser *m.* prometedor (proh-meh-teh-DOHR) ◯*f.* -ra◯

promontory *m.* promontorio (proh-mohn-TOH-ryoh)

promote (*advertise*) (to) promocionar (proh-moh-syoh-NAHR)

promote (*further*) / tout (to) promover (proh-moh-BEHR)

promoter *m.* promotor (proh-moh-TOHR) ◯*f.* -ra◯

promotion (*furtherance*) *f.* promoción (proh-moh-SYOHN)

promotional (adj.) promocional (proh-moh-syoh-NAHL)

prompt / fast / quick (adj.) pronto (PROHN-toh) / rápido (RAH-pee-doh)

promptness / promptitude *f.* prontitud (prohn-tee-TOOD)

pronounce / enunciate (to) pronunciar (proh-noon-SYAHR)

pronounced / marked (adj.) pronunciado (proh-noon-SYAH-doh)

pronunciation *f.* pronunciación (proh-noon-syah-SYOHN)

propaganda *f.* propaganda (proh-pah-GAHN-dah)

propel (to) propulsar (proh-pool-SAHR)

propensity / penchant *f.* propensión (proh-pehn-SYOHN)

property *f.* propiedad (proh-pyeh-DAHD)

prophecy *f.* profecía (proh-feh-SEE-ah)

prophesy / foretell (to)   profetizar (proh-feh-tee-SAHR)

prophet   *m.* profeta (proh-FEH-tah)

prophetess *f.* profetisa (proh-feh-TEE-sah)

prophetic / prophetical / portentious (adj.)   profético (proh-FEH-tee-koh)

propitious (adj.)   propicio (proh-PEE-syoh)

proportion / ratio (!) *f.* proporción (proh-pohr-SYOHN)

proportionate (adj.)   proporcional (proh-pohr-syoh-NAHL)

proposal (*general*)   *f.* propuesta (proh-PWEHS-tah)

propose (*suggest*) (to)   proponer (proh-poh-NEHR)

proposition *f.* proposición (proh-poh-see-SYOHN)

proprietary (adj.)   propietario (proh-pyeh-TAH-ryoh)

proprietor / owner   *m.* propietario (proh-pyeh-TAH-ryoh) ↻*f.* -ria↺

prosaic (adj.)   prosaico (proh-SEYE-koh)

proscribe (to)   proscribir (prohs-kree-_BEER_)

prose   *f.* prosa (PROH-sah)

proselyte / convert   *m.* prosélito (proh-SEH-lee-toh)

prosper / thrive (to)   prosperar (prohs-peh-RAHR)

prosperity / (*economic*) boom   *f.* prosperidad (prohs-peh-ree-_DAHD_)

prosperous / successful / well-to-do (adj.)   próspero (PROHS-peh-roh)

prosthesis *f.* prótesis (PROH-teh-sees)

prostitution *f.* prostitución (prohs-tee-too-SYOHN)

prostrate (adj.)   postrado (pohs-TRAH-_d_oh)

prostrate (to)   postrar (pohs-TRAHR)

prostration *f.* postración (pohs-trah-SYOHN)

protagonist   *m. & f.* protagonista (proh-tah-goh-NEES-tah)

protect / shelter / shield / mother (!) (to)   proteger (proh-teh-HEHR)

protection / safekeeping *f.* protección (proh-tehk-SYOHN)

protective / protecting (adj.)   protector (proh-tehk-TOHR)

protector   *m.* protector (proh-teht-TOHR) ↻*f.* **protectress** -ra↺

protégé *m.* protegido (proh-teh-HEE-doh) ↻*f.* **protégée** –da↻

protein *f.* proteína (proh-teh-EE-nah)

protest / outcry *f.* protesta (proh-TEHS-tah)

protest / remonstrate with (to) protestar (proh-tehs-TAHR)

protocol *m.* protocolo (proh-toh-KOH-loh)

prototype *m.* prototipo (proh-toh-TEE-poh)

protuberance / protrusion *f.* protuberanza (proh-too-_beh_-RAHN-sah)

prove / demonstrate / taste (to) probar (proh-_BAHR_) 💣

proverb *m.* proverbio (proh-_BEHR_-_byoh_)

proverbial (adj.) proverbial (proh-_behr_-_BYAHL_)

provide / supply (to) proveer (proh-_beh_-EHR)

providence *f.* providencia (proh-_bee_-_DEHN_-syah)

providential (adj.) (proh-_bee_-_dehn_-SYAHL)

provider / supplier *m.* proveedor (proh-_beh_-eh-_DOHR_) ↻*f.* –ra↻

province *f.* provincia (proh-_BEEN_-syah)

provincial (adj.) provincial (proh-_been_-SYAHL)

provincialism *m.* provincialismo (proh-_been_-syah-LEEZ-moh)

provision *f.* provisión (proh-_bee_-SYOHN)
    ① **provisions**—*f. pl.* provisiones (proh-_bee_-SYOH-nehs) / comestibles (koh-mehs-TEE-_blehs_) / víveres (BEE-_beh_-rehs) / vituallas (bee-TWAH-yahs)

provision (with) (to) aprovisionar (con / de) (ah-proh-_bee_-syoh-NAHR [kohn / deh]) / proveer (pro-_beh_-HER) 💣

provisional / temporary (adj.) provisional (proh-_bee_-syoh-NAHL)

provocation *f.* provocación (proh-_boh_-kah-SYOHN)

provocative (adj.) provocativo (proh-_boh_-kah-TEE-_boh_)

provoke / prompt (*induce*) (to) provocar (proh-_boh_-KAHR)

prow / bow (*of ship*) *f.* proa (PROH-ah)

proximate / near to (adj.) próximo (PROHK-see-moh)

proximity / closeness / nearness *f.* proximidad (prohk-see-mee-_DAHD_)

prudence / caution / providence (!) *f.* prudencia (proo-_DEHN_-syah)

prudent / politic / provident (!) (adj.) prudente (proo-_DEHN_-teh)

pseudonym / pen name   *m.* seudónimo (sehoo-<u>D</u>OH-nee-moh) 💣

psyche   *f.* psique (SEE-keh)

psychiatric (adj.)   psiquiátrico (see-KYAH-tree-koh)

psychiatrist   *m. & f.* psiquiatra (see-KYAH-tra)

psychiatry   *f.* psiquiatría (see-kyah-TREE-ah)

psychic / psychical (adj.)   psíquico (SEE-kee-koh)

psychoanalyse (to)   psicoanalizar (see-koh-ah-nah-lee-SAHR)

psychoanalysis   *f.* psicoanálisis (see-koh-ah-NAH-lee-sees)

psychoanalyst   *m. & f.* psicoanalista (see-koh-ah-nah-LEES-tah)

psychological (adj.)   psicológico (see-koh-LOH-hee-koh)

psychologist   *m.* psicólogo (see-KOH-loh-goh) ↺*f.* -ga↺

psychology   *f.* psicología (see-koh-loh-HEE-ah)

psychopath   *m. & f.* psicópata (see-KOH-pah-tah)

psychopathic (adj.)   psicopático (psee-koh-PAH-tee-koh)

psychosis   *f.* psicosis (see-KOH-sees)

psychotic   *m.* psicótico (see-KOH-tee-koh) ↺*f.* -ca↺ ↺(adj.) ▯↺

puberty   *f.* pubertad (poo-<u>b</u>ehr-TAH<u>D</u>)

public   *m.* público (POO-<u>b</u>lee-koh) ↺(adj.) ▯↺

publication / periodical   *f.* publicación (poo-<u>b</u>lee-kah-SYOHN)

publicist   *m. & f.* publicista (poo-<u>b</u>lee-SEES-tah)

publicity   *f.* publicidad (poo-<u>b</u>lee-see-<u>D</u>AH<u>D</u>)
  ① **hype** (*publicity*)—*m.* bombo publicitario (BOHM-boh poo-<u>b</u>lee-see-TAH-ryoh)

publicize (to)   publicitar (poo-<u>b</u>lee-see-TAHR)

publish / release (*book or statement*) (to)   publicar (poo-<u>b</u>lee-KAHR)

pudding   *m.* pudín (poo-<u>D</u>EEN)

puerile (adj.)   pueril (pweh-REEL)

pulley   *f.* polea (poh-LEH-ah)

pulmonary (adj.)   pulmonar (pool-moh-NAHR)

pulmonary organ / lung   *m.* pulmón (pool-MOHN)

pulp *f.* pulpa (POOL-pah)

pulpit *m.* púlpito (POOL-pee-toh)

pulsation *f.* pulsación (pool-sah-SYOHN)

pulse *m.* pulso (POOL-soh)

pulverize (to) pulverizar (pool-<u>b</u>eh-ree-SAHR)

pulverized material / dust / powder *m.* polvo (POHL-<u>b</u>oh)
   ① **(cosmetic) powder**—*m. pl.* polvos (POHL-<u>b</u>ohs)

punch (*fruit-based drink*) *m.* ponche (POHN-cheh)

punctual / prompt (adj.) puntual (poon-TWAHL)

punctuality *f.* puntualidad (poon-twah-lee-<u>D</u>AH<u>D</u>)

punctuate (to) puntuar (poon-TWAHR)

punctuation *f.* puntuación (poon-twah-SYOHN)

punishable (adj.) punible (poo-NEE-<u>b</u>leh)

punitive (adj.) punitivo (poo-nee-TEE-<u>b</u>oh)

pupil (*of the eye*) *f.* pupila (poo-PEE-lah)

pure / pristine / sheer (adj.) puro (POO-roh)

puree *m.* puré (poo-REH)

purgatory *m.* purgatorio (poor-gah-TOH-ryoh)

purge (to) purgar (poor-GAHR)

purification *f.* purificación (poo-ree-fee-kah-SYOHN)

purify (to) purificar (poo-ree-fee-KAHR)

puritan *m.* puritano (poo-ree-TAH-noh) ↻*f.* -na↻

puritan / puritanical (adj.) puritano (poo-ree-TAH-noh)

puritanism *m.* puritanismo (poo-ree-tah-NEEZ-moh)

purity *f.* pureza (poo-REH-sah)

purpose / intention *m.* propósito (proh-POH-see-toh)

putrid / rotten (adj.) podrido (poh-<u>D</u>REE-<u>d</u>oh) / pútrido (POO-tree-<u>d</u>oh)

putrefaction / rot *f.* putrefacción (poo-treh-fahk-SYOHN)

putrify / rot (to) pudrirse (poo-<u>D</u>REER-seh)

pyramid *f.* pirámide (pee-RAH-mee-<u>d</u>eh)

pyromania *f.* piromanía (pee-roh-mah-NEE-ah))

pyromaniac / firebug *m.* pirómano (pee-ROH-mah-noh) ⟳*f.* -na⟳

pyrotechnics / fireworks *f.* pirotecnia (pee-roh-TEHK-nyah)

—Q—

quadragenarian (adj.) *m.* cuadragenario (kwah-<u>d</u>rah-heh-NAH-ryoh) ⟳*f.* -ria⟳ ⟳(adj.) *f*⟳

Quadragesima (*religion*) *f.* Cuadragésima (kwah-<u>d</u>rah-HEH-see-mah)

quadrant *m.* cuadrante (kwah-<u>D</u>RAHN-teh) ●

quadratic / square (adj.) cuadrado (kwah-<u>D</u>RAH-<u>d</u>oh)

quadrille (*dance*) *f.* cuadrilla (kwah-DREE-yah) / (*card game*) *m.* cuatrillo (kwah-TREE-yoh)

quadruped *m.* cuadrúpedo (kwah-<u>D</u>ROO-peh-<u>d</u>oh) ⟳(adj.) ▯⟳●

quadruple (to) cuadruplicar (kwah-<u>d</u>roo-plee-KAHR) ●

quality / attribute *f.* cualidad (kwah-lee-<u>D</u>AH<u>D</u>) ●

quantity *f.* cantidad (kahn-tee-<u>D</u>AH<u>D</u>) ●

quarantine *f.* cuarentena (kwah-rehn-TEH-nah) ●

quart (*measure*) *m.* cuarto (de galón) (KWAHR-toh [deh gah-LOHN]) ●

quarter (*one fourth*) / room (*of house*) *m.* cuarto (KWAHR-toh) ●

quartet *m.* cuarteto (kwahr-TEH-toh) ●

question *f.* cuestión (kwehs-TYOHN) ●

questionable (adj.) cuestionable (kwehs-tyoh-NAH-<u>b</u>leh) ●

questionnaire *m.* cuestionario (kwehs-tyoh-NAH-ryoh) ●

quiet (*motionless*) (adj.) quieto (KYEH-toh)

quietude (*stillness*) *f.* quietud (kyeh-TOO<u>D</u>)

quintet *m.* quinteto (keen-TEH-toh)

quintuple (adj.) quíntuplo (KEEN-too-ploh)

quota *f.* cuota (KWOH-tah) ●

quotation (*of price*) *f.* cotización (koh-tee-sah-SYOHN) ●

quote (*a price*) (to)   cotizar (koh-tee-SAHR) 💣

quotidian / daily (adj.)   cotidiano (koh-tee-_DYAH-noh)

quotient   *m.* cociente (koh-SYEHN-teh) 💣

—R—

rabbi   *m.* rabí (rah-BEE) / *m.* rabino (rah-_BEE-noh)

rabid (adj.)   rabioso (rah-BYOH-soh)

rabies   *f.* rabia (RAH-byah)

race (*anthropological*)   *f.* raza (RAH-sah)

racial (adj.)   racial (rah-SYAHL)

racism   *m.* racismo (rah-SEEZ-moh)

racist   *m. & f.* racista (rah-SEES-tah)

racket (*for sports*)   *f.* raqueta (rah-KEH-tah)

radar   *m.* radar (rah-_DAHR)

radial (adj.)   radial (rah-_DYAHL)

radiant (adj.)   radiante (rah-_DYAHN-teh)

radiate (to)   irradiar (ee-rrah-_DYAHR) 💣

radiation   *f.* radiación (rah-_dyah-SYOHN)

radiator   *m.* radiador (rah-_dyah-_DOHR)

radical (*political*)   *m. & f.* radical (rah-_dee-KAHL) ↻(adj.) ☐↻

radio (*science, broadcasting*)   *f.* radio (RAH-dyoh)
    ① **radium / radius**—*m.* radio (RAH-_dyoh)

radioactive (adj.)   radiactivo (rah-_dyahk-TEE-_boh)

radioactivity   *f.* radiactividad (rah-dyahk-tee-_bee-_DAHD)

ramification   *f.* ramificación (rah-mee-fee-kah-SYOHN)

ramify (to)   ramificarse (rah-mee-fee-KAHR-seh)

ramp   *f.* rampa (RAHM-pah)

rancid (adj.)   rancio (RAHN-syoh)

rancor / spite / spleen   *m.* rencor (rehn-KOHR) 💣

rancorous (adj.)   rencoroso (rehn-koh-ROH-soh)

rank (*relative standing*)   *m.* rango (RAHN-goh)

rapacious (adj.)   rapaz (rah-PAHS)

rapid / fast (adj.)   rápido (RAH-pee-doh)

rapidity / speed   *f.* rapidez (rah-pee-DEHS)

rapids   *m. pl.* rápidos (RAH-pee-dohs)

rare / odd (adj.)   raro (RAH-roh)

rarity   *f.* rareza (rah-REH-sah)

rasp / scrape / scratch (to)   raspar (rahs-PAHR)
   ① **scratch**—*m.* rasguño (rahs-GOO-nyoh)

rat (*zoology*)   *f.* rata (RAH-tah)
   ① **mouse**—ratón *m.* (rah-TOHN)

rat trap / mousetrap   *f.* ratonera (rah-toh-NEH-rah)

ratification   *f.* ratificación (rah-tee-fee-kah-SYOHN)

ratify (to)   ratificar (rah-tee-fee-KAHR)

ration   *f.* ración (rah-SYOHN)

ration (to)   racionar (rah-syoh-NAHR)

rational (adj.)   racional (rah-syoh-NAHL)

rationalization   *f.* racionalización (rah-syoh-nah-lee-sah-SYOHN)

rationalize (to)   racionalizar (rah-syoh-nah-lee-SAHR)

rationalized / streamlined (adj.)   racionalizado (rah-syoh-nah-lee-SAH-doh)

ratty / worn / shabby (adj.)   raído (rah-EE-doh)

ray / beam / thunderbolt (!)   *m.* rayo (RAH-yoh)
   ① **streak / stripe**—*f.* raya (RAH-yah)

rayon   *m.* rayón (rah-YOHN)

react (to)   reaccionar (reh-ahk-syoh-NAHR)

reaction   *f.* reacción (reh-ahk-SYOHN)

reaffirm (to)   reafirmar (reh-ah-feer-MAHR) 💣

real / actual / true (adj.)   real (reh-AHL) / verdadero (behr-dah-DEH-roh)

realism   *m.* realismo (reh-ah-LEEZ-moh)

realist   *m. & f.* realista (reh-ah-LEES-tah)

realistic / matter-of-fact (adj.)   realista (reh-ah-LEES-tah)

reality *f.* realidad (reh-ah-lee-<u>DAHD</u>)

realization *f.* realización (reh-ah-lee-sah-SYOHN)

realize (*accomplish or gain*) (to) realizar (reh-ah-lee-SAHR)

really / truly realmente (reh-ahl-MEHN-teh)

reappearance *f.* reaparición (reh-ah-pah-ree-SYOHN) 💣

reason (*rationality*) *f.* razón (rah-SOHN)

reasonable (adj.) razonable (rah-soh-NAH-<u>bl</u>eh)

reasoning *m.* razonamiento (rah-soh-nah-MYEHN-toh)

rebel *m. & f.* rebelde (reh-<u>B</u>EHL-deh) ↻(adj.) **rebellious / wayward** ☐↻

rebel / revolt (to) rebelarse (reh-<u>b</u>eh-LAHR-seh)

rebellion / revolt *f.* rebelión (reh-<u>b</u>eh-LYOHN) 💣

recalcitrant (adj.) recalcitrante (reh-kahl-see-TRAHN-teh)

recapitulate / sum up (to) recapitular (reh-kah-pee-too-LAHR)

recede (to) retroceder (reh-troh-seh-<u>D</u>EHR) 💣

receipt (*voucher / act of receiving*) *m.* recibo (reh-SEE-<u>b</u>oh)

receive (to) recibir (reh-see-<u>B</u>EER)

receiver *m.* receptor (reh-sehp-TOHR) ↻*f.* -ra↻ / recibidor (reh-see-bee-DOHR) ↻*f.* -ra↻

recent (adj.) reciente (reh-SYEHN-teh)

receptacle *m.* receptáculo (reh-sehp-TAH-koo-loh)

reception (*receipt of / formal event*) *f.* recepción (reh-sehp-SYOHN)

receptionist *m. & f.* recepcionista (reh-sehp-syoh-NEES-tah)

receptive / responsive (!) (adj.) receptivo (reh-sehp-TEE-<u>b</u>oh)

recession *f.* recesión (reh-seh-SYOHN)

recharge (to) recargar (reh-kahr-GAHR)

rechargeable (adj.) recargable (reh-kahr-GAH-<u>bl</u>eh)

recipe *f.* receta (reh-SEH-tah)

recipient *m. & f.* recipiente (reh-see-PYEHN-teh) ↻(adj.) ☐↻ / *m.* recibidor (reh-see-<u>b</u>eh-DOHR) ↻*f.* -ra↻ ↻(adj.) ☐↻

reciprocal (adj.) recíproco (reh-SEE-proh-koh)

reciprocate (to) reciprocar (reh-see-proh-KAHR)

reciprocity *f.* reciprocidad (reh-see-proh-see-<u>D</u>AH<u>D</u>)

recital (*performance*) *m.* recital (reh-see-TAHL)

recitation *f.* recitación (reh-see-tah-SYOHN)

recite (to) recitar (reh-see-TAHR)

recline (on) (to) reclinarse (en) (reh-klee-NAHR-she [ehn])

recognition / acknowledgment / identification *m.* reconocimiento (reh-koh-noh-see-MYEHN-toh)

recognizable (adj.) reconocible (reh-koh-noh-SEE-<u>b</u>leh)

recognize (*acknowledge or identify*) (to) reconocer (reh-koh-noh-SEHR)

recommence / resume (to) recomenzar (reh-koh-mehn-SAHR)

recommend (to) recomendar (reh-koh-mehn-<u>D</u>AHR)

recommendation / testimonial *f.* recomendación (reh-koh-mehn-<u>d</u>ah-SYOHN)

recompense / reward *f.* recompensa (reh-kohm-PEHN-sah)

recompense / reward (to) recompensar (reh-kohm-pehn-SAHR)

reconcile (to) reconciliar (reh-kohn-see-LYAHR)

reconciliation *f.* reconciliación (reh-kohn-see-lyah-SYOHN)

recondition (to) reacondicionar (reh-ah-kohn-dee-syoh-NAHR)

reconnaissance *m.* reconocimiento (reh-koh-noh-see-MYEHN-toh)

reconnoiter / scout (to) reconocer (reh-koh-noh-SEHR)

reconsider (to) reconsiderar (reh-kohn-see-<u>d</u>eh-RAHR)

reconsideration *f.* reconsideración (reh-kohn-see-<u>d</u>eh-rah-SYOHN)

recourse *m.* recurso (reh-KOOR-soh)

recover / repossess (to) recobrar (reh-koh-<u>B</u>RAHR)

re-create (to) recrear (reh-kreh-AHR)

recreation (*playtime in school*) *m.* recreo (reh-KREH-oh)

recreational (adj.) recreativo (reh-kreh-ah-TEE-<u>b</u>oh)

recrimination *f.* recriminación (reh-kree-mee-nah-SYOHN)

recruit *m.* recluta (reh-KLOO-tah) 💣
   ⓘ **recruitment**—*f.* recluta (reh-KLOO-tah)

recruit (to) reclutar (reh-kloo-TAHR) 💣

recruitment / recruiting *m.* reclutamiento (reh-kloo-tah-MYEHN-toh) 💣

rectangle *m.* rectángulo (rehk-TAHN-goo-loh)

rectangular (adj.) rectangular (rehk-tahn-goo-LAHR)

rectify (to) rectificar (rehk-tee-fee-KAHR)

rectitude / righteousness *f.* rectitud (rehk-tee-TOO<u>D</u>)

rectory / parsonage *f.* rectoría (rehk-toh-REE-ah)

recuperate / recover / recoup (!) (to) recuperar (reh-koo-peh-RAHR)

recuperation / retrieval (!) *m.* recuperación (reh-koo-peh-rah-SYOHN)

recurrent (adj.) recurrente (reh-koo-RREHN-teh)

recycle (to) reciclar (reh-see-KLAHR) 💣

redeem (to) redimir (reh-<u>d</u>ee-MEER)

redeemer *m.* redentor (reh-<u>d</u>ehn-TOHR) ↻*f.* -ra↻ 💣

redemption *f.* redención (reh-<u>d</u>ehn-SYOHN) 💣

rediscover (to) redescubrir (reh-<u>d</u>ehs-koo-<u>BR</u>EER)

reduce (*lessen*) (to) reducir (reh-<u>d</u>oo-SEER)

reduction (*lowering*) *f.* reducción (reh-<u>d</u>ook-SYOHN)

redundant (adj.) redundante (reh-<u>d</u>oon-<u>D</u>AHN-teh)

reevaluate (to) revaluar (reh-<u>b</u>ah-LWAHR) 💣

reevaluation *f.* revaluación (reh-<u>b</u>ah-lwah-SYOHN) 💣

refer (to) (to) referirse (a) (reh-feh-REER-she [ah])

reference *f.* referencia (reh-feh-REHN-syah)
    ⓘ **references / credentials**—*f. pl.* referencias (reh-feh-REHN-syahs)

referendum *m.* referéndum (reh-feh-REHN-doom)

refinance (to) refinanciar (reh-fee-nahn-SYAHR)

refine (to) refinar (reh-fee-NAHR)

refined / cultured (adj.) refinado (reh-fee-NAH-<u>d</u>oh)

refinement *m.* refinamiento (reh-fee-nah-MYEHN-toh)

refinery *f.* refinería (reh-fee-neh-REE-ah)

reflect / mirror (to) reflejar (reh-fleh-HAHR)

reflection (*image*) *m.* reflejo (reh-FLEH-hoh)

reflection (*meditation*)   *f.* reflexión (reh-flehk-SYOHN)

reflecting (*physical*) (adj.)   reflectante (reh-flehk-TAHN-teh)

reflective (adj.)   (*physical quality*) reflector (reh-flehk-TOHR) / (*state of mind*) reflexivo (reh-flehk-SEE-<u>b</u>oh)

reflector / searchlight (!)   *m.* reflector (reh-flehk-TOHR)

reflex   *m.* reflejo (reh-FLEH-hoh)

reform / reformation   *f.* reforma (reh-FOHR-mah)

reform (to)   reformar (reh-fohr-MAHR)

reformatory   *m.* reformatorio (reh-fohr-mah-TOH-ryoh)

reformer   *m.* reformador (reh-fohr-mah-<u>D</u>OHR) ◑*f.* -ra◐

refresh / freshen (to)   refrescar (reh-frehs-KAHR)

refreshments / light snacks   *m. pl.* refrescos (reh-FREHS-kohs)

refrigerate (to)   refrigerar (reh-free-heh-RAHR)

refrigeration   *f.* refrigeración (reh-free-heh-rah-SYOHN)

refrigerator / freezer (!)   *m.* refrigerador (reh-free-heh-rah-<u>D</u>OHR)

refuge / haven / sanctuary   *m.* refugio (reh-FOO-hyoh)

refugee   *m.* refugiado (reh-foo-HYAH-<u>d</u>oh) ◑*f.* -da◐

refuse / decline / deny (to)   rehusar (reh-oo-SAHR)
  ① Related noncognate: **refusal**—*m.* rechazo (ree-CHAH-soh) 💣

refutation / rebuttal   *f.* refutación (reh-foo-tah-SYOHN)

refute / disprove / rebut (to)   refutar (reh-foo-TAHR)

regenerate (to)   regenerar (reh-heh-neh-RAHR)

regeneration   *f.* regeneración (reh-heh-neh-rah-SYOHN)

regimen / regime   *m.* régimen (REH-hee-mehn)

regiment   *m.* regimento (reh-hee-MEHN-toh)

region / (geographic) area   *f.* región (reh-HYOHN)

regional (adj.)   regional (reh-hyoh-NAHL)

register / registry   *m.* registro (reh-HEES-troh)

register / record (to)   registrar (reh-hees-TRAHR)

registration   *m.* registro (reh-HEES-troh)

registry / records　*m.* registro (reh-HEES-troh)

regress / return (to)　regresar (reh-greh-SAHR) / retroceder (reh-troh-seh-DEHR)

regressive (adj.)　regresivo (reh-greh-SEE-<u>b</u>oh)

regular / fair / normal (adj.)　regular (reh-goo-LAHR)

regularity　*f.* regularidad (reh-goo-lah-ree-<u>D</u>AH<u>D</u>)

regulate (to)　regular (reh-gooh-LAHR)

regulation (*process of*)　*f.* regulación (reh-goo-lah-SYOHN)

regulation / rule / ruler　*f.* regla (REH-glah)

regurgitate (to)　regurgitar (reh-goor-hee-TAHR)

rehabilitate (to)　rehabilitar (reh-ah-<u>b</u>ee-lee-TAHR)

reign　*m.* reinado (ray-NAH-<u>d</u>oh)
　① **kingdom / realm**—*m.* reino (RAY-noh)

reign / rule (to)　reinar (ryeh-NAHR)

reimburse / repay / refund (to)　reembolsar (reh-ehm-bohl-SAHR)

reimbursement / refund　*m.* reembolso (reh-ehm-BOHL-soh)

reincarnation　*f.* reencarnación (reh-ehn-kahr-nah-SYOHN)

reinforce / stiffen (to)　reforzar (reh-fohr-SAHR) 💣

reinforcement　*m.* refuerzo (reh-FWEHR-soh) 💣

reiterate (to)　reiterar (reh-ee-teh-RAHR)

rejoice (to)　regocijarse (reh-goh-see-HAHR-seh)

rejuvenate (to)　rejuvenecer (reh-hoo-<u>b</u>eh-neh-SEHR)

rejuvenation　*m.* rejuvenecimiento (reh-hoo-<u>b</u>eh-neh-see-MYEHN-toh)

relate / recount / report (to)　relatar (reh-lah-TAHR)

relate (*associate things*) (to)　relacionar (reh-lah-syoh-NAHR)

relate to (*interact with*) (to)　relacionarse a / con (reh-lah-syoh-NAHR-seh ah / kohn)

related (adj.)　relacionado (reh-lah-syoh-NAH-<u>d</u>oh)

relation (*retelling*)　*m.* relato (reh-LAH-toh)

relation / connection / relevance *f.* relación (reh-lah-SYOHN)

   ① **relation / relative / kinsman**: *m. & f.* familiar (fah-mee-LYAHR) / *m.* pariente (pah-RYEHN-teh) ◑*f.* -ta◐. Note that Spanish *pariente / -ta* does not mean English *parent*. When referring to parents, in Spanish one speaks of one's **padre** or **madre** or—collectively—one's **padres**.

relative (*comparative*) (adj.) relativo (reh-lah-TEE-<u>b</u>oh)

relativity *f.* relatividad (reh-lah-tee-<u>b</u>ee-<u>D</u>AH<u>D</u>)

relax (to) relajarse (reh-lah-HAHR-seh)

relaxation *f.* relajación (reh-lah-hah-SYOHN)

relaxing / restful (adj.) relajante (reh-lah-HAHN-teh)

relegate (to) relegar (reh-leh-GAHR)

relevant / germane (adj.) relevante (reh-leh-<u>B</u>AHN-teh)

reliability *f.* fiabilidad (fyah-<u>b</u>ee-lee-<u>D</u>AH<u>D</u>) 💣

reliable (adj.) fiable (FYAH-<u>b</u>leh) 💣

relic *f.* reliquia (reh-LEE-kyah)

religion *f.* religión (reh-lee-HYOHN)

religious (adj.) religioso (reh-lee-HYOH-soh)

remedy / cure *m.* remedio (reh-MEH-<u>d</u>yoh)

remedy / redress (to) remediar (reh-meh-<u>D</u>YAHR)

reminiscence *f.* reminiscencia (reh-mee-nees-SEHN-syah)

reminiscent *f.* reminiscente (reh-mee-nees-SEHN-teh)

remission *f.* remisión (reh-mee-SYOHN)

remit (to) remitir (reh-mee-TEER)

remittance *f.* remesa (reh-MEH-sah)

remitter / sender *m. & f.* remitente (reh-mee-TEHN-teh)

remnant / remainder *m.* remanente (reh-mah-NEHN-teh) 💣

remorse *m.* remordimiento (reh-mohr-<u>d</u>ee-MYEHN-toh)

remote / far away / far-off (adj.) remoto (reh-MOH-toh)

remunerable (adj.) remunerable (reh-moo-neh-RAH-<u>b</u>leh)

remunerate (to) remunerar (reh-moo-neh-RAHR)

remuneration / compensation *f.* remuneración (reh-moo-neh-rah-SYOHN)

remunerative (adj.) remunerativo (reh-moo-neh-rah-TEE-<u>b</u>oh)

remunerator *m.* remunerador (reh-moo-neh-rah-DOHR) ☯*f.* -ra☯

renaissance / revival *m.* renacimiento (reh-nah-see-MYEHN-toh)

renegade *m.* renegado (reh-neh-GAH-<u>d</u>oh) ☯*f.* -da☯

renounce / forego / relinquish (to) renunciar (reh-noon-SYAHR)

renovate / redecorate (to) renovar (reh-noh-<u>B</u>AHR)

renovation / renewal *f.* renovación (reh-noh-<u>b</u>ah-SYOHN)

renown *m.* renombre (reh-NOHM-breh)

renowned (adj.) renombrado (reh-nohm-BRAH-<u>d</u>oh)

rent *f.* renta (REHN-tah)

rent (to) (*Americanism*) rentar (rehn-TAHR)

renunciation / waiver *f.* renuncia (reh-NOON-syah)

reorganization / shake-up *f.* reorganización (reh-ohr-gah-nee-sah-SYOHN)

reorganize (to) reorganizar (reh-ohr-gah-nee-SAHR)

repair *m.* reparo (reh-PAH-roh)

repair / fix / mend (to) reparar (reh-pah-RAHR)

reparation / repair *f.* reparación (reh-pah-rah-SYOHN)

repeat (to) repetir (reh-peh-TEER)

repel / repulse / reject (!) (to) repeler (reh-peh-LEHR)

repellent / repulsive (adj.) repelente (reh-peh-LEHN-teh)

repent (to) arrepentirse (ah-rreh-pehn-TEER-seh) 💣

repentance *m.* arrepentimiento (ah-rreh-pehn-tee-MYEHN-toh) 💣

repentant (adj.) arrepentido (ah-rreh-pehn-TEE-<u>d</u>oh) 💣

repercussion *f.* repercusión (reh-pehr-koo-SYOHN)

repertoire / repertory *m.* repertorio (reh-pehr-TOH-ryoh)

repetition / recurrence *f.* repetición (reh-peh-tee-SYOHN)

repetitive / repetitious (adj.) repetitivo (reh-peh-tee-TEE-<u>b</u>oh)

replace / substitute (to) reemplazar (reh-ehm-plah-SAHR)

replaceable (adj.)   reemplazable (reh-ehm-plah-SAH-<u>b</u>leh)

replacement / substitute   *m.* reemplazo (reh-ehm-PLAH-soh)

replica / rejoinder (!)   *f.* réplica (REH-plee-kah)

reply / retort (to)   replicar (reh-plee-KAHR)

report   *m.* reporte (reh-POHR-teh)

report (*on / about*) (to)   reportar (reh-pohr-TAHR)

report (*at post / for duty*) (to)   reportarse (reh-pohr-TAHR-seh)

reportage / article   *m.* reportaje (reh-pohr-TAH-heh)

reporter   *m.* reportero (reh-pohr-TEH-roh) ◑*f.* -ra◐

repose / rest / relaxation   *m.* reposo (re-POH-soh)

repose / rest (to)   reposar (reh-poh-SAHR)

reprehensible (adj.)   reprensible (reh-prehn-SEE-<u>b</u>leh)

represent (*act on behalf or portray*) (to)   representar (reh-preh-sehn-TAHR)

(political) representation / performance / portrayal   *f.* representación (reh-preh-sehn-tah-SYOHN)

representative / deputy   *m. & f.* representante (reh-preh-sehn-TAHN-teh)

representative (adj.)   representativo (reh-preh-sehn-tah-TEE-<u>b</u>oh)

repress (to)   reprimir (reh-pree-MEER)

repression / (external) restraint   *f.* represión (reh-preh-SYOHN)

repressive (adj.)   represivo (reh-preh-SEE-<u>b</u>oh)

reprimand / rebuke   *f.* reprimenda (reh-pree-MEHN-dah)

reprimand / rebuke (to)   reprender (reh-prehn-DEHR)

reprint (to)   reimprimir (reh-eem-pree-MEER)

reprisal   *f.* represalia (reh-preh-SAH-lyah)

reproach / rebuke   *m.* reproche (reh-PROH-cheh)

reproach / chide (to)   reprochar (reh-proh-CHAHR)

reprobation / reproof   *f.* reprobación (reh-proh-<u>b</u>ah-SYOHN)

reproduce (to)   reproducir (reh-proh-<u>d</u>oo-SEER)

reproducible (adj.)   reproducible (reh-proh-doo-SEE-<u>b</u>leh)

reproduction   *f.* reproducción (reh-proh-<u>d</u>ook-SYOHN)

reproductive (adj.)   reproductor (reh-proh-<u>d</u>ook-TOHR)

reptile   *m.* reptil (rehp-TEEL)

republic   *f.* república (reh-POO-<u>b</u>lee-kah)

republican   *m.* republicano (reh-poo-<u>b</u>lee-KAH-noh) ◖*f.* -na◗

republican (adj.)   republicano (reh-poo-<u>b</u>lee-KAH-noh)

repudiate (to)   repudiar (reh-poo-<u>D</u>YAHR)

repudiation   *f.* repudiación (reh-poo-dyah-SYOHN) / *m.* repudio (reh-POO-<u>d</u>yoh)

repugnance / disgust   *f.* repugnancia (reh-poog-NAHN-syah)

repugnant / obnoxious (adj.)   repugnante (reh-poog-NAHN-teh)

repulsive (adj.)   repulsivo (reh-pool-SEE-<u>b</u>oh)

reputation / repute   *f.* reputación (reh-poo-tah-SYOHN)
　　① (adj.) **reputable** (*having a good reputation*)—acreditado (ah-kreh-dee-TAH-<u>d</u>oh)

reputed (adj.)   reputado (reh-poo-TAH-<u>d</u>oh)

requiem (*religion*)   *m.* réquiem (REH-kyehm)

require / need (to)   requerir (reh-keh-REER)

requisite   *m.* requisito (reh-kee-SEE-toh)

requisition   *f.* requisición (reh-kee-see-SYOHN)

requisition (to)   requisar (reh-kee-SAHR)

rescue / ransom (!)   *m.* rescate (rehs-KAH-teh)

rescue / save / redeem (to)   rescatar (rehs-kah-TAHR)

resent (to)   resentirse de (reh-sehn-TEER-seh deh)

resentful (adj.)   resentido (reh-sehn-TEE-<u>d</u>oh)

resentment / grudge   *m.* resentimiento (reh-sehn-tee-MYEHN-toh)

reservation (*advance booking*)   *f.* reservación (reh-sehr-<u>b</u>ah-SYOHN)

reservation (*misgiving / doubt*)   *f.* reserva (reh-SEHR-<u>b</u>ah)

reserve (*emotional restraint*)   *f.* reserva (reh-SEHR-<u>b</u>ah)

reserve (*hold back or book*) (to)   reservar (reh-sehr-<u>B</u>AHR)

reserved / self-contained (adj.)   reservado (reh-sehr-<u>B</u>AH-<u>d</u>oh)

reside / dwell (to)   residir (reh-see-<u>D</u>EER)

residence / abode *f.* residencia (reh-see-<u>D</u>EHN-syah)

resident *m. & f.* residente (reh-see-<u>D</u>EHN-teh) ↻(adj.) ☐↻

residential (adj.) residencial (reh-see-dehn-SYAHL)

residual (adj.) residual (reh-see-<u>D</u>WAHL)

residue *m.* residuo (reh-SEE-<u>d</u>woh)

resign oneself to (to) resignarse a (reh-seeg-NAHR-seh ah)

resignation (*loss of hope*) *f.* resignación (reh-seeg-nah-SYOHN)

resist (*withstand*) (to) resistir (reh-sees-TEER)

resistance / stamina (!) *f.* resistencia (reh-sees-TEHN-syah)

resistant / tough (adj.) resistente (reh-sees-TEHN-teh)

resolute / resolved / steadfast (adj.) resuelto (reh-SWEHL-toh)

resolution / resolve / determination *f.* resolución (reh-soh-loo-SYOHN)

resolve (*determine or solve*) (to) resolver (reh-sohl-<u>B</u>EHR)

resonance *f.* resonancia (reh-soh-NAHN-syah)

resonant / resounding (adj.) resonante (reh-soh-NAHN-teh)

resonate / resound / ring (to) resonar (reh-soh-NAHR)

resource *m.* recurso (reh-KOOR-soh)

respect / esteem *m.* respeto (rehs-PEH-toh)

respect (*esteem or obey*) (to) respetar (rehs-peh-TAHR)

respectability *f.* respetabilidad (rehs-peh-tah-bee-lee-<u>D</u>AH<u>D</u>)

respectable (adj.) respetable (rehs-peh-TAH-<u>b</u>leh)

respectful / deferential (adj.) respetuoso (rehs-peh-TWOH-soh)

respectfulness *f.* respetuosidad (rehs-peh-twoh-see-<u>D</u>AH<u>D</u>)

respective (adj.) respectivo (rehs-pehk-TEE-<u>b</u>oh)

respiration / breathing *f.* respiración (rehs-pee-rah-SYOHN)

respirator (*medicine*) *m.* respirador (rehs-pee-rah-<u>D</u>OHR)

respire / breathe (to) respirar (rehs-pee-RAHR)

respite / break *m.* respiro (rehs-PEE-roh)

resplendent (adj.) resplandeciente (rehs-plahn-<u>d</u>eh-SYEHN-teh) 💣

respond (*reply*) **/ retaliate (!)** (to) responder (rehs-pohn-<u>D</u>EHR)

response / answer / reply   *f.* respuesta (rehs-PWEHS-tah)

responsibility / accountability   *f.* responsabilidad (rehs-pohn-sah-bee-lee-DAH<u>D</u>)

responsible / accountable / liable (adj.)   responsable (rehs-pohn-SAH-<u>b</u>leh)

(the) rest (of) / remainder   *m.* resto (REHS-toh)
   ① **leftovers**—*m. pl.* restos (REHS-tohs)

restaurant   *m.* restaurante (rehs-taow-RAHN-teh)

restitution / reinstatement (!)   *f.* restitución (rehs-tee-too-SYOHN)

restoration / repair   *f.* restauración (rehs-taow-rah-SYOHN)

restore / reestablish / repair (to)   restaurar (rehs-taow-RAHR)

restriction / restraint / constraint   *f.* restricción (rehs-treek-SYOHN)

restrictive (adj.)   restrictivo (rehs-treek-TEE-<u>b</u>oh)

result / consequence   *m.* resultado (reh-sool-TAH-<u>d</u>oh)

result in / follow (*as a result*) (to)   resultar (reh-sool-TAHR)

résumé / summary / synopsis   *m.* resumen (reh-SOO-mehn)

resurgence   *m.* resurgimiento (reh-soor-hee-MYEHN-toh)

resuscitate / revive (to)   resucitar (reh-soo-see-TAHR)

resuscitated (adj.)   resucitado (reh-soo-see-TAH-<u>d</u>oh)

resuscitation   *f.* resucitación (reh-soo-see-tah-SYOHN)

retain / keep (to)   retener (reh-teh-NEHR)

retaliation   *f.* retaliación (reh-tah-lyah-SYOHN)

retard / delay (to)   retardar (reh-tahr-<u>D</u>AHR)

retention   *f.* retención (reh-tehn-SYOHN)

reticence / reluctance   *f.* reticencia (reh-tee-SEHN-syah)

reticent / reluctant (adj.)   reticente (reh-tee-SEHN-teh)

retire (*from work*) / retreat (to)   retirarse (reh-tee-RAHR-seh)

retract / recant (to)   retractarse (de) (reh-trahk-TAHR-she [deh])

retreat (*withdrawal or place of refuge*)   *f.* retiro (reh-TEE-roh)

retroactive (adj.)   retroactivo (reh-troh-ahk-TEE-<u>b</u>oh)

retrospective (adj.)   retrospectivo (reh-trohs-pehk-TEE-<u>b</u>oh)

return (*a going to or coming back*)   *m.* retorno (reh-TOHR-noh)

return (*go back*) (to)   retornar (reh-tohr-NAHR)
  ① (to) **return (*give back*)**—devolver (deh-bohl-BEHR)

reunion / assembly / gathering   *f.* reunión (rehoo-NYOHN)

reunite / assemble / congregate (to)   reunirse (rehoo-NEER-seh)

reusable (adj.)   reutilizable (rehoo-tee-lee-SAH-bleh)

reveal / disclose / divulge (to)   revelar (reh-beh-LAHR)

revelation / disclosure   *f.* revelación (reh-beh-lah-SYOHN) 💣

reverberate (to)   reverberar (reh-behr-beh-RAHR)

reverberation   *f.* reverberación (reh-behr-beh-rah-SYOHN)

reverence   *f.* reverencia (reh-beh-REHN-syah) ↻(adj.) **reverent** –nte↻

reverence / revere (to)   reverenciar (reh-beh-rehn-SYAHR)

reverend (*religion*) (adj.)   reverendo (reh-beh-REHN-doh)

reverential (adj.)   reverencial (reh-beh-rehn-SYAHL)

reversal (*of fortune*) / setback   *m.* revés (reh-BEHS)

reverse   *m.* reverso (reh-BEHR-soh) ↻(adj.) ☐↻

reversible (adj.)   reversible (reh-behr-SEE-bleh)

revert (to)   revertir (reh-behr-TEER)

revise (to)   revisar (reh-bee-SAHR)

revision   *f.* revisión (reh-bee-SYOHN)

revive (to)   reavivar (reh-ah-bee-BAHR)

revocation / repeal   *f.* revocación (reh-boh-kah-SYOHN)

revoke / repeal / rescind (to)   revocar (reh-boh-KAHR)

revolt   *f.* revuelta (reh-BWEHL-tah)

revolution   *f.* revolución (reh-boh-loo-SYOHN)

revolutionary   *m.* revolucionario (reh-boh-loo-syoh-NAH-ryoh) ↻*f.* –ria↻
  ↻(adj.) ☐↻

revolutionize (to)   revolucionar (reh-boh-loo-syoh-NAHR)

revolver / handgun   *m.* revólver (reh-BOHL-behr)

rhetoric   *f.* retórica (reh-TOH-ree-kah) ↻(adj.) **rhetorical** –co↻

rhyme   *f.* rima (REE-mah)

rhyme (to)   rimar (ree-MAHR)

rhythm   *m.* ritmo (REET-moh)

rhythmic / rhythmical (adj.)   rítmico (REET-mee-koh)

ridicule   *m.* ridículo (ree-DEE-koo-loh)

ridiculous / ludicrous (adj.)   ridículo (ree-DEE-koo-loh)

rifle   *m.* rifle (REE-fleh)

rigid / stiff / inflexible (adj.)   rígido (REE-hee-doh)

rigidity / stiffness   *f.* rigidez (ree-hee-DEHS)

rigor   *m.* rigor (ree-GOHR)

rigorous (adj.)   rigoroso (ree-goh-ROH-soh)

risk / hazard   *m.* riesgo (RYEHS-goh)

risk / hazard (to)   arriesgar (ah-rryehs-GAHR) 💣

risky / chancy / hazardous (adj.)   arriesgado (ah-rryehs-GAH-doh) 💣

rite   *m.* rito (REE-toh)

ritual   *m.* ritual (ree-TWAHL) ↻(adj.)☐↻

rival / competitor / nemesis   *m. & f.* rival (ree-BAHL) ↻(adj.)☐↻

rival (to)   rivalizar con (ree-bah-lee-SAHR kohn)

rivalry   *f.* rivalidad (ree-bah-lee-DAHD)

riverbank / riverside   *f.* ribera (ree-BEH-rah)

roast beef   *m.* rosbif (rohs-BEEF)

rob / steal (to)   robar (roh-BAHR)
    ① **robber / thief**—*m.* ladrón (lah-DROHN) ↻*f.* -ona↻

robbery / burglary   *m.* robo (ROH-boh)

robot   *m.* robot (roh-BOHT)

robust / hale / hardy (adj.)   robusto (roh-BOOS-toh)

rock / (large) stone   *f.* roca (ROH-kah)

rocky (adj.)   rocoso (roh-KOH-soh)

rodent   *m.* roedor (roh-eh-DOHR)

roll / coil / scroll   *m.* rollo (ROH-yoh)

roller / rolling pin   *m.* rodillo (roh-DEE-yoh)

romance / affair *m.* romance (roh-MAHN-seh)

romantic (adj.) romántico (roh-MAHN-tee-koh)

rosary (*religion*) *m.* rosario (roh-SAH-ryoh)

rose (*flower*) *f.* rosa (ROH-sah) ↻(adj.) **rose / of the color rose** []↻

rotation *f.* rotación (roh-tah-SYOHN)

roulette *f.* ruleta (roo-LEH-tah)

round (*of drinks, negotiations, and so forth*) *f.* ronda (ROHN-dah)

round (adj.) redondo (reh-<u>D</u>OHN-doh)

round (to) redondear (reh-<u>d</u>ohn-deh-AHR)

route / way *f.* ruta (ROO-tah)

routine *f.* rutina (roo-TEE-nah)

routine / mundane (adj.) rutinario (roo-tee-NAH-ryoh)

royal / regal (adj.) real (reh-AHL) 💣

royalty *f.* realeza (reh-ah-LEH-sah)

ruby *m.* rubí (roo-<u>BEE</u>)

rude / coarse / rough (adj.) rudo (ROO-<u>d</u>oh)
   ① (adj.) **noisy**—ruidoso (rwee-<u>D</u>OH-soh)

rudiment *m.* rudimento (roo-<u>d</u>ee-MEHN-toh)

rudimentary / elementary (adj.) rudimentario (roo-<u>d</u>ee-mehn-TAH-ryoh)

ruin *f.* ruina (RWEE-nah)

ruin / wreck (to) arruinar (ah-rrwee-NAHR) 💣

ruinous (adj.) ruinoso (rwee-NOH-soh)

rule *f.* regla (REH-glah)
   ① **as a rule / generally / usually**—por regal general (pohr REH-glah heh-neh-RAHL)

rum *m.* ron (ROHN) 💣

ruminate (to) ruminar (roo-mee-NAHR)

rumor *m.* rumor (roo-MOHR)

rupture / severance *f.* ruptura (roop-TOO-rah)

rupture (to) romper (ROHM-pehr)

rural (adj.)   rural (roo-RAHL)

rustic (*person*)   *m.* rústico (ROOS-tee-koh) ↻*f.* -ca↻ ↻(adj.)☐↻

—S—

sabotage   *m.* sabotaje (sah-boh-TAH-heh)

sabotage (to)   sabotear (sah-boh-teh-AHR)

sack / bag / satchel   *m.* saco (SAH-koh)
 ① (to) **sack (*put into sacks*)**—ensacar (ehn-sah-KAHR)

sack / pillage / despoil (to)   saquear (sah-keh-AHR)

sacrament   *m.* sacramento (sah-krah-MEHN-toh)

sacramental (adj.)   sacramental (sah-krah-mehn-TAHL)

sacred / sanctified / holy (adj.)   sagrado (sah-GRAH-doh)

sacrifice   *m.* sacrificio (sah-kree-FEE-syoh)

sacrifice (to)   sacrificar (sah-kree-fee-KAHR)

sacrilege   *m.* sacrilegio (sah-kree-LEH-hyoh)

sacrilegious (adj.)   sacrílego (sah-KREE-leh-goh)

sacristan (*religion*) / sexton   *m.* sacristán (sah-krees-THAN)

sacrosanct (adj.)   sacrosanto (sah-kroh-SAHN-toh)

sadism   *m.* sadismo (sah-DEEZ-moh)

sadist   *m.* sádico (SAH-dee-koh) ↻*f.* -ca↻ ↻(adj.) **sadistic** ☐↻

safeguard   *f.* salvaguardia (sahl-bah-GWAHR-dyah) 💣

safeguard (to)   salvaguardar (sahl-bah-gwahr-DAHR) 💣

saga   *f.* saga (SAH-gah)

sagacious / sage / shrewd (adj.)   sagaz (sah-GAHS)

sagacity / shrewdness   *f.* sagacidad (sah-gah-see-DAHD)

sage / wise person   *m.* sabio (SAH-byoh) ↻*f.* -ia↻

saint   *m.* santo (SAHN-toh) ↻*f.* -ta↻ ↻(adj.) **saintly / holy** ☐↻

saintliness   *f.* santidad (sahn-tee-DAHD)

salacious (adj.)   salaz (sah-LAHS)

salaciousness / salacity *f.* salacidad (sah-lah-see-<u>D</u>AH<u>D</u>)

salad *f.* ensalada (ehn-sah-LAH-<u>d</u>ah) 💣

salary / wage(s) *m.* salario (sah-LAH-ryoh)

salient (adj.) saliente (sah-LYEHN-teh)

saline (adj.) salino (sah-LEE-noh)

saliva / spit / spittle *f.* saliva (sah-LEE-<u>b</u>ah)

salivary (adj.) salival (sah-lee-<u>B</u>AHL)

salivate (to) salivar (sah-lee-<u>B</u>AHR)

salmon *m.* salmón (sahl-MOHN)

salon / room / (meeting) hall *m.* salón (sah-LOHN)

salt *f.* sal (SAHL)

salt (to) salar (sah-LAHR)

salty (adj.) salado (sah-LAH-<u>d</u>oh)

salubrious / salutary (adj.) salubre (sah-LOO-<u>b</u>reh)

salutation / greeting *f.* salutación (sah-loo-tah-SYOHN)

salute / greet / hail (to) saludar (sah-loo-<u>D</u>AHR)

salvage (to) salvar (sahl-<u>B</u>AHR)

salvation *f.* salvación (sahl-<u>b</u>ah-SYOHN)

salvo *f.* salva (SAHL-<u>b</u>ah)

sanitarium / sanatorium *m.* sanatorio (sah-nah-TOH-ryoh)

sanctify / hallow (to) santificar (sahn-tee-fee-KAHR)

sanction (to) sancionar (sahn-syoh-NAHR)

sanctity *f.* santidad (sahn-tee-<u>D</u>AH<u>D</u>)

sanctuary / shrine (!) *m.* santuario (sahn-TWAH-ryoh)

sandal *f.* sandalia (sahn-DAH-lyah)

sandwich *m.* sándwich (SAHND-weech)

sanitary (adj.) sanitario (sah-nee-TAH-ryoh)

sanitation *f.* sanidad (sah-nee-<u>D</u>AH<u>D</u>)

sarcasm *m.* sarcasmo (sahr-KAHZ-moh)

sarcastic / snide (adj.) sarcástico (sahr-KAHS-tee-koh)

sardine *f.* sardina (sahr-<u>DEE</u>-nah)

sardonic (adj.) sardónico (sahr-<u>DOH</u>-nee-koh)

Satan *m.* Satán (sah-TAHN) / *m.* Satanás (sah-tah-NAHS)

satanic (adj.) satánico (sah-TAH-nee-koh)

Satanism *m.* satanismo (sah-tah-NEEZ-moh)

satellite *m.* satélite (sah-TEH-lee-teh)

satin *m.* satén (sah-TEHN)

satire *f.* sátira (SAH-tee-rah)

satiric / satirical (adj.) satírico (sah-TEE-ree-koh)

satirize / lampoon (to) satirizar (sah-tee-ree-SAHR)

satisfaction *f.* satisfacción (sah-tees-fahk-SYOHN)

satisfactory (adj.) satisfactorio (sah-tees-fahk-TOH-ryoh)

satisfy (to) satisfacer (sah-tees-fah-SEHR)
   ① (adj.) **satisfied**—satisfecho (sah-tees-FEH-choh)

saturate (to) saturar (sah-too-RAHR)

saturation *f.* saturación (sah-too-rah-SYOHN)

sauna *f.* sauna (SAOW-nah)

sausage *f.* salchicha (sahl-CHEE-chah)

savage *m. & f.* salvaje (sahl-<u>BAH</u>-heh) ↻(adj.) ☐↻ 💣

savagery / savageness *m.* salvajismo (sahl-<u>b</u>ah-HEEZ-moh) 💣

save (*rescue*) (to) salvar (sahl-<u>BAHR</u>)
   ① (to) **save (*money, for later use*) / save up (for)**—ahorrar (para) (ah-oh-RRAHR [PAH-rah])

savior / rescuer *m.* salvador (sahl-<u>b</u>ah-<u>DOHR</u>) ↻*f.* -ra↻💣

savor / flavor / taste *m.* sabor (sah-<u>BOHR</u>)

saxophone *m.* saxofón (sahk-soh-FOHN)

scald (to) escaldar (ehs-kahl-DAHR)

scale (*extent, proportion*) *f.* escala (ehs-KAH-lah) 💣

scale (*ascend*) / climb (to) escalar (ehs-kah-LAHR) 💣
   ① Related: **ladder** and **stairway**—*f.* escalera (ehs-kah-LEH-rah)

scalpel *m.* escalpelo (ehs-kahl-PEH-loh)

scandal / (emotional) scene *m.* escándalo (ehs-KAHN-dah-loh) 💣

scandalize (to)   escandalizar (ehs-kahn-dah-lee-SAHR) 💣

scandalous / outrageous (adj.)   escandaloso (ehs-kahn-dah-LOH-soh)

scarce / scant / meager (adj.)   escaso (ehs-KAH-soh)
○(adj.) **scanty** ☐○ 💣

scarceness /scarcity   *f.* escasez (ehs-kah-SEHS) 💣

scene (*commotion, section of drama, or view / vista*)   *f.* escena (ehs-SEH-nah) 💣

scene (*local situation / doings*)   *m.* escenario (ehs-seh-NAH-ryoh) 💣

schism   *m.* cisma (SEEZ-mah) 💣

scholar (*pupil*)   *m. & f.* escolar (ehs-koh-LAHR)

school / schoolhouse   *f.* escuela (ehs-KWEH-lah)
① Related: **preschool**—*f.* preescuela (preh-ehs-KWEH-lah); **element-ary school**—*f.* escuela primaria (ehs-KWEH-lah pree-MAH-ryah); **high school**—*f.* escuela superior (ehs-KWEH-lah soo-peh-RYOHR); **public school**—*f.* escuela pública (ehs-KWEH-lah POO-blee-kah)

science   *f.* ciencia (SYEHN-syah) 💣

scientist   *m.* científico (syehn-TEE-fee-koh) ○(adj.) **scientific** ☐○ 💣

scintillate / sparkle (to)   centellear (sehn-teh-yeh-AHR)

scribe   *m.* escriba (ehs-KREE-bah) 💣
① Importantly related: (to) **write**—escribir (ehs-kree-BEER); **writer**— *m.* escritor (ehs-kree-TOHR) ○*f.* -ra○ 💣

script   *f.* escritura (ehs-kree-TOO-rah) 💣

scruple   *m.* escrúpulo (ehs-KROO-poo-loh) 💣

scrupulous (adj.)   escrupuloso (ehs-kroo-poo-LOH-soh) 💣

scrutinize (to)   escrutar (ehs-kroo-TAHR) / escudriñar (ehs-koo-dree-NYAHR) 💣

scrutiny   *m.* escrutinio (ehs-kroo-TEE-nyoh) 💣

sculpt / sculpture (to)   esculpir (ehs-kool-PEER) 💣

sculptor   *m.* escultor (ehs-kool-TOHR) ○*f.* **sculptress** -ra○ 💣

sculpture   *f.* escultura (ehs-kool-TOO-rah)

seal (*security closure*)   *m.* sello (SEH-yoh) 💣

seal (to)   sellar (seh-YAHR)

season / flavor / spice (to)   sazonar (sah-soh-NAHR)

seasoning (*flavoring*)   *f.* sazón (sah-SOHN)

secondary / subsidiary (adj.)   secundario (seh-koon-DAH-ryoh)

secret / secrecy   *m.* secreto (seh-KREH-toh) ⭗(adj.) **secret** ☐⭗

secretary   *m.* secretario (seh-kreh-TAH-ryoh) ⭗*f.* –ia⭗

secrete (*discharge*) (to)   secretar (seh-kreh-TAHR)

secretion   *f.* secreción (seh-kreh-SYOHN)

sect   *f.* secta (SEHK-tah)

sectarian   *m.* sectario (sehk-TAH-ryoh) ⭗*f.* –ia⭗ ⭗(adj.) ☐⭗

section   *f.* sección (sehk-SYOHN)

sector   *m.* sector (sehk-TOHR)

secular (adj.)   secular (seh-koo-LAHR)

secure / safe / confident of (adj.)   seguro (seh-GOO-roh)

security / safety / sureness   *f.* seguridad (seh-goo-ree-<u>D</u>AH<u>D</u>)

sedate (to)   sedar (seh-<u>D</u>AHR)

sedation   *f.* sedación (seh-<u>d</u>ah-SYOHN)

sedative   *m.* sedante (seh-<u>D</u>AHN-teh) ⭗(adj.) ☐⭗

sedentary (adj.)   sedentario (seh-<u>d</u>ehn-TAH-ryoh)

seduce (to)   seducir (seh-<u>d</u>oo-SEER)

seduction   *f.* seducción (seh-<u>d</u>ook-SYOHN)

seductive (adj.)   seductivo (seh-<u>d</u>ook-TEE-<u>b</u>oh)

segment   *m.* segmento (sehg-MEHN-toh)

segmented (adj.)   segmentado (sehg-mehn-TAH-<u>d</u>oh)

segregate (to)   segregar (seh-greh-GAHR)

segregation   *f.* segregación (seh-greh-gah-SYOHN)

select (to)   seleccionar (seh-lehk-syoh-NAHR)

select / choice (adj.)   selecto (seh-LEHK-toh)

selection / choice / pick   *f.* selección (seh-lehk-SYOHN)

selective (adj.)   selectivo (seh-lehk-TEE-<u>b</u>oh)

self-defense   *f.* defensa personal (deh-FEHN-sah pehr-soh-NAHL)

semantic / semantical (adj.) semántico (seh-MAHN-tee-koh)

semantics *f.* semántica (seh-MAHN-tee-kah)

semen *m.* semen (SEH-mehn)

semester *m.* semestre (seh-MEHS-treh)

semifinal (*sports*) *f.* semifinal (seh-mee-fee-NAHL)

semifinal (*sports*) (adj.) semifinalista (seh-mee-fee-nah-LEES-tah)

semifinalist *m. & f.* semifinalista (seh-mee-fee-nah-LEES-tah)

seminary (*religion*) / **seminar** (*of students, of experts*) *m.* seminario (seh-mee-NAH-ryoh)

seminarian / seminarist (*religion*) *m.* seminarista (seh-mee-nah-REES-tah)

seminarian / seminarist (*students or experts taking a seminar*) *m. & f.* seminarista (seh-mee-nah-REES-tah)

Semite *m. & f.* semita (seh-MEE-tah) ↻(adj.) ☐↻

Semitic (adj.) semítico (seh-MEE-tee-koh)

Semitism *m.* semitismo (seh-mee-TEEZ-moh)

senate *m.* senado (seh-NAH-doh)

senator *m.* senador (seh-nah-DOHR) ↻*f.* -ra↻

senile (adj.) senil (seh-NEEL)

senility *f.* senilidad (seh-nee-lee-DAHD)

sensation / (physical) feeling *f.* sensación (sehn-sah-SYOHN)

sensational (adj.) sensacional (sehn-sah-syoh-NAHL))

sensationalism *m.* sensacionalismo (sehn-sah-syoh-nah-LEEZ-moh)

sensationalist *m. & f.* sensacionalista (sehn-sah-syoh-nah-LEES-tah)

sense (*sensation, impression; meaning of*) *m.* sentido (sehn-TEE-doh)
①(adj.) **senseless** (*without meaning or rational basis*)—sin sentido (seen sehn-TEE-doh)

sense (to) sentir (sehn-TEER)

(rational) sensibility *f.* sensibilidad (sehn-see-bee-lee-DAHD)

sensible / sensitive / delicate (adj.) sensible (sehn-SEE-bleh)

sensible / practical / reasonable (adj.) sensato (sehn-SAH-toh)

sensitivity / sensitiveness (*responsiveness*) *f.* sensibilidad (sehn-see-<u>bee</u>-lee-<u>DAHD</u>)

sensorial / sensory (adj.)   sensorial (sehn-soh-RYAHL) / sensorio (sehn-SOH-ryoh)

sensual / sensuous (adj.)   sensual (sehn-SWAHL)

sensualism   *m.* sensualismo (sehn-swah-LEEZ-moh)

sensualist   *m. & f.* sensualista (sehn-swah-LEES-tah)

sensuality / sensuousness   *f.* sensualidad (sehn-swah-lee-<u>DAHD</u>)

sentence / judgment   *f.* sentencia (sehn-TEHN-syah)
  ① **sentence (*grammatical structure*)**—*f.* frase (FRAH-seh) / *f.* **oración** (oh-rah-SYON)

sentence (to)   sentenciar (sehn-tehn-SYAHR)

sentiment   *m.* sentimiento (sehn-tee-MYEHN-toh)

sentimental (adj.)   sentimental (sehn-tee-mehn-TAHL)

sentimentality   *f.* sentimentalismo (sehn-tee-mehn-tah-LEEZ-moh)

sentinel / sentry / lookout   *m. & f.* centinela (sehn-tee-NEH-lah) ✹

separable (adj.)   separable (seh-pah-RAH-<u>b</u>leh)

separate / detached (adj.)   separado (seh-pah-RAH-<u>d</u>oh)

separate / detach / force apart (to)   separar (seh-pah-RAHR)

separate (*come apart*) (to)   separarse (seh-pah-RAHR-seh)

separation / detachment   *f.* separación (seh-pah-rah-SYOHN)

serenade   *f.* serenata (seh-reh-NAH-tah)

serene (adj.)   sereno (seh-REH-noh)

serenity   *f.* serenidad (seh-reh-nee-<u>DAHD</u>)

sergeant   *m.* sargento (sahr-HEHN-toh)

serial (adj.)   seriado (seh-RYAH-<u>d</u>oh)

serial (*on radio or television*)   *m.* serial (seh-RYAHL)

series / sequence   *f.* serie (SEH-ryeh)

serious / earnest / grave (adj.)   serio (SEH-ryoh)

seriousness   *f.* seriedad (seh-ryeh-<u>DAHD</u>)

sermon   *m.* sermón (sehr-MOHN)

serpent / snake *f.* serpiente (sehr-PYEHN-teh)

serrated (adj.) serrado (seh-RRAH-<u>d</u>oh)

servant (*domestic help, maid, valet*) *m.* sirviente (seer-<u>B</u>YEHN-teh) ↻*f.* -ta↺

serve / dish out (to) servir (sehr-<u>B</u>EER)

service (*act of serving*) *m.* servicio (sehr-<u>B</u>EE-syoh)

servile / obsequious (adj.) servil (sehr-<u>B</u>EEL)

servitude *f.* servidumbre (sehr-<u>b</u>ee-<u>D</u>OOM-breh)

session *f.* sesión (seh-SYOHN)

severe / harsh / strict / stern (adj.) severo (seh-<u>B</u>EH-roh)

severity / harshness *f.* severidad (seh-<u>b</u>eh-ree-<u>D</u>AH<u>D</u>)

sex / gender *m.* sexo (SEHK-soh)

sexism *m.* sexismo (sehk-SEEZ-moh) 💣

sexist *m. & f.* sexista (sehk-SEES-tah) ↻ (adj.) ▢↻ 💣

sexologist *m.* sexólogo (sehk-SOH-loh-goh) ↻*f.* -ga↺

sexology *f.* sexología (sehk-soh-loh-HEE-ah)

sexual (adj.) sexual (sehk-SWAHL) 💣

sexuality *f.* sexualidad (sehk-swah-lee-<u>D</u>AH<u>D</u>)

sexy (adj.) sexy (SEHK-see)

shampoo *m.* champú (cham-POO) 💣

shawl *m.* chal (CHAHL) 💣

sheriff *m. & f.* sheriff (sheh-REEF)

sigh *m.* suspiro (soos-PEE-roh)

sigh (*emit a sigh*) (to) suspirar (soos-pee-RAHR) 💣

sign (*indication*) *m.* signo (SEEG-noh)

signal *f.* señal (seh-NYAHL) 💣

signal (to) señalar (seh-nyah-LAHR) 💣

significance (*meaning of*) *m.* significado (seeg-nee-fee-KAH-<u>d</u>oh)

significance (*importance*) *f.* significación (seeg-nee-fee-kah-SYOHN)

significant / meaningful (adj.) significativo (seeg-nee-fee-kah-TEE-<u>b</u>oh)

signify / denote (to) significar (seeg-nee-fee-KAHR)

silence / hush   *m.* silencio (see-LEHN-syoh)

silence / quiet (to)   silenciar (see-lehn-SYAHR)

silent / noiseless (adj.)   silencioso (see-lehn-SYOH-soh)

silhouette   *f.* silueta (see-LWEH-tah)

simian / ape   *m.* simio (SEE-myoh)

similar / kindred (adj.)   similar (see-mee-LAHR)

similarity / similitude   *f.* similitud (see-mee-lee-TOO<u>D</u>)

simile   *m.* símil (SEE-meel)

simple / easy / straightforward (adj.)   simple (SEEM-pleh)

simplicity   *f.* simplicidad (seem-plee-see-<u>D</u>AH<u>D</u>)

simplification   *f.* simplificación (seem-plee-fee-kah-SYOHN)

simplify (to)   simplificar (seem-plee-fee KAHR)

simulate (to)   simular (see-moo-LAHR)

simulated / mock (adj.)   simulado (see-moo-LAH-<u>d</u>oh)

simultaneous (adj.)   simultáneo (see-mool-TAH-neh-oh)

sincere / earnest (adj.)   sincero (seen-SEH-roh)

sincerity / earnestness   *f.* sinceridad (seen-seh-ree-<u>D</u>AH<u>D</u>)

single man / bachelor   *m.* soltero (sohl-TEH-roh) ↻(adj.) ▯↻

single woman / bachelorette   *m.* soltera (sohl-TEH-rah) ↻(adj.) ▯↻

singular / peculiar (adj.)   singular (seen-goo-LAHR)

sinister (adj.)   siniestro (see-NYEHS-troh)

siphon   *m.* sifón (see-FOHN)

siren   *f.* sirena (see-REH-nah)

site / specific spot / place   *m.* sitio (SEE-tyoh)

situate / position (to)   situar (see-TWAHR)

situation (*circumstance*)   *f.* situación (see-twah-SYOHN)

skeleton   *m.* esqueleto (ehs-keh-LEH-toh) 💣

skeptic / skeptical (adj.)   escéptico (ehs-SEHP-tee-koh)

skeptic   *m.* escéptico (ehs-SEHP-tee-koh) ↻*f.* -ca↻ 💣

skepticism   *m.* escepticismo (ehs-sehp-tee-SEEZ-moh) 💣

(theatrical) sketch / skit *m.* sketch (ehs-KEHCH)

ski *m.* esquí (ehs-KEE) 💣

ski (to) esquiar (ehs-KYAHR) 💣

skier *m.* esquiador (ehs-kyah-<u>D</u>OHR) ↻*f.* –ra↻ 💣

slave *m.* esclavo (ehs-KLAH-<u>b</u>oh) ↻*f.* –va↻ 💣

slavery *f.* esclavitud (ehs-klah-<u>b</u>ee-TOO<u>D</u>) 💣

slogan *m.* eslogan (ehs-loh-GAHN) 💣

smog *m.* smog (SMOHG)

snob *m. & f.* esnob (ehs-NOH<u>B</u>) ↻(adj.) **snobbish** *f*↻ 💣

snobbery / snobbishness *m.* esnobismo (ehs-noh-<u>B</u>EEZ-moh) 💣

sober / staid (adj.) sobrio (SOH-<u>b</u>ryoh)

sociable / companionable (adj.) sociable (soh-SYAH-<u>b</u>leh)

social (*societal*) (adj.) social (soh-SYAHL)

socialism *m.* socialismo (soh-syah-LEEZ-moh)

socialist *m. & f.* socialista (soh-syah-LEES-tah) ↻(adj.) ☐↻

socialization *f.* socialización (soh-syah-lee-sah-SYOHN)

socialize (to) socializar (soh-syah-lee-SAHR)

society (*association or populace*) *f.* sociedad (soh-syeh-<u>D</u>AH<u>D</u>)

sociologic / sociological (adj.) sociológico (soh-syoh-LOH-hee-koh)

sociologist *m.* sociólogo (soh-SYOH-loh-goh) ↻*f.* –ga↻

sociology *f.* sociología (soh-syoh-loh-HEE-ah)

soda *f.* soda (SOH-<u>d</u>ah) / *f.* sosa (SOH-sah)

sodium *m.* sodio (SOH-<u>d</u>yoh)

sofa / couch / settee *m.* sofá (soh-FAH)

(physically) soft / smooth (adj.) suave (SWAH-<u>b</u>eh) / blando (BLAHN-doh)

software *m.* software (sohft-WHERE)

soil *m.* suelo (SWEH-loh)

solar (adj.) solar (soh-LAHR)

soldier *m.* soldado (sohl-<u>D</u>AH-<u>d</u>oh)

sole (*of shoe*)   *f.* suela (SWEH-lah)

sole / only / exclusive (adj.)   solo (SOH-loh)

solemn (adj.)   solemne (soh-LEHM-neh)

solemness / solemnity   *f.* solemnidad (soh-lehm-nee-DAHD)

solicit / ask for / request (to)   solicitar (soh-lee-see-TAHR)

solicitor / canvasser   *m.* solicitador (soh-lee-see-tah-DOHR) ↻*f.* –ra↻

solicitous (adj.)   solícito (soh-LEE-see-toh)

solid   *m.* sólido (SOH-lee-doh) ↻(adj.) **solid / sturdy / firm** ☐↻

solidarity   *f.* solidaridad (soh-lee-dah-ree-DAHD)

solidify (to)   solidificar (soh-lee-dee-fee-KAHR)

solidity / sturdiness   *f.* solidez (soh-lee-DEHS)

solitary / loner / recluse   *m.* solitario (soh-lee-TAH-ryoh) ↻*f.* –ria↻

solitary / single / lone (adj.)   solitario (soh-lee-TAH-ryoh)

solitude / loneliness   *f.* soledad (soh-leh-DAHD)

solo (*unaccompanied performance*)   *m.* solo (SOH-loh)

solo / alone / by oneself / lonely/ only (adj.)   solo (SOH-loh)

soloist   *m. & f.* solista (soh-LEES-tah)

solstice   *m.* solsticio (sohls-TEE-syoh)

soluble (adj.)   soluble (soh-LOO-bleh)

solution (*answer*)   *f.* solución (soh-loo-SYOHN)

somber / glum / gloomy (adj.)   sombrío (sohm-BREE-oh)
   ① Importantly semirelated: **shade / shadow**—*f.* sombra (SOHM-brah);
   (adj.) **shaded / shady**—sombreado (sohm-breh-AH-doh)

somnambulism   *m.* sonambulismo (soh-nahm-boo-LEEZ-moh) /
   somnambulismo (sohm-nahm-boo-LEEZ-moh)

somnambulist   *m. & f.* sonámbulo (soh-NAHM-boo-loh) ↻*f.* –la↻/
   somnámbulo (sohm-NAHM-boo-loh) ↻*f.* –la↻

somnolence / sleepiness   *f.* somnolencia (sohm-noh-LEHN-syah)

somnolent / sleepy (adj.)   somnoliento (sohm-noh-LYEHN-toh)

sonata   *f.* sonata (soh-NAH-tah)

sonnet   *m.* soneto (soh-NEH-toh)

sonorous (adj.)   sonoro (soh-NOH-roh)

sophisticated / worldly (adj.)   sofisticado (soh-fees-tee-KAH-<u>d</u>oh)

sophistication / urbanity (adj.)   sofisticación (soh-fees-tee-kah-SYOHN)

soprano   *m. & f.* soprano (soh-PRAH-noh) ○(adj.) □○

sordid / seamy / seedy (!) (adj.)   sórdido (SOHR-<u>d</u>ee-<u>d</u>oh)

so-so / bland (adj.)   soso (SOH-soh) / así así (ah-SEE ah-SEE)

soufflé   (*French*) *m.* soufflé (soo-FLEH)

sound / noise   *m.* sonido (soh-NEE-<u>d</u>oh)

soup   *f.* sopa (SOH-pah)

south   *m.* sur (SOOR)

south (adj.)   del sur (dehl SOOR)

southeast   *m.* sudeste (soo-<u>D</u>EHS-teh)

southeast (*of the southeast*) (adj.)   del sudeste (dehl soo-<u>D</u>EHS-teh)

southwest   *m.* sudoeste (soo-<u>d</u>oh-EHS-teh)

southwest (*of the southwest*) (adj.)   del sudoeste (dehl soo-<u>d</u>oh-EHS-teh)

souvenir   (*French*) *m.* souvenir (soo-<u>b</u>eh-NEER)

sovereign / ruler   *m.* soberano (soh-<u>b</u>eh-RAH-noh) ○*f.* -na○ ○(adj.) □○

sovereignty / rulership   *f.* soberanía (soh-<u>b</u>eh-rah-NEE-ah)

space (*area, room*)   *m.* espacio (ehs-PAH-syoh) 🍷

spacious / roomy (adj.)   espacioso (ehs-pah-SYOH-soh) 🍷

spasm / pang / throe   *m.* espasmo (ehs-PAHZ-moh) 🍷

spasmotic / jerky (adj.)   espasmódico (ehs-pahz-MOH-<u>d</u>ee-koh) 🍷

special (adj.)   especial (ehs-peh-SYAHL) 🍷

specialist / expert   *m. & f.* especialista (ehs-peh-syah-LEES-tah)

specialty   *f.* especialidad (ehs-peh-syah-lee-<u>D</u>AH<u>D</u>) 🍷

specialization   *f.* especialización (ehs-peh-syah-lee-sah-SYOHN)

specialize (to)   especializarse (ehs-peh-syah-lee-SAHR-seh)

species (*kind / sort*)   *f.* especie (ehs-PEH-syeh) 🍷

specific (adj.)   específico (ehs-peh-SEE-fee-koh) 🍷

specification   *f.* especificación (ehs-peh-see-fee-kah-SYOHN) 🍷

specify (to)   especificar (ehs-peh-see-fee-KAHR) 💣

specimen / sample / example   *m.* espécimen (ehs-PEH-see-mehn) 💣

spectacle   *m.* espectáculo (ehs-pehk-TAH-koo-loh) 💣

spectacular (adj.)   espetacular (ehs-pehk-tah-koo-LAHR) 💣

spectator / bystander   *m.* espectador (ehs-pehk-tah-<u>D</u>OHR) ↻*f.* –ra↻ 💣

speculate (to)   especular (ehs-peh-koo-LAHR) 💣

speculation   *f.* especulación (ehs-peh-koo-lah-SYOHN) 💣

speculative (adj.)   especulativo (ehs-peh-koo-lah-TEE-<u>b</u>oh) 💣

speculator   *m.* especulador (ehs-peh-koo-lah-<u>D</u>OHR) ↻*f.* –ra↻ 💣

sphere (*globe or range of*)   *f.* esfera (ehs-FEH-rah) 💣

spherical (adj.)   esférico (ehs-FEH-ree-koh)

spice   *f.* especia (ehs-PEH-syah) 💣

spinach (*botanical*)   *f.* espinaca (ehs-pee-NAH-kah) 💣
   ① **spinach** (*culinary*)—*f. pl.* espinacas (ehs-pee-NAH-kahs)

spine (*anatomical*)   *f.* espina dorsal (ehs-PEE-nah dohr-SAHL) 💣

spine (*botanical*) / **thorn**   *f.* espina (ehs-PEE-nah) 💣
   ① (adj.) **thorny** (*referring to plant or problem*)—espinoso (ehs-pee-NOH-soh)

spiral / swirl / whorl   *f.* espiral (ehs-pee-RAHL) ↻(adj.) ▯↻ 💣

spirit (*personal mood or ghost*)   *m.* espíritu (ehs-PEE-ree-too) 💣

spiritual (*religious song*)   *m.* espiritual (ehs-pee-ree-TWAHL) ↻(adj.) ▯↻ 💣

spiritualism   *m.* espiritualismo (ehs-pee-ree-twah-LEEZ-moh) 💣

spirituality   *f.* espiritualidad (ehs-pee-ree-twah-lee-<u>D</u>AH<u>D</u>) 💣

splendid / magnificent (adj.)   espléndido (ehs-PLEHN-dee-<u>d</u>oh) 💣

splendor   *m.* esplendor (ehs-plehn-DOHR) 💣

sponge   *f.* esponja (ehs-POHN-hah) 💣

spontaneity   *f.* espontaneidad (ehs-pohn-tah-nay-<u>D</u>AH<u>D</u>) 💣

spontaneous (adj.)   espontáneo (ehs-pohn-TAH-neh-oh) 💣

sporadic (adj.)   esporádico (ehs-poh-RAH-<u>d</u>ee-koh) 💣

sport   *m.* deporte (deh-POHR-teh) 💣

sportsman / sportswoman / sports fan   *m. & f.* deportista (deh-pohr-TEES-tah) 💣

sporty (adj.)   deportivo (deh-pohr-TEE-<u>b</u>oh) 💣

spouse / husband   *m.* esposo (ehs-POH-soh) 💣

spouse / wife   *f.* esposa (ehs-POH-sah) 💣

sprint   *m.* esprint (ehs-PREENT) 💣

sprint (to)   esprintar (ehs-preen-TAHR) 💣

spurious (adj.)   espurio (ehs-POO-ryoh) 💣

spy   *m. & f.* espía (ehs-PEE-ah) 💣

spy / peek (!) (to)   espiar (ehs-pee-AHR)

stability   *f.* estabilidad (ehs-tah-<u>b</u>ee-lee-<u>D</u>AH<u>D</u>) 💣

stabilize (to)   estabilizar (ehs-tah-<u>b</u>ee-lee-SAHR) 💣

stable / barn   *m.* establo (ehs-TAH-<u>b</u>loh) 💣

stable / solid (adj.)   estable (ehs-TAH-<u>b</u>leh) 💣

staccato (adj.)   staccato (ehs-tahk-KAH-toh)

stadium   *m.* estadio (ehs-TAH-<u>d</u>yoh) 💣

stake / post   *f.* estaca (ehs-TAH-kah) 💣

stampede   *f.* estampida (ehs-tahm-PEE-<u>d</u>ah) 💣

standard / common / normal (adj.)   estándar (ehs-TAHN-dahr) 💣

standardize (to)   estandarizar (ehs-tahn-dah-ree-SAHR) 💣

state (*nation or condition*)   *m.* estado (ehs-TAH-<u>d</u>oh) 💣

statesman (*man or woman*)   *m. & f.* estadista (ehs-tah-DEES-tah) 💣

static (*electronic*)   *f.* estática (ehs-TAH-tee-kah) 💣

static (*stationary*) (adj.)   estático (ehs-TAH-tee-koh) 💣

station depot / season   *f.* estación (ehs-tah-SYOHN) 💣

station / park (to)   estacionar (ehs-tah-syoh-NAHR) 💣

stationary / unmoving (adj.)   estacionario (ehs-tah-syoh-NAH-ryoh) 💣

statistic   *f.* estadística (ehs-tah-<u>D</u>EES-tee-kah) 💣

statistic / stastical (adj.)   estadístico (ehs-tah-<u>D</u>EES-tee-koh)

statue   *f.* estatua (ehs-TAH-twah) 💣

statuette / figurine *f.* estatuilla (ehs-tah-TWEE-yah) 💣

stature / height / standing *f.* estatura (ehs-tah-TOO-rah) 💣

status *m.* estatus (ehs-TAH-toos) 💣

statute / law *m.* estatuto (ehs-tah-TOO-toh) 💣

(beef) steak *m.* bistec (bees-TEHK)

stereotype *m.* estereotipo (ehs-teh-reh-oh-TEE-poh) 💣

stereotype (to) estereotipar (ehs-teh-reh-oh-tee-PAHR) 💣

sterile / barren (adj.) estéril (ehs-TEH-reel) 💣

sterility / barrenness *f.* esterilidad (ehs-teh-ree-lee-<u>DAHD</u>) 💣

stigma *m.* estigma (ehs-TEEG-mah) 💣

stigmatize (to) estigmatizar (ehs-teeg-mah-tee-SAHR) 💣

stimulant *m.* estimulante (ehs-tee-moo-LAHN-teh) 💣

stimulate (to) estimular (ehs-tee-moo-LAHR) 💣

stimulating / stimulative (adj.) estimulante (ehs-tee-moo-LAHN-teh)

stimulation *f.* estimulación (ehs-tee-moo-lah-SYOHN) 💣

stimulus *m.* estímulo (ehs-TEE-moo-loh) 💣

stipend *m.* estipendio (ehs-tee-PEHN-dyoh) 💣

stipulate / provide (that) (to) estipular (ehs-tee-poo-LAHR) 💣

stipulation / condition *f.* estipulación (ehs-tee-poo-lah-SYOHN) 💣

stoic *m.* estoico (ehs-TOHY-koh) ⟳*f.* -ca⟳ 💣

stoic / stoical (adj.) estoico (ehs-TOHY-koh)

stoicism *m.* estoicismo (ehs-tohy-SEEZ-moh) 💣

stole *f.* estola (ehs-TOH-lah) 💣

stomach *m.* estómago (ehs-TOH-mah-goh)

stove (for area heating) *f.* estufa (ehs-TOO-fah) 💣

strange / bizarre / odd (adj.) extraño (ehs-STRAH-nyoh) 💣

stranger / foreigner *m.* extranjero (ehs-strahn-HEH-roh) 💣

strangle / throttle (to) estrangular (ehs-trahn-goo-LAHR)

strangler *m.* estrangulador (ehs-trahn-goo-lah-<u>DOHR</u>) ⟳*f.* -ra⟳

strategic / strategical (adj.) estratégico (ehs-trah-TEH-hee-koh) 💣

strategy *f.* estrategia (ehs-trah-TEH-hyah) 💣

stratification *f.* estratificación (ehs-trah-tee-fee-kah-SYOHN)

stratified (adj.) estratificado (ehs-trah-tee-fee-KAH-<u>d</u>oh) 💣

stratefy (to) estratificar (ehs-trah-tee-fee-KAHR)

stress *m.* estrés (ehs-TREHS) 💣

stressful (adj.) estresante (ehs-treh-SAHN-teh) 💣

stretch (*expanse*) *m.* trecho (TREH-choh) 💣

stretch / extend (to) estirar (ehs-tee-RAHR) 💣

strict / stringent (adj.) estricto (ehs-TREEK-toh) 💣

strident / shrill (adj.) estridente (ehs-tree-<u>D</u>EHN-teh) 💣

structure *f.* estructura (ehs-trook-TOO-rah) ⟳(adj.) **structural** -al⟳ 💣

structure (to) estructurar (ehs-trook-too-RAHR)

stucco *m.* estuco (ehs-TOO-koh) 💣

student / learner *m. & f.* estudiante (ehs-too-<u>D</u>YAHN-teh) 💣

studio / study (*workroom or act of learning*) *m.* estudio (ehs-TOO-<u>d</u>yoh) 💣

studious (adj.) estudioso (ehs-too-<u>D</u>YOH-soh) 💣

study (to) estudiar (ehs-too-<u>D</u>YAHR) 💣

stupefied / amazed / astonished (adj.) estupefacto (ehs-too-peh-FAHK-toh) 💣

stupendous (adj.) estupendo (ehs-too-PEHN-<u>d</u>oh) 💣

stupid (*person*) / dummy *m.* estúpido (ehs-TOO-pee-<u>d</u>oh) ⟳*f.* -da⟳ 💣

stupid / dumb / foolish (adj.) estúpido (ehs-TOO-pee-<u>d</u>oh) M

stupidity / foolishness *f.* estupidez (ehs-too-pee-<u>D</u>EHS)

stupor / amazement *m.* estupor (ehs-too-POHR) 💣

style / manner / stylus (!) *m.* estilo (ehs-TEE-loh) 💣

stylize (to) estilizar (ehs-tee-lee-SAHR) 💣

subconscious *m.* subconsciente (soob-kohns-SYEHN-teh) ⟳(adj.) ▢⟳

subcontract *m.* subcontrato (soob-kohn-TRAH-toh)

subcontract (to) subcontratar (soob-kohn-trah-TAHR)

subcontracting *f.* subcontratación (soob-kohn-trah-tah-SYOHN)

subcontractor   *m. & f.* subcontratista (soob-kohn-trah-TEES-tah)

subdivide (to)   subdividir (soob-<u>d</u>ee-<u>b</u>ee-<u>D</u>EER)

subdivision   *f.* subdivisión (soob-<u>d</u>ee-<u>b</u>ee-SYOHN)

subject (*person under rulership*)   *m.* súbdito (SOOB-<u>d</u>ee-toh) ↻*f.* -ta↻ ♦⃝

subject (*to superior control*) (adj.)   subyugado (soob-yoo-GAH-<u>d</u>oh) /sojuzgado (soh-hoos-GAH-doh) ♦⃝

subject / prone to (adj.)   sujeto (soo-HEH-toh) ♦⃝

subjection / subjugation   *m.* sometimiento (soh-meh-tee-MYEHN-toh) / *m.* sojuzgamiento (soh-hoos-gah-MYEHN-toh) ♦⃝

subjective (*nonobjective*) (adj.)   subjetivo (soob-heh-TEE-<u>b</u>oh)

subjectivity   *f.* subjetividad (soob-heh-tee-<u>b</u>ee-<u>D</u>AH<u>D</u>)

subjugate (to)   subyugar (soob-yoo-GAHR) / sojuzgar (soh-HOOS-GAHR)

sublime (adj.)   sublime (soo-<u>B</u>LEE-meh)

submerge / immerse (to)   sumergir (soo-mehr-HEER) ♦⃝

submersion / immersion   *f.* sumersión (soo-mehr-SYOHN) ♦⃝

submission / surrender   *f.* sumisión (soo-mee-SYOHN)
   ① **submission** (*something submitted to others*)—*f.* presentación (preh-sehn-tah-SYOHN)

submissive / meek (adj.)   sumiso (soo-MEE-soh) ♦⃝

submit (*to authority or condition*) (to)   someter (soh-meh-TEHR) ♦⃝
   ① (to) **submit** (*something to others*)—presentar (preh-sehn-TAHR)

subordinate   *m.* subordinado (soo-<u>b</u>ohr-<u>d</u>ee-NAH-<u>d</u>oh) ↻*f.* -da↻

subordinate (to)   subordinar (soo-<u>b</u>ohr-<u>d</u>ee-NAHR)

subordination   *f.* subordinación (soo-<u>b</u>ohr-<u>d</u>ee-nah-SYOHN)

subscribe (to)   suscribirse (soos-skree-<u>B</u>EER-seh) ♦⃝

subscription   *f.* suscripción (soos-skreep-SYOHN)

subsequent (adj.)   subsiguiente (soob-see-GHYEN-teh)

subsidiary   *f.* subsidiaria (soob-see-<u>D</u>YAH-ryah)

subsidize (*a family*) (to)   subsidiar (soob-see-<u>D</u>YAHR)
   ① (to) **subsidize** (*an enterprise*)—subvencionar (soob-<u>b</u>ehn-syoh-NAHR)

subsidy (*to a family, to a person*)   *m.* subsidio (soob-SEE-<u>d</u>yoh)
   ① **subsidy** (*to an enterprise, to a country*)—*f.* subvención (soob-<u>b</u>ehn SYOHN)

subsist (to) subsistir (soob-sees-TEER)

subsistence *f.* subsistencia (soob-sees-TEHN-syah)

substance *f.* substancia (soobs-TAHN-syah)

substantial (*of substance*) (adj.) substancial (soobs-tahn-SYAHL)

substantial (*abundant*) (adj.) sustancioso (soos-tahn-SYOH-soh) 💣

substitute / surrogate (!) *m.* sustituto (soos-tee-TOO-toh) 💣

substitute (to) sustituir (soos-tee-TWEER) 💣

substitution *f.* sustitución (soos-tee-too-SYOHN) 💣

subterfuge *m.* subterfugio (soob-tehr-FOO-hyoh)

subterranean / underground (adj.) subterráneo (soob-teh-RRAH-neh-oh)

subtle (adj.) sutil (soo-TEEL) 💣

subtlety *f.* sutileza (soo-tee-LEH-sah) 💣

subtotal *m.* subtotal (soob-toh-TAHL)

subtract (to) sustraer (soos-trah-EHR) 💣

subtraction *f.* sustracción (soos-trahk-SYOHN) 💣

suburb *m.* suburbio (soo-<u>B</u>OOR-byoh)

suburban (adj.) suburbano (soo-<u>b</u>oor-BAH-noh)

subversion *f.* subversión (soob-<u>b</u>ehr-SYOHN)

subversive (adj.) subversivo (soob-<u>b</u>ehr-SEE-<u>b</u>oh)

subvert (to) subvertir (soob-<u>b</u>ehr-TEER)

subverter *m.* subversor (soob-<u>b</u>ehr-SOHR)↻*f.* -ra↻

subway (*transit system*) *m.* subterráneo (soob-teh-RRAH-neh-oh)
   ① In some locales, the preferred term is *m.* **metro** (MEH-troh).

succeed (*follow*) (to) suceder (soo-seh-<u>D</u>EHR) 💣

succession / sequence / series *f.* sucesión (soo-seh-SYOHN) 💣

successive (adj.) sucesivo (soo-seh-SEE-<u>b</u>oh) 💣

successor *m.* sucesor (soo-seh-SOHR) ↻*f.* -ra ↻ 💣

succinct (adj.) sucinto (soo-SEEN-toh) 💣

succulent (adj.) suculento (soo-koo-LEHN-toh) 💣

succulent (*plant*) *f.* suculenta (soo-koo-LEHN-tah) 💣

succumb (to) sucumbir (soo-koom-BEER) 💣

sucrose *f.* sacarosa (sah-kah-ROH-sah) 💣

suction *f.* succión (sook-SYOHN) 💣

suffer / undergo (!) (to) sufrir (soo-FREER)

suffering *m.* sufrimiento (soo-free-MYEHN-toh)

sufficient / ample / enough (adj.) suficiente (soo-fee-SYEHN-teh)

suffocate / smother / stifle (to) sofocar (soh-foh-KAHR) 💣

suffrage (*vote*) *m.* sufragio (soo-FRAH-hyoh) 💣

sugar *m. or f.* azúcar (ah-SOO-kahr) 💣

sugar / put sugar in / sweeten (to) azucarar (ah-soo-kah-RAHR)

sugary (adj.) azucarado (ah-soo-kah-RAH-<u>d</u>oh) 💣

suggest (*propose*) (to) sugerir (soo-heh-REER) 💣

suggestible (adj.) sugestionable (soo-hehs-tyoh-NAH-<u>b</u>leh) 💣

suggestion *f.* sugestión (soo-hehs-TYOHN) 💣

suicidal (adj.) suicida (swee-SEE-dah)

suicide *m.* suicidio (swee-SEE-<u>d</u>yoh)

suite *f.* suite (SWEET)

sum / addition / total *f.* suma (SOO-mah)
   ① (to) **add / find sum of**—sumar (soo-MAHR)

summit / top *f.* cima (SEE-mah) 💣

sumptuous / palatial (adj.) suntuoso (soon-TWOH-soh) 💣

sunblock *m.* filtro solar (FEEL-troh soh-LAHR)

super (*outstanding*) (adj.) súper (SOO-pehr)

superb (adj.) superbo (soo-PEHR-<u>b</u>oh)

superficial / perfunctory (adj.) superficial (soo-pehr-fee-SYAHL)

superfluous (adj.) superfluo (soo-PEHR-flwoh)

superhuman (adj.) sobrehumano (soh-<u>b</u>reh-oo-MAH-noh) 💣

superintendent *m. & f.* superintendente (soo-peh-reen-tehn-DEHN-teh)
   ① Generally, in the Hispanic world this term relates to a police official; the
   superintendent of any large building is *m.* **portero (pohr-TEH-roh)**
   ○*f.* **-ra**○; and of a school, *m.* **director (dee-rehk-TOHR)** ○*f.* **-ra**○.

superior   *m.* superior (soo-peh-RYOHR) ⟲(adj.) ☐⟲
  ⓵ **superior** (*religion*)—*m.* superior (soo-peh-RYOHR) ⟲*f.* -ra⟲

superiority   *f.* superioridad (soo-peh-ryoh-ree-<u>D</u>AH<u>D</u>)

superlative (adj.)   superlativo (soo-pehr-lah-TEE-<u>b</u>oh)

supermarket   *m.* supermercado (soo-pehr-mehr-KAH-<u>d</u>oh)

supernatural (adj.)   sobrenatural (soh-<u>b</u>reh-nah-too-RAHL) 💣

superstition   *f.* superstición (soo-pehrs-tee-SYOHN)

superstitious (adj.)   superticioso (soo-pehrs-tee-SYOH-soh)

supervise / oversee (to)   supervisar (soo-pehr-<u>b</u>ee-SAHR)

supervision   *f.* supervisión (soo-pehr-<u>b</u>ee-SYOHN)

supervisor / overseer   *m.* supervisor (soo-pehr-<u>b</u>ee-SOHR) ⟲*f.* -ra⟲

supplant (to)   suplantar (soo-plahn-TAHR) 💣

supplementary (adj.)   suplementario (soo-pleh-mehn-TAH-ryoh) 💣

supplicate / beseech (to)   suplicar (soo-plee-KAHR) 💣

supplication / appeal   *f.* súplica (SOO-plee-kah) 💣

(physical) support / prop   *m.* soporte (soh-POHR-teh) 💣

suppose / assume / guess / surmise (to)   suponer (soo-poh-NEHR) 💣

supposition   *f.* suposición (soo-poh-see-SYOHN) 💣

suppository (*medicine*)   *m.* supositorio (soo-poh-see-TOH-ryoh) 💣

suppression   *f.* supresión (soo-preh-SYOHN) 💣

supremacy   *f.* supremacía (soo-preh-mah-SEE-ah)

supreme / paramount (adj.)   supremo (soo-PREH-moh)

surgeon   *m.* cirujano (see-roo-HAH-noh) ⟲*f.* -na⟲ 💣

surgery   *f.* cirugía (see-roo-HEE-ah) 💣

surpass / surmount (to)   superar (soo-peh-RAHR) 💣

surprise   *f.* sorpresa (sohr-PREH-sah) 💣

surprise (to)   sorprender (sohr-prehn-DEHR) 💣

surprising (adj.)   sorprendente (sohr-prehn-DEHN-teh) 💣

surrender (*yield or give up*) (to)   rendirse (rehn-DEER-seh) 💣

surreptitious (adj.)   subrepticio (soob-rehp-TEE-syoh) 💣

suspect   *m.* sospechoso (sohs-peh-CHOH-soh) ○*f.* -sa○ ○(adj.) ▢○ 💣

suspect (to)   sospechar (sohs-peh-CHAHR) 💣

suspend / discontinue / dismiss (to)   suspender (soos-pehn-DEHR)

suspense   *m.* suspenso (soos-PEHN-soh)

suspension / dimissal   *f.* suspensión (soos-pehn-SYOHN)

suspicion / inkling   *f.* sospecha (sohs-PEH-chah) 💣

suspicious / questionable (adj.)   sospechoso (sohs-peh-CHO-soh) 💣

suspicious / distrustful (adj.)   suspicaz (soos-pee-KAHS)

sustain / nourish (to)   sustentar (soos-tehn-TAHR)

sustain / prolong / support / hold up / maintain / endure (to)   sostener (sohs-teh-NEHR) 💣

sustenance / nourishment   *m.* sustento (soos-TEHN-toh)

sweater / pullover   *m.* suéter (SWEH-tehr)

syllable   *f.* sílaba (SEE-lah-bah) 💣

symbol / sign   *m.* símbolo (SEEM-boh-loh) 💣

symbolic / symbolical (adj.)   simbólico (seem-BOH-lee-koh) 💣

symbolism   *m.* simbolismo (seem-boh-LEEZ-moh) 💣

symbolize (to)   simbolizar (seem-boh-lee-SAHR) 💣

symmetric / symmetrical (adj.)   simétrico (see-MEH-tree-koh) 💣

symmetry   *f.* simetría (see-meh-TREE-ah) 💣

symphonic (adj.)   sinfónico (seen-FOH-nee-koh) 💣

symphony   *f.* sinfonía (seen-foh-NEE-ah) 💣

symposium   *m.* simposio (seem-POH-syoh) 💣

symptom   *m.* síntoma (SEEN-toh-mah) 💣

symptomatic (adj.)   sintomático (seen-toh-MAH-tee-koh) 💣

syndicalism   *m.* sindicalismo (seen-dee-kah-LEEZ-moh)

syndicalist   *m. & f.* sindicalista (seen-dee-kah-LEES-tah) ○(adj.) ▢○

syndicate / trade union   *m.* sindicato (seen-dee-KAH-toh)

syndicate (to)   sindicar (seen-dee-KAHR)

synagogue   *f.* sinagoga (see-nah-GOH-gah) 💣

synchronize (to)   sincronizar (seen-kroh-nee-SAHR) 💣

syncopate (*grammar, music*) (to)   sincopar (seen-koh-PAHR) 💣

syncopation (*grammar, music*)   *f.* síncopa (SEEN-koh-pah) 💣

syndrome   *m.* síndrome (SEEN-droh-meh) 💣

synonym   *m.* sinónimo (see-NOH-nee-moh) ↻(adj.) **synonymous** ☐↻

synthesis   *f.* síntesis (SEEN-teh-sees) 💣

synthesize (to)   sintetizar (seen-teh-tee-SAHR) 💣

synthetic / synthetical (adj.)   sintético (seen-TEH-tee-koh) 💣

syphilis (*medicine*)   *f.* sífilis (SEE-fee-lees) 💣

syringe   *f.* jeringa (heh-REEN-gah) 💣

system   *m.* sistema (sees-TEH-mah)

systematic / systematical (adj.)   sistemático (sees-teh-MAH-tee-koh) 💣

systematize / systemize (to)   sistematizar (sees-teh-mah-tee-SAHR)

systemic (adj.)   sistémico (sees-TEH-mee-koh) 💣

—T—

table (*of figures*) **/ tabulation**   *f.* tabla (TAH-<u>b</u>lah)

tablet (*pill*)   *f.* tableta (tah-<u>B</u>LEH-tah)

tabloid   *m.* tabloide (tah-<u>B</u>LOY-<u>d</u>eh)

taboo   *m.* tabú (tah-<u>B</u>OO) ↻(adj.) *f*↻

tabulate (to)   tabular (tah-<u>b</u>oo-LAHR) ↻(adj.) **tabular** ☐↻

tacit (adj.)   tácito (TAH-see-toh)

taciturn / sullen (!) (adj.)   taciturno (tah-see-TOOR-noh)

tact   *m.* tacto (TAHK-toh)

tactic / tactical (adj.)   táctico (TAHK-tee-koh)

tactic / tactics   *f.* táctica (TAHK-tee-kah)

tactile (adj.)   táctil (TAHK-teel)

tactility / (sense of) touch   *m.* tacto (TAHK-toh)

talc / talcum powder   *m.* talco (TAHL-koh)

talent / (personal) gift   *m.* talento (tah-LEHN-toh)

talented / gifted (adj.)   talentoso (tah-lehn-TOH-soh)

talisman / (lucky) charm   *m.* talismán (tah-lees-MAHN)

tangible (adj.)   tangible (tahn-HEE-<u>b</u>leh)

tank (*container*)   *m.* tanque (TAHN-keh)

tapestry   *m.* tapiz (tah-PEES)

tardiness / lateness   *f.* tardanza (tahr-<u>D</u>AHN-sah)

tardy / late / overdue (adj.)   tardío (tahr-<u>D</u>EE-oh)

tariff   *f.* tarifa (tah-REE-fah)

tart (*pastry*)   *f.* tartaleta (tahr-tah-LEH-tah)

tattoo   *m.* tatuaje (tah-TWAH-heh)

tavern / saloon   *f.* taberna (tah-<u>B</u>EHR-nah)

tea   *m.* té (TEH)

technic / technical (adj.)   técnico (TEHK-nee-koh)

technic / technics   *f.* técnica (TEHK-nee-kah)

technicality   *f.* tecnicidad (tehk-nee-see-<u>D</u>AH<u>D</u>)

technician   *m.* técnico (TEHK-nee-koh) ↻*f.* -ca↺

technique   *f.* técnica (TEHK-nee-kah)

technologic / technological (adj.)   technológico (tehk-noh-LOH-hee-koh)

technology   *f.* technología (tehk-noh-loh-HEE-ah)

technocracy   *f.* tecnocracia (tehk-noh-KRAH-syah)

technocrat   *m. & f.* tecnócrata (tehk-NOH-krah-tah) ↺(adj.) **technocratic** ☐↻

tedious / tiresome (adj.)   tedioso (teh-<u>D</u>YOH-soh)

tedium / tediousness   *m.* tedio (TEH-<u>d</u>yoh)   ·

telegraph   *m.* telégrafo (teh-LEH-grah-foh)

telegraph / wire (to)   telegrafiar (teh-leh-grah-FYAHR)

telegrapher / telegraph operator / telegraphist   *m. & f.* telegrafista (teh-leh-grah-FEES-tah)

telegraphic (adj.)   telegráfico (teh-leh-GRAH-fee-koh)

telegraphy *f.* telegrafía (teh-leh-grah-FEE-ah)

telegram / wire   *m.* telegrama (teh-leh-GRAH-mah)

telepathic (adj.)   telepático (teh-leh-PAH-tee-koh)

telepathy *f.* telepatía (teh-leh-pah-TEE-ah)

telephone / phone   *m.* teléfono (teh-LEH-foh-noh)

telephone / phone (to)   telefonear (teh-leh-foh-neh-AHR)

telescope   *m.* telescopio (teh-lehs-KOH-pyoh)

televise / telecast (to)   televisar (teh-leh-bee-SAHR)

television *f.* televisión (teh-leh-bee-SYOHN)

temblor / tremor / earthquake   *m.* temblor (de tierra) (tehm-BLOHR [deh TYEH-rrah])
   ① Other words for **earthquake**: *m.* terremoto (teh-rreh-MOH-toh); *m.* sismo (SEEZ-moh)

temerity *f.* temeridad (teh-meh-ree-DAHD)

temper (*moderate*) (to)   temperar (tehm-peh-RAHR)

temperament   *m.* temperamento (tehm-peh-rah-MEHN-toh)

temperamental / mercurial (adj.)   temperamental (tehm-peh-rah-mehn-TAHL)

temperate (adj.)   templado (tehm-PLAH-doh) 💣

temperature *f.* temperatura (tehm-peh-rah-TOO-rah)

tempest / storm *f.* tempestad (tehm-pehs-TAHD)

tempestuous / stormy (adj.)   tempestuoso (tehm-pehs-TWOH-soh)

temple (*religious*)   *m.* templo (TEHM-ploh)

tempo   *m.* tempo (TEHM-poh)

temporal / temporary (adj.)   temporal (tehm-poh-RAHL)

tempt (to)   tentar (tehn-TAHR)

temptation *f.* tentación (tehn-tah-SYOHN)

tempter   *m.* tentador (tehn-tah-DOHR) ↻*f.* **temptress** –ra↻

tenacious (adj.)   tenaz (teh-NAHS)

tenacity / tenaciousness *f.* tenacidad (teh-nah-see-DAHD)

tend (to) / be apt (to) (to)   tender (a) (tehn-DEHR [ah])

tendency   *f.* tendencia (tehn-DEHN-syah)

tender / affectionate / caring (adj.)   tierno (TYEHR-noh)

tenderness   *f.* ternura (tehr-NOO-rah)

tendon   *m.* tendón (tehn-DOHN)

tennis   *m.* tenis (TEH-nees)

tenor (*singer or voice range*)   *m.* tenor (teh-NOHR)

tense / tighten (to)   tensar (tehn-SAHR)

tense / taut / tight (adj.)   tenso (TEHN-soh)

tension / strain / stress   *f.* tensión (tehn-SYOHN)

tepee   *m.* tipi (TEE-pee)

tepid / lukewarm (adj.)   tibio (TEE-byoh)

term (*word or period of duration*)   *m.* término (TEHR-mee-noh)

terminal   *m.* terminal (tehr-mee-NAHL) ⊅(adj.) ☐⊅

terminate / finish (to)   terminar (tehr-mee-NAHR)
    ① (to) **come to an end**—terminarse (tehr-mee-NAHR-seh)

terminated / finished / over (adj.)   terminado (tehr-mee-NAH-doh)

termination / ending   *f.* terminación (tehr-mee-nah-SYOHN)

terminology   *f.* terminología (tehr-mee-noh-loh-HEE-ah)

terminus / end point   *m.* término (TEHR-mee-noh)

terrace / balcony   *f.* terraza (teh-RRAH-sah)

terra-cotta   *f.* terracota (teh-rrah-KOH-tah)

terrain   *m.* terreno (teh-RREH-noh)

terrestrial (adj.)   terrestre (teh-RREHS-treh)

terrible / awful / dreadful (adj.)   terrible (teh-RREE-bleh)

terrific (adj.)   terrífico (teh-RREE-fee-koh)

terrify / terrorize (to)   aterrorizar (ah-teh-rroh-ree-SAHR) 💣

territory / region   *m.* territorio (teh-rree-TOH-ryoh)

terror   *m.* terror (teh-RROHR)

terrorism   *m.* terrorismo (teh-rroh-REEZ-moh)

terrorist   *m. & f.* terrorista (teh-rroh-REES-tah ↻(adj.) ▢↻

test   *m.* test (TEHST)

testament / will   *m.* testamento (tehs-tah-MEHN-toh)

testicle   *m.* testículo (tehs-TEE-koo-loh)

testify (to)   testificar (tehs-tee-fee-KAHR)

testifier / witness (*in court*)   *m. & f.* testigo (tehs-TEE-goh)

testimony / attestation   *m.* testimonio (tehs-tee-MOH-nyoh)

theater (*edifice or genre*)   *m.* teatro (teh-AH-troh)

theatrical (adj.)   teatral (teh-ah-TRAHL) / dramático (drah-MAH-tee-koh)

theme / subject / topic   *m.* tema (TEH-mah)

theologian   *m.* teólogo (teh-OH-loh-goh) ↻*f.* -ga↻

theological / theologic (adj.)   teológico (teh-oh-LOH-hee-koh)

theology   *f.* teología (teh-oh-loh-HEE-ah)

theorem (*mathematics*)   *m.* teorema (the-oh-REH-mah)

theoretic / theoretical (adj.)   teórico (teh-OH-ree-koh)

theorize (to)   teorizar (teh-oh-ree-SAHR)

theory / theoretics   *f.* teoría (teh-oh-REE-ah)

therapeutic / therapeutical (adj.)   terapéutico (teh-rah-PEHOO-tee-koh)

therapist   *m. & f.* terapeuta (teh-rah-PEHOO-tah)

therapy   *f.* terapia (teh-RAH-pyah)

thermometer   *m.* termómetro (tehr-MOH-meh-troh)

thermos   *m.* termo (TEHR-moh)

thermostat   *m.* termostato (tehr-mohs-TAH-toh)

thesis   *f.* tesis (TEH-sees)

throne   *m.* trono (TROH-noh)

tic   *m.* tic (TEEK)

timbre / tone / (small) bell   *m.* timbre (TEEM-breh)

timid / bashful / coy (adj.)   tímido (TEE-mee-<u>d</u>oh)

timidity / timidness / shyness   *f.* timidez (tee-mee-<u>D</u>EHS)

timorous / fearful (adj.)   temeroso (teh-meh-ROH-soh)

timorousness / dread / fear   *m.* temor (teh-MOHR)

tint / dye / tinge   *m.* tinte (TEEN-teh)

tint / dye / tinge (to)   teñir (teh-NYEER)

tissue (*biological*) / textile   *m.* tejido (teh-HEE-<u>d</u>oh)

titanic / gargantuan (adj.)   titánico (tee-TAH-nee-koh)

title   *m.* título (TEE-too-loh)

title (to)   titular (tee-too-LAHR)

tobacco   *m.* tobaco (toh-BAH-koh)

tolerable / endurable (adj.)   tolerable (toh-leh-RAH-<u>b</u>leh)

tolerance / toleration   *f.* tolerancia (toh-leh-RAHN-syah)

tolerant (adj.)   tolarante (toh-leh-RAHN-teh)

tolerate (to)   tolerar (toh-leh-RAHR)

tomato (*fruit and plant*)   *m.* tomate (toh-MAH-teh)

tomb / grave   *f.* tumba (TOOM-bah)

ton   *f.* tonelada (toh-neh-LAH-<u>d</u>ah)

tone (*of sound, not color*) / pitch   *m.* tono (TOH-noh)

tongue (*organ or language*)   *f.* lengua (LEHN-gwah)

tonic   *m.* tónico (TOH-nee-koh) ↻(adj.) ☐↻

tonic water   *f.* tónica (TOH-nee-kah)

top (*of container*) / lid   *f.* tapa (TAH-pah)

topaz   *m.* topacio (toh-PAH-syoh)

topic   *m.* tópico (TOH-pee-koh)

topographic / topographical (adj.)   topográfico (toh-poh-GRAH-fee-koh)

topography   *f.* topografía (toh-poh-grah-FEE-ah)

torch   *f.* antorcha (ahn-TOHR-cha)

torment   *m.* tormento (tohr-MEHN-toh)

torment (to)   atormentar (ah-tohr-mehn-TAHR) 💣

tormentor   *m.* atormentador (ah-tohr-mehn-tah-<u>D</u>OHR) ↻*f.* -ra↻ 💣

tornado *m.* tornado (tohr-NAH-<u>d</u>oh)

torpedo *m.* torpedo (tohr-PEH-<u>d</u>oh)

torpedo (to) torpedear (tohr-peh-<u>d</u>eh-AHR)

torrent *m.* torrente (toh-RREHN-teh)

torrential *m.* torrencial (toh-rrehn-SYAHL)

torrid (adj.) tórrido (TOH-rree-<u>d</u>oh)

torso *m.* torso (TOHR-soh)

tortoise / turtle *m.* tortuga (tohr-TOO-gah)

tortuous (adj.) tortuoso (tohr-TWOH-soh)

torture *f.* tortura (tohr-TOO-rah)

torture (to) torturar (tohr-too-RAHR)

torturer *m.* torturador (tohr-too-rah-<u>D</u>OHR) ○*f.* -ra○
  ○(adj.) **torturous / torturing** □○

total *m.* total (toh-TAHL) ○(adj.) **total / complete** □○

total / tally (to) totalizar (toh-tah-lee-SAHR)

totalitarian *m.* totalitario (toh-tah-lee-TAH-ryoh) ○*f.* –ia○
  ○(adj.) □○

totalitarianism *m.* totalitarismo (toh-tah-lee-tah-REEZ-moh)

totality / entirety *f.* totalidad (toh-tah-lee-<u>D</u>AH<u>D</u>)

touch / feel (to) tocar (toh-KAHR)

tourism / sightseeing *m.* turismo (too-REES-moh)

tourist / sightseer *m. & f.* turista (too-REES-tah)

tourney / tournament *m.* torneo (tohr-NEH-oh)

tourniquet *m.* torniquete (tohr-nee-KEH-teh)

towel *f.* toalla (toh-AH-yah)

tower / steeple *f.* torre (TOH-rreh)

traction *f.* tracción (trahk-SYOHN)

tractor (*agricultural*) *m.* tractor (trahk-TOHR)

trademark / brand *f.* marca (MAHR-kah)

tradition *f.* tradición (trah-<u>d</u>ee-SYOHN)

traditional (adj.) tradicional (trah-<u>d</u>ee-syoh-NAHL)

traditionalism *m.* tradicionalismo (trah-<u>d</u>ee-syoh-nah-LEEZ-moh)

traditionalist *m. & f.* tradicionalista (trah-<u>d</u>ee-syoh-nah-LEES-tah)

traffic (*vehicular flow*) *m.* tráfico (TRAH-fee-koh)

tragedy *f.* tragedia (trah-HEH-<u>d</u>yah)

tragic / tragical (adj.) trágico (TRAH-hee-koh)

train *m.* tren (TREHN)

train / coach (to) entrenar (ehn-treh-NAHR) 💣

traitor / double-crosser *m.* traidor (try-<u>D</u>OHR) ⟳*f.* -ra⟳ ⟳(adj.) ☐⟳
① Another word for **traitor** is: *m. & . f.* traicionero (treye-syoh-NEH-roh) ⟳*f.* -ra⟳ ⟳(adj.) ☐⟳. As an adjective the term means **treacherous / traitorous / treasonous.**

tram / trolley / streetcar *m.* tranvía (trahn-BEE-ah)

trampoline / springboard *m.* trampolín (trahm-poh-LEEN)

tramway (*streetcar line or tracks*) *m.* tranvía (trahn-BEE-ah)

tranquil / calm / peaceful (adj.) tranquilo (trahn-KEE-loh)

tranquillity / calm / quiet *f.* tranquilidad (trahn-kee-lee-<u>D</u>AH<u>D</u>)

transfer *f.* transferencia (trahns-feh-REHN-syah) 💣

transfer (to) transferir (trahns-feh-REER) 💣

transfusion *f.* transfusión (trahns-foo-SYOHN) 💣

transit (*passage*) *m.* tránsito (TRAH N-see-toh)

transition *f.* transición (trahn-see-SYOHN)

transmission / broadcast *f.* transmisión (trahnz-mee-SYOHN)

transmit / (electronically) convey (to) transmitir (trahnz-mee-TEER) 💣

transparent / sheer (adj.) transparente (trahns-pah-REHN-teh)

transport / transportation *m.* transporte (trahns-POHR-teh)

transport / convey (to) transportar (trahns-pohr-TAHR)

transvestite *m.* travestido (trah-<u>b</u>ehs-tee-<u>d</u>oh)

trap / snare / pitfall *f.* trampa (TRAHM-pah)

trap / snare (to) atrapar (ah-trah-PAHR)

traverse / crossing *f.* travesía (trah-<u>b</u>eh-SEE-ah)

traverse (to) atravesar (ah-trah-<u>b</u>eh-SAHR)

treasure *m.* tesoro (teh-SOH-roh)

treasury (*governmental office*) *f.* tesorería (teh-soh-reh-REE-ah)

treat (*behave toward*) (to) tratar (trah-TAHR)

treatment (*behavior toward*) *f.* manera de tratar (mah-NEH-rah deh trah-TAHR)

treatment (*medical attention*) *m.* tratamiento (trah-tah-MYEHN-toh)

treaty *m.* tratado (trah-TAH-doh)

tremble / shake / quake (to) temblar (tehm-BLAHR)

tremendous (adj.) tremendo (treh-MEHN-doh)

trench *f.* trinchera (treen-CHEH-rah)

triangle *m.* triángulo (TRYAHN-goo-loh)

tribe *f.* tribu (TREE-boo)

tribunal / court of law *m.* tribunal (tree-boo-NAHL)

tributary (*person*) *m.* tributario (tree-boo-TAH-ryoh) ⟳*f.* -ria⟳ ⟳(adj.) ☐⟳

tributary (*river*) *m.* tributario (tree-boo-TAH-ryoh)

tribute / testimonial *m.* tributo (tree-BOO-toh)

trick *m.* truco (TROO-koh) ◐⁛

trip / stumble *m.* tropezón (troh-peh-SOHN) ◐⁛

trip / stumble (to) tropezar (troh-peh-SAHR) ◐⁛

triple (adj.) triple (TREE-pleh)

triple (to) triplicar (tree-plee-KAHR)

trite / hackneyed (adj.) trillado (tree-YAH-doh)

triumph / win *m.* triunfo (TRYOON-foh)

trolley / streetcar *m.* tranvía (trahn-BEE-ah)

trombone *m.* trombón (trohm-BOHN)

troops *f. pl.* tropas (TROH-pahs)

trophy *m.* trofeo (troh-FEH-oh)

tropic *m.* trópico (TROH-pee-koh) ⟳(adj.) **tropical** ☐⟳ ① **Tropics**—*m. pl.* trópicos (TROH-pee-kohs)

trot *m.* trote (TROH-teh)

trot (to) trotar (troh-TAHR)

troubador / minstrel *m.* trovador (troh-<u>b</u>ah-<u>D</u>OHR)

trumpet *f.* trompeta (trohm-PEH-tah)

trunk (*of tree*) *m.* tronco (TROHN-koh)

trust (*cartel*) *m.* trust (TROOST)

tube / (plumbing) pipe *m.* tubo (TOO-<u>b</u>oh)

tulip *m.* tulipán (too-lee-PAHN)

tumor *m.* tumor (too-MOHR)

tumult / hubbub *m.* tumulto (too-MOOL-toh)

tune / melody *f.* tonada (toh-NAH-<u>d</u>ah)

tunnel *m.* túnel (TOO-nehl)

turban *m.* turbante (toor-<u>B</u>AHN-teh)

turbine *f.* turbina (toor-<u>B</u>EE-nah)

turtle *f.* tortuga (tohr-TOO-gah)

type / ilk / kind / sort *m.* tipo (TEE-poh)

typical (adj.) típico (TEE-pee-koh)

tyrannic / tyrannical (adj.) tiránico (tee-RAH-nee-koh)

tyranny *f.* tiranía (tee-rah-NEE-ah) ●

tyrant *m. & f.* tirano (tee-RAH-noh) ↻(adj.) ☐↻

—U—

ulcer *f.* úlcera (OOL-seh-rah)

ultimate / last / final (adj.) último (OOL-tee-moh)
  ① Related adverb: **most recently**—últimamente (ool-tee-mah-MEHN-teh)

unable / incapable / unfit (adj.) incapaz (een-kah-PAS)

unanimous (adj.) unánime (oo-NAH-nee-meh)

uncertain (adj.) incierto (een-SYEHR-toh)

unconscious / mindless (adj.)   inconsciente (een–kohns-SYEHN-teh) 💣

undecided (adj.)   indeciso (een-deh–SEE-soh) 💣

undulate / flutter / ripple (to)   ondular (ohn-doo-LAHR)

undulation / ripple   *f.* ondulación (ohn-doo-lah-SYOHN)

unequal (adj.)   desigual (deh-see-GWAHL) 💣

unemployment   *m.* desempleo (deh-sehm-PLEH-oh)

ungrateful / thankless (adj.)   ingrato (een-GRAH-toh) 💣

unguent / ointment / salve   *m.* ungüento (oon-GWEHN-toh)

uniform (*official garb*)   *m.* uniforme (oo-nee-FOHR-meh)

uniform / even (adj.)   uniforme (oo-nee-FOHR-meh)

uniformity / evenness   *f.* uniformidad (oo-nee-fohr-mee-<u>D</u>AH<u>D</u>)

unilateral / one-sided (adj.)   unilateral (oo-nee-lah-teh-RAHL)

union (*joining*) / splice   *f.* unión (oo-NYOHN)

unit   *f.* unidad (oo-nee-<u>D</u>AH<u>D</u>)

unite (*by external action*) / connect (to)   unir (oo-NEER)

unite (*by internal force*) / merge (to)   unirse (oo-NEER-seh)

unity   *f.* unidad (oo-nee-<u>D</u>AH<u>D</u>)

universal (adj.)   universal (oo-nee-<u>b</u>ehr-SAHL)

universe   *m.* universo (oo-nee-<u>B</u>EHR-soh)

university / college   *f.* universidad (oo-nee-<u>b</u>ehr-see-<u>D</u>AH<u>D</u>)

unjust / unfair / wrong (adj.)   injusto (een-HOOS-toh) 💣

unjustified / unwarranted (adj.)   injustificado (een-joos-tee-fee-KAH-<u>d</u>oh) 💣

unnecessary / needless (adj.)   innecesario (een-neh-seh-SAH-ryoh) 💣

unoccupied / unemployed (adj.)   desocupado (deh-soh-koo-PAH-<u>d</u>oh)

unquiet / uneasy / anxious / restless (adj.)   inquieto (een-KYEH-toh)
   ① (to) **be unquiet / disturbed / worried / upset**—inquietarse (een-kyeh-TAHR-seh) 💣

unreasonable (adj.)   irrazonable (ee-rrah-soh-NAH-<u>b</u>leh)

unserviceable / unusable (adj.)   inservible (een-sehr-<u>B</u>EE-<u>b</u>leh) 💣

unstable / unsteady (adj.)   inestable (ee-nehs-TAH-<u>b</u>leh) 💣

unuseful / useless / idle (adj.)   inútil (ee-NOO-teel)

uranium   *m.* uranio (oo-RAH-nyoh)

urban / urbane(!) / suave (!) (adj.)   urbano (oor-BAH-noh)

urbanism   *m.* urbanismo (oor-bah-NEEZ-moh)

urgency   *f.* urgencia (oor-HEHN-syah)

urgent / pressing (adj.)   urgente (oor-HEHN-teh)

urinal   *m.* orinal (oh-ree-NAHL) 💣

urinate (to)   orinar (oh-ree-NAHR) 💣

urine   *f.* orina (ohr-REE-nah) 💣

urn   *f.* urna (OOR-nah)

usage   *f.* usanza (oo-SAHN-sah)

use (of) / utilization   *m.* uso (OO-soh)

use / employ (*make use of*) (to)   usar (oo-SAHR)

useful (adj.)   útil (OO-teel)

useless (adj.)   inútil (ee-NOO-teel)

user   *m.* usuario (oo-SWAH-ryoh) ◑*f.* -ria◑ 💣

usual (adj.)   usual (oo-SWAHL)

usually   usualmente (oo-swahl-MEHN-teh)

utensil / tool   *m.* utensilio (oo-tehn-SEE-lyoh)

uterus / womb   *m.* útero (OO-teh-roh)

utile / utilitarian / useful (adj.)   útil (OO-teel)

utility (of) / usefulness   *f.* utilidad (oo-tee-lee-<u>D</u>AH<u>D</u>)

utilize / employ (*make use of*) (to)   utilizar (oo-tee-lee-SAHR)

—V—

vacation   *f. pl.* vacaciones (bah-kah-SYOH-nes)

vaccinate (to)   vacunar (bah-koo-NAHR)
   ① **to be vaccinated**—vacunarse (bah-koo-NAHR-seh)

vaccination   *f.* vacunación (bah-koo-nah-SYOHN)

vaccinator (*person*)   *m.* vacunador (bah-koo-nah-DOHR) ◑*f.* -ra◑

vaccine *f.* vacuna (bah-KOO-nah)

vacillate / hesitate / waver (to)   vacilar (bah-see-LAHR)

vacillating (adj.)   vacilante (bah-see-LAHN-teh)

vagabond / drifter   *m.* vagabundo (bah-gah-<u>B</u>OON-doh) ↻*f.* -da↻
    ↻(adj.) **vagabond / vagrant** ▢↻

vagina *f.* vagina (bah-HEE-nah)

vague (adj.)   vago (BAH-goh)

vain / conceited (adj.)   vanidoso (bah-nee-<u>D</u>OH-soh)

vain / futile (adj.)   vano (BAH-noh)
    ① **(in) vain**—in vano (een BAH-noh)

valid (adj.)   válido (bah-LEE-<u>d</u>oh)

valiant / brave / courageous (adj.)   valiente (bah-LYEHN-teh)

valise / suitcase *f.* valija (bah-LEE-hah)

valley *m.* valle (BAH-yeh)

valor / courage / mettle (!)   *m.* valor (bah-LOHR)

valorous / valiant (adj.)   valeroso (bah-leh-ROH-soh)

valuable / of value (adj.)   valioso (bah-LYOH-soh)

valuation / appraisal / evaluation   *f.* valoración (bah-loh-rah-SYOHN)

value / worth   *m.* valor (bah-LOHR)

value (*evaluate or price*) (to)   valuar (bah-LWAHR)

vandal   *m.* vándalo (BAHN-dah-loh)

vandalism   *m.* vandalismo (bahn-dah-LEEZ-moh)

vanguard / forefront   *f.* vanguardia (bahn-GWAHR-<u>d</u>yah)

vanilla   *f.* vainilla (beye-NEE-yah)

vanish (to)   desvanecerse (dehs-<u>b</u>ah-neh-SEHR-seh)

vanity / conceit   *f.* vanidad (bah-nee-<u>D</u>AH<u>D</u>)

vapor / steam   *m.* vapor (bah-POHR)

varied / diverse / motley (adj.)   variado (bah-RYAH-<u>d</u>oh)

variety / diversity   *f.* variedad (bah-ryeh-<u>D</u>AH<u>D</u>)

various / several (!) / sundry (adj.)   *m. pl.* varios (BAH-ryohs)

vary (*change*) (to)   variar (bah-RYAHR)

vascillate / hesitate (to)   vacilar (bah-see-LAHR)

vascillation / hesitancy   *f.* vacilación (bah-see-lah-SYOHN)

vascillating / halting / hesitant (adj.)   vacilante (bah-see-LAHN-teh)

vase   *m.* vaso (BAH-soh)

vast (adj.)   vasto (BAHS-toh)

vegetarian   *m.* vegetariano (beh-heh-tah-RYAH-noh) ↻*f.* -na↻ ↻(adj.) ☐↻

vegetarianism   *m.* vegetarianismo (beh-heh-tah-ryah-NEEZ-moh)

vegetation   *f.* vegetación (beh-heh-tah-SYOHN)

vehemence   *f.* vehemencia (beh-eh-MEHN-syah) ↻(adj.) **vehement** -nte↻

vehicle   *m.* vehículo (beh-EE-koo-loh)

veil   *m.* velo (BEH-loh)

vein   *f.* vena (BEH-nah)

velocity / rate / speed   *f.* velocidad (beh-loh-see-<u>D</u>AH<u>D</u>)
   ① **speed limit**—*m.* límite de velocidad (LEE-mee-teh deh beh-loh-see-<u>D</u>AH<u>D</u>); *m.* **speedometer**—velocímetro (beh-loh-SEE-meh-troh)

velveteen (*cloth*)   *m.* velludillo (beh-yoo-DEE-yoh)

venal (adj.)   venal (BEH-nal)

venality   *f.* venalidad (beh-nah-lee-<u>D</u>AH<u>D</u>)

vend / sell (to)   vender (behn-DEHR)

vendetta   *f.* vendetta (behn-DEHT-tah)

vendition / sale   *f.* venta (BEHN-tah)

vendor / peddler   *m.* vendedor (behn-deh-<u>D</u>OHR) ↻*f.* -ra↻

veneration / reverence   *f.* veneración (beh-neh-rah-SYOHN)

vengeance / revenge   *f.* venganza (behn-GAHN-sah)

(take) vengeance / revenge (to)   vengar (behn-GAHR)

venom / poison   *m.* veneno (beh-NEH-noh)

venomous / poisonous (adj.)   venenoso (beh-neh-NOH-soh)

ventilate (to)   ventilar (behn-tee-LAHR)

ventilation   *f.* ventilación (behn-tee-lah-SYOHN)

ventilator / fan　*m.* ventilador (behn-tee-lah-<u>D</u>OHR)

　　① Related noncognates: **wind**—*m.* viento (BYEHN-toh); (adj.) **windy**—ventoso (behn-TOH-soh); and **window**—*f.* ventana (behn-TAH-nah)

venture　*f.* ventura (behn-TOO-rah)

veranda / porch (*of house*)　*f.* veranda (beh-RAHN-<u>d</u>ah)

verb　*m.* verbo (BEHR-<u>b</u>oh)

verbose / wordy (adj.)　verboso (behr-<u>B</u>OH-soh)

verbosity / wordiness　*f.* verbosidad (behr-<u>b</u>oh-see-<u>D</u>AH<u>D</u>)

verbal (adj.)　verbal (behr-<u>B</u>AHL)

verify (to)　verificar (beh-ree-fee-KAHR)

verily / truly / in truth　verdaderamente (behr-<u>d</u>ah-<u>d</u>eh-rah-MEHN-teh) / en verdad (ehn behr-<u>D</u>AH<u>D</u>)

verity / truth　*f.* verdad (behr-<u>D</u>AH<u>D</u>)

　　① Important related noncognates: (adj.) **true (*actual*)**—verdadero (behr-<u>d</u>ah-<u>D</u>EH-roh) / (adj.) **truthful**—verídico (behr-REE-<u>d</u>ee-koh)

vernacular　*m.* vernáculo (behr-NAH-koo-loh) ↻ (adj.) ☐ ↻

versatile (adj.)　versátil (behr-SAH-teel)

versatility　*f.* versatilidad (behr-sah-tee-lee-<u>D</u>AH<u>D</u>)

verse　*m.* verso (BEHR-soh)

versed (adj.)　versado (behr-SAH-doh)

versification　*f.* versificación (behr-see-fee-kah-SYOHN)

versify / verse (to)　versificar (behr-see-fee-KAHR)

vertebra　*f.* vértebra (BEHR-teh-brah)

vertebral (adj.)　vertebral (behr-teh-BRAHL)

vertebrate　*m.* vertebrado (behr-teh-<u>B</u>RAH-<u>d</u>oh) ↻(adj.) ☐↻

vertical (adj.)　vertical (behr-tee-KAHL)

verticality　*f.* verticalidad (behr-tee-kah-lee-<u>D</u>AH<u>D</u>)

vertigo / dizziness　*m.* vértigo (BEHR-tee-goh)

vessel (*receptacle*)　*f.* vasija (bah-SEE-hah)

vestibule / foyer / lobby　*m.* vestíbulo (behs-TEE-<u>b</u>oo-loh)

vestige / remnant / trace　*m.* vestigio (behs-TEE-hyoh)

vestments / clothes *f.* vestimenta (behs-tee-MEHN-tah) / *f.* vestidura (behs-tee-DOO-rah)

① **vestments** (*ecclesiastical*)—*f. pl.* vestimentas (behs-tee-MEHN-tahs) / *f. pl.* vestiduras (behs-tee-DOO-rahs)

veteran *m.* veterano (beh-teh-RAH-noh) ⟳(adj.) ▯⟳

veterinarian *m.* veterinario (beh-teh-ree-NAH-ryoh)

veterinary (adj.) veterinario (beh-teh-ree-NAH-ryoh)

via (*by*) vía (BEE-ah)

viability *f.* viabilidad (byah-bee-lee-DAHD)

viable (adj.) viable (BYAH-bleh)

viaduct *m.* viaducto (byah-DOOK-toh)

vibrate / pulsate / throb (to) vibrar (bee-BRAHR)

vibrating (adj.) vibrante (bee-BRAHN-teh)

vibration / jiggle / throb / vibrancy *f.* vibración (bee-brah-SYOHN)

vibrator *m.* vibrador (bee-brah-DOHR)

vicar (*religion*) *m.* vicario (bee-KAH-ryoh)

vicariate *m.* vicariato (bee-kah-RYAH-toh)

vice (*moral fault*) *m.* vicio (BEE-syoh)

vicinity / community (!) *f.* vecindad (beh-seen-DHAD)

① Related noncognate: **neighbor**—*m.* vecino (beh-SEE-noh) ⟳*f.* -na⟳

vicious (adj.) vicioso (bee-SYOH-soh) 💣

victim *f.* víctima (BEEK-tee-mah)

victorious (adj.) victorioso (beek-toh-RYOH-soh)

① Closely related noncognate: **victor**—*m.* vencedor (behn-seh-DOHR) ⟳*f.* -ra⟳

victory *f.* victoria (beek-TOH-ryah)

vigil *f.* vigilia (bee-HEE-lyah)

(keep) vigil / watch / guard (to) vigilar (bee-hee-LAHR)

vigilance / surveillance (!) *f.* vigilancia (bee-hee-LAHN-syah)

vigilant / alert / wakeful / watchful (adj.) vigilante (bee-hee-LAHN-teh)

vignette *f.* viñeta (bee-NYEH-tah)

vigor / stamina   *m.* vigor (bee-GOHR)

vigorous / forceful / strenuous (adj.)   vigoroso (bee-goh-ROH-soh)

vile (adj.)   vil (BEEL)

vileness   *f.* vileza (bee-LEH-sah)

villain   *m.* villano (bee-YAH-noh) ↻*f.* -na↻ ↻(adj.) **villainous** ☐↻

vinegar   *m.* vinagre (bee-NAH-greh)

vineyard   *f.* viña (BEE-nyah)

viola   *f.* viola (BYOH-lah)

violate / rape (to)   violar (byoh-LAHR)

violation / rape   *f.* violación (byoh-lah-SYOHN)

violator (*of the law*) **/ rapist**   *m.* violador (byoh-lah-<u>D</u>OHR) ↻*f.* -ra↻

violence   *f.* violencia (byoh-LEHN-syah)

violent (adj.)   violento (byoh-LEHN-toh)

violet   *f.* violeta (byoh-LEH-tah)

violin / fiddle   *m.* violín (byoh-LEEN)

violinist   *m. & f.* violinista (byoh-lee-NEES-tah)

virgin   *f.* virgen (beer-HEHN)

virginity   *f.* virginidad (beer-hee-nee-<u>D</u>AH<u>D</u>)

virile / manly (adj.)   viril (bee-REEL)

virility / manliness   *f.* virilidad (bee-ree-lee-<u>D</u>AH<u>D</u>)

virtual (adj.)   virtual (beer-TWAHL)

virtue   *f.* virtud (beer-TOO<u>D</u>)

virtuous (adj.)   virtuoso (beer-TWOH-soh)

virus   *m.* virus (BEE-roos)

visa   *f.* visa (BEE-sah)

viscous / thick / sticky (adj.)   viscoso (bees-KOH-soh)

visible (adj.)   visible (bee-SEE-<u>b</u>leh)

vision / (viewed) sight   *f.* vista (BEES-tah)

vision (*apparition*)   *f.* visión (bee-SYOHN)

visionary   *m.* visionario (bee-syoh-NAH-ryoh) ↻*f.* -ria↻ ↻(adj.) ☐↻

visit / visitor *f.* visita (bee-SEE-tah)

visit (to)   visitar (bee-see-TAHR)

visual (adj.)   visual (bee-SWAHL)

vital (adj.)   vital (bee-TAHL)

vitality *f.* vitalidad (bee-tah-lee-<u>D</u>AH<u>D</u>)

vitamin *f.* vitamina (bee-tah-MEE-nah)

vitiate (to)   viciar (bee-SYAHR)

vitreous / glassy (adj.)   vítreo (BEE-treh-oh)

vivacious / animated / jaunty (adj.)   vivaz (bee-<u>B</u>AHS)

vivacity / liveliness / ebullience *f.* vivacidad (bee-<u>b</u>ah-see-<u>D</u>AH<u>D</u>)

vivid (adj.)   vívido (BEE-<u>b</u>ee-<u>d</u>oh)

vivify / give life to (to)   vivificar (bee-<u>b</u>ee-fee-KAHR)

vocabulary *m.* vocabulario (boh-kah-boo-LAH-ryoh)

vocal (adj.)   vocal (boh-KAHL)

vocation / calling *f.* vocación (boh-kah-SYOHN)

vogue *f.* boga (BOH-gah)
    ① (to) **be in vogue**—estar en boga (ehs-TAHR ehn BOH-gah)

voice / rumor (!) *f.* voz (BOHS)

voice / shout (!) (to)   vocear (boh-seh-AHR)

volcano *m.* volcán (bohl-KAHN)

volition *f.* volición (boh-lee-SYOHN)

volume (*loudness*) / bulk *m.* volumen (boh-LOO-mehn)

voluminous / bulky (adj.)   voluminoso (boh-loo-mee-NOH-soh)

volunteer / voluntary *m.* voluntario (boh-loon-TAH-ryoh) ↺*f.* -ria↺
    ↺(adj.) ☐↺

voluptuous (adj.)   voluptuoso (boh-loop-TWOH-soh)

voluptuousness *f.* voluptuosidad (boh-loop-twoh-see-<u>D</u>AH<u>D</u>)

vomit *m.* vómito (BOH-mee-toh)

vomit / spew (to)   vomitar (boh-mee-TAHR)

voracious (adj.)   voraz (boh-RAHS)

voraciousness / voracity *f.* voracidad (boh-rah-see-<u>D</u>AH<u>D</u>)

vortex / whirlpool *m.* vórtice (BOHR-tee-seh)

vote / vow (!) *m.* voto (BOH-toh)

vote (to) votar (boh-TAHR)

vulgar / coarse / common (adj.) vulgar (bool-GAHR)

vulgarism (*word, expression*) *m.* vulgarismo (bool-gah-REEZ-moh)

vulgarity (*lack of refinement*) *f.* vulgaridad (bool-gah-ree-DAHD)

vulgarization / popularization *f.* vulgarización (bool-gah-ree-sah-SYOHN)

vulgarize / popularize / make vulgar (to) vulgarizar (bool-gah-ree-SAHR)

vulgarizer / popularizer *m.* vulgarizador (bool-gah-ree-sah-DOHR)
◔*f.* –ra◔ ◔(adj.) **popularizing** ☐◔

vulnerable / susceptible / liable (adj.) vulnerable (bool-neh-RAH-bleh)

vulnerability / susceptibility *f.* vulnerabilidad (bool-neh-rah-bee-lee-DAHD)

—W—

waffle *m.* wafle (WAH-fleh) 💣

walkie-talkie *m.* walkie-talkie (woh-kee-TOH-kee)

waltz *m.* vals (BAHLS) 💣

waltz (to) valsar (bahl-SAHR) 💣

wasp / yellow jacket *f.* avispa (ah-BEES-pah) 💣

watt *m.* watt (WAHT)

water closet *m.* water (BAH-tehr) / *m.* water closet (BAH-tehr KLOH-seht) / *m.* WC (OO-beh DOH-bleh SEH)

water polo *m.* waterpolo (bah-tehr-POH-loh)

weekend *m.* weekend (WEEK-ehnd)

west *m.* oeste (oh-EHS-teh) ◔(adj.) ☐◔ 💣

western (*movies*) *m.* western (WEHS-tehrn)

whiskey *m.* whisky (WEES-kee)

—X—

xenophile *m.* xenófilo (seh-NOH-fee-loh) ↻*f.* -la↺

xenophilia *f.* xenofilia (seh-noh-FEE-lyah)

xenophobe *m.* xenófobo (seh-NOH-foh-<u>b</u>oh) ↻*f.* -ba↺

xenophobia *f.* xenophobia (seh-noh-FOH-<u>b</u>yah)

xenophobic (adj.) xenófobo (seh-NOH-foh-<u>b</u>oh

xerox (to) xerocopiar (seh-roh-koh-PYAHR)
 ① **photocopy**—*f.* xerocopia (seh-roh-KOH-pyah)

X-ray (*beam or process*) *m.* rayo X (RAH-yoh eh-KEES)

X-ray (*plate or image*) *f.* radiografía (rah-<u>d</u>yoh-grah-FEE-ah)

X-ray (*take X-ray of*) (to) radiografiar (rah-<u>d</u>yoh-grah-FYAHR)

xylography *f.* xilografía (see-loh-grah-FEE-ah)

xylophone *m.* xilófono (see-LOH-foh-noh)

—Y—

yacht *m.* yate (YAH-teh)

yard (*measure*) *f.* yarda (YAHR-<u>d</u>ah)

yoga *m.* yoga (YOH-gah)

yogurt *m.* yogur (YOH-goor)

yoke *m.* yugo (YOO-goh)

yucca *f.* yuca (YOO-kah)

—Z—

zeal *m.* celo (SEH-loh) 💣

zealous (adj.) celoso (seh-LOH-soh) 💣

zebra *f.* cebra (SEH-<u>b</u>rah) 💣

zenith *m.* cenit (SEH-neet)

zephyr *m.* céfiro (SEH-fee-roh) 💣

zeppelin   *m.* zepelín (seh-peh-LEEN)

zero   *m.* cero (SEH-roh) ↻(adj.) ☐↻

zigzag   *m.* zigzag (seeg-SAHG)

zigzag (adj.)   en zigzag (ehn seeg-SAHG)

zigzag (to)   zigzaguear (seeg-sah-gweh-AHR)

zinc   *m.* cinc (SEENK) ☀

zircon   *m.* circón (seer-KOHN) ☀

zodiac   *m.* zodíaco (soh-<u>DEE</u>-ah-koh)

zodiacal (adj.)   zodiacal (soh-dyah-KAHL)

zombie   *m. & f.* zombi (SOHM-bee)

zone   *f.* zona (SOH-nah)

zoo   *m.* zoo (SOO)

zoological (adj.)   zoológico (soh-oh-LOH-hee-koh)

zoologist   *m.* zoólogo (soh-OH-loh-goh) ↻*f.* -ga↻

zoology   *f.* zoología (soh-oh-loh-HEE-ah)

zoom (to)   zumbar (soom-BAHR)

zygote   *m.* zigoto (see-GOH-toh) / cigoto (see-GOH-toh)